Pears
Guide to
Today's World

Pears
Guide to
Today's World

compiled by
Edward Blishen
and
Chris Cook

PELHAM BOOKS
LONDON

First published in Great Britain by
Pelham Books Ltd
52 Bedford Square
London WC1B 3EF
1979

ISBN 0 7207 0947 4

Printed in Great Britain by
Butler & Tanner Ltd, Frome

Jacket design: top, left to right: Lenin, Mao Tse-Tung, Mme Curie; *middle, left to right:* President Kennedy, James Joyce, Sigmund Freud; *bottom, left to right:* Kwame Nkrumah, General Marshall, Fidel Castro.

Contents

List of Illustrations

Introduction

The world today is changing so fast that many feel, from time to time, that they have somehow lost track of what is happening. It may even seem that life has become too complex to be really understood. But the character of the modern world, for all this atmosphere of furious change, is firmly rooted in the events of the last 200 years or so. It was at the turn of the eighteenth century that the industrial revolution began to transform the lives of people in the West; the process was under way which would turn nations that had always lived by agriculture into industrial nations – a process that has not yet ended, and that has had its effect on the earth from one end to the other. It was accompanied by, and was itself the cause of, great political changes, which also are not yet exhausted and lie behind much that is happening in the last quarter of the twentieth century.

The purpose of this book is to give a picture of today's world in terms of the way it has grown over these past two centuries. Though not primarily a history, it contains a great deal of history. It looks at the world of politics, the state of science and technology, the general condition of the arts; at special modern problems, like those that cluster round the term 'the environment'; at space travel, that remarkable twentieth-century extension of the Age of Exploration; at the major religions, and the part they play in the present pattern of things; and at the background and development of modern medicine.

The aim, very simply, is to make the present-day world easier to understand. And because new ideas and important events throughout this period, indeed throughout all human history, can be traced back to the lives of remarkable men and women, many pages of brief biographies are included. Each section is designed to make satisfactory reading in itself, as a separate item: but the various parts of the book are meant, together, to compose a general, interlocking picture of the modern world and the way it has become what it is.

1

The Making
of the
Modern World

Summary of Chapter

Map 1. Europe in 1789.

The Ancien Régime

The French Revolution of 1789 can reasonably be considered to mark the beginning of the modern age, politically and socially. To understand the development of modern Europe we need to look at the fabric of pre-Revolutionary Europe, to look back at what was called the *ancien régime*, to the time when the major states of Europe – France, Prussia, Austria and Russia – were governed by enlightened despots. These terms are often used too loosely, and we need to understand clearly what is meant by them. *Ancien régime* literally meant the old rule, the established system of politics and society. It implied a rigid and inflexible social order, in which people's occupations, rights and consequently power were established from birth. At the head of particular states were the despots: single rulers set above faction, men and women in whom the ultimate authority rested. They controlled the armed forces, the civil service and the law, they presided over their governments, and as a result they were the initiators of such reforms as were passed. It was their desire at this time for innovation and the efficient running of the state, under the influence of the new philosophy of the eighteenth century, which earned them the description 'enlightened'.

The basis of *ancien régime* Europe was the structure of its society, whose clear and rigid divisions are best illustrated by Russia. At the bottom of the social scale were the peasants, many of whom were still serfs by law – they had no political rights and no real chance of advancement. Long hours, poor pay and bad housing were also their lot. They had no freedom of movement, each being tied to a particular nobleman's estates. The situation was similar in Austria and Prussia, though attempts, some partially successful, were made in these countries to improve the peasants' standard of living and to give them some political freedom.

Above the Third Estate, as they were called in France, were the middle classes or the *bourgeoisie*, who consisted of business and professional people. Their rights, too, were defined by birth and occupation. The most important posts in the government and in the armed forces were usually filled by the landed aristocracy. This pattern emerged most clearly in Prussia, where Frederick the Great consciously excluded able members of the middle class from high office; the aristocracy were, in his words, 'the fairest jewels in his crown' and 'the foundations and pillars of the state'. The Prussian General Code, though passed in 1791, five years after his death, embodied these principles. The Act stated that everyone had rights, but that they varied according to one's position in society and, consequently, one's occupation.

In France, where social mobility was greater, members of the *bourgeoisie* were able to rise to the higher posts in government. Turgot, who served under Louis XV and became Controller-General (chief minister) under Louis XVI during 1774–6, is a case in point. The majority of *Intendants* (the officials responsible for each *pays*) were men of middling status, promoted on the basis of merit and experience.

Ancien régime Europe, then, existed mainly with stability in mind. Change was its enemy. Rapid promotion was discouraged. A strict hierarchy ensured that there was no violent alteration in government or in the structure of society.

It was against this background of established conservatism that the enlightened despots tried to modernize their states. They acquired their ideas and their justification principally from the *philosophes*. The term *philosophes* is really a convenient label to attach to a varied body of revolutionary thinkers who lived at this time, each with a similar approach to problems but with widely differing solutions. Unlike their predecessors, these philosophers did not believe in the sanctity of antiquity: everything had to be tested and if it was not possible to find a reason for something's existence, it had to be destroyed. Customs and conventions were irrational and, therefore, pointless. Privilege was considered to be indefensible; equality before the law and religious toleration were particular points of issue. The rule of reason was their keystone. Foremost among these influential thinkers was Voltaire. It is significant that he corresponded regularly with Catherine the Great of Russia and Frederick the Great of Prussia. All the major European despots kept close contact with leading enlightened thinkers. Montesquieu's *De l'esprit des lois* (1748) was largely the source for Catherine's law code, the *Nahaz* or *Instructions*.

Josef II of Austria was probably the despot most influenced by the thought of the *philosophes*, and certainly the best able to put it into practice. He believed passionately in the concept of running the state for the greatest good of all. Consequently it was his aim to improve the general condition of the peasants, to give them liberties, to educate them and to raise their living standards. To do this he had to attack the privileges of their masters and of the Roman Catholic Church, both of which involved him in difficult and lengthy battles. He introduced a programme of religious toleration, destroying the monopoly of the papacy in worship and education. He ended censorship of the press. Breaking the power of provincial assemblies dominated by the aristocracy, he attempted to centralize all power in Vienna, which he thought would benefit the majority of the subjects in his dominions. Josef II was the essentially modern element in the Austrian Empire at the end of the eighteenth century. It was unfortunate, in his case, that he did not realize the strength of conservatism. Even the peasants, who had most to gain from his reforms, were sufficiently set in their ways that they too opposed many of his edicts, especially those concerned with religion and custom.

Catherine the Great, who had deposed her husband, Tsar Peter III, in 1762, understandably was not so well established as Josef, which meant that she was unable to institute such far-reaching reforms. The strength of the nobility made it impossible for her to do anything substantial for the serfs. She did, however, weaken the hold of the Church, creating a measure of religious toleration, and she established a number of state schools and colleges.

Frederick the Great, the least enlightened of the three, remained at heart a conservative. His reforms were of a minor nature, and were confined to the judiciary (the drafting of a national code of laws and the establishment of a hierarchy of courts), a measure of religious toleration and some limited social welfare legislation.

The principle common to these well-known despots was a belief in the subordination of all to the state. They regarded themselves merely as guardians of their people's best interests. Everything must be run so as to provide the greatest good for the greatest number. Sectional interests were to be nullified wherever possible. It was this view which prompted Josef II to declare that 'a single head, however mediocre, is better fitted to run a political organization than ten far more competent who have to act as a body'; the latter, he felt, would be side-tracked and tend to act for the good of the few alone.

The rule of a single person by these beliefs meant that, under the enlightened despots, government agencies tended to grow in size and scope. Frederick's bureaucracy expanded somewhat haphazardly. New departments were added to the existing administration to deal with specialized problems, often only to cause greater confusion. Similarly, Josef placed great faith in an efficient centralized bureaucracy. He did his utmost to destroy local assemblies and to bring all of his various dominions under a single head.

It is not surprising, therefore, given their attitude to the organization of the state and its society, that the enlightened despots pursued expansive foreign policies. Rulers who desired centralization and order within their boundaries were concerned to push back those boundaries to protect their interests. Since they believed that theirs was the best form of government, they were also anxious to convert others to such a regime. This philosophy goes some way to explain the progressive carving up of Poland in 1772, 1793 and 1795 by Austria, Prussia and Russia.

Both Frederick and Josef took a close personal interest in their armed forces. It has been convincingly argued that Josef's tax reforms were based on a desire to increase the state's revenue in order to support an expanded army. Catherine's energies were in some measure directed towards Russian expansion, particularly against the Ottoman Empire; two vicious wars were conducted by her generals in the Crimea and the Caucasus, throughout the 1760s, 70s and 80s. Frederick's notable territorial gains were in central Europe, beginning with Silesia in 1741, won from Austria; he, too, gained strategically important lands from the partitioning of Poland.

While historians often speak of Europe under the *ancien régime*, it should be remembered that there were important national differences between individual nations. It is not a term that can be used for the whole continent without reservation and exception. France, though it is rightly said to have been a society of the *ancien régime* before the Revolution of 1789, did not have an enlightened despot of Josef's kind. Louis XV, who ruled from 1715 to 1774, was politically weak when faced by vested opposition from the nobility. Although he possessed a sound administrative system based on the *Intendants*, his governments lacked the cash and, therefore, the power to institute enlightened reforms. France was as different from Austria as Prussia was from Russia. Each nation responded to the force of reformist philosophy in its own fashion.

Thus Europe on the eve of the French Revolution had already begun to assume characteristics which can be called modern. The old order was beginning to break down, though resistance to change was still winning the day.

The French Revolution

The French Revolution is one of the most complex modern historical events. Debate has not been confined to an interpretation of events and the significance which may be attached to them; it has extended to the Revolution's broader influence on culture, government and values throughout Europe and America. Indeed, historians have disputed its very starting point. Napoleon dated the French Revolution from the sensational affair of the Queen's necklace. In August 1785 Cardinal de Rohan was arrested at Versailles and charged with using Marie Antoinette's name to obtain a fantastically expensive diamond necklace from the court jewellers without payment. He claimed his right to be tried by the *Parlement* (local assembly) of Paris, a body composed of the bitterest enemies of the monarchy. The actual trial and the scandals which it exposed linked the Queen's name with the rogues of Parisian society. She, it was supposed by the public, was to have sold her favours to the cardinal for the necklace and then refused to pay the price. The part all this played in discrediting her in general opinion and so preparing the way for the fall of the monarchy is not to be underestimated. Yet it would be wrong to argue that this episode was a fundamental cause in bringing on the 1789 uprising. It was merely one more symptom of instability and malaise in France, produced by much bigger issues. Our purpose is to try to pinpoint the factors which produced this protracted revolt; what actually took place and what, briefly, were its effects.

The French Revolution really had its origins in the structure of eighteenth-century French society, which was divided into three orders (or 'estates'): the peasantry, the *bourgeoisie* and the nobility, and, set outside these three, the king and his close advisors. As the century passed, each group developed particular grievances which were basically irreconcilable. The peasantry, though no longer forced to carry out their feudal obligations, were heavily taxed and denied political rights. Theirs was an unenviable position. In the event of high food prices, they were the ones to provide mass support for an uprising. The *bourgeoisie* – educated, monied and also subject to high taxation – were increasingly excluded from political office by the restrictions imposed on them by the nobility. For example, in 1762 the *Parlement* of Grenoble, now run exclusively by the aristocracy, ruled that henceforth members must have a 'parlementary' ancestry of four noble generations in the paternal line. The able, middle-class Grenoble lawyers were thus excluded from the political office they desired and merited.

The aristocracy, who were exempt from direct taxation, jealously guarded their rights. Louis XIV had been forced by bad debts to sell seats in the *parlements*, and these had become, as a result, noble strongholds instead of the broader, more democratic institutions they were originally designed to be. The nobility's main complaint was directed towards the monarchy, which was continually trying to erode their highly privileged position. They were the richest element in the state and yet they contributed nothing to its upkeep. Both Louis

XIV (1643–1715) and Louis XV were hampered by financial weakness. They could not reform because they could not afford the cost, while the upper classes would not increase their minimal contributions because they realized that this would threaten their very existence.

In 1750 the King had authorized the creation of a *noblesse militaire* by which *bourgeois* army officers, on the completion of thirty years' service, could be ennobled. Yet in 1781, just as the thirty-year period was coming to an end, the aristocracy put sufficient pressure on the monarch to make him issue an ordinance effectually cancelling the scheme. Turgot, one of the most enlightened of Louis XV's ministers, devoted his efforts to restoring the royal finances; but having launched this opening phase of an attack on noble privilege, he was removed by the weak-willed Louis, again under pressure from the aristocracy. It was the unacceptable structure of French society which made France ripe for revolt when economic misfortune hit in the late 1780s.

From about 1710 to 1778 France experienced a period of almost unbroken prosperity. Agricultural production rose slowly while industrial output increased with greater rapidity, more than keeping pace with the growing population concentrated in the towns. However, from 1778 onwards France entered into a phase of economic contraction. Prices, profits and wages all fell. Though the economy recovered briefly in 1787, the crisis returned in 1788–9 with increased severity.

The rising in Paris and the overthrow of the government resulted in the establishment of a 'Constituent Assembly' in July 1789. It was of middle-class composition. Its reforms and decrees were essentially designed to create a society where the *bourgeoisie* might thrive. The granting of broad political, economic and social freedoms was their aim. Unfortunately many people, and especially the Third Estate, were not prepared for this legislation. This assembly, too, was dogged by financial weakness. Its attempts to redistribute taxation were pointless since, as a result of the disorders, no one was continuing to pay taxes at all. The *sans-culottes* (the working class in Paris) felt that the projected free-enterprise society would benefit the *bourgeoisie* at their expense. They felt that the old privilege of birth was being replaced by a new privilege of business and professional wealth.

Republican notions gradually gained support throughout 1791 and 1792. These were aggravated by Louis XVI's attachment to the traditional religious system, especially in view of the prevailing criticism of the privileged status of the Roman Catholic Church. Tension was heightened by Austrian hostility, ostensibly created by the dynastic ties between Queen Marie Antoinette and the Hapsburg monarchy. In April 1792 France declared war on Austria. The winter of 1792–3 saw an invading army repulsed and political power move to the Girondins, under Brissot. The Girondins were largely well-educated, professional men who supported foreign war as a means of uniting the people with the republican cause. Their attitude towards the monarchy vacillated but it was at their command that Louis XVI was executed in January 1793. A still more radical group, the Jacobins, then used the failure of the French army as an excuse to remove the Girondins from power and establish an emergency Revolutionary government. It was at this time that Robespierre rose to the

The execution of Marie Antoinette. From an engraving in the Mansell Collection.

fore. Ruthless in the pursuit of power, he came to dominate the so-called Committee of Public Safety through the elimination of his enemies. Some 2,600 people were guillotined in Paris alone, and there were further 'terrors' in the provinces. Robespierre's basic support came from the Parisian *sans-culottes*. His final overthrow and murder resulted from his inability to satisfy this group when economic depression closed its grip. For, in contrast to the earlier Assembly, he operated a policy of strict wage and price controls. While these worked in more moderate periods, the enforcement of such a complicated plan in times of real hardship was beyond the administrative resources even of the Jacobins. Parisian riots became frequent in the spring of 1794. A further desperate attempt to limit wages added to the anger of the workers, and he was deposed. With military support, a more moderate republicanism, which merged into the period known as the rule of the Directory, followed until Napoleon took over in 1799.

Through all these changes in political fortune, one thing stands out: the supreme importance of Paris. What happened in the capital was critical for the rest of the country. Paris was not only the seat of government and administration, it was a business and financial centre. It was the only city with a really influential mass of working people, some of whom, through their involvement in industry and commerce, had become very articulate. The provinces, accustomed to Parisian dominance in political affairs, tended to fall in line with its dictates as particular parties rose and fell.

What then, were the effects of this great upheaval, first on France and then on the rest of Europe? As a result of this great social reorganization France had become involved in an ideological war which was to last until 1815. This is important in its own right and we shall look at it in the section on Napoleon. More permanent, the Revolution conferred political power on the middle classes and reduced the burdens placed on the peasantry. The power of the Roman Catholic Church, though not broken, had been considerably reduced.

Revolution as a means of instituting political change was now established in France; it was resorted to throughout the nineteenth century – in 1830, 1848 and 1870.

The effects on the rest of Europe were also important. Beyond involving all the major European powers, including Great Britain, in a lengthy and costly war, the Revolution had a profound effect upon peoples' values and ideas. On the one hand, there were those who were frightened by its destructiveness. They became all the more determined to resist change and maintain the status quo. These included politicians like Metternich in Austria, Edmund Burke in England and Tsar Alexander II in Russia; they personified the forces of reaction which were now put on their mettle. Against these were those liberals who were encouraged by the achievements of the Revolution and wished to see similar results throughout Europe. They included Hegel and Novalis in Germany, Byron, Keats and Shelley in England, and Victor Hugo and Balzac in France. These were the writers and organizers who were to agitate for the independence of so many subjugated European states and to fight for the granting of liberal and national freedoms of the kind that the Revolution had produced in France. Its influence, therefore, was not a simple one.

Thus the French Revolution does deserve the lavish attention that it has been given by historians. It was a major event in European politics. It merits the title 'revolution' because it did initiate far-reaching and profound changes in French society and, possibly more important, alter men's attitudes to society throughout the continent. If it did not always change them altogether, it did at least make them think hard and reconsider.

Napoleonic Europe

Napoleon Bonaparte was only thirty years old when he became First Consul and absolute ruler of France in 1799. Though born on the island of Corsica, he was a French citizen as a result of its annexation from the Genoese in 1768, a year before his birth. From there he entered the army and was trained as an artillery officer. By 1793 he had been converted to Revolutionary ideals and had distinguished himself as a soldier by repulsing the British from the port of Toulon. His fame grew as he won a series of victories in Italy, particularly at the battles of Lodi and Rivoli. He himself dictated the peace terms with the Austrians at Campo-Formio. There followed an unsuccessful campaign in Egypt; the battle of the Nile was his first disastrous brush with Nelson. He returned, in 1799, to overthrow the French government – the Directory – and was appointed First Consul. By this act he established himself as sole ruler of the country. His efforts from this time till his final imprisonment on the island of St Helena were ruthlessly directed towards consolidating his position at home and extending France's power throughout the rest of Europe. He had an over-riding belief in his own abilities and fitness to rule.

Lejeune's painting of the Battle of Aboukir Bulloz (1799) where Napoleon drove the Turkish army into the sea. Mansell Collection. (*Photo: Photographie Bulloz*)

We shall divide the study of Napoleon into two parts. The first section tries to discover what were Napoleon's activities as an administrator within France and, later, his Empire – how effective his government was, and what its achievements were. The second part looks at him as a soldier and conqueror of half of Europe, and asks why he was so successful for so long and why, in the end, he failed.

The essential point about Napoleon's administration was that it was eclectic – that is, he drew his ideas, policies and personnel from many sources, and did not confine himself to particular vested interests as the old monarchy and Revolutionary committees had tended to do. Napoleon revived a centralized administrative system such as had existed under the Bourbons. He created ten ministries and related satellite bodies, putting them under the direction of members of the State Council. He reintroduced the old departmental system, by which the country was divided up into ninety-eight similar geographical districts, each controlled by a prefect (*préfet*), reminiscent of the old *Intendants* of Louis XV.

As the new prefects, he appointed men of experience and ability, who were chosen for their talents and not for their past political allegiances. The success of the Consulate was partly based on his success in recruiting the ablest men for his government. Former royal civil servants rubbed shoulders with ex-Revolutionaries. Fouché, his chief of police, had served both Robespierre and the Directory before serving Bonaparte. Though the nobility lost their ancient privileges, it has recently been shown that they by no means lost their real influence over their localities. Many old nobles who returned when an amnesty was declared in 1801 took important offices in the Consulate. This ability to mix together such various elements was a very important part of Napoleon's success. His autocratic rule helped to impose a powerful, unified will on the French people.

The cornerstone of his actual policy-making was the *Code Napoléon*, which was the name given in 1807 to the civil code first introduced in 1804. Before the Revolution, and certainly while it was in progress, there had been no real unity in France. Unsuccessful attempts to formulate a uniform code had been made on five occasions by the Directory. This new code was a compromise solution not limited merely to legal definition; it was designed to affect the whole of society. On the one hand it confirmed the disappearance of the outward trappings of the aristocracy and confirmed the social principles of 1789. It stressed the liberty of the individual and equality before the law. On the other hand it was concerned with the interests of the *bourgeoisie*; it sanctified and confirmed rights of property and did its best to strengthen the institution of marriage. Napoleon himself was not so much responsible for the individual articles as for bringing together the members who composed its sessions and the ideas which these came to embody through their deliberations. The *Code* was later applied to all territories which France either annexed or came to rule through conquest. For Napoleon it was one of the basic bonds of Empire.

So Napoleon was consciously aware that he was an heir to a monarchy as well as a republic. The constitution of the life Consulate (1802) gave him the power of an absolute monarch; it only remained to add the facade of the imperial title in 1804. By crowning himself Emperor in front of the Pope in Paris, he immeasurably strengthened his position. For this satisfied the old aristocracy, who were still attached to notions of royalty, while it allayed the fears of those who had benefited from its overthrow. For the regicides (the men, that is, responsible for the execution of Louis XVI), Revolutionary *bourgeoisie* and peasantry could never feel safe so long as their present regime rested on the life of one man. A hereditary Empire meant a stable and guaranteed future.

This tactic was reinforced by the creation of the Legion of Honour in 1802. It is significant that both in shape and colour, the medal resembled the old Order of Saint Louis. In 1808 an imperial nobility was introduced. Napoleon attached great importance to these outward forms. When Thibaudeau, one of his advisors who had worked on the civil code, referred to his new order as merely 'baubles', Napoleon retorted, 'You are pleased to call them baubles; well, it is with baubles that mankind is governed'. Again, in this respect of his policy we see his desire to synthesize the old and the new.

Napoleon's achievements as a soldier were considerable. After his Italian campaign and the defeat of the Austrians in 1797, he enjoyed a period of quiet until becoming involved in the war of the Third Coalition of 1805–7. First he beat the Austrians at Austerlitz; then he defeated the Prussians at Jena and Auerstadt. The Russians continued to resist alone till 1807, when they concluded an alliance at Tilsit. His invasion of Spain in 1808 involved him in an unsuccessful war with the British and with local guerrilla movements. Yet he

The execution of Spanish patriots by Napoleon's soldiers. '13 May 1808' by Goya. Museo del Prado, Madrid.

was able to win his fourth campaign against the Austrians by a victory at Wagram in 1809. His invasion of Russia in 1812 was a failure, though he reached Moscow; the strain imposed on France by this venture led to his defeat by Austria, Russia and Prussia at Leipzig in 1814. He was imprisoned on Elba, but escaped in February 1815 to rule in France again as Emperor. His final bid for European supremacy ended on the field of Waterloo, where an Allied army, for the first time including English troops under Wellington, utterly destroyed the French forces.

Napoleon's success in battle was due, in considerable measure, to the adoption of policies which worked well on the home front. Throughout the eighteenth century it had become increasingly difficult for a commoner to acquire commissioned rank. Napoleon furthered the system thrown up by the French Revolutionary Wars of promotion by merit. His more notable generals, such as Lannes, Davout, Massena and Murat, were all of non-noble background.

Napoleon also pushed the strategy developed at that time to its logical conclusion. Breaking with traditions of eighteenth-century warfare, he favoured very large armies and a ruthless strategy designed to annihilate the enemy by swift and intricate manœuvres. At the battles of Ulm and Jena his forces totalled between 180,000 and 190,000 men. It has been calculated that two million Frenchmen saw service between the years 1804 and 1815. Napoleon was also noted for marching 210,000 men from the Rhine to the Danube and from there to Ulm in only seventeen days, which would have been inconceivable fifty years before, in the days of long baggage trains, when armies were reluctant to stray far from fortresses. Once the enemy had been engaged Napoleon believed, like Nelson, in its annihilation. Clausewitz, in his work *Vom Krieg* (1832), recorded his sentiments: 'A principle of moderation would be an absurdity [so] let us not hear of generals who would conquer without bloodshed.' It should be stressed, however, that these notions were not original to Napoleon; they had been advocated by French theorists in the later years of the eighteenth century.

Napoleon also believed in 'total war'. For him conflict was not to be confined to soldiers alone; the whole nation had in some respect to be mobilized. He attached great significance to propaganda. The policy begun in 1793 to involve everyone in France was pursued. 'All Frenchmen', it was announced, 'are called to their country to defend liberty ... young men will go to the front; married men will forge arms and carry food; women will make tents and clothing and work in hospitals; children will turn old linen into bandages; old men will be carried into the squares to teach the hatred of kings and republican unity.' This was Napoleon's doctrine, too. His eventual downfall was due primarily to an over-reaching ambition; he took on too many nations and, in stretching his forces to the limit in Russia, left himself open to defeat.

Map 2. Europe in 1812.

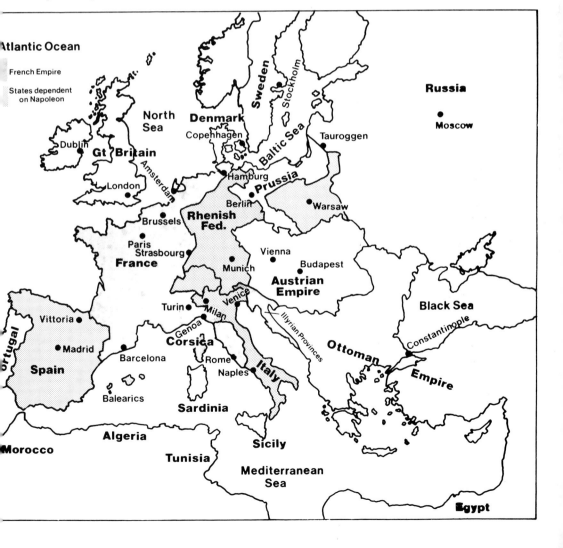

So, when we look at his career as a whole from 1799 to 1815, we may conclude that historical accounts have often overstated Napoleon's achievements. He has been seen too often as an enlightened innovator. It has been argued that his particular genius lay in an ability to draw on both traditional and modern ideas; it was in the successful combination of these that his special talents lay. It should not be forgotten that in many respects Napoleon was tyrannical. He did not favour democratic government; his ambitions for conquest were without limit, and he was ruthless in his drive for European supremacy. It can also be argued that his domestic reforms were all conditioned, if not wholly inspired, by the desire to stabilize and confirm his dictatorial hold over France.

The Industrialization of Europe

'The Industrial Revolution' is a phrase often used but rarely defined. Though it has much wider social implications, it is strictly an economic term meaning a sharp acceleration in the average rate at which wealth is produced by individuals. This jump is considered to be sufficient to justify the description 'revolutionary'. Therefore it is not a phenomenon that can be observed throughout Europe at any one time. Particular nations experienced industrial revolutions at different times. Britain was the first, with a dramatic expansion in the economy that took place in the early 1780s. Belgium was the next to follow in the 1830s, while France was not to achieve a sustained and rapid increase in GNP (Gross National Product, a measure of total wealth in the state) until the 1840s. Germany followed in the 1870s, roughly at the same time as America. The problem, therefore, is to explain this timetable. Why was Britain a hundred years in advance of Germany and why did the other European states follow in the order they did? Why, indeed, did Russia fail throughout the whole nineteenth century to produce anything which may be termed an industrial revolution? Recent scholarship has shown that there are no simple reasons. To answer the question we have to take a broad view of society; it cannot be seen in terms of coal mines, iron foundries and cotton factories alone.

This period of European history was characterized by dramatic population growth. Here lies a clue to an understanding of the process of industrialization. Though this was a trend that had begun back in the middle of the eighteenth century, it really only became strikingly evident after the end of the Napoleonic Wars. Britain, it is interesting to note, set the pace: rapid growth began in the 1780s, and from 1811 to 1891 its population grew from $18\frac{1}{4}$ to $37\frac{1}{2}$ million; that is, by about 10 per cent per decade as compared with 4 per cent per decade before 1780. France, similarly, enjoyed an uncharacteristic increase in population between 1840 and 1860, falling off as the century progressed; it corresponded with that country's fastest period of economic growth in the nineteenth century. The German population also shows a remarkable acceleration from the 1870s onwards. In other words, there would appear to be an intimate connection between an industrial revolution and a rapid increase in population. But it would be wrong to say that the first caused the second, or vice versa; the two are interconnected. Population expansion is simply one factor in this process of economic growth; it helps to start the movement off and, once under way, it in turn is stimulated. More people means a bigger market for producers, which encourages specialization and greater efficiencies in the organization of labour. The factory system could never have worked in medieval Europe because there were too few customers, poorly connected by communications. The Industrial Revolution itself, involving the creation of new industries and the expansion of old ones, encouraged further population increase by creating more jobs. In addition, the improved diets that this economic expansion brought for many artisans may also have reduced the level of infant mortality. It is a complex and mutually satisfying process.

Just as important and as much a part of this phenomenon were improvements in farming techniques, again sufficient to be called revolutionary. A growing population, tending to be occupied in the new industrial towns and cities of Europe, had to be fed. The only way this could be achieved was for each farm to produce more per acre. As early as 1750 in Europe, and earlier in Britain, improved agricultural techniques were adopted. The wider application of crop rotations, involving an end to fallowing and the use of more kinds of grain, resulted in greater output. Better breeding methods for livestock and a trend towards specialization meant higher yields of higher-quality produce. Robert Bakewell, the British agricultural reformer, declared that his purpose was to produce better meat not for the gentry but for the masses. Without these improvements it would have been impossible for Britain or any other European state to support a growing proportion of the population devoting its working hours solely to commerce and industry. The beginnings of industrialization in Russia at the end of the nineteenth century, for example, were conditioned by the general expansion of agriculture together with the rapid extension of cultivation into the south-eastern provinces. So economic growth was a broad process that necessarily affected all aspects of production.

It would, of course, be wrong to ignore industry altogether. For while this sector may not be viewed as being of primary importance, the iron, coal and textile industries are of some strategic significance. Cotton goods and mass-produced manufactures were valuable not only for exports but in stimulating home demand in the 1780s and beyond. Germany's development in the 1880s was based in a similar way on chemicals, electrical goods, optics and precision engineering. It was the expanding demand for English textiles, and particularly cotton, which led to the full development of the factory system in the 1830s. Workers were now organized in their masses to do specific tasks on the production line, rather than doing the complete job themselves. Hours were strictly regulated and a new work discipline was imposed.

In fact a late industrial revolution was highly beneficial to Germany. For she was able to adopt the latest machinery and techniques, while older established countries were still using outdated equipment. This must be an important reason why Germany did so well in the new highly technical fields such as electricals and chemicals; she was able to benefit from British experience without having to replace obsolete stock. America, developing at roughly the same time with the completion of the railroads opening up the interior, had the same advantage.

Given industry's importance, geographical factors must clearly have played a part in the relative timing of industrial revolutions. The steam engine, an important energy source, demanded inputs of iron, water and coal, so that areas which combined these resources were often the first to progress. Britain had a clear advantage in this respect. France's lack of coal was one of the factors affecting her relatively late 'take-off'. Belgium, by comparison, had ample supplies of raw materials. When conditions came right in Germany it was not surprising that the Ruhr region became an important industrial area, since it combined coal and iron ore deposits and the Rhine provided an excellent route-way. Jacob Mayer chose Bochum for his new steel works in 1842 for these very reasons.

Clearly, an efficient communications network is an essential factor. Again geography plays its part. Britain was better placed than most, and tended to innovate more quickly and widely than the rest of Europe. She began in the 1750s with a good river system, backed up by an already growing network of turnpike roads. The canals followed in the forty years after the 1760s. Britain was again the first European country to construct a railway network, followed significantly on the Continent by Belgium and then France. Russian expansion was evidently impeded by its sheer size. It was only with French financial help that it was able to make the beginnings of a railway system in the 1880s.

Other factors which must be taken into consideration are slightly more institutional. Mercantile and financial connections were influential in establishing Britain's early lead. As with France, her broadly-based colonial possessions gave her a ready-built export market and access to a wide range of raw materials. They also helped London as an insurance and mercantile centre. Supremacy in banking followed on this basis. The Bank of England grew in stature throughout the nineteenth century, becoming internationally important. By 1900 London was the leading commercial, banking, insurance, shipping and investment centre of the world. Income from these services was a considerable element in the British balance of payments, as much as 44 per cent in 1800. (This figure includes income from interest and dividends.) Other countries, including France in 1800, tried to create efficient financial systems based on a national, central bank. But none was as successful as Britain until America began to develop Wall Street at the end of the nineteenth century.

The last remaining factor is the least tangible; economists call it 'the residuum'. It really means those ingredients which are left over and which may be seen to have exercised some influence on industrialization. For example, in some European states there was a deliberate stifling of the entrepreneurial class. That is, it is possible that protection against foreign competition in France after 1815 tended to deaden initiative and spirit amongst businessmen. The guild system in central Europe resisted attempts to create large-scale enterprises and opposed the introduction of new techniques. In Russia, the strict hierarchy of social orders prevented humble men of merit from getting on in business. (It is important to remember that many leading English industrialists were from the middling orders and often of a non-conformist background.)

The political organization of various European states did not encourage economic growth. The fragmentation of Germany, Austria and Italy after 1815 retarded progress, though the Customs Union or *Zollverein* initiated in 1834 went some way to giving Germany unity and cohesion. Governments themselves could foster growth. During the period of most rapid French expansion in the nineteenth century (1840–60), the construction of a railway system was promoted by the state. The Railway Law of 1842 stated that the government would pay for the land on which the track was to be laid and one-third of the cost of buildings and equipment. Technical education was also encouraged at this time.

The 120 years between 1780 and 1900 witnessed a remarkable transformation in Europe's economic structure. All the major continental states had industries of some sort, even if their predominant activity was still agricultural; while Britain, France, Belgium and Germany had become truly industrial nations. It was a development which was to have wide repercussions. It caused far-reaching social consequences through the creation of a new business elite and an urban working class; it affected politics and diplomacy by speeding up communications for both people and information; it brought a fresh destructiveness to war. In answering old problems of famine, disease and poor living conditions, it produced a new series of problems of its own (see *Science and Technology*, p. 91, and *Environment*, p. 205).

The Rise of the Nation State

In 1789 the nation state was not well defined in Europe. France suffered from too many internal divisions. The Holy Roman Empire was, in reality, a mixed group of peoples with differing cultures, values and governments. Germany was a mass of individual small states. Even by 1815 this situation had not changed substantially for some Continental countries, including Italy and Germany. The process by which these nations came to be united and conscious of that unity was a long one, but by the 1850s the most important part of this evolution was virtually complete. For, by this time, the rule of law had developed; governments were being organized not to resist change but to initiate reforms themselves. The nature of this legislation had also altered. It tended to affect everybody in the state rather than particular groups. The state was viewed in a new way. No longer was it regarded solely as a machine to carry out specialized jobs, such as the rule of law and order; in addition, it was viewed as a focus for emotion, duties and morality. The German philosopher Hegel thought that it alone could give being to the individual. The problem remains to try to trace how this came about and, in doing so, to understand why.

Map 3. Europe after the Congress of Vienna: 1815.

What were the forces making for change? The progressive industrialization of Europe and the population expansion which this involved were crucial to the rise of the nation state. European economic growth produced a new *bourgeoisie* – men of middling status and of an inventive and independent disposition who had made their fortunes from the opportunities offered by the opening up of fresh markets in industry and commerce. They were monied, educated and, by virtue of their position over their workers, influential. Yet, because of the continued existence of the outward legal form of *ancien régime* society, they were denied the political status which their actual position merited. The old, landed aristocracy continued to rule and rights were still defined by birth. It is not surprising, therefore, that these *nouveaux riches* (newly rich people) were discontented, and were often at the centre of the cries for reform.

These were the classes to whom ideas of both liberalism and nationalism had a ready appeal. Liberalism really meant the struggle for greater freedom of action. For not only did they want wider constitutional powers, they also desired broader opportunities to express themselves. Censorship still operated in varying degrees throughout nineteenth-century Europe. In Austria, under Chancellor Metternich, every single book, paper or advertisement had to be approved by the official censor. Rossini's march for the newly elected Pope Pius IX could not be played in 1846 because His Holiness was thought to be a liberal. It is significant that the 1848 uprising in Vienna was triggered off by medical and engineering students who had drafted a petition to abolish censorship and to establish freedom of teaching. 'The intellectual food allowed to the nation' (and here Marx in the *Communist Manifesto* of 1848 is speaking specifically of Austria) 'was selected with manifest caution and dealt out as sparingly as possible.' Repression of liberties, practised in varying degrees throughout Europe, was an important factor in producing such a universal response among the *bourgeoisie* in 1848. Every city with more than about 100,000 inhabitants experienced some form of uprising in that year.

The other movement influencing the rise of the nation states, and which also had a special appeal to the discontented middle classes, was nationalism. Many peoples in Europe were subject to dynastic subjugation: for instance the Germans, Italians, Czechs, Slovaks, Hungarians, Greeks, Poles and Belgians. In the eighteenth century enlightened thought had argued that internationalism and cosmopolitanism were ideals. While not rejecting the idea of co-operation between nations, men now focused their attention more immediately on the sovereignty of particular peoples. The struggles of the small Balkan states against the Ottoman Empire were compared with Holy Wars; Lord Byron was not alone in his involvement in the wars for Greek independence. Mazzini informed Italian workers that their 'chief and most essential duty of all, is to your country. To secure the freedom and unity of your nation is your duty; and it is also a necessity.' There was, therefore, a fresh pride in nationalism, in being a member of a particular 'race' or *Volk*. A special appeal was made to the past to emphasize any group spirit by reference to old folk tales and ancient heroisms. Hence the new thinkers were termed Romantics; they believed in more than pure reason. Important in this respect were Goethe, Novalis and Hegel in Germany, Sir Walter Scott, Wordsworth, Byron, and Keats in England, and in France Victor Hugo, Balzac, Saint-Simon and Châteaubriand.

By this reference to tradition, nationalism appealed to sentiments of separatism; it reminded men of all that was special, individual and personal. Hegel, bound up with the national movement, developed this argument further. He suggested that men could only realize their full potential as individuals by being part of a coherent state. Thus, nationalism was not adopted by the discontented *bourgeoisie* as simply another means of securing careers open to talent, though clearly independence for many central European states would produce this result. It was more than that; their patriotism was part of deeply held beliefs about man and society. The steady industrialization of Europe was also important in another respect. For it involved not only population growth but also the creation of the factory system and the rapid expansion of towns. It created an urban working class. Again this made for discontent with existing conditions. The technical advance which was all part of the Industrial Revolution also produced the skilled artisan. It was this group of educated and comparatively well-paid workers who first thought about their conditions of work and general place in society; these were the early organizers and policy makers. They were able to spare the time to collect funds, publish newspapers, run political societies and agitate for reforms. In England, they included such men as William Lovett and Thomas Cooper, both Chartists. In Europe, however, during this period, the outstanding working class leaders tended to be of a middle-class background: Louis Blanc, son of a high government official; Mazzini, son of a doctor; Karl Marx, a graduate of Bonn and Berlin; and Bakunin, a former Russian officer of aristocratic family.

These were the thinkers who were to reject liberal notions in favour of socialism and then communism. They argued that the loose freedoms advocated by the liberals were a sign of weakness; they preferred group solidarity and tight bonds between individuals of the same class. It is not surprising that they often referred to the Middle Ages where they pinpointed the interdependence of members of society, each having duties and obligations to others. But theirs was an influence not to be felt with any great force till the end of the nineteenth century.

The effect of industrialization on the rest of the workforce was also significant, though more for the latter part of the nineteenth century than for the middle. The rapid expansion of population tended to concentrate the new industrial workforce in specific areas; overcrowding and poor sanitation were normal. This partly explains why the 1848 revolutions were urban in character. For, in addition to these disgusting living conditions, the workers had to accept a new and harsh labour discipline. The application of machinery and the splitting up of production tasks among groups meant that hours and rates of work were strictly regulated. No longer were parents responsible for their children. Factory masters imposed tight rules, which were resented by people accustomed to regulating their own pace of work and apprenticing their own children into their trades. So here was a massed body of discontent which could easily be aroused by those who were better educated and more highly motivated towards change.

Yet despite all these pressures for reform, the conservatives did not give in easily. The 1848 revolutions were not a success. A leading figure in the ranks of reaction and opposition to change was Prince Klemens Metternich, Chancellor and therefore effective ruler of the Austrian Empire from 1809 to 1848. He was concerned not only to see that liberal sentiments remained ineffectual, but also to preserve the balance of power within Europe as a whole. He was a prime mover in establishing the so-called Congress System, which consisted of a series of meetings involving the foreign ministers of the five major powers (Britain, Austria, France, Prussia and Russia) to maintain the status quo and prevent the emergence of the forces of nationalism amongst dependent states. Though it was very successful until the early 1820s, stifling, for example, Italian and Spanish uprisings, Metternich's influence declined over time. His failure in 1826 to prevent Greek independence was symptomatic of the growing power of liberalism and nationalism in Europe. The out-

Uprising in Berlin, 1848. Mansell Collection.

break of revolution in 1848 saw his personal downfall and a weakening of the system he stood for.

The actual timing of these continent-wide revolts is significant and worthy of attention. They were caused by economic depression. The growth of international trade and the progressive commitment to industry meant that the slumps caused by the trade cycle were more acute. The 1846–7 trough was deeper than that of 1825 and was made all the more harsh by additional harvest failures, intensified further by the poor potato crop. So mass support was stirred up by dearth – though it should be noted that people actually rose in revolt not when prices were at their highest (in 1846–7) but when they had fallen slightly and when distress was not so acute and the people had the ability to act. The rate at which prices changed also affected people's reactions. It is also probably true that towns followed the example of other towns, (and that when Paris rose in February, Italian cities in February–March and Vienna in March and May, German and Hungarian towns tended to copy them).

Thus, by the middle of the nineteenth century these forces making for the full development of the nation states were well established. Though nationalist movements were defeated in 1848, the power of reaction was not sufficient to extinguish them; they suffered a temporary setback and no more. For the second half of the century was to see the liberation of Italy by Garibaldi, the uniting of Germany under Bismarck, and the break-up of the Austrian Empire. Possibly the really surprising thing is that these movements were so long delayed. The conservatives were tenacious fighters. As Mazzini wrote in 1835: 'Old Europe is dying, the old order is passing away. But it is a long time on the death bed.'

The Unification of Italy and Germany

The history of nineteenth-century Europe is in many respects the story of how loosely bound groups of people, at the mercy of dynastic subjugation, came to form united and independent nations eager to assert themselves within the continental balance of power. The progressive development of both Italy and Germany are clear examples of this trend. It is, however, a process which had its roots in the Europe of Napoleon, for both the Italian (from 1804) and German states were subject to his all-embracing rule. The application of the Code Napoleon and the Continental System (the closing of the whole of Europe to British trade, established by the decrees of Berlin and Milan and designed to crush British commerce) meant that each of these countries experienced a political, social and economic unity which they had yet to acquire under Austrian domination. Nationalist movements were inspired by this example. Yet with Bonaparte's defeat in 1815 and the conclusion of the Treaty of Vienna this very real unity was destroyed. The victors sought a return to the eighteenth-century political system; they were anxious to resurrect Austria as a major power. Hence the German and Italian states were deliberately divided up in order to make them weak and readily subject to the will of Metternich, the Austrian Chancellor. Germany was divided into a loose confederation of thirty-nine states, with no central administration. In Italy the individual principalities were revived: notably those of Naples, Piedmont, Tuscany and Modena, while the new 'kingdom' of Lombardy-Venetia was directly placed under the rule of the Hapsburg Emperor. So the story of the next fifty or so years, in these two countries, is that of the struggle between national patriots trying to achieve coherence and independence, and the more conservative ruling aristocracy who rigidly opposed this development.

The first problem faced by patriots such as Mazzini and Cavour in Italy and Hegel and Bismarck in Germany was the geographical variations that resulted from the Vienna peace settlement in 1815. Metternich's assertion that the Italian state was simply a 'geographical expression' was not wholly true. For Italy, like Germany, suffered from being divided by mountain and river systems. The striking contrast in the economic fortunes of southern and northern Italy was based on a great difference in the quality of the soil and climate, together with dearth, in one case, and, in the other, richness in mineral deposits. Sicily, the furthest south of the Italian principalities, was particularly poor in these respects. Contrasting agricultural and industrial development created internal rivalries. This situation was not so very unlike that in Germany. Here, too, states varied considerably in their economic development. The more progressive agricultural and industrial states bordering on the Rhine, including Prussia and Hanover, offered a sharp contrast to those eastern and less richly endowed states, dominated by Austria, including Bavaria and the duchies of Saxe-Coburg and Saxe-Weimar. German unity was further hindered by a weak east–west river system and an absence of good roads, canals and later railways. It was Metternich's intention that Germany should remain backward, which would make it easier to dominate.

This problem was partly overcome in the 1830s and 40s by trade agreements concluded between individual states. Hitherto, German economic development and unity had been hampered by outdated tariff barriers. Within Prussia alone there were sixty-seven different tariffs in 1815. Internal Prussian duties were abolished in 1818. This was so successful that other German states formed customs unions of their own in 1828. But as the resources of the Prussian union were greater, they all came together to form a single *Zollverein* (customs union) in 1834. Other states continued to join in the years that followed. It would be wrong to see this union as being politically inspired. Its authors were concerned in the first place to encourage industry and trade. The fact that it indirectly conferred a measure of administrative unity on a series of states was an important result, but incidental to their purpose.

In Italy, Count Camillo Cavour, leader of the movement for unification or *risorgimento*, offered a similar solution to this problem. He had originally entered politics in 1850 as the Piedmontese Minister of Agriculture, Marine and Commerce. Becoming Minister of Finance and then Prime Minister, his policies were directed towards encouraging commerce, improving the financial system and constructing strategic roads, railways and canals. He also concluded a series of trade treaties with Great Britain, Belgium, the German *Zollverein* and Holland. In other words, he believed first in making Piedmont a prosperous and progressive nation (comparable in this respect with Prussia), which could then be used to dominate and so to unify the remaining Italian states. He saw the importance of railways, hoping to make Piedmont part of an international network, and initiating a scheme for piercing Mont Cénis by a railway tunnel and turning Genoa into a great commercial port.

Hand in hand with this attempt to unify Germany and Italy geographically and economically went the struggle for national independence. Both countries failed to achieve this goal in 1848, when revolution broke out in their major cities. Neither was yet powerful enough to escape from the Austrian grip. It was in the period between 1850 and 1870 that the movement began to yield concrete results. Its leaders had to deal with a common enemy – the Austro-Hungarian Empire; a common ally was France under the Second Empire of Napoleon III.

In Italy, Cavour, the leading politician in the fragmented peninsula, realized, as a result of the failure of 1848, that Italy needed assistance. His first preference was for British aid. Britain was, in general, sympathetic to the cause of liberal nationalism in Italy, and had no immediate demands or conditions to make in return. But Britain would not help with vital military support. The most Cavour could expect from her was a benevolent neutrality if a war against Austria should develop. So Cavour's most likely ally was Napoleon III, who had widely broadcast his sympathies for the cause of Italian unification and had shown readiness to embark on foreign adventures in order to gain fresh prestige for his own regime. In July 1858 Napoleon and Cavour sealed an agreement which came to be known as the Pact of Plombières. Its essential clauses involved the offer to France of Savoy and Nice in return for her military support against Austria.

Piedmontese mobilization in the spring of 1859 precipitated an Austrian declaration of war. After six weeks' fighting, the Piedmontese and French forces won two battles at Magenta and Solferino, driving the Austrians out of Lombardy. They were decisive. A quick peace concluded at Villafranca resulted in the partial unification of Italy with the creation of an Italian Confederation under the presidency of the Pope. Many individual principalities remained, and Cavour resigned in disgust. But when Piedmont was granted Parma and Modena, in addition to Lombardy, he returned to office.

The final phase of unification was largely the work of Garibaldi. Having fought against the Austrians, in May 1860 he sailed from Genoa with his thousand 'redshirts' to invade Sicily and work north in the name of a united Italy. He defeated the large Bourbon army of Francis II of Naples, taking that city in September. Cavour was worried not only that this campaign would attract European intervention, but also that Garibaldi's success would destroy Piedmontese leadership in the peninsula. So, after securing Napoleon's support, Cavour sent a large Piedmontese force south to destroy the papal forces and to occupy Naples, thus checking Garibaldi's progress. This final movement resulted in unification, and in January 1861 the first all-Italian parliament met in Turin.

The means by which Prussia under Bismarck was able to unite the German states, also against Austrian opposition, were not precisely the same, though there are important similarities. At the time when Victor Emmanuel of Piedmont-Sardinia was being made king of all Italy, Prussia gained a new leader in William I. Though he was a deeply conservative man in most matters of internal policy, he believed that it was part of his mission to see that Prussia unified Germany. It was for this reason that both nationalists and liberals welcomed his coming to the throne. As in Italy, the movement began with a scheme for partial unification. It was proposed by Prussia that the two northern army corps should be placed under her control and the two southern corps under Austrian control. In this way Prussia was really asking for the splitting of the German Confederation between these two dominant powers – at least for the time being.

In July 1861 Otto von Bismarck (1815–98) began to make his mark in German politics. He was of a landed, aristocratic family, though he himself first became a civil servant. Having acquired political experience in the Prussian Diet in Berlin (where he showed himself to be a determined reactionary, opposing all liberal measures), he rose to power as the Prussian representative to the German Bundestag. He was a man with a quick and sensitive mind of great strength. In July he produced his famous Baden Memorandum on the defence and organization of Germany, arguing for a strong and united nation.

Like Cavour, Bismarck realized that an alliance with France would be an advantage in any dispute with Austria. He was aware that Prussia herself, like Piedmont, needed strengthening. So the army was enlarged, re-equipped and reorganized. Now Bismarck wanted a war. He saw that a Prussian war against Denmark in 1864 would achieve similar results to Cavour's entry into the

Crimean War in 1854. It would indicate where future leadership lay and raise Prussia's prestige. The result of the victorious war was that Prussia took Schleswig and Austria Holstein in 1865. Bismarck's plan was now to secure French neutrality (achieved by a meeting with Napoleon III at Biarritz in October 1865) so that he could tackle Austria unhampered. There is no doubt that Bismarck, backed by the army chiefs Moltke and Roon, wanted and planned for conflict with Austria.

In June 1866 Bismarck forced events by proposing that the Bundestag should be dissolved and that Austria should be excluded from the affairs of a new German nation. War resulted. The Austrians were decisively beaten at the battle of Sadowa and the outcome, formalized by the Treaty of Prague, was the independence of the German states. The gradual consolidation of these groups could now proceed without the restraining hand of Austria, and culminated in the new German Reich (kingdom) of 1871. It is difficult to say whether Bismarck had a single plan drawn up in the 1860s designed to achieve this end by exactly these means. Some historians have argued that this was so, using the evidence of a report by the British statesman, Disraeli, who said that in 1862 Bismarck had told him of his whole scheme for the unification (exactly as it was to take place) in a conversation over dinner. This forms a contrast with the methods of Cavour. The Italian was much more of an opportunist; he was forced to act in 1860 when Garibaldi invaded from the south, while his comparative military weakness forced him to rely much more heavily than Bismarck on French support.

So there are some clear similarities in the processes by which Germany and Italy became unified. Though a contrast can be drawn between Bismarck, the long-term planner, and Cavour, the opportunist, they both had similar aims to which they devoted their greatest efforts. These were a Prussian-controlled North German Confederation and a united Italy dominated by Piedmont. Their common enemy was Austria. Within their borders, another common adversary was the Roman Catholic Church, which vigorously opposed any attempt by the state to assume a greater control of events and administration. Bismarck and Cavour were supreme exponents of *realpolitik* (that is, acting in the best interests of one's state, whatever means one has to employ). Their successes are to be explained more by this masterly grasp of the realities of the balance of power and the potentialities of their own countries than by any preconceived plans they may have laid. As events exercised their influence, so they were forced to modify their general strategy. These unifications provide an example of how men of great influence react together with events, such as wars and conferences, and not in a vacuum, to alter the actual political map of Europe. Their efforts were responsible for speeding up the rise of Germany and Italy and Austria's consequent fall from supremacy in central Europe.

The Rise and Development of Imperialism

Imperialism has its origins in many earlier centuries of colonial expansion. From the sixteenth century onwards Spain, Portugal, Holland, France and, latterly, Britain had established colonial dominions. These adventures had involved not only mercantile interests but were based to varying degrees upon missionary zeal, national pride, adventure and plain greed. So in 1870, when this movement suddenly developed, there was nothing essentially new about the extension of European control over other areas of the globe. Yet the scale on which it was carried out was new; also the very idea of 'imperialism' was fresh. The word itself was a mid-nineteenth-century invention. By 1914 there were very few countries not under European rule, or onetime colonies which had seized their independence. And during this period Germany, Italy, Belgium, America and Japan had joined Britain and France as imperial states. It would seem that no one single motive was responsible for this phenomenon; the reasons included the desire for international status, the need for wider and more diverse markets, the paternalistic belief in European democracy and Christianity, and a simple desire for adventure and riches.

Both the Russian revolutionary leader Lenin in his pamphlet *Imperialism the Highest Stage of Capitalism* (1916) and contemporary economists have suggested that the main reason for this process of expansion was economic. The period from the late eighteenth to the mid-nineteenth century had seen the progressive industrialization of most of Europe. New large-scale industrial concerns required large markets; they also needed broader and larger inputs of raw materials. Their profits needed fresh fields for investment, and new areas to exploit. The vast African and Asian heartlands provided an answer. The special attractions of these continents were that they offered the raw materials needed by the rapidly proliferating factories of Europe, including cotton, silk, rubber, vegetable oils and certain minerals. In the nineteenth century Britain could still manufacture cotton cloth cheaper than the Indians, despite the fact that the raw materials and finished goods had to be transported half way around the globe. It would be wrong, however, to see the movement wholly in self-seeking economic terms. The British were responsible for supplying the Indian continent with its railway system, designed and installed by British engineers. The new imperial states were also a valuable outlet for rapidly expanding populations. There was steady migration from England, for example, to Australia and Canada, and on a smaller scale to Africa and Asia. So it was not a process from which only the ruling state benefited. Economically backward countries received a modernizing boost which it is difficult to imagine they would have received otherwise. Besides engineering projects the investment of foreign capital was important after 1880. Of the annual investment of British capital between 1909 and 1913, 36 per cent went into British overseas territories. It has recently been argued that this money was not in fact deployed in the best interests of the British themselves; it could have been better spent had it been invested at home rather than abroad.

The first railway in British Burma – opening of the Rangoon and Irrawaddy State Railway at Rangoon, 1877. Mary Evans Picture Library.

Another important reason why rising European nations were keen to develop imperial interests was that they felt a country acquired a certain international status based upon the extent of its possessions. In this respect, the empire was similar to the size and strength of a nation's armed forces. Indeed, the two often went hand in hand. Britain's economic and military strength largely lay, throughout the nineteenth century, with her navy and mercantile marine. So her desire to expand her colonial empire not surprisingly tended to focus on lands with good anchorages and strategic command of shipping lanes. The acquisition of Cyprus, a fine Mediterranean base, and the Cape of Good Hope, to safeguard East African and Asian trade, are cases in point. The French were more interested (as a European land power with a large army) in securing additional sources of manpower; thus they annexed large areas of central Africa. The importance of colonies as a measure of status is illustrated by Disraeli's changed attitude. In 1852 he had decried them as being 'millstones around our necks'; yet by 1877 he had come to consider India so important that he suggested to Queen Victoria that she take the new title of Empress of

India. It was a move which excited popular imagination, both at home and overseas, and strengthened his and the Queen's standing.

Of course, not every colonizer or explorer was a self-seeking plunderer interested only in wealth. Many explorers were also missionaries and teachers, anxious to 'improve' the native populations they encountered. The most famous was David Livingstone. A medical missionary, originally sent to Africa by the London Missionary Society, he later returned to Africa as an official government representative 'to open a path for commerce and Christianity'. He was one among many. The French to a greater degree sent organized missions to Africa to convert the natives to Christianity. Missionaries were not limited to the African continent, but were equally active in India and China. Similar to the religious explorer was the administrator who welcomed what he saw as an opportunity to bring order and efficient and good government out of primitive muddle. Among them were men who believed firmly in the rightness of the English parliamentary system: Lord Cromer in Egypt, Lord Lugard in Nigeria and Lord Milner in the Cape.

Not surprisingly the quest for fresh territory, and the clash of interests between imperial states, produced tensions and disputes among European nations. These incidents were in part produced by the creation of the colonies themselves; in part, they reflected existing rivalries amongst the major continental powers. In Africa there was particular rivalry between England and France over the Sudan, which reached a crisis in the Fashoda Incident of 1898. The dispute dated back to the 1850s, when British and French interests had both been involved in the construction of Egyptian railways and the Suez Canal. Throughout the 1880s Britain had been advancing her interests south into the Sudan. The French took up the challenge and sent an expedition under Captain Marchand from West Africa to establish French interests. On reaching Fashoda, he concluded a trade treaty with the local chief and annexed the territory for France. Shortly afterwards a victorious Kitchener arrived with a British military force which surrounded the tiny French garrison. The incident brought France and Britain to the brink of war. Fortunately (and wisely) the French foreign minister backed down. Other incidents followed, not only between Britain and France. Germany supported Paul Kruger, President of the Transvaal, in his fight against British rule. Britain and Russia fell out when Russia continually stirred up trouble in Afghanistan, threatening British control of the Indian North-West Frontier. Germany and France were involved in an imperial dispute over the control of Morocco, which had managed to remain in a semi-independent state; each sought to impose it rule, and crises broke out in 1905 and 1908. In fact, it can be argued that much of the tension which built up eventually to erupt into the First World War was produced by colonial rivalry and dispute. Certainly the war itself provided an opportunity for European states in Africa to try to capture each other's colonies.

The history of imperialism after the First World War is one of the rise, in the colonies, of nationalistic fervour and the desire for independence. During the war, native troops had often played an active part; troops from British colonies actually served on the Western Front. The period between the wars is a story of concession and of movement towards limited independence. Imperial governments were naturally reluctant to hand over power. In India, for example, it was only as a result of a determined campaign of passive resistance led by Mahatma Gandhi that certain concessions were given. The India Act of 1935 granted self-government to the provinces in local matters. The Viceroy, however, remained in control of the important matters of state, including the armed forces and foreign affairs. The Second World War resulted in the granting of full independence to most former colonies, replaced in Britain's case with the Commonwealth. As the balance of world power has shifted away from Britain and the other major European powers, so they have been forced to surrender their leadership over the underdeveloped areas of the world. In their place the three super-powers Russia, America and China have assumed the role of protective and paternalistic imperial leaders.

The Origins of the First World War

The war of 1914–18, though often called a World War, was the result of the failure of the great European nations – Russia, Britain, France, Germany, Austria-Hungary and Italy – to maintain peaceful relations during a period of significant change. Though many of the issues which divided them concerned territory elsewhere in the world, it was these powers who determined the great issues of peace and war, formed systems of alliances, acquired colonial possessions, made claims to influence in certain areas of Europe, and built up powerful armies and navies.

Though all of them can be described as great powers, they were very different from one another internally, in their outlook on the rest of the world, and in their past histories. Germany and Britain were, by the outbreak of war, clearly the most economically and socially advanced states. They both had a high output of coal and iron, the industries that then formed the backbone of a country's military strength. Both had developed the basis of what we now call a welfare system: free elementary education, pensions and unemployment benefits that were effective in preventing the instability that other industrial societies, particularly Russia, were soon to suffer as a result of workers' discontent. Both Germany and Britain had large military capacities with which to defend their colonial possessions. But even these states, so similar in many respects, were very different in others. After 1890 and the dismissal of the German Chancellor, Bismarck, Germany was effectively led by a monarch, Kaiser Wilhelm II, who was not content to see Germany's international position improve gradually; he became, instead, the leader of a state that wished to transform its fast-growing economic strength into effective international power – to become, in other words, the dominant state on the European continent. Britain's interests lay with European stability. Then, as now, its leaders were influenced by a feeling of being near Europe but not of it. Britain had extensive colonial interests in Africa, India and the Far East. Its economic prosperity was based upon the peaceful continuance of European trade, and access to British colonies. Britain was therefore the natural enemy of any nation that wished to dominate Europe and of any whose strength and ambitions appeared to threaten Britain's route to its colonies. Germany did both; but this only became really clear at the beginning of the twentieth century.

So Britain and Germany found themselves participating in alliances which opposed one another. These, known as the Triple Alliance (Germany, Austria-Hungary and Italy) and the Triple Entente (Great Britain, France and Russia), evolved at different times and for different historical reasons. But the important thing about them was that, though states within each alliance had their disagreements, the two groups represented the collective power of Europe divided into two factions on almost every important issue in the ten years before the First World War. France and Russia were united by having, as potential enemies, Germany and Austria-Hungary.

France and Germany were enemies for many reasons. They were powerful states that shared a long, common border, a simple geographical fact that meant much in those days. Germany was well aware of the attempts made by Napoleon at the beginning of the nineteenth century to extend his rule over all Europe. France, on the other hand, had never forgotten that two of the provinces that emerged in the new Germany that had defeated France in the Franco-Prussian War of 1870 were the French-speaking areas of Alsace and Lorraine. This was an issue that was to prevent every German statesman from arriving at a friendly understanding with the French.

Russia and Austria-Hungary were divided on many questions, but the most persistent source of conflict between them – and, indeed, the one that was to provide the starting gun for the First World War – was the problem of the Balkans, or the Eastern Question. Their disagreement over the Balkan territories was partly a matter of geography, partly a matter of religion. The Balkans had been controlled for centuries by the Ottoman (Turkish) Empire which, by the end of the nineteenth century, was bankrupt, corrupt, and torn by squabbles among its leaders. It was the only Moslem empire in Europe, and remained impervious to the wind of change that had affected other European empires on questions such as religious and political freedom. The territories ruled by Turkey in the Balkans contained large groups of Christian inhabitants who wanted the freedom to worship according to their own faith, and who saw in the nationalist movements that had united Italy and Germany the inspiration for political independence on national lines. The national characteristics of these minorities were Slav. They derived from Slavic ancestors, and were part of the Russian Orthodox Church. It was natural, therefore, for the Balkan Slavs to look to Russia for assistance against the Turks, and for many Russians to see it as an almost religious duty that such assistance should be given. In addition to sympathy for the Balkan Slavs, the Russians had a compelling geopolitical reason for wanting the downfall of the Ottoman Empire. The heart of that Empire lay in a region long coveted by those who dreamed of an expanded, greater Russia: the Dardanelles – a stretch of water

Map 4. The Balkans 1880–1914.

that would give the Russians a direct outlet into the Mediterranean and to Constantinople, the city best equipped to protect it. The Austrian part of the Austro-Hungarian Empire was particularly vulnerable to the form of nationalism displayed by the Balkan Slavs. The Austrians had large Slavic minorities, which themselves were showing signs of dissatisfaction with rule from Vienna. In addition to this, anything that strengthened the Russian Empire, as the acquisition of influence around Constantinople certainly would, strengthened a potential enemy. Austria therefore stood first for the status quo, for the Ottoman Empire as a bulwark against Russian expansion and Slav nationalism. But, if this were not to be possible, and if the Ottoman Empire collapsed, then Austria would demand increased influence to balance the increased strength of Russia.

In this situation lay the germ of a real crisis. Germany was not directly interested in the Balkan problem, but she needed the alliance with Austria to prevent the French from attempting to secure by force the return of the lost provinces of Alsace-Lorraine. The French also had little direct interest in the Balkans – indeed they may have been concerned at the Russian threat to their influence in the Mediterrenean. But if France was ever to be involved again in a war with Germany, the existence of an Eastern Front for the Germans to tackle would probably make the difference between victory or defeat; French interests therefore lay more strongly with Russia, the more probable war with Germany became. Britain's interest in the Eastern Question was substantial: at least, Britain thought it was. Russian aims were viewed with the deepest suspicion; and particularly vulnerable to a change in the political balance in the region was the Suez Canal, often described as the lifeline of the Empire, because it connected Europe with the route to Britain's African and Indian possessions. Therefore, while Britain felt secure from a threat from one of Russia's enemies, it stood opposed to Russia; when other issues loomed larger, both Russia and Britain diminished their interest in their respective Balkan aims. This was the situation by the turn of the century. Although Russia would stand opposed to the oppression of the Balkan minorities, and in particular to the expansion of Austrian influence in that direction, it did not show signs of the expansionism that had previously troubled the British.

In this way the great nations of Europe chose sides, and formed a precarious balance of power. But a balance of power cannot be effective if one side or the other is determined to change the existing order despite the opposition of the other elements in the balance. Both Germany and Austria-Hungary wanted to do precisely this. In Germany's case, the changes it was after were of a general nature: it wanted to become the dominant European nation. Historians in Germany have shown that their military and political leaders drew up plans for the annexation of territory to the east. They also challenged the naval supremacy which Britain regarded as essential to her security by an enormous ship-building programme that began in the early 1890s and continued until the outbreak of war. This led Britain to accelerate her own arms-building programmes, and inevitably produced in both countries a popular clamour for aggressive foreign policies which the British found harder and harder to resist and which the German leadership found politically convenient. It also forced Britain away from its traditional policy of splendid isolation from European affairs and into a peace-time alliance with the Japanese (in 1902), the entente with France (1904), and alliance with Russia (1907).

Austria-Hungary also sought to change the European order, despite knowing that such attempts would be resisted and were therefore likely to produce war. Its ambitions were, as we have seen, concerned with the Balkans. In 1897 Austria-Hungary established a protectorate over Bosnia and Herzegovina, two Balkan provinces. It also increased pressure against the Russian attempts to prevent more persecution of Turkish-ruled Christians in 1912. By 1914 the Balkans had become a powder-keg, and hostility beyond the Balkans, between Germany on the one hand and France and Britain on the other, was increasing fast. So when, on 28 June 1914, the Austrian Archduke Ferdinand was assassinated by a Bosnian terrorist in the Serbian town of Sarajevo, the power which Germany had been able to use to restrain Austria in, for example, 1912, was either spent or was not used. The Austrian government responded to the assassination with an ultimatum to Serbia, the terms of which were so severe that the Austrians must have known they would be rejected. Russia felt compelled to assure Serbia of its support. Serbia was only a small Slav country, but nevertheless one of many areas against which Austria might apply pressure if Russia did not show its resolve. Despite a last-minute correspondence between Tsar Nicholas II of Russia and his cousin Kaiser Wilhelm, Russia's opposition to Austria meant German opposition to Russia and therefore to France; because in order to tackle Russia, the German military planners envisaged a knock-out blow at France through the territory of neutral Belgium.

Historians continue to speculate about whether Britain would have joined the war against Germany, Austria-Hungary and Italy if the German army had not violated Belgian neutrality. But when war did come to Britain, it was greeted with such popular enthusiasm that it seems unlikely that any British government could have kept Britain out even if the attack had come through France. The war was seen as one of German aggression; and the fact that this aggression affected Belgium only magnified the offence, which in the eyes of the British public Germany had been preparing for many years. British entry into the war on 4 August 1914 meant that the Triple Entente was to face the Triple Alliance; the two sides of the balance of power would struggle to determine what the European continent should look like, and how many of the changes desired by Germany and Austria-Hungary could be won by force. But to those who dreaded the outcome of such a war between the world's most powerful nations (and there were surprisingly few who felt such dread), the balance of power itself seemed to be responsible for the outbreak of war, and not the individuals who determined the policies of the warring nations. This as we shall see, was to have profound effects on the attitudes of some of the peacemakers.

The First World War

On 28 July 1914, Austria declared war on Serbia and in doing so set off a general European war based on the well-established system of alliances. During July, Russia and Austria both decreed the general mobilization of their forces, while Germany sent an ultimatum to Russia and France, followed by declarations of war against Russia on 1 August and against France on 3 August. Germany had already delivered an ultimatum to Belgium, demanding a free passage for her troops. This threat made up the mind of the hesitant British government, which now despatched an ultimatum that Germany should respect Belgium neutrality; the German refusal to do so involved Britain in the war on 4 August. Thus only one of the great powers of Europe had managed to keep out of what was to come to be known as the First World War, and that was Italy – though she was to join in 1915.

The outbreak of war in 1914, and its protracted nature over the next four years, set in motion armies more gigantic than any previous war had seen At the outset, two million Germans were on the march, and there were a further three million trained men in reserve to back them up. France had an army of four million, though she relied in the first engagements on only a quarter of this force. Through the progressive conscription of all able-bodied men, France eventually raised an army of eight million. Russia had the largest (though most poorly equipped) army. Her total numbers were around six and a half million in 1914, expanding by 1917 to double this figure. Britain, starting with a small but well-trained elite, the British Expeditionary Force (BEF), expanded her land forces by compulsory conscription (introduced in 1916) to nine million. A world-wide character was given to the war by the fact that not only the campaigns but also the recruits were of a diverse nature. For the British forces encompassed troops from all over the Empire – Indian, Australian, African and Canadian soldiers were active, not only on the Western Front. One of the outstanding features of the war was, therefore, the immense size of the forces involved. This trend in warfare, and ideas about warfare, are observable already in 1832 in the writings of Clausewitz, where superiority in numbers was proclaimed as an essential constituent of victory. It was a doctrine which had very real force in the minds of the European generals of 1914.

As well as an increase in the size of armies, the First World War produced great technical innovations. The development of the machine gun is an outstanding example. The average proportion of machine guns (once described as 'the concentrated essence of infantry') in the major European armies of 1914 was only two per 1,000 men; they were included in the armoury of the BEF almost as an afterthought. Yet bitter experience was soon to show that two machine guns in defence were often capable of paralysing the attacking power of 1,000 men, forcing them to take refuge in the trenches. And so the number of these weapons multiplied, and special machine gun regiments were formed. Armaments, generally, were improved. As it became accepted that this was not going to be a war of lightning cavalry charges and quick manœuvres, artillery came to play an increasingly important part in the new trench warfare.

These improvements in the technical level at which war could be waged were essentially based on the progressive industrialization of Europe. Improved methods of forging, refining and machining metals meant that shells and guns alike could be made to more accurate specifications. The growth of the factory system meant that greater numbers of shells could be produced for ever-larger armies. Men could be equipped more cheaply and more effectively than ever before. The introduction of the steel helmet (in place of a cloth cap) saved countless lives.

The use of the helmet was made possible by mass-production techniques and the ability to produce steel, at a low cost, hard enough to resist shrapnel. More refined aspects of these spin-offs from the Industrial Revolution included the first large-scale submarine and air campaigns. Previously these two weapons – the submarine and the aeroplane – had been used in restricted numbers, to little effect. In the air, as techniques were developed for firing accurately through propellors and to improve aerobatic handling, planes were used not only as reconnaissance vehicles, but also as bombers and fighters in their own right. Shipping was for the first time seriously hampered by submarines. The general improvements in their engines, seaworthiness and armaments meant that they could cruise further away from their bases, stay submerged for longer periods, and attack enemy merchantmen and warships with greater force and accuracy. It was in response to this new threat that the British, under the guidance of Lloyd George, were forced to devise the convoy system in 1917. One thing clearly demonstrated by the heavier British losses at the battle of Jutland in 1916 was German technical superiority at sea. Not only were German ships better armoured, but their guns were more carefully manufactured and hence more accurate at superior ranges, and their general standard of organization and efficiency was higher. Britain maintained her dominance at sea only by the overwhelming numbers of her ships, and by the superior morale based on tradition and experience.

Briefly, the Germans in 1914 followed the Schlieffen Plan. They intended to defeat France by a lightning offensive, concentrating on the encirclement of Paris and advancing from the north through Belgium. In fact the advance was too rapid, and their westernmost forces were held off at the battle of the Marne by combined British and French forces. The French then retreated into good defensive positions, leaving the Germans to come on in some disorder. There followed the so-called 'race for the sea', each army trying to outflank the other until they reached the Channel and stalemate. From this time on, the character of the war was set. Trenches were dug from the Alps to the Channel coast.

The characteristic system of trench warfare sprang from the inability of either side to produce an effective piercing attack. It arose from a reluctance to make imaginative use of the new techniques of waging war. The traditional cavalry charge had been rendered useless by the machine gun and the repeater rifle (now with a rifled barrel for greater accuracy). The only answer which occurred to the generals was the massed infantry assault. Even when attacking forces were in an overwhelming majority troops protected by trenches and barbed-wire fortifications and equipped with machine guns found it easy to beat off attacks. Not until the invention of the tank by the British (first used in pitifully small numbers at the battle of Cambrai in November 1917) was there any effective alternative to this strategy. Naturally enough, conditions in the trenches were appalling. They were often waterlogged, a consequence of the muddy nature of the Flanders plain, and were bitterly cold in winter; while living conditions remained primitive. Frostbite, dysentery, 'trench-foot' and suicide were not uncommon. Conditions were much the same for all the armies.

The story of the next four years is essentially one of deadlock, each side trying unsuccessfully to break through the other's lines. Battles, by the very nature of the way they were conducted, were costly in lives. The usual pattern was to open with an extensive and prolonged artillery barrage which, in theory, was supposed to flatten the enemy's positions. It rarely did so, and

Devastation of the battleground between Bapaume and Arras, first Battle of the Somme. (*Photo: Radio Times Hulton Library*)

only served to point out which area of the front could expect an attack so that reserves could be assembled in advance. The actual offensive followed; wave after wave of troops were sent over the top into the open to rush at the enemy's trenches. Here the machine gun took its toll. The odds were usually in favour of the defenders, and the only answer the generals had was to send ever larger numbers of men into the attack. At the battle of the Somme there were 60,000 casualties (20,000 of them killed' on the first day – the highest ever recorded in the history of the British army. The battles of Ypres and Verdun were similarly notable for the incredibly high number of dead and wounded. Indeed, it was because of the appalling casualty lists that many French units mutinied at the beginning of 1917. It was because of the actual toll in lives that the fresh, well-trained American troops were welcomed when they came into action in France in 1918. The Germans, though they would be freed from war on their eastern side after the Russian Revolution produced a peace at Brest-Litovsk, did not have this advantage. Indeed, by this time the Austrians, their main ally, were weakening; at the battle of Caporetto, General Cadorna lost 250,000 prisoners to the Italians. Certainly by 1918 Germany was experiencing considerable economic difficulties at home. Discontent and hardship finally produced an uprising when Ludendorff's final spring offensive was held and broken by an allied counter-attack. The demand was for peace.

The stalemate produced by trench warfare in Europe produced various schemes to try to win the war elsewhere. The most notable attempt was at

Gallipoli. It was felt by both Lloyd George (then Minister for Munitions, later to succeed Asquith as Prime Minister in 1916) and Winston Churchill, First Lord of the Admiralty, that Germany's defeat might be secured by first knocking out her ally Turkey and then, with the help of the other Balkan nations, attacking Austria from the south-east. The Gallipoli peninsula was chosen for an attack, but the initial venture was abandoned, largely because of a preoccupation with a western victory, when the Turks were on the verge of collapse. The task was then handed over to General Sir Ian Hamilton; a slim chance remained, but his failure to exploit the opportunity offered by surprise allowed the Turks to reinforce and establish good defensive positions. Supplies of further British and Commonwealth troops were thus wasted. The only really creditable aspect of the whole campaign was the withdrawal, which was superbly executed.

The Germans similarly tried to defeat the Allies away from the Western Front by starving Britain and France into defeat with their concerted U-Boat campaign against shipping in the Atlantic. The offensive was begun in 1917 to try to prevent much-needed American supplies from reaching western Europe. In April 1917 Germany scored a maximum number of sinkings when half a million tons were sunk – more than all the ships leaving British ports. In response, Britain introduced food rationing and adopted the convoy system. By September, American destroyers were involved in protection work, while special 'submarine chasers', aircraft and mines were brought into service. These reduced the effectiveness of this form of campaign; while the sinking of American merchant ships was, in part, instrumental in producing America's declaration of war on Germany (6 April 1917).

German defeat was the result of a combination of circumstances. When Germany announced its unrestricted submarine campaign, America, under President Woodrow Wilson, broke off relations. The publication of the Zimmerman telegram (detailing a fantastic scheme proposing German assistance to secure the independence of New Mexico from America) precipitated a reluctant United States into war. Since the security of the country was not endangered, Americans had to treat the war as a moral crusade. So when the Russians concluded their own peace with the Germans in December 1917, Wilson was prompted to announce his Fourteen Points – a sketch of a programme for peace which, he hoped, would make another war impossible. Now the Allies could boast some righteous justification for their cause, and their leaders no longer thought only in terms of defeating the Germans. Among the familiar points were clauses calling for freedom of the seas, a reduction of armaments and the restoration of an independent Belgium.

The Russian withdrawal from the war was a matter of great importance for the modification of political boundaries in eastern Europe. After the overthrow of Tsar Nicholas II in March 1917, political and military control fell into the hands of militant bourgeois officers and politicians who were still in favour of continuing the war against Germany. But unabated hardship and a series of defeats stirred up the desire for peace. The Bolsheviks were now beginning to threaten the Russian administration led by Kerensky.

Revolution broke out in November, under Lenin's leadership, and once

Lenin had established himself in power Trotsky was empowered to conclude an armistice on 15 December at Brest-Litovsk. In return for peace the Russians surrendered their control over Poland, the Baltic provinces, the Ukraine, Finland and the Caucasus. Because the treaty was declared invalid on the German surrender, fresh problems of sovereignty were created for these now independent states.

On the Western Front, the Allies broke through the Hindenburg Line on 29 September. In Palestine, General Allenby recaptured Damascus from the Turks with the aid of T. E. Lawrence (of Arabia), causing Turkey to surrender. With the Italian penetration of the Austrian front, Germany's main ally also capitulated on 4 November. The German High Seas Fleet mutinied when ordered into action after a respite of over two years in port. Revolution began to spread from the naval barracks to the towns. Ludendorff, recovering from a breakdown, urged Germany's new head of state, Prince Max of Baden (Kaiser Wilhelm II had fled to Holland) to sue for an armistice. And so, at the eleventh hour of the eleventh day of the eleventh month of 1918, the peace was concluded. Curiously, there were no Allied troops on German soil.

The Russian Revolution

In Russia in 1917 two revolutions took place. The first signalled the end of the Tsarist monarchy that had governed Russia for centuries; the second brought to power the party which has governed it ever since.

Like Russia today, these revolutions expressed a curious mixture of modern revolutionary theory and traditional Russian political behaviour. The works of Karl Marx, which influenced the revolutionists were modern in that they dealt principally with the consequences of industrialization, Briefly, they argued that in industrialized or capitalist societies a small group of people made a great deal of money through the ownership of industry; while a large number of others lived on the edge of poverty, as workers in those industries. This difference in wealth and interest and numbers between the 'exploiters' or owners, and the 'exploited' or workers was, in Marx's view, both essential to the capitalist system of production and, ultimately, the source of its inevitable collapse. The collapse of capitalism would come, he argued, because eventually the difference in wealth between the two groups would become intolerable; the workers, given their superior numbers, would take over the ownership of industry and use it for the collective benefit of the people.

These ideas influenced the revolutionaries who came to be known as the Bolshevik (or majority) faction of the Russian Social Democrats, who were the victors in the power struggle that resulted in the second, or October, Revolution of 1917. But, all theory aside, the circumstances that made revolution possible bore the characteristics of previous turbulent periods in Russian history. At the turn of the century Russia was both a backward country and a great power. She had the resources to wage war, to expand her frontiers, and to count as a major factor in the European balance of power. But despite the outward appearance of strength, her industrial production was lower than that of France, a country with only a fifth of Russia's population. A small urban working class, like that considered by Marx to characterize a capitalist economy, was forming in new factories being built with the help of foreign investors. But most of this working class was of recent peasant origin, and the bulk of the population consisted of peasants. The country was ruled by the Tsar, or Emperor, and a bureaucracy responsible only to him.

Partly in response to internal pressures, and partly as a result of eastern ambitions, the Tsar pushed his country into war with Japan in 1904. Almost unbelievably, by 1905 the armies, and more especially the navies, of one of the world's most powerful nations had been humiliatingly defeated by a small and only recently-emerged Asian power. The defeat touched off revolution in the cities and peasant riots in the villages. After a first severe response, the Tsar granted a constitution which created a Duma or parliament. By 1907, however, he had found the relative radicalism of the Duma too unpalatable, and he introduced into it a safe majority for the wealthy landowners, a group over which he exercised effective control. But at the same time a period of government-sponsored reform in the villages was taking place. Under the moderately progressive prime minister Stolypin, a large number of peasants (nearly two million) became small landowners. This seemed to promise greater stability in the countryside. Industrial development continued after the 1905 disturbances and enjoyed a considerable boom until the outbreak of war in 1914. These favourable economic conditions had led many – including the man to emerge as leader of the Bolsheviks, Lenin – to believe that revolution was a distant and diminishing prospect. The prosperity which industrial expansion and agricultural reform had stimulated seemed to have 'derevolutionized' the ordinary peasant and workers.

But the First World War changed all that. Russia's military strength was largely the result of two advantages, space and manpower. Space had made it vulnerable to only the most persistent and powerful of enemies, while its vast and largely obedient population had traditionally provided it with huge armies. But the first major war of the twentieth century was different from those which had shaped the Russian military tradition. The existence of more efficient transport meant that opposing armies enjoyed much longer and better equipped lines of communication, which diminished the old advantages of Russia's great territories. Second, the development of mechanical weaponry, and in particular of the field gun and machine gun, rendered front-line troops much more vulnerable to swift, large-scale slaughter. The rate at which Russia's men were decimated was much greater than at any time in the past; therefore its armies had to be much larger, which meant that men were taken away from the villages, and the consequent loss of food production led to the starvation of both Russian armies and civilians. On top of all this, Russia's generals seemed to lack the sophistication and brilliance of their German adversaries.

In 1915 German armies advanced well into Russian territory, and by the end of 1916 they had managed to quieten their Eastern Front sufficiently to increase their efforts against the British and French armies in the west. These Russian failures, and the apparent inability of the Tsar to produce any initiative likely to counter them, led to the collapse of the monarchy in February 1917. A provisional government was established; its first actions were to release political prisoners, and to decide to continue the war. In short, it set the revolutionaries free and presented them with the conditions of revolution. For among those released from exile or permitted to return from abroad were the Bolshevik leaders, Lenin, Trotsky and Stalin. Their party immediately adopted the slogans of 'peace' and 'land'. Soldiers began to desert in vast numbers, returning to their villages to join in the land seizures that had become rife; and even the social legislation instigated by the provisional government could do nothing to restore order. The Bolsheviks showed no faith in the elected constituent assembly and called instead for the transfer of power to the 'Soviets' – rough-and-ready assemblies, containing workers, soldiers and peasants, which by and large supported the Bolshevik party. The legitimacy of the new government was insufficient to win it the support of either the monarchist right, who in the person of General Kornilov plotted to overthrow it, or the revolutionary left who devoted all their energies to replacing it with an administration of their own. On 25 October by the old Russian calendar (7 November by the new one) the Bolsheviks overthrew the provisional government, took control of the strategic centres of Petrograd, the Russian capital, and vested authority in the Soviets. 'We shall now proceed to construct the Socialist Order,' announced Lenin to a crowd of his supporters.

But this statement was premature. Until 1921 Russia was fighting invaders determined to assist those Russians who wanted to overthrow the Bolshevik government. The Russian Civil War had a profound influence on subsequent Soviet policy. Though much of the reason for intervention by other powers in the Civil War had to do with ideological distaste for the new government, still the British and American intervention was connected with the Russian decision to leave the war against Germany and Austria in late 1917. But in later years Stalin seemed convinced that the behaviour of the western nations in 1917–21 would be repeated at the first opportunity. It also meant that the Revolution was born in an atmosphere of terror and brutality and this seemed to have conditioned the men, such as Stalin, who, as the Civil War ended, emerged as the senior leaders.

The period immediately after the Civil War saw the purging of those who had assisted the Bolsheviks but who had later come to oppose the absolute control which the Bolsheviks attempted to exercise over all aspects of life; and the rigours of the Civil War also produced a period of general economic restriction known as 'War Communism' which set the pattern for future control of economic development. The resurrection of the kind of state security organization that had existed under the Tsar, now known as the Cheka, gave the Bolshevik leadership an additional instrument with which to impose their will.

By Lenin the revolution was seen as merely the beginning of a general uprising of European workers. Lenin's interpretation of Marxism emphasized the role of war between 'imperalist' states as the most significant weakness of the system, and one to be exploited by revolutionaries. In Germany an attempted revolution in 1918 was quelled by the use of force. In France and Britain, though discontent existed it was anticipated and successfully appeased by both governments. To her leaders' surprise, Russia in 1921 emerged from bloody civil war economically weakened and isolated among the capitalist nations who, contrary to prediction, had not been consumed by revolution. Moreover, the Bolshevik party was split into rival factions. The building of the socialist order would have to take place, not amid the acclamation of a united country in a socialist Europe, but in the face of opposition from within and hostility from outside.

In 1923, with these dilemmas unresolved, Lenin, architect of the Bolshevik revolution, suffered a severe stroke that prevented him from continuing his leading role. A muffled power struggle began almost at once between Stalin, the political organizer, and Trotsky, founder of the Red Army and a brilliant ideologist, and this struggle exploded into the open with Trotsky's expulsion from the Communist party in 1927. After 1927 Stalin's dominant position in the Soviet Communist party was never really challenged. The infrequency with which his party central committees met was an indication of how absolute his control became. But outside the Soviet Union, the Russian Revolution was a powerful stimulant for radical left-wing activity. Until the secret speech of 1956, in which Nikita Kruschev denounced the repression and personality cult for which Stalin was responsible, the left in Europe, with a few but notable exceptions, saw in the Soviet Union what one American journalist expressed soon after October 1917 when he said: 'I have seen the future, and it works.' Communist parties everywhere acknowledged the ideological leadership of the Union of Soviet Socialist Republics in demonstrating the value of socialism as the cure for social and economic ills. It is reasonable to suppose, therefore, that if the Revolutionary government in Russia had not survived the rigours of 1917–21, the portion of the globe now governed by Communist parties would have been significantly smaller than it is. Though partly shrouded by the First World War, the Bolshevik Revolution lays strong claim to being the most important political development of the twentieth century.

The Peace Treaties

The peace treaties that ended the First World War were hammered out at the Paris Peace Conference. The conference opened on 18 January 1919 and officially ended on 21 January 1920. The terms of the various treaties were, in the main, decided by four out of the five Allied powers that had won the war; France, Great Britain, Italy and the United States of America. The frontiers and peace treaties of the conference were those that concerned the Allies on the one hand, and the defeated enemy states: Germany, Austria, Hungary,

Bulgaria and Turkey on the other. The frontiers of Russia were dealt with in the less formal forum of the Russian Civil War, which continued after the Paris Peace Conference had closed.

The organization of the Conference was rather chaotic: much effort went into the development of national policies to be pursued at the Conference, but little attention had been paid to the procedure to be followed. The most important bargaining was undertaken by the 'Big Five', Britain, France, Italy, the United States and Japan – even though Japan had not been directly involved in the war. On 24 March 1919 Japan quit the negotiations, leaving the four other countries represented by their respective leaders: President Wilson of the US, Prime Minister Lloyd George of Britain, President Clemenceau of France and Prime Minister Orlando of Italy. When Fiume, a territory disputed by Yugoslavia and Italy, was not awarded to Italy, Orlando left in protest and decisions were left to the remaining three. There was a separate treaty for each of the defeated nations. The first to be signed was the Treaty of Versailles, which concerned the future of Germany and the establishment of the League of Nations. After its signature, at the end of June 1919, President Wilson returned to the United States to attempt to persuade Congress (the American parliament) to accept America's participation in the new international organization that was largely his creation.

The Treaty of Versailles

Germany did not surrender unconditionally, as at the end of the Second World War. In October 1918 the German Chancellor sought an armistice, or cessation of hostilities, on the basis of President Wilson's fourteen points. On 4 November the Allies accepted peace on that basis, but with reservations on the question of reparations, or payments for war damage. The territorial provisions of the Treaty were severe. Alsace-Lorraine, the area taken from France after the Franco-Prussian War of 1870, was returned to France; the Saar, Germany's most productive coal-mining area, was placed under international control; the mines of the Saar were transferred to French ownership in part payment for damage to French coal mines; and three small territories were transferred to Belgium. The French had demanded all German territory to the west of the river Rhine; but after opposition from the other Allies, they accepted Allied occupation of the area for a limited time, and its demilitarization by Germany. In the north, Denmark received the territory of northern Schleswig; in the east, German territories were transferred to the new Polish state. Germany also lost territory to the Baltic state of Lithuania and to Czechoslovakia. Her colonies were transferred to the control of the League of Nations, which in turn distributed them among other nations with colonial possessions in Africa. In addition to this massive loss of territory, Germany was required by the Treaty to accept responsibility or guilt for the war and to pay compensation for war damage inflicted upon the Allied victors.

This section of the Treaty caused more trouble than any other, both at the Peace Conference and afterwards. Too large a sum might be unpayable and cause the Germans to refuse to sign the Treaty, which would mean a return to fighting. Too small a sum would infuriate public opinion both in France and Britain and place the governments or their representatives in danger. No final sum was actually stated in the Treaty; instead a Reparations Commission was established and charged with responsibility for determining the sums to be paid and the timing of payments. The French particularly insisted, and the other Allies agreed, that Germany should be stripped of all military forces not absolutely necessary to the maintenance of order within Germany itself. The army was limited to 100,000 men, who had to serve for a minimum of twelve years. The navy was limited, and submarines were prohibited altogether. Germany was forbidden to build a military air force, and the armaments industry was to be subject to the closest control and inspection. The severity of these terms made the German negotiators extremely reluctant to sign the Treaty, but because the Allies had maintained a blockade against Germany from the beginning of the armistice, living conditions in Germany were extremely difficult. There was nothing for it but to sign.

The signature did not end the story. Successive German governments sought to reverse the restrictions of Versailles. Only differences about method and timing separated them in their attitudes to foreign policy.

Peace Treaties with Austria, Bulgaria and Hungary

The Treaty of St Germain between Austria and the Allies was similar in scope to the Treaty of Versailles. Austrian armed forces also were limited and Austria was forbidden to merge with Germany, despite the fact that President Wilson's fourteen points stressed the importance of nationalism as a force for peace. Territory was ceded to Italy, and the new nation of Czechoslovakia was hewn out of territory that had previously been under Austrian control. Like Germany, Austria was required to accept guilt for the war, though it was recognized that her capacity to pay reparations was considerably less.

The Treaty of Trianon between Hungary and the Allies was signed on 4 June 1920. Much of Hungary's territory had been taken by force before the Peace Conference by Romania, Yugoslavia, Czechoslovakia and Italy. Altogether, she lost more than 60 per cent of her pre-war land. Her army was limited to 35,000 men; and, like Austria and Germany, she was required to pay reparations and accept responsibility for the war.

The Treaty of Neuilly with Bulgaria required the withdrawal of Bulgarian forces to their pre-war frontier and the transfer of territory to Romania, Yugoslavia and Greece. Reparations were also required, and her army was reduced to a maximum of 33,000 men.

A treaty along the same lines, the Treaty of Sèvres, was signed with Turkey in August 1920. But there was simultaneously a change of government within Turkey. The new Turkish leaders did not accept that their country should be punished for the actions of the previous regime, and they decided to fight rather than capitulate. First, they settled their eastern frontier independently of the Allies by a separate treaty with the Soviet Union. This show of strength was enough to persuade the Allies against attempting to impose the Treaty by force. France and Turkey signed the Treaty of Ankara in October 1921, and hostility between French and Turkish forces ceased. This break in Allied unity allowed the Turks to turn their armies against the Greeks; as a result, the Turks acquired territory and recognition of their control of Constantinople. The Treaty of Lausanne, signed in July 1923, represented a victory for resistance to the Allies, and Turkey alone amongst the ex-enemy states was not required to pay reparations. The lesson of the Turkish action to revise the initial treaty cannot have been lost on the leaders of other defeated states. Despite the high moral principles in which the treaties had been phrased, the exertion of force could – and in Germany's case during the 1930s did – change the attitude of the western Allies, and force them to accept the defeated states as equals.

The League of Nations

The aim of the League of Nations was to provide an effective organization devoted to the peaceful resolution of international crises. President Wilson believed that the First World War had started because of the development of hostile systems of alliance between the great powers. They had engaged in a series of commitments to their partners that were kept secret from their opponents, and as a result, small issues concerning any two members of the opposing alliances threatened to start a major war. Additionally, the pre-war system had enabled power to be the arbiter of disputes between nations; the weaker, smaller countries would not enjoy protection from aggression until they could rely upon the support of other nations. If the members of the League would oppose aggression anywhere, by anyone, then even the largest nation could not safely coerce any other, for fear of evoking reprisals from nations everywhere.

So the League came to be based on two fundamental principles which were written into its Covenant as follows: 1) 'No nation shall go to war with any other nation until every other possible means of settling the dispute shall have been fully or fairly tried'; and 2) 'Under no circumstances shall any nation seek forcibly to disturb the territorial settlement to be arrived at as the consequence of this peace or to interfere with the political independence of any of the states of the world.' But the League could not change the nature of the international system without changing the nature of the states that composed it. Alliances or understandings directed against other nations existed between countries supporting the concept of the League. For example, Britain and France. Large nations wielded more political and economic power than the smaller states, and so were more difficult for the League to resist. And if the League was to resist any aggressor, its major nations, before they agreed to participate, would have to be persuaded that it was in their respective interests. So in all important respects the League was structurally ill-equipped to change the nature of international relations. It also failed actually to include many important nations. Russia joined only in 1934; Germany joined in 1926 but left in 1933, as did Japan. Italy left in 1937; and, most ironic of all, the Americans never joined.

On a less important level the League did enjoy some success in promoting international co-operation on non-political matters such as health-care, through the World Health Organization (WHO), and industrial relations, through the International Labour Organization (ILO). It tried, with some limited success, to assist the national minorities that emerged from the new post-war states, and to assist the settlement of refugees.

In April 1946, after the creation of the United Nations Organization, the League of Nations was dissolved.

The failure of the League to prevent the renewal of war was closely connected with the peace treaties themselves. The Treaty of Versailles had incorporated the techniques of power politics which the League was designed to do away with. Germany had much territory taken from her with the simple purpose of weakening her and depriving her of the capacity, rather than the will, to make war. The payment of reparations was a partial cause of the economic crisis called the Great Depression that did so much to heighten the tensions that the League proved powerless to control. As long as some nations had a strong desire to change the existing order, the danger that they might turn to force if all else failed was ever-present. In such circumstances, appeals to the League could be an excuse for inaction. This was the case with the Japanese invasion of Manchuria in 1931 and the Italian invasion of Ethiopia in 1936. As long as the pretence was kept up then the League was as an effective alternative to older methods of diplomacy, the issues were not faced and aggression was allowed to go unchecked. If the League's advocates had been more modest in developing the scope of the League's power, restricting its role perhaps to arbitration, it might have exerted a more powerful influence for the good. As it was, it had large aims and limited abilities – the surest recipe for frustrated ambition and disappointed hopes.

The Rise of Fascism

Germany

Hitler first caught the public eye with his ill-fated Munich *putsch* of 1923. Munich was the capital city of Bavaria, under whose Prime Minister, Kahr, and military chief, General von Lossow, it had virtually declared its independence from the rest of Germany. Hitler, who was beginning to test the strength of his National Socialist (Nazi) Party, had planned to gain control of the Bavarian state as a means of wresting power from the democratic government. On the evening of 8 November 1923 he and his followers burst into the Bürgerbräu beer cellar in Munich, forcing Lossow, at pistol point, to declare for a march on Berlin. The next day, once freed from this compulsion, the Bavarian leaders withdrew their support, and the Bavarian police overpowered Hitler and his Nazis. Hitler was imprisoned in Landsberg Castle for five months. It was his first and only abortive attempt to become ruler of Germany. The whole affair demonstrated the weakness of the elected

Republic and the potentially unstable political situation, two factors which helped to turn Germany in a few years into a totalitarian dictatorship.

The emergence of Fascism in Germany had its origins in the results of the First World War. The political system created around the Versailles Peace Settlement of 1919 was never strong. In place of the powerful control offered by the Kaiser, a socialist government under Ebert was formed in November 1918. This new Republic (called Weimar after its meeting place) was thought by many Germans to be both anti-national and unpatriotic. It came into being in an atmosphere of defeat. Almost its first job was to accept a humiliating armistice. Germany lost lands which it rightly regarded as its own, the Rhineland and her colonies, and had to endure the separation of Danzig and East Prussia. It also suffered a massive reduction in the size of its armed forces. Equally galling to the German people was Article 231 of the Treaty, the so-called 'War Guilt' clause. The obligation to pay reparations of an enormous and unlimited amount was, to German minds, bad enough. To be made to admit that the sole responsibility for the war rested on their shoulders was far worse. The Weimar Republic was tarred with a brush of defeat and humiliation.

At the same time, the Weimar Republic was the first democratic system the Germans had known. Because of this, and because of the divided opinion surrounding the peace settlement, there were no strong political parties. A coalition of socialists and Catholic centrists and democrats formed the government which accepted the peace terms. A difference of opinion grew up between the liberal politicians who sat in parliament, and the civil servants, judges and officers of the depleted forces. This latter group remained in sympathy with the past and aspired to the restoration of a strongly nationalist Germany. It was a divided and unstable country which went forward from 1919.

Instability was made worse by the deep post-war depression. The middle classes lost most of their savings through rapidly rising prices; there were 9.5 million unemployed workers in 1931. The traditional right-wing parties helped to discredit the Republic by their ceaseless calls for a new heroic leader who would save Germany from Communism and uncontrolled inflation. It was in this atmosphere of unrest that Hitler's National Socialists gained popular support.

Hitler's programme was designed to appeal to a broad spectrum of discontented opinion. He offered, on the one hand, the fulfilment of nationalist desires, the recovery of all German lands lost as a result of the Peace Treaty, and the expulsion of all alien elements – especially the Jews who were now blamed for all ills in the state. This was a policy which particularly appealed to the officer corps, large landowners, and the businessmen and industrialists who wished to see a strong, independent Germany and feared a Communist takeover. On the other hand, Hitler advocated a particular brand of socialism, which involved the 'abolition of incomes unearned by work', the 'abolition of the thraldom of interest' and the formation of a unified nation in which the whole economy was run by the state for maximum efficiency. It was this policy, in large part, which won widespread support for Hitler from the middle classes, concerned for their savings and businesses.

Under Hitler's regime a Jew is forced to walk through the streets with the placard 'I am a Jew, but I won't complain about the Nazis.' (*Photo: Radio Times Hulton Library*)

Hitler's main opponents in the late 1920s were the Communists who, like the Nazis, had mass support. His victory over them was based on the breadth of his programme. The Communists really appealed only to the working classes, while the Nazis attracted funds and political influence from professional classes. So, at the 1932 elections, when the unemployed numbered six million, the Nazis became the biggest party in the Reichstag (parliament) with 230 seats. The Communists gained only 89, the Social Democrats 133 and the Centre Party 97. The continued threat of the Communists, and the apparent legitimacy of the Nazis (that is, their readiness to take their place in the existing political pattern) caused the right wing under President Hindenburg (former German commander-in-chief during the First World War) to invite Hitler to become Chancellor in January 1933. On Hindenburg's death a year later Hitler amalgamated the posts of President and Chancellor.

Once in power, Hitler refused to be tied down by the limitations that the established politicians wished to impose. The move towards an absolute dictatorship continued. He now had the authority as well as the means to control the country as completely and ruthlessly as he wished. His private armies, the SA (brownshirts) and the SS (blackshirts), were used to crush any opposition. The press, radio and public meetings were controlled. As early as 1928 a Nazi Lawyers' and Teachers' Association had been created; and, most important, there was the Hitler Youth to inspire and direct Germany's

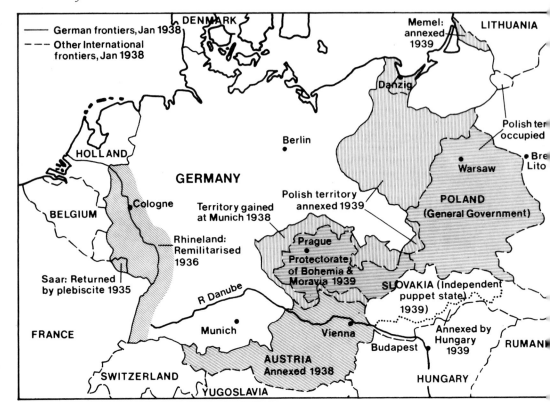

Map 5. Greater Germany 1933–9.

children. A propaganda ministry was one of the earliest creations of the new regime. Strikes were forbidden in May 1933, and trade unions were dissolved. In 1934 the Nazi Labour Front was established. Concentration camps were opened and vicious purges begun. Hitler's own party was not safe from these attacks; on 30 June 1934 Hitler had prominent SA men, including the leader Rohm and other leading politicians and soldiers of the 'Old Guard', put to death without trial. It was an opportunity to get rid of rivals. Notions of *Lebensraum* (living space) and *Herrenrasse* (master race) were fostered, and fascism spread under German influence as Hitler acquired further territories: the Saar (1935), the Rhineland (1936), Austria (1938) and Czechoslovakia (1938).

Italy

Italy was the other major European power where Fascism triumphed, and its success was based on similar circumstances. As in Germany, economic difficulties were important. Italy produced discontented millions when the post-war depression began to take its grip in 1919. These were the men to whom Mussolini appealed and who were to join his para-military body, the 'blackshirts'.

Again, Italian Fascism had its roots in extreme nationalism. Though the Italians had been on the winning side in the First World War, they felt that the peace settlement had not been particularly favourable to them. These feelings were heightened by the weak economic situation into which the country slipped. Strikes and industrial violence became common. The alarm and outraged feelings of the middle classes, who saw themselves derided at home and thwarted abroad, and whose savings were destroyed by inflation, explains much of the weakness of Italian politicians when confronted by the Fascists.

By 1920 Mussolini had organized about 300,000 supporters. As in Germany, violence often erupted when they met Communist groups on the streets. On the surface Mussolini, like Hitler, sought to achieve power by lawful means and to establish his party in the Italian parliament: though his final rise to dominance was based on his physical strength. In October 1922, while reviewing 40,000 Fascists at Naples, he challenged the government to solve the country's problems or to surrender power to his party. Two days later, he announced that his blackshirts were to march on Rome. The weak King Victor Emmanuel and a feeble right-wing government surrendered to Mussolini.

Once in power, Mussolini's tactics were very similar to Hitler's. He concentrated his efforts on subordinating all interests to the state and putting himself at the head of the country. Particularly in the early years, Mussolini's rule brought important economic advances and social improvements – Mussolini really *did* make the trains run on time. In 1925 he abolished the democratic system and made 'the head of government' responsible only to the King. Terror, though not on the scale practised by the Nazis in Germany, was an important weapon. Like Hitler, Mussolini tried to solve the shortage of jobs by programmes of public works, though Italian efforts were on a much smaller scale. Both partly answered the problem through the expansion of their armed forces and vastly increased bureaucracies.

Spain

The country in which the rise of Fascism created most resistance and attracted most contemporary notice was in Spain. Here its emergence produced a ferocious and lengthy civil war. Again, as in Germany and Italy, internal weaknesses and aspirations can be detected before the outbreak of war in July 1936. There was no coherent government. Politics in Spain were characterized, as they so often had been, by a whole spectrum of different groups ranging from extreme right-wingers to Communists. There were also intense local allegiances that helped to prevent any national unity. Spain's political history from 1930 (the date of the establishment of the Republic and a constitution) to 1936 was one of division and disturbance, as the traditional elements – the monarchists, the aristocratic landowners and the Roman Catholic church – resisted attempts at liberal reforms by the Republican government. Violence became chronic. In the end, three generals, Franco, Mola and

The celebration of the VII anniversary of 'The March Towards Rome'. Mussolini speaks to the Blackshirts and representatives of national strengths from the Palazzio Venezia. (*Photo: Radio Times Hulton Library*)

Sanjurjo, launched a military coup from their base in Spanish Morocco; it was only half a success, and civil war resulted.

The war's amazing length was the result of the even nature of the forces ranged on either side. It was in fact the later Italian and German intervention, in the form of generous supplies of equipment and men, which was one crucial factor in winning the war for the Fascists, now led by Franco alone. Although the Republican side attracted left-wing supporters from Europe, notably France and Britain, in the form of International Brigades, they were volunteers untrained and largely unequipped. German planes and Italian troops (100,000 by 1938) were used with great effect. Notable at the time was the cruel dive-bombing of the defenceless market town, Guernica, by the German Condor Legion. In 1939, weight of numbers and superior equipment won Franco the day. The cost of the war had been appalling. Three quarters of a million Spaniards had been killed, and political purges followed the Fascist victories. Franco proceeded to ally himself with Hitler and Mussolini through the Anti-Comintern Pact (that is, the pact against the countries belonging to the Communist International) signed by Spain in 1939.

Other Countries

Fascism was never any real threat in England. Under Sir Oswald Mosley, its influence was confined to the East End of London and some south coast towns. Numbers were never sufficient to cause the police any serious worries, and they never became a force to be reckoned with in Parliament. They failed in England for the same reasons that they succeeded in Europe. Britain emerged victorious from the First World War, and though it suffered from the Depression, it never experienced quite the same unemployment and hardship as Italy or Germany. The British political system was well established and respected by the majority. Mosley never achieved control of the media to extend his tenuous hold.

It is an interesting exercise to ask why France never became a Fascist state. A set of circumstances existed which were favourable to the rise of fascism. The country lacked unity, its governments were weak and short-lived, its public institutions were in low repute, and it had no great leaders. Lapses into violence, obvious in 1934 and 1936, became common till 1939. The country resembled Italy before Mussolini came to power. Yet Fascism, though there were some extreme right-wing and nationalist groups, never took root in France. On the whole it remained, by inclination, left-wing. This was probably the result of a strong mass dislike of Germany and anything characteristically German. The French, as France's impressive eastern fortications (the Maginot Line) demonstrated, were preoccupied with the fear of a German resurgence, and so were hardly likely to adopt Germany's political system. Fascism was not, therefore, a blanket movement that could be applied to Europe wholesale; different nationalities responded in their own individual ways to its challenge.

The most important fact about these Fascist dictatorships was political. Italy, Germany and Spain were governed by men who, more completely than any other rulers before them, wielded absolute power. They were totalitarian states. Fascism involved the concentration of power in the hands of a tiny ruling group which sought to control every aspect of life from education to religion, industry and politics itself. The success of the Fascists rested on two main pillars – the ability to control public opinion, and the ability to crush by force any form of opposition or criticism of the state. Loyalty was directed towards individual leaders, whether *Duce* (Mussolini) or *Führer* (Hitler). The Fascist states were societies combining traditional weapons of fear and persuasion with modern technology that allowed them to dominate and regulate, more effectively than ever before, masses of people rather than small groups.

The Great Depression

The symbolic beginning of the Great Depression came in 1929 with the collapse in the price of shares on the New York stock exchange, known as the Great Crash. This led to a breakdown of American confidence in future economic prosperity, and caused American investors to withdraw the loans they had made to European enterprises. Combined with the same form of uncertainty in the minds of European investors, this resulted in withdrawals from the banking system, and to a reduction in the money available for the building of new industries and the creation of jobs. Throughout the industrialized world, the Great Depression was marked by a large rise in the number of people out of work, and by the existence of extreme poverty in some areas of all industrialized nations. But its economic consequences were not confined to industrialized nations. Producers of food all over the world had to accept a sharp decline in the prices paid for their products, and a decline in the income of the people who produced them. In Japan, for example, the drop in the amount of silk purchased by the United States alone was responsible for the reduction in agricultural (silk-producing) family incomes of between 40 and 50 per cent. In Eastern Europe, those countries which relied upon the export of raw materials to industrialized countries had to accept a fall both in the price and the volume of their exports. But although the Great Crash was an important element in the timing and depth of the Depression, for its actual causes we must look more closely at the economic consequences of the First World War.

The futility of that war for the European nations who took part in it from the outset is nowhere more clearly visible than in its effects on the ordinary person's ability to earn a living. Britain, whose territory was less affected by the actual fighting than was that of any of the chief European participants, suffered an enormous loss in the amount of trade to which it had grown accustomed in pre-war years. Many of its industries had been devoted to the production of war material, for which there was no sizeable post-war market. In addition, markets which had been British before the war – for instance, Latin America – had been neglected and were occupied by other producers.

Britain's transactions with the Empire had been disrupted as a result of the war and, of course, many of its most productive working men had been killed or crippled. In France and Belgium, human casualties had also been enormous, but in addition they had had to endure fighting on their own territory; as, of course, did Russia. The Treaty of Brest-Litovsk of 1917 gave the Russians peace, but at a high price in territory and in productive resources which were transferred to Germany. Though Germany's territory was largely undamaged, its economy had been gradually adapted to the requirements of war and so was ill-equipped for recovery after the peace treaties. With the disruption of the trading relations on which Europe's prosperity and economic growth had been built, that task of post-war recovery was daunting. But the measures designed to promote it were far from suitable.

The Treaty of Versailles placed guilt for the war firmly on Germany's shoulders. The economic implication was clear; if it was Germany that had caused the shambles, it was Germany who would have to compensate for the lives and the production that had been lost. The treaty established a Reparations Commission which was to present a bill for war damage to the Allies before 1 May 1921, and a payment of twenty million gold marks was demanded in addition in advance of this date. The sums proposed by the Reparations

Commission were invariably so large that the Germans could not, or would not, pay. To do so would have meant wrecking their economy; and, in any case, they did not accept the idea of war guilt upon which reparations were based. One distinguished historian of the period has written that 'the reparations question darkened the sky of Europe with uncertainty and bitterness'; and this is no exaggeration. But it also involved the United States. The Allies' war effort had been helped by large-scale loans from American bankers and the American government. At the end of the war, particularly after doubts had been raised in America about certain aspects of the peace treaties, these sources of credit demanded repayment. The reaction of both the French and the British was to link the repayment of US loans to the payment of German reparations. Though America had chosen to have nothing to do with the new League of Nations, she could not ignore Europe's economic problems. In effect, European recovery depended upon America's willingness to become Europe's banker. In 1924 the Americans advanced the Dawes Plan, which co-ordinated American funds to Germany and was intended to help Germany to fulfil her treaty obligations. This plan helped to soothe the problem of international monetary confusion; but it did not change the basic principles underlying the problem – namely, that French demands for reparations would not be met, and that American demands for the repayment of loans would not be heeded. The relative prosperity of the years from 1924 to 1929 concealed this weakness from the casual eye. But with the crash of the US stock market, the way America's economy and Europe's were connected became clear. At the same time, the large-scale withdrawal of America's European investments showed that the Americans were unaware just how important their economic relations with Europe were. With America retreating economically as well as politically behind her own frontiers, hopes of further co-operation vanished. In 1929 the Germans cancelled reparation payments, and the rest of Europe responded by cancelling repayment of loans to the United States. The World Economic Conference scheduled for 1933 was effectively torpedoed, and hopes for the establishment of a new and more rational system of international economic relations had to wait until the end of the next world war. It is in the political impact of these economic developments that the significance of the Great Depression lies in the history of international relations between the wars.

As we have seen, the Great Depression was responsible for making worse the disagreements between the European and American Allies after the First World War, for the failure of the World Economic Conference, and also for the cancellation of German reparations payments, which undid most of the improvement in German–French and German–British relations. Put in a less direct way, the Depression was responsible for bringing to power governments who cared far less than their predecessors about the need for international harmony. In the United States, President Franklin D. Roosevelt was elected to office in November 1932 against the previous holder of the office, Herbert Hoover, who was defeated because he was associated with the economic consequences of the Depression. There can be no doubt that Roosevelt was more of an isolationist than Hoover. He was prepared to support legislation to introduce tariffs against European imports; he would not involve himself with attempts to bring the United States into the major international crises after 1930, and busied himself instead with the policies of his New Deal – his plan to provide immediate economic relief for the unemployed as well as urgent reforms in agriculture, labour, finance and housing. This, though successful, did nothing to prevent American involvement in another war of European origin less than ten years after his election to the Presidency.

In Germany, the Depression produced conditions favourable to the rise of the extremist parties. In the elections of September 1930, the Communists increased their parliamentary representation from fifty-four to seventy-seven seats, while the Nazi Party shot up from twelve to 107, becoming the second largest party in the Reichstag after the Socialists. In March 1932 Adolf Hitler, leader of the Nazi Party, polled thirteen and a half million votes in the election for the Presidency of the Weimar Republic; this support, added to the support he received in the Reichstag, led to the fatal decision of 30 January 1933 when Hitler was appointed Chancellor (the German equivalent of a prime minister). Nazi power, thus rewarded, was consolidated in the elections of March 1933. The Nazi's gained 45 per cent of the vote; as the vote was divided among a large number of small parties, this gave them effective control of both government and parliament. The tremendous increase in support for the Nazis was closely related to the despair felt by ordinary people when faced with the economic circumstances of the Depression. So the way became clear for Hitler systematically to repudiate Germany's treaty obligations; to rearm the country, to remilitarize the Rhineland; to agitate for the return of provinces lost as a result of the peace treaties: in other words, to undermine the basis of Europe's stability.

Hyperinflation made visible. Laundry baskets were necessary to collect the bulky pay packets in Berlin in 1923. (*Photo: Popperfoto*)

Hitler's was the most spectacular rise to power; but there were others. In Japan, the immense hardship that resulted from the fall in Japanese exports was most damaging to the small peasant landowners from whose ranks were drawn most of the army's junior officers. The authority of an already weak civilian government grew even less, enabling the army to take matters into their own hands. Believing that Japan would never be truly secure while she depended on economic prosperity in Europe and North America, the army decided to seize control of large areas of China in order to acquire a secure supply of raw materials and labour, and a large and growing market. So in 1931, on the pretext of replying to an attack on Japanese-owned railway equipment in Mukden, Manchuria, the Japanese army moved to control the province of Manchuria. Despite condemnation by the League of Nations, they consolidated their hold and began to plan a future area of Japanese imperial influence named The Greater East Asia Co-Prosperity Sphere. From this time onwards the Japanese expanded in the Pacific Ocean, threatening American and European interests and developing the aims that were eventually to bring them to war with the United States and Britain.

As well as causing the rise of predatory and nationalistic regimes, the Depression also sapped the will of the powers who stood for stability and order. In both Britain and France, the two pillars of European order, internal politics became more and more nervously tense; yet the orthodox treatment of the Depression, which required governments to be passive in the hope that renewed business confidence would lead to more investment and more jobs, served only to delay recovery and discourage the strengthening of the military resources of both nations. Yet at the same time, despair at the ability of their government to solve the economic problems led many Frenchmen and Englishmen to look to the Soviet Union. Russia, isolated from the international community, seemed to have discovered an answer to economic problems. The effect of this attraction exacted by Russia was to make their governments even more fearful of Communism than they had been, and the French and British opposed co-operation with Russia against Germany. Though the Soviet Union was admitted to the League of Nations in 1933, the appeals of the Soviet Foreign Minister, Litvinov, for a common front against Fascism went unheeded. The smaller non-communist states of eastern Europe, such as Czechoslovakia, Poland, Romania, and Yugoslavia, reacted to the Depression by building tariff walls against each other's products; and their relations, never good, worsened to the point where they were of little value as allies against Germany. In addition to their trade problems, all these countries had national minorities within their territories which, as their economic condition worsened, grew more resentful of the central governments.

The impact of the Depression cannot be overestimated. Though accurate predictions can never be made about what might have been, it seems clear in retrospect that in the years before 1929 Europe and America were groping towards the solution to the tangled questions of reparations and war debts. If this had been followed by an attempt to construct the kind of international economic institutions that emerged at the end of the Second World War, the sort of national economic crisis that produced the Nazi government in

Germany might have been avoided. As it was, the forces of extremism and militarism were strengthened, and the strength of those who might have resisted them was greatly weakened. Because of this, future historians might well consider that the Second World War began as much in the economic crisis of 1929 as in the political crisis that followed a decade later.

The Origins of the Second World War

Like the First World War, the Second World War had its general causes and its specific ones. The general causes were those that created a climate of conflict and antagonism between the countries that eventually went to war with one another; and the specific causes were those which translated that general hostility into direct conflict over particular issues. But there is an added factor in the analysis of the origins of the Second World War. Unlike the First War, it was truly a world war, encompassing the five continents. A European war broke out in 1939, spreading to the Middle East in 1940. In 1941 the German armies turned eastwards against the Soviet Union, and later in that year Japan attacked the United States, bringing her into the war in both the Pacific and (following Germany's declaration of hostilities) in Europe. While only a matter of weeks separated the assassination of the Archduke Ferdinand in Sarajevo and the involvement of the major participants in a continental war, there were years separating the outbreak of hostilities in Europe and the involvement of the major belligerents in what has come to be called the Second World War. The problem was nicely expressed in an exchange between General de Gaulle and a soldier in the Free French Army, of which he was leader. 'When did you join the war?' the General asked him. 'Well before you, *Mon Général*', he replied, for he had fought against the Fascists in Spain in 1936. In this section we will confine ourselves to examining the first full mobilization of the German armies for a war with a European country in September 1939, and the Japanese attack upon the American navy in Pearl Harbour in December 1941.

Europe

International conflict continued after the end of the First World War despite the hopes of those who made the peace. Wilson, the architect of the principles upon which the peace was made and of the League of Nations, had hoped to put an end to the Great Power politics that, in his view, had led to war and would always do so. The League institutionalized the theoretical equality of all nations, regardless of size and strength. Its purpose was to provide an effective deterrent to aggression. Wilson's desire to try an alternative system of international relations was understandable. But the system he proposed was not basically different from the power politics he hoped to get away from.

Nations still had to be convinced that opposition to another was not in their national interests. If some states chose to be friendly with some and unfriendly towards others, there was nothing the League could do to stop them. And if states had the military capacity to wage war, it only remained for their political leaders to create favourable conditions; and this, of course, could mean similar conditions within the League. By basing his hopes for a new international order on the League of Nations, Wilson and those who thought as he did avoided serious consideration of the underlying tensions in international relations; instead, they concentrated on what was most superficial in the problem of peace-keeping. It is at these underlying tensions that we must now look.

As well as trying to restructure the international system around a new institution, Wilson lent his support to measures designed to punish Germany, who lost large tracts of territory to Czechoslovakia and Poland, while other areas such as the industrial region of the Saar, were placed under international supervision. Germany was forbidden to try to re-incorporate any of these areas within the Reich, or to attempt to form a union with the tiny, rather pathetic post-war state of Austria. Germany's armies were limited in manpower and in the types of weapons they might use. In addition to these measures, which might misguidedly be justified as attempts to ensure that a militaristic Germany would never again trouble Europe, the Allies also made it accept the full responsibility for beginning the war and therefore for all the destruction that resulted. Germany was required to pay reparations and treated, initially at any rate, as an outcast.

Though the territories it had conquered by force in the west were returned to their owners, German conquests in the east were never returned to Russia by the Allies; (many years later, Russia grew strong enough to take them back by force). Not only was Germany punished for waging war against the Allies, but Russia was punished for being defeated by her. The effects of these events were to influence the European political climate profoundly. The territories inhabited by Germans but transferred to other countries were a constant source of difficulty. They undermined the authority of the governments of states into which they had been incorporated, and they served as a constant reminder to Germans of the humiliation which they had endured, and therefore as a constant barrier to good relations between Germany and those states, such as Poland and Czechoslovakia, which ruled their populations. The restrictions placed on the German army did not break down the structure on which a larger conscript force was later built; and they were in any case an inducement to the Germans to avoid fulfilling their treaty obligations. The war guilt clause of the Treaty of Versailles was immediately and continuously attacked by German historians, who spent the inter-war period proving to the satisfaction of their fellow Germans that the clause was historically inaccurate and the conditions that flowed from it, such as reparations, therefore quite unjust. The reparations demanded by the Allies served as a constant excuse for German politicians to conceal their inability to manage the economy. Indeed, reparations had an adverse effect on the ability of the Germans to rebuild their economic strength. By excluding Russia from the international community, the Allies made them turn towards the Germans; a fact that was to lead to military co-operation between the two countries under the Treaty of Rapallo (1922), which permitted the German army to hold on Russian territory manœuvres forbidden under the Versailles Treaty, and to the Nazi-Soviet Pact of August 1939.

Some effort was made after 1925 to face up to the problems posed by the Versailles Treaty. The Locarno Treaties of 1925 attempted to prepare ground for the rehabilitation of Germany. Some progress was made in sorting out the quantities and the timing of reparation payments, and the policy of securing the fulfilment of Germany's obligations by force was ended. In 1927 the inspection of German military installations ceased; and by 1930 the Rhineland had been evacuated by the Allied occupation force. But the economic problems caused by the world-wide Depression led to a massive increase in the popularity of the Nazi Party, which stood for the unilateral denunciation of all the restrictive items in the Versailles Treaty and for the creation of a new and stronger German Reich. By 1933 Hitler was in power as Chancellor, and by 1934 the Nazi Party had consolidated its control over all aspects of the country's political life.

The first sign of the difficulties that this new government was to present came with its refusal to continue the international disarmament conference of 1933. But other signs were soon to follow. In 1935, contrary to the Versailles Treaty, and without consulting other signatories, Hitler announced the re-introduction of conscription. In 1936 he remilitarized the Rhineland, again in defiance of German treaty obligations, and again with no more than verbal opposition from France and Britain. During these years Germany also succeeded in breaking up the series of alliances between France and the small nations on Germany's eastern borders. The paper relationship between France and those countries continued, but, by extending economic links and demonstrating the timidity of French diplomacy, Hitler developed much closer relations with the east European nations, though they were not relations based upon equality.

He also succeeded in making a friend out of a potential ally of Britain and France – Italy. Benito Mussolini, a man with great ambitions for Italy, came to admire Hitler's daring, the discipline he exerted within Germany, and, above all, his success. In the Spanish Civil War that began in June 1936, both Italian and German forces assisted the rebels, led by General Franco in what came to be seen as a rehearsal for the world war. The year before, Italy had defied the League of Nations and world opinion with the invasion of Abyssinia (now called Ethiopia); this intervention in Spain sealed a bond between the two dictators: its basis lay in their common disregard for the peaceful pursuit of change. In 1936, the description by Mussolini of Berlin and Rome as an 'axis around which can revolve all those European states with a will to collaboration and peace' signalled the existence of an alliance between two ambitious and greedy national leaders. So when, in 1938, Hitler moved to secure the return of the Sudetenland, an area of Czechoslovakia with a predominantly German population, the successes he had previously enjoyed made him bolder and dispirited his opponents. Despite feeling in both France and Britain that Hitler was insatiable and would soon have to be stopped, the government of neither country felt militarily strong enough; and, in any case, they hoped the Sudetenland might be Hitler's last claim.

With this in mind, the British and French negotiated an agreement at Munich in September 1938 returning the Sudetenland to Germany. But by early 1939 it became clear even to the most ardent believers in the policy of appeasing Hitler that he would not stop at the Sudetenland. His armies occupied the rest of Czechoslovakia, beginning in February 1939. It seemed that his next target might be the German-populated areas of Poland; so the British Prime Minister, Neville Chamberlain offered the Polish government a guarantee of Polish territory which was accepted. And so it happened that when Germany declared war on Poland in October 1939, both Britain and France found themselves committed to defending territory which their armies could not reach.

As a result of western Europe's reluctance to take seriously any of the Soviet Union's warnings about the danger of German expansion, Stalin signed a pact of non-aggression with Hitler in August 1939. Thus, just over twenty years after the optimistic attempts of the makers of the Versailles Treaty to construct a European order that would permanently abolish war, Britain and France were once again at war with Germany.

The Far East

In the Far East, as in Europe, the combination of a dissatisfied power and an economic depression produced conflict and instability which the League of Nations was powerless to prevent. Japan's disillusionment with the post-war settlements was strengthened by the Washington naval conferences of 1921–2, which limited the size of the Japanese navy to approximately half of the navy of either Britain or the United States. At the peace conferences Japan had asked that a declaration on racial equality be made by the victorious powers; they had refused. Measures designed to restrict the Japanese navy were therefore viewed by Japan as an example of the western nations contempt for orientals, and of their desire to control developments in the Far East. Japan's economy was based upon the import of raw materials and the export of finished goods. If supplies of raw materials dried up or demand for exports diminished, Japanese producers would suffer, and the government would be able to do nothing.

The consequence of this simple and widely understood fact of economic life was that Japan looked towards China as a potential source of economic security. For many years China had been internally divided, with some sections beyond the control of any central government, but in the 1920s it had gone through the throes of political modernization. Japanese economic interests in China, and especially in Manchuria, were a source of political influence. The success of an effective Chinese nationalist movement would threaten those interests and might also create a China powerful enough to dominate the whole Pacific region. It was these considerations that shaped Japan's attitude towards China and the Far East in general. When the Depression occurred in Europe and North America, the market for Japanese exports collapsed, and with it the living standards of the Japanese people. With the civilian government powerless, the Japanese army in Manchuria, where it was protecting Japanese railway interests, moved to occupy the whole province. The conquest of Manchuria began in 1931; and from that time until the end of the Second World War substantial Chinese territories fell under Japanese control. When the League of Nations condemned the Japanese attack on Manchuria in 1933, Japan responded by leaving the League. In 1937, Japanese armies moved south from Manchuria and by 1939 were in occupation of most of the Chinese coast. Now Japan's expansion seemed to threaten British and French colonial possessions in Burma and Indochina, as well as American interests in the Pacific. But the European nations were preoccupied with events in Europe, and America was left to face Japan alone.

Throughout 1940 and 1941 negotiations took place beween the two countries, but no progress was made. After coming to terms with the Soviet Union in 1941, Japan determined to resolve by force the struggle with America for mastery of the Pacific. In a surprise attack on the American fleet in Pearl Harbour, Japan began a war with the United States which was to be fought with the utmost ferocity.

It also freed from the restraining hand of isolationism those in the US who wished to fight with the British against the Germans. In 1940, after the collapse of France, Britain had stood virtually alone. By the end of 1941 she had acquired two powerful Allies, America and Russia (whose territory the Germans had invaded during the summer) at the cost of one new enemy – Japan. This fortunate turn of events was, for Britain, the beginning of a long struggle that could end only in victory.

The Second World War

The beginning of the Second World War is usually dated by British historians from Britain's declaration of war on Germany in September 1939. This is not an entirely satisfactory definition. For if this war is taken to be a truly global conflict, then it is fair to say that Britain's declaration did not produce worldwide hostilities. At this stage the major combatants were limited to Britain, Germany and France. It was not until the surprise attack in December 1941 on Pearl Harbour, the American Pacific naval base, that the USA and Japan were locked into this complex struggle. Given, then, that there was a gradual build-up to a world war situation, culminating in the declarations of 1941, it can be argued that September 1939 is not the date to choose as the starting-point for this process. German aggrandizement had its origins in Hitler's return to the Rhineland in 1936, or at least in his invasions of Austria and Czechoslovakia in 1938, before the push into Poland in the following year. In the same way, Japanese expansion was not a process which began suddenly in 1941. The

Japanese had been pursuing an imperial, aggressive advance ever since the invasion of Manchuria in 1931. They had extended their influence by force throughout China and southwards into the South-East Asian peninsula, and so into the American-held Pacific islands. As for the Russians, they started the war as allies of Germany in the invasion of Poland; it was not until 1941 that Hitler's invasion of Russia caused them to join with Britain and America.

The Second World War, then, is a vast problem with which to grapple. Its complexity is due to the scale on which it was fought, and the fact that it involved unusual and changing alliances, produced many distinct and different campaigns, and resulted in a huge shift in the balance of power throughout the world.

The Second World War produced many and more various campaigns than the First simply because of its geographical diversity. The 1914–18 war was decided in the end in one theatre of action: the Western Front. The Gallipoli campaign had resulted in deadlock, and the German attempts at forcing a decisive sea engagement at Jutland had also failed. By contrast, the 1939–45 war was notable for the variety of its battlefields. Among the separate campaigns were the Atlantic, the European, the Mediterranean and the North African, the Far East and the Pacific. In these campaigns, both air and sea forces were to play a significant part to an extent unknown in the First World War, when their potentialities were still undeveloped.

The European campaign was probably the one in which the really decisive battles of the war were fought. It was in western and central Europe that Hitler first established his empire. With the invasion and fall of France in 1940, no European country remained which was not tied directly to Germany by military rule, or attached to her indirectly by alliance or because it was economically necessary. Though Switzerland remained a neutral country throughout the war, its freedoms were clearly limited by its encirclement by Nazi countries. So, when Hitler decided in the spring of 1941 to invade Russia, his old ally against Poland, he was the virtual master of Europe. Only Britain stood clearly outside his grasp. It is a matter for debate whether Hitler had seriously considered invading England in 1940. Certainly, the defeat of Goering's Luftwaffe in the Battle of Britain made him decide to drop any such plans, serious or not. His policy towards Britain from then on was one of consistent heavy bombing of major cities – the Blitz campaign – in an effort to break the people's spirit. But from 1940 onwards (and indeed probably till the very end of the war) Hitler's chief interests were concentrated on the defeat of the Russians. He took personal command of the invasion of Russia and the battles that followed.

The first push into Russia was overwhelmingly successful, owing much to the successful strategy of Blitzkrieg (lightning war). This involved concentrating the attacking forces, which now included dive bombers designed to soften up and intimidate the enemy, at one point on the enemy's front. By contrast, campaigns in the First World War had been preceded by lengthy warning barrages, and then took place along miles of front line. Another new element was the use of highly mechanized units. The ideas behind this strategy were those of shock, surprise and speed. The vast Russian plains lent themselves particularly well to this tactic of rapid mechanized advance. Hitler's tanks, in fact, succeeded in reaching the outskirts of Leningrad and Moscow. But they arrived too late, and the harsh Russian winter took its toll. The German armies, expecting the war to be over in six months, had come unprepared for such low temperatures. The troops suffered from frostbite, while ill-protected tanks froze up and machine guns jammed. Hitler never succeeded in capturing Moscow.

In September 1942 he altered his objective and advanced on Stalingrad. This campaign directed towards the Caucasus was ostensibly designed to secure valuable oil supplies. It may also have been planned for ideological reasons; Stalingrad, the city of Stalin, was an important Russian symbol, as Verdun had been for the French in 1916; perhaps Hitler hoped to bleed the Russians dry here. In the event the attack was a failure. After a fierce battle the Germans were repulsed and were themselves surrounded by a Russian relief force under the command of General Zhukov. General von Paulus, the German commander, was forced to surrender in January 1943 after terrible hardships; the Russians took 90,000 prisoners. It was a crushing blow for the Germans, and demonstrated clearly that they were losing the war.

Another campaign of importance was that waged in the Mediterranean and North Africa. It was inspired in the first place by the Italian invasion of Egypt from Ethiopia. British forces under General Wavell easily defeated an enemy of superior size. Italian failures prompted Hitler to help his ally Mussolini, and the Africa Korps under Rommel was formed. German successes followed, and the British were beaten back around Alexandria and Tobruk. It was only with the appointment of General Montgomery and the building up of massively superior forces that the British succeeded in defeating Rommel, the 'desert fox', at El Alamein in October 1942: a victory which Winston Churchill described as 'the beginning of the end'. This campaign then merged into the European theatre of war as the Allies invaded Italy in September 1943 and pushed northeastwards into Austria. At sea, the Mediterranean had been the scene of fierce fighting between the Germans and British. British convoys and fighters slowly defeated German and Italian submarines and planes, and the island of Malta never fell despite ferocious attacks. The Italian navy, defeated early on at the battle of Cape Matapan (1941), was never a serious threat.

The war in the west was also fought across the Atlantic. Indeed this was the means by which Hitler hoped to defeat Britain after 1940. Through his unrestricted U-Boat campaign Hitler hoped to sink so many merchant ships that Britain would be starved into submission. He almost succeeded, but the refinements made to the convoy system were in the end responsible for the failure of Hitler's submarines. Better radar, underwater detection apparatus, improved depth charges, faster and bigger escort ships, air cover from Coastal Command and new tactical formations all reduced sinkings to a minimum by 1944.

The next major blow to Hitler came from the west, with the Allied invasion of Normandy in June 1944. Again Hitler had been deceived. He had thought that an invasion force would land in northern France, and here his defensive forces were strongest. Brittany had been further weakened by the continuing demands of the failing Russian front. Hence the Allies were able to get as far as Belgium (the Ardennes campaign) before they met the full force of a desperate German counter-attack. Resistance continued as they fought their way over the Rhine and into Germany. By this time the end was in sight; there were few German troops left capable of fighting. In April 1945 Hitler shot himself in his Berlin headquarters just as the Russians from the East and the Allies from the West entered the ruined city.

Finally, there was the Far Eastern campaign, which at first involved only Britain against Japan. America was involved after 1941. The underrated Japanese armies continued their invasion of China, moving south into British-held territories. In 1941–2, Japan's forces captured Hong Kong, Malaya, Burma and Borneo, as well as the American-held Pacific islands. Particularly galling for the English was the fall of Singapore, which was Britain's chief naval and mercantile port for the Pacific and had come to be regarded as an invincible stronghold. Yet Japanese troops crossing from the mainland of Malaya in February 1942 overwhelmed the island's defences, and over 70,000 British and Australian troops were forced to surrender. Churchill described the event as 'the worst disaster and largest capitulation in British history'. From this time on, American and British troops (based in India) fought a tough jungle war to regain south-east Asia. It was not until 1945 that the British under General Slim reconquered Burma and Malaya. The American marines under General MacArthur landed on the Pacific islands one by one and recaptured them against exceptionally tenacious Japanese resistance. Unconditional surrender was in the end the result of the dropping of the atomic bomb on the cities of Hiroshima and Nagasaki in August 1945. The world war was at an end.

Generally speaking, the Second World War was an increasingly technical war; in itself it promoted scientific discovery. The atom bomb and the German V1 and V2 rockets were examples of scientific advance being deliberately applied to warfare. Weapons were refined to give greater range, accuracy and hitting power. Similarly, defensive positions were strengthened. The coastal defences of northern France, in contrast to the mud trenches of the First World War, were a complex formation of reinforced concrete bunkers improved by radar and more efficient radio links. Possibly the most obvious refinements came in the air. Because aircraft were now more powerful and more reliable and had a greater flying range, they were able to make heavy bombing raids on cities deep in Germany and Britain. Night-flying was made possible by advanced electronics and engineering. The schnorkel, combined with more efficient batteries and electric motors, enabled German submarines to remain at sea for almost indefinite periods, providing they could be supplied when afloat.

The Second World War again witnessed a further move towards a 'total war' situation where nobody living in a combatant country would be immune. Rationing and conscription were introduced from the outset. Long-range bombing raids meant that civilians were involved in the front line of the fighting. The propaganda war was also intensified. Broadcasting took on a fresh importance. Not only were people subject to exhortations from their own leaders, but the enemy, using powerful transmitters, sought to influence their thinking.

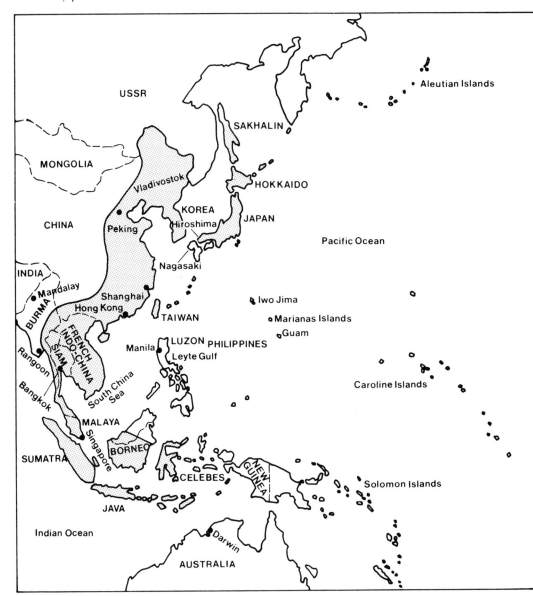

Map 6. The surrender of Japan.

What did the Second World War really accomplish? Its essential result was to alter the balance of power over the globe. The two rising forces in 1939, Japan and Germany, had both been utterly crushed and their economies, for the moment, left in ruins. In their place, Russia and America had arisen as the two dominant world forces. By virtue of the peace settlements America was committed to helping to protect and to subsidize its war-torn European allies. In the years following the war, America, through the Marshall Aid Plan, poured money and expertise into the western European nations, now formed into a defensive pact against Communism. Russia had advanced in 1945 through eastern Europe to Berlin, and now insisted on maintaining its control over these occupied countries. Czechkoslovakia, Poland, Hungary, East Germany and the Baltic states exchanged Nazi domination for Russian all becoming Communist. The Second World War had therefore accelerated a process that had been under way throughout the inter-war years. Russia and America, by virtue of their size and geological riches, were probably destined to become world leaders anyway; the war, by destroying the power of Germany and Japan, pushed the other two forward as both military and economic giants. By 1945, with the ending of the Second World War, the scene was set for the new era of post-war politics.

Map 7. The division of Germany into zones, 1945.

Prominent People

Adams, Samuel (1722–1803), American revolutionary statesman. He advocated 'no taxation without representation' as early as 1765; in 1766 he anticipated Napoleon by calling the English 'a nation of shopkeepers'; he promoted the Boston tea-party; and in 1776 he signed the Declaration of Independence.

Alexander II (1818–81), reforming Tsar of Russia, who succeeded his father Nicholas I in 1855. In 1861 he emancipated the 23 million serfs and in 1865 established provincial elective assemblies. Later his government became openly repressive, and he was killed by a Nihilist bomb.

Allenby, 1st Viscount (Edmund Henry Hyman) (1861–1936), British general. He served in South Africa between 1884 and 1902, on the Western Front 1914–16. Promoted general in 1917, as commander-in-chief of the Egyptian Expeditionary Force he took Jerusalem on 9 December and drove the Turks out of Palestine.

Angell, Sir Norman (1872–1967), British political commentator and pacifist, author of *The Great Illusion* (1910), in which he argued the economic futility of war even for the winners. Nobel Peace Prize 1933.

Asquith, Herbert Henry (1852–1928), Liberal Prime Minister of Britain 1908–1916. His government was notable for old age pensions (1908), payment of MPs, the Parliament Act, Irish home rule and unemployment insurance (1911), but as War Minister he gave way to Lloyd George. He resigned the leadership in 1926.

Astor, Viscountess (Nancy Witcher Astor) (1879–1964), the first woman MP to sit in the British House of Commons, when she succeeded her husband as MP for Plymouth in 1919.

Atatürk, Kemal (1881–1938), builder of modern Turkey. He drove the Greeks out of Turkey in 1922 and was President of the Turkish Republic 1923–38.

Bagehot, Walter (1826–77), British economist and journalist, editor of *The Economist* 1860–77. He wrote *The English Constitution* (1867).

Baldwin, Stanley (1867–1947), Conservative Prime Minister of Britain, 1923–4, 1924–9, and 1935–7.

Balfour, Arthur James (1848–1930), British statesman and writer, was Conservative Prime Minister of Britain 1902–6. As Foreign Secretary under Lloyd George he was responsible for an important declaration on Palestine in 1917. His works include *A Defence of Philosophic Doubt*.

Benes, Eduard (1884–1948), Czechoslovak statesman; co-founder with Thomas Masaryk of the Czech Republic after the break-up of the Austro-Hungarian monarchy in 1918; premier 1921–2, 1935–8.

Bentham, Jeremy (1748–1832), British utilitarian philosopher and writer on jurisprudence. His main works are *Government* (1776) and *Principles of Morals and Legislation* (1789). In Mill's words, 'He found the philosophy of law a chaos, and left it a science.'

Bernadotte, Jean Baptiste (1763–1844), worked his way up from a common soldier in the French army to a successful commander under Napoleon.

Bonaparte was jealous and distrustful of Bernadotte's military success, and in 1810 he was chosen heir to the throne of Sweden. In 1818 he succeeded as Charles XIV, and was known as a good and wise king.

Birkenhead, Lord (Frederick Edwin Smith) (1872–1930), British lawyer and politician; championed Ulster as Unionist MP (1906–19), and rose to be Solicitor-General (1915), Attorney-General (1915–1919), Lord Chancellor (1919–22), and Secretary for India (1924–8).

Bismarck, Otto Eduard Leopold von (1815–98), German (Prussian) diplomat and statesman, chief architect of the German empire. He used a dispute over Schleswig-Holstein to defeat Austria at Königgrätz in 1866, and he provoked the Franco-Prussian war of 1870–1, dictating the terms of peace to a defeated France. He was created a prince and Chancellor of the new German empire, and began a colonial policy in 1884. Known as the Iron Chancellor, he survived two assassination attempts only to be dismissed by Emperor William II in 1890.

Blanqui, Louis Auguste (1805–81), French revolutionary leader, master of insurrection. He was one of the foremost fighters in all three French revolutions of the nineteenth century, in 1830, 1848 and 1871; for his share in the Commune (1872) he was sentenced to life imprisonment, but was released after seven years. He spent altogether thirty-seven years in prison and invented the term 'dictatorship of the proletariat'; his social theories, stressing the class struggle, influenced Marx.

Blum, Léon (1872–1950), French statesman, leader of the French Socialist Party. He held office briefly in 1936–7 and his efforts strengthened the growth of the Popular Front and the campaign against appeasement of Hitler. After the war (when he was interned in Germany), he formed a short-lived Socialist government in 1946.

Bolivar, Simon (1783–1830), South American revolutionary, called The Liberator. He led independence movements in the north-west of South America against Spanish rule and founded Grand Colombia (now Venezuela, Colombia, Panama, Ecuador). He was for a while President of Colombia and Peru; Upper Peru was made a separate state, and called Bolivia in his honour. He died in poverty, of tuberculosis, and is still revered as one of the heroes of the South American continent.

Bondfield, Margaret Grace (1873–1953); as Minister of Labour, 1929–31, she was the first woman to enter the British cabinet and to be a member of the Privy Council.

Bose, Subhas Chandra (1897–1945), Indian nationalist leader; killed in a plane crash.

Botha, Louis (1862–1919), South African soldier and statesman. In command of the Transvaal forces 1899–1902 in the Boer War, he became Prime Minister of the Transvaal colony under the new constitution in 1907. In 1910 he became the first premier of the Union of South Africa, and conquered German South-West Africa in 1914–15.

Bright, John (1811–89), British Quaker statesman and orator. Friend of Cobden, with whom he promoted the movement for free trade and the anti-corn law league. Served as MP for Durham, Manchester and Birmingham; he was one of the most eloquent speakers of his time.

Brougham, Lord (Henry Peter Brougham) (1778–1868), British legal reformer. Advocate of Queen Caroline against George IV (1820); helped found *The Edinburgh Review* in 1802, and later, London University.

Brown, John (1800–59), American abolitionist. His action in inciting black slaves to revolt in 1859 led to the Civil War. In October he and eighteen men broke into the US armoury at Harper's Ferry in Virginia; he was tried for insurrection, treason and murder, and hanged at Charlestown on 2 December 1859. He is the hero of the Civil War song *John Brown's Body*, and is regarded as a martyr.

Burke, Edmund (1729–97), Irish Whig writer and political philosopher. He advocated the emancipation of the American colonies and better administration in India, but was violently opposed to the French Revolution, using the government not only to fight it but also to suppress free opinions at home.

Buxton, Sir Thomas Fowell (1786–1845), British social reformer; MP for Weymouth 1818–37, he succeeded Wilberforce as head of the anti-slavery group in 1824.

Campbell-Bannerman, Sir Henry (1836–1908), Liberal statesman, Prime Minister of Britain 1905–8. A pro-Boer, he granted the self-government to the Transvaal (1906) and the Orange River Colony (1907). During his office there was increasing friction between the Liberal-dominated House of Commons and Conservative-controlled House of Lords over reform legislation.

Canning, George (1770–1827), British statesman. Served under Pitt and Portland, and was an advocate of Catholic emancipation. He was the first to recognize the free states of Spanish America. In 1827 Lord Liverpool resigned and Canning formed an administration with the Whigs, but died soon after.

Carson, Edward Henry (1854–1935), Irish barrister, Solicitor-General for Ireland 1892; Conservative MP for Dublin University 1892–1918; Attorney-General 1915; First Lord of the Admiralty 1916–17; member of the war cabinet 1917–18. He organized the Ulster Volunteers, and violently opposed home rule.

Cartwright, John (1740–1824), British political writer, brother of Edmund Cartwright the inventor, known as the 'Father of Reform'. His writings advocated annual parliaments, the ballot, manhood suffrage, abolition of slavery, and the liberties of Spain and Greece. In 1820 he was fined £100 for sedition.

Castlereagh, Viscount (Robert Stewart) (1769–1822), Irish-born British statesman, was first a Whig, but turned Tory. A supporter of Catholic emancipation, he was War Minister 1805–9, and then Foreign Secretary under Lord Liverpool from 1812, taking a leading part in the Napoleonic wars. He was, however, deeply hated; repressor of the Irish rebellion and instigator of the Peterloo massacre, he committed suicide with a penknife.

Cavour, Camillo Benso di (1810–61), Italian statesman who, as premier of Piedmont, helped to bring about the unification of Italy.

Cecil, Lord Robert (1864–1958), British politician who helped draft the charter of the League of Nations. Nobel Peace Prize 1937.

Chamberlain, Joseph (1836–1914), British statesman. At first a Liberal under Gladstone, but his objections to home rule led to his resignation and he became a Unionist. As secretary for the colonies in the coalition government

ment of 1895 he acquired the reputation of a great colonial administrator.

Chamberlain, (Arthur Neville) (1869–1940), son of Joseph, was Chancellor of the Exchequer 1923–4, 1931–7; Minister for Health 1924–9, and Prime Minister 1937–40. He appeased Hitler with the Munich agreement of 1938, returning with the notorious promise 'peace in our time', and was succeeded by Churchill in 1940.

Chiang Kai Shek (1887–1975), Chinese general and statesman; with the fall of the Manchu dynasty in 1911 he became military adviser to President Sun Yat-sen and, after the latter's death (1925), became commander of the Kuomintang army and president, 1928–31. Torn between fighting the Japanese invaders and the Chinese Communists, but intent above all on holding on to power and wealth, he was defeated by the Communists and retired to Formosa (Taiwan) in 1949.

Churchill, Lord Randolph Henry Spencer (1849–95), British Conservative politician, who held brief office as Secretary for India (1885–6) and as Chancellor of the Exchequer and leader of the Commons (1886). Father of Winston.

Churchill, Sir Winston Leonard Spencer (1874–1965), British statesman and author, son of the above. He entered Parliament in 1900 and served as a junior officer with the British forces abroad, and was war correspondent for the *Morning Post*. He held the following ministerial posts: Under-Secretary for the Colonies 1905–8; President of the Board of Trade 1908–10; Home Secretary 1910–11; First Lord of the Admiralty 1911–15; 1939–40; Chancellor of the Duchy of Lancaster, 1915; Minister of Munitions 1917; Minister of War 1918–1921; Minister of Air 1919–21; Secretary of State for the Colonies 1921–2; Chancellor of the Exchequer 1924–9; Prime Minister and Minister of Defence 1940–5; Prime Minister 1951–5. His main achievement was as leader during the Second World War; his defeat immediately after the war, when he ran the election on a 'red scare campaign', showed however that his limitations were understood.

Clarkson, Thomas (1760–1846), British philanthropist who devoted his life to the abolition of slavery, both in Africa and the West Indies. He shares the credit with Wilberforce for the passing of the 1807 Act abolishing the British slave trade.

Clausewitz, Karl von (1780–1831), Prussian general and military expert whose *Vom Kriege (On War)* revolutionized the theory of war and dominated Prussian military thinking in the nineteenth century.

Clemenceau, Georges (1841–1929), French statesman of radical views; twice premier, 1906–9, 1917–20. He was a defender of Dreyfus. In old age he presided at the peace conference of 1919, where he was hostile to Germany.

Cobden, Richard (1804–65), British advocate of free trade. He led agitation against the laws restricting import of corn, and they were repealed in 1846.

Cole, George Douglas Howard (1889–1959), British economist and political journalist, Professor of Social and Political Theory at Oxford, 1944–57. Among his writings are *The Intelligent Man's Guide Through World Chaos* and a five-volume *History of Socialist Thought*.

Collins, Michael (1890–1922), Irish politician and Sinn Fein leader. He successfully organized guerrilla warfare against the British, and was largely responsible for the negotiation of the treaty with Britain in 1921. Signing it, he said, 'I am signing my own death warrant.' He was killed in an ambush on his return to Ireland.

Crispi, Francesco (1819–1901), Italian (Sicilian) statesman. Organized the successful movement of 1859–60, and re-entered Sicily with Garibaldi. In the restored kingdom of Italy he became deputy, president of the chamber, minister, and premier in 1887–90 and 1894. He was strongly anti-clerical.

Cromer, Lord (Evelyn Baring) (1841–1917), British diplomat who, as British comptroller-general in Egypt 1883–1907, did much to maintain order and improve finances.

Curzon, Lord (George Nathaniel Curzon) (1859–1925), statesman and administrator; Viceroy of India 1898–1905; member of Lloyd George's war cabinet 1916–18; Foreign Secretary 1919–24.

Dalhousie, Lord (James Andrew Broun Ramsay) (1812–60); governor-general of India from 1847, he annexed the Punjab and other states; railways, roads and canals were planned and built; and he opened the civil service to Indians and acted against suttee (whereby Indian wives immolated themselves on their husband's funeral pyre), and the slave trade.

Davis, Jefferson (1808–89), American Civil War leader. Born in Kentucky, he was made President of the Confederate States when the Civil War broke out. Captured and imprisoned, he was tried after the war for treason, but discharged. In 1881 he published *The Rise and Fall of the Confederate Government*.

Davitt, Michael (1846–1906), Irish nationalist. Son of a peasant, his family was evicted from their smallholding and moved to Lancashire. Working in a cotton factory Michael lost his right arm in an accident; in 1866 he joined the Fenians and in 1870 was sentenced to fifteen years' penal servitude. Released in 1877, he began an anti-landlord crusade which culminated in the Land League in 1879. Again imprisoned, he published his *Leaves from a Prison Diary* in 1885, and was returned to Parliament in 1892 as an anti-Parnellite.

De Valéra, Eamon (1882–1974), Irish statesman, b. New York of Spanish and Irish parentage. Brought up in Limerick, he was imprisoned for his part in the 1916 Easter uprising. He led the Republican Sinn Feiners 1917–26, and then the Irish Free State opposition (Fianna Fail). His party gained the elections of 1932 and he became President of the Executive Council 1932–8, and Prime Minister 1938–48, 1951–4, 1957–9, and President again 1959–73.

Disraeli, Benjamin, Earl of Beaconsfield (1804–81), British statesman and novelist of Jewish parentage who helped to shape modern Conservatism in England. He entered Parliament in 1837 and was Prime Minister in 1868 and 1874–80. In 1875 he made Britain half-owner of the Suez Canal, and in 1876 made the Queen Empress of India. He was the rival of Gladstone and a friend of Queen Victoria. Among his novels are *Vivian Grey* (1826), *Coningsby* (1844) and *Sybil* (1845).

Dreyfus, Alfred (1859–1935), French (Jewish) victim of injustice. While an artillery captain on the General Staff he was accused in 1894 of divulging national secrets to a foreign power and sentenced to life imprisonment on the

Cayenne Île du Diable. Vigorous efforts by his wife and friends to prove his innocence plunged France into furious arguments about militarism and anti-semitism. Reinstated in 1906, he was awarded the Legion of Honour in 1919.

Durham, Lord (John George Lambton) (1792–1840), British Whig MP who served as governor-general of Canada after the disturbances of 1837, and two years later presented to parliament his *Durham Report*, which laid down the principles of colonial self-government.

Edward VII (1841–1910), King of England, the eldest son of Queen Victoria. He married Princess Alexandra of Denmark in 1863, and succeeded his mother in 1901.

Edward VIII (1894–1972), King of England, succeeded his father George V in 1936, and abdicated later that year because of hostility to his planned marriage with an American divorcee, Mrs Simpson. He was created Duke of Windsor and the marriage took place in June 1937. He was governor of the Bahamas 1940–5.

Engels, Friedrich (1820–95), German socialist, son of a wealthy textile manu-facturer, lifelong friend of Karl Marx. They met in Paris in 1844 and col-laborated in writing the *Communist Manifesto* of 1848. In 1845, Engels' *The Condition of the Working Class in England* was published, and it was through him that Marx acquired his knowledge of English labour conditions.

Fawcett, Millicent Garrett (1847–1929), educational reformer and leader of the movement for women's suffrage. A sister of Elizabeth Garrett Anderson (doctor and founder of a medical school for women), she was made president of the Women's Unionist Association in 1889.

Fichte, Johann Gottlieb (1762–1814), German philosopher of the nationalistic Romantic school who prepared the way for modern totalitarianism.

Fourier, Charles (1772–1837), French socialist who propounded a system of associated enterprise which, although utopian, stimulated social reform.

Franco, Francisco (1892–1975), Spanish general and dictator. He led the Fascist rebellion against the Republican government (1936) and with the help of the German and Italian Fascists won the Spanish Civil War and took power. In a letter to Hitler he wrote: 'The destiny of history has united you with myself and the Duce in an indissoluble way.' His dictatorship was ruthlessly repressive up to the time of his death.

Gandhi, Mohandas Kamamchand (Mahatma) (1869–1948), Indian patriot, social reformer and moral teacher. Lived in South Africa 1893–1914, opposing discrimination against Indians. A leader of the independence movement in India, he dominated Congress, instituted civil disobedience, advocated non-violence and sought to free India from its caste system. He was sentenced to six years' imprisonment for civil disobedience in 1922. After independence he sought to unite all Indians, but in 1948 was assassinated on his way to a prayer meeting.

Garibaldi, Giuseppe (1807–82), Italian soldier and patriot, who with Mazzini and Cavour created a united Italy. In 1834 he was condemned to death for taking part in an attempt to seize Genoa, but escaped to South America where he distinguished himself as a guerrilla fighter. He returned in 1848 to fight for Mazzini but was again forced to flee, returning in 1851 to support Cavour and take part in the Austrian war. In 1860, with his thousand volunteers, the 'Red Shirts', he freed Sicily, took Naples, and handed over the Two Sicilies to Victor Emmanuel, who was proclaimed king.

George III (1738–1820), King of England, grandson of George II, reigned 1760–1820. During his reign his desire to govern led to much friction, and his support for Pitt ended the supremacy of the old Whig families. Decisive battles were fought in America, India and Europe; despite his efforts, American independence was achieved in 1776. He suffered from bouts of insanity.

George IV (1762–1830), King of England, eldest son of George III, reigned 1820–30. He affected to be a Whig to annoy his father, but governed as his father had done with the aid of the Tories. His reign was a time of distress and of demand for reform; George was an undutiful son, a bad husband, and a callous father, but was known as 'the first gentleman of Europe'. He first became Regent because of his father's insanity.

George V (1865–1936), King of England, the second son of Edward VII and Queen Alexandra, becoming heir to the throne on the death of his elder brother in 1892. He succeeded in 1910.

George VI (1895–1952), King of England, second son of George V, called to the throne in 1936 on the abdication of his elder brother, Edward VIII. His reign was marked by the Second World War and rapid social change.

George, Henry (1839–97), American political economist, whose fundamental remedy for poverty was a 'single tax' levied on the value of land exclusive of improvements, and the abolition of all taxes which fall upon industry and thrift.

Gladstone, William Ewart (1809–98), British Liberal statesman, orator and author. He entered Parliament in 1832 as a Tory and held office under Peel. From 1852 he served several terms as Chancellor of the Exchequer and was Liberal Prime Minister 1868–74, when his legislation included the Education Act of 1870, the Ballot Act, the disestablishment of the Irish church and an Irish Land Act. Again Prime Minister 1880–5, 1886 and 1892–4, he carried a Parliamentary Reform Act, and unsuccessfully advocated home rule for Ireland. He left behind him probably the longest and most successful record of practical legislation by any minister, and as a parliamentary debater he has never had a superior.

Gordon, Charles George (1833–85), British soldier. After service in the Crimea and China, where he was known as 'Chinese Gordon', he was made governor of the Equatorial provinces of Egypt in 1873, and attempted to suppress slavery. He was a notable governor of the Sudan, 1877–80, but was killed at Khartoum in 1884 while trying to put down the rebel troops of the Mahdi.

Grant, Ulysses Simpson (1822–85), American general of the Civil War, and 18th President of the United States (1869–76). Under his administration the rights of suffrage without regard to race, colour or previous servitude were guaranteed.

Grattan, Henry (1746–1820), Irish statesman who struggled for Irish legislative independence, Catholic emancipation (he was a Protestant) and parliamentary reform; he was thwarted, largely because of the corruption and unrepresentativeness of the Irish Parliament.

Haldane, Lord (Richard Burdon Haldane) (1856–1928), British Liberal states-man. He advocated educational reform, and as Secretary for War (1905–12) he remodelled the army and founded the Territorials.

Hamilton, Alexander (1755–1804), American statesman and economist. In 1787 he conceived the series of essays afterwards collected as *The Federalist*, and in 1792 became the leader of the Federalists, a party hostile to the Republicans under Jefferson. As Secretary of the Treasury (1789–95) he put Washington's government on a firm financial footing. He was killed in a duel with his rival in the Federal Party, Aaron Burr.

Hardie, James Keir (1856–1915), British (Scottish) Labour leader. Founded the Independent Labour Party (1893). He worked in a coal-mine from childhood and, victimized as champion of the miners (whom he organized), moved away and became a journalist. In 1892 he was the first socialist to be elected to the Commons (for West Ham South). He started and edited *The Labour Leader* 1887–1904, and was the first chairman of the parliamentary Labour party, 1906. Opposition to the Boer War cost him his seat.

Hastings, Warren (1732–1818), British administrator in India. As governor-general of the East India Company he revised the finances and led inquiries into corruption, but found on his return to England that a parliamentary inquiry was set up to impeach him for corruption. After seven years he was acquitted, but was financially ruined.

Henderson, Arthur (1863–1935), British (Scottish) Labour politician. Secretary of the Labour Party and Chairman 1908–10, 1914–17, 1931–2, was in coalition cabinets 1915–17, Home Secretary in the Labour government 1924, Foreign Secretary 1929–31. Working mainly for disarmament, he was President of the World Disarmament Conference, 1932–5. Nobel Peace Prize 1934.

Herzl, Theodor (1860–1904), founder of modern political Zionism, was born in Budapest, but lived mostly in Vienna. His tomb is in Jerusalem.

Hindenburg, Paul von (1847–1934), German field-marshal, became a national hero by defeating the Russians at Tannenberg in 1914. He was President of Germany 1925–34.

Hitler, Adolf (1889–1945), German dictator, founder of National Socialism, b. in Austria. He came to Munich in 1912 and enlisted in the Bavarian infantry. After the war he became leader of the German National Socialist (Nazi) move-ment. He attempted a *coup d'etat* in Bavaria in 1923 but failed and, while in prison, wrote *Mein Kampf* (1925). He became Reich Chancellor in 1933 and, on the death of Hindenburg in 1934, Führer; commander-in-chief of the Wehrmacht 1935. Under his rule, working-class movements were ruthlessly destroyed; all opponents and non-Aryan racial elements – Communists, socialists, Jews, gypsies – were persecuted and murdered. By terrorism and propaganda and the rhetoric of intense German nationalism, he made the German state a powerful machine for aggression. There followed the occupa-tion of the Rhineland (1936), support for the Spanish Fascists, the annexa-tion of Austria and Czechoslovakia (1938–9), the invasion of Poland and declaration of war by Britain and France (1939), the invasion of Russia (1941). Hitler, convinced of his own greatness and Germany's destiny, survived an assassination attempt by his own officers, but met final defeat in 1945; on 30

April he committed suicide as the Russian troops closed in on Berlin.

Jefferson, Thomas (1743–1826), third American President, 1801–9. He created the Republican Party and helped to draft the Declaration of Independence; he also tried unsuccessfully to put an end to slavery.

Kropotkin, Prince Peter (1842–1921), Russian anarchist, geographer and explorer, who was imprisoned in 1874 for favouring the political action of a working men's association, but escaped after two years to England. At Lyons he was condemned in 1883 to five years' imprisonment for anarchism; released after three years he settled in England until the 1917 revolution took him back to Russia. He wrote on anarchism, the French Revolution, Russian literature, Asia, and mutual aid in revolution; and wrote an autobiography, *Memoirs of a Revolutionist* (1900).

Kruger, Stephanus Johannes Paulus (1825–1904), Boer leader who, in 1881, was appointed head of the provisional government against Britain. In 1883 he was elected president of the Transvaal or South African Republic, and again in 1888, 1893 and 1898. When the war of 1899–1902 turned against the Boers, he vainly sought help in Europe.

Law, Andrew Bonar (1858–1923), b. New Brunswick, Canada; British Unionist MP from 1900; in 1911 he succeeded Balfour as Unionist leader in the House of Commons, was Colonial Secretary 1915–16, then a member of the war cabinet, Chancellor of the Exchequer 1916–18, Lord Privy Seal 1919, and from 1916 leader of the House of Commons. He retired in March 1921, but despite ill-health was Conservative Prime Minister from October 1922 to May 1923.

Lawrence, Thomas Edward (1888–1935) (Lawrence of Arabia), British soldier who led the Arabs against the Turks in the 1914–18 war, and wrote *The Seven Pillars of Wisdom*, among other works. He was killed in a motor-cycle accident.

Lenin (Vladimir Ilyich Ulyanov) (1870–1924), Russian revolutionary leader and statesman, born in Simbirsk on the middle Volga, son of the local inspector of education. From 1893 to 1917 he worked underground in Russia and abroad for the revolutionary cause, being exiled to E. Siberia in 1895. The leading spirit of the Bolsheviks, a revolutionary group within the Social Democratic Party, he and his fellow exiles returned to Russia in April 1917; and after the October revolution which overthrew Kerensky, he headed the new government. He faced a difficult task, with world war, civil war, and anarchy. He wrote many political tracts, including *'Left Wing' Communism: an Infantile Disorder, The State and Revolution, What is to be done?*

Liebknecht, Karl (1871–1919), son of a social democrat, he became a barrister. During the First World War he was imprisoned as an independent, anti-militarist, social democrat. In 1918 he and Rosa Luxemburg founded the German revolutionary Communist Workers' Party (KPD) in Berlin. They were both murdered by German Freikorps officers in 1919.

Lincoln, Abraham (1809–65), sixteenth President of the USA. Born in Kentucky, he was returned to Congress from Illinois in 1846. He was a leader of the Republican party which was formed in 1856 to oppose slavery. He became president in 1861, the year in which the Civil War broke out, and he planned and urged the thirteenth amendment to the constitution which was passed in 1865. The phrase 'government of the people, by the people, for the people' comes from his Gettysburg speech of 1863. On 14 April 1865 at Ford's Theatre, Washington, he was shot by J. Wilkes Booth, an actor, and died next morning.

Lloyd George of Dwyfor, 1st Earl (David Lloyd George) (1863–1945), British Liberal statesman of Welsh origin. He was MP for Caernarvon 1890–1944; President of the Board of Trade 1905–8; and as Chancellor of the Exchequer he introduced social insurance, old age pensions, and the momentous budget of 1909–10, whose rejection by the Lords led to the constitutional crisis and the Parliament Act of 1911. In 1916 he superseded Asquith as Prime Minister, and was one of the 'Big Four' in the peace negotiations. He conceded the Irish Free State in 1921.

Lugard, Lord (Frederick John Dealtry Lugard) (1858–1945), British colonial administrator in Africa, especially Nigeria, and exponent of the system of indirect rule through native chiefs.

Luxemburg, Rosa (1871–1919), Polish political activist who, like Trotsky, believed in the need for 'permanent revolution'. Co-founder with Liebknecht of the KPD, the Communist Workers' Party, in Germany, she was murdered with him in 1919.

MacDonald, James Ramsay (1866–1937), British Labour politician of Scottish origin who was, from January to November 1924, Prime Minister and Foreign Secretary of the first Labour government, a minority government at the mercy of the Liberals. He was Prime Minister again, 1929–31, but met the financial crisis of 1931 by forming a predominantly Conservative 'National' government, splitting his own party. He stayed in power until 1935, and from then until his death was Lord President under Baldwin.

Marx, Karl (1818–83), German founder of modern international Communism. He studied law, philosophy and history at the universities of Bonn and Berlin, and went to Paris to study economics, where he met Engels. Expelled from France, he settled in Brussels and, with Engels, reorganized the Communist League and wrote the *Communist Manifesto* in 1848. Actively involved in the revolutionary movement, he was forced to move to London in 1849; there he wrote *Das Kapital*, a new theory of society in which he interpreted history in terms of economics and explained the evolution of society in terms of class struggle. In 1864 he helped to found the first International. He ranks as one of the most original and influential thinkers of modern times.

Masaryk, Thomas Garrigue (1850–1937), Czech statesman and independence leader. He was the first President of Czechoslovakia, 1918–35.

Mazzini, Giuseppe (1805–72), Italian patriot who advocated a free and united Italy. Expelled from Italy, France and Switzerland for political agitation, he took refuge in London in 1837. In 1848 he returned to Italy and became dictator of the short-lived Roman republic, put down by French forces. He prepared the way for Italian unity.

Molotov, Vyacheslav Mikhailovitch (b. 1890), Russian statesman. He succeeded Litvinov as Commissar for Foreign Affairs, 1939–49, but was expelled from the Communist Party in 1964. He changed his name from Scriabin to Molotov (the hammer) early in his career to escape the imperial police; the molotov cocktail (a kind of small bomb) is named after him.

Montgomery of Alamein, 1st Viscount (Bernard Law Montgomery) (1887–1976), British field-marshal; commanded 8th Army in North Africa, Sicily and Italy, 1942–4; C-in-C, British Group of Armies and Allied Armies in Northern France, 1944. He served as Deputy Supreme Allied Commander Europe (NATO), 1951–8.

Mussolini, Benito (1883–1945), Fascist dictator of Italy, 1922–43, 'Il Duce', son of a blacksmith. From 1935 an aggressive foreign policy (Abyssinia and Spain) was at first successful, and in June 1940 he entered the war on the side of Hitler. The two dictators never trusted each other – and defeat in North Africa and the invasion of Sicily brought down Mussolini's government. He was shot dead by partisans while attempting to flee to Switzerland.

Napoleon I (Bonaparte) (1769–1821), French Emperor and general, of Corsican birth. Trained in French military schools from the age of ten, by the age of twenty-seven he was commander of the army in Italy and defeated the Austrians, giving France control of Lombardy. He then led an expedition to Egypt, but Nelson destroyed his fleet at the battle of the Nile. After further Italian victories, he carried out a *coup d'etat* in 1799, and in 1804 became Emperor. After further aggressions he became the arbiter of Europe and made his brothers kings of Naples, Holland and Westphalia; but in Spain he provoked the Peninsular War and was driven back; his invasion of Russia ended in the disastrous winter retreat from Moscow; and in 1814 the Allies forced him to abdicate and retire to Elba. He emerged again in 1815 to be defeated by Wellington at Waterloo and was exiled to St. Helena, where he died of cancer of the stomach.

Napoleon III (1808–73), French Emperor, son of Napoleon I's brother Louis. Imprisoned for five years for his attempts on the throne of France, he returned in the revolution of 1848, and in 1851 came to power by a *coup d'etat*. Tough repression at home was linked to an adventurous foreign policy – the Crimean War (1854–6), intervention in Mexico, war against Austria (1859), and expeditions to China (1857–60): but when he was manœuvred by Bismarck into the Franco-Prussian war he was defeated at Sedan in 1870. The Second Empire was ended and he retired to England.

Nelson, 1st Viscount (Horatio Nelson) (1758–1805), British admiral. Son of a Norfolk clergyman, he went to sea at twelve and became a captain in 1793. In the French revolutionary wars he lost his right eye in 1794 and his right arm in 1797. Decorated and promoted to rear-admiral, he defeated the French at Aboukir Bay in 1798, became vice-admiral in 1801, and was at the bombardment of Copenhagen. In 1805 he destroyed the French fleet at Trafalgar, in which battle he was killed.

Owen, Robert (1771–1858), British (Welsh) social reformer. As manager, and later owner, of New Lanark cotton mills he tried to put his philanthropic views into effect, with slight success. He challenged the doctrine of *laissez-faire* and inaugurated the co-operative movement.

Paine, Thomas (1737–1809), English-born radical political writer. He spent the years 1774–87 in America helping the American revolutionary cause, and was made secretary to the committee of foreign affairs. On his return to England he wrote *The Rights of Man* (1791–2), was condemned for treason, and fled to France. He entered French politics, was sent to prison and wrote *The Age of Reason*, advocating deism. He died in New York.

Pankhurst, Emmeline (1858–1928), English suffragette who, with her daughters Christabel (1880–1958) and Sylvia (1882–1960), worked for women's suffrage; in 1903 she founded the National Women's Social and Political Union; following suffragette demonstrations in London in 1913, Emmeline was sentenced for inciting persons to place explosives in Lloyd George's house.

Peel, Sir Robert (1788–1850), British Tory statesman, who first held office in 1811. As Home Secretary he reorganized London police (called, after him, 'Peelers' or 'Bobbies'), and in 1829 the Wellington-Peel government's great measure was toleration of Roman Catholics. He was Prime Minister from November 1834 to April 1835, and during 1841–6. In 1846, largely as a result of the Irish famine, he repealed the corn laws which protected English agriculture. He died after a riding accident.

Pitt, William (the Younger) (1759–1806), British Tory statesman, Prime Minister 1783–1801, 1804–6. Although he secured important parliamentary reforms and was an able finance minister, he cared more for power than for measures. Not understanding the importance of the French Revolution, he introduced repressive measures at home and was forced into a long struggle with France. He vacillated over Irish policy and the emancipation of the Catholics, and, broken in health, died before he was fifty.

Rasputin, Grigori Yefimovich (1871–1916), Russian peasant monk who at the court of Tsar Nicholas II exerted a malign influence over the Tsarina through his apparent ability to improve the health of the sickly Tsarevich Alexis. He was murdered by a group of nobles at the Yussupoff Palace.

Rhodes, Cecil John (1853–1902), British empire-builder who went to Natal for health reasons and made a fortune in the diamond mines. In 1890 he became Prime Minister of Cape Colony and secured British expansion in what is now Rhodesia. His policy was the ultimate establishment of a federal South African dominion under the British flag, but he withdrew from politics after the failure of the ill-advised 1896 Jameson Raid into the Transvaal. He left large sums to found scholarships at Oxford for overseas students.

Roosevelt, Franklin Delano (1882–1945), American statesman, a distant cousin of Theodore Roosevelt. During the First World War he held office under Wilson and was Democratic candidate for the presidency in 1920. Stricken by polio he became governor of New York (1928–32) and, in the presidential election of 1932, defeated Hoover, repeal of prohibition being made a vital party issue. He met the economic crisis of 1933 with a policy for a 'New Deal'. Re-elected in 1936, he held office until his death near the end of the Second World War, during which he had held many meetings with Churchill and Stalin.

Roosevelt, Theodore (1858–1919), President of USA, b. of Dutch and Scottish descent in New York. Popular because of his exploits in the Spanish–American War, when he raised and led 'Roosevelt's Rough-riders', he was appointed Vice-President for the Republicans in 1900. He became President when McKinley was assassinated in 1901, and was re-elected in 1905. His promotion of peace between Russia and Japan gained him the Nobel Peace Prize, 1906.

San Martin, José de (1778–1850), South American national leader, b. Argentina; during 1812–22 he played a great part, as general and statesman, in winning independence from Spanish rule for his native land and for Chile and Peru.

Smuts, Jan Christian (1870–1950), South African statesman and soldier, born in Cape Colony, who fought on the Boer side as Botha's right-hand man in the Boer War. He was premier of the Union, 1919–24, conquering German S.W. and E. Africa, and uniting the South African and Unionist parties in 1920. Premier again, 1939–48, he worked for co-operation within the Commonwealth and in the world, but his party was defeated in 1948 by the Nationalists under Malan.

Stalin (Joseph Vissarionovich Djugashvili) (1879–1953), b. Georgia, Soviet statesman who for nearly thirty years was leader of the Russian people. He originally studied at Tiflis for the priesthood, but became an active revolutionary and took part in the Civil War after 1917. In 1917 he became general secretary of the Communist Party and, after Lenin's death, he ousted Trotsky to take complete command. He modernized agriculture on socialist lines by ruthless methods, and conducted purges and show trials in which many thousands of opponents died or disappeared. On the German invasion in 1941 he assumed military leadership. George Lukacs said that Stalin 'turned Marxism on its head' by twisting it into theories and strategies which fitted his own tactics on any particular occasion. Trotsky, whose murder Stalin arranged, said: 'It was the supreme expression of the mediocrity of the apparatus that Stalin himself rose to his position.'

Sun Yat-sen (1867–1925), Chinese revolutionary, idealist and humanitarian. After a rising failed in 1895 he lived abroad, but in 1911 the Manchus were overthrown and he became president. In 1912 he founded the Kuomintang (Chinese National Party), but soon resigned in favour of Yuan Shih-kai. His 'Three Principles' were nationalism, democracy and livelihood.

Talleyrand-Périgord, Charles Maurice de (1754–1838), French politician and diplomat, who was educated for the church but turned against it and was excommunicated. He was at first very close to Napoleon and was instrumental in consolidating his power as Emperor. Foreign Minister from 1797 to 1807, he deserted Napoleon, and represented France at the Congress of Vienna.

Trotsky, Leo (Lev Davidovich Bronstein) (1879–1940), Russian revolutionary, b. of Jewish parents in the Ukraine, one of the leaders of the Bolshevik revolution. He was twice (1901, 1905) exiled to eastern Siberia, but escaped to London. With Lenin he led the Bolshevik revolution in October 1917, being commissar for foreign affairs till March 1918, then of war till 1924. He differed from Stalin on policy, believing in 'permanent revolution', according to which socialism could not be achieved in Russia without revolution elsewhere, and was dismissed from office in 1925 and expelled from the Communist Party in 1927. Exiled from Russia, he sought refuge across Europe, and was finally granted asylum in Mexico. Tried in his absence, he was murdered by one of Stalin's agents with a blow from an ice-pick. A prolific writer and political philosopher, his *History of the Russian Revolution* was translated in 1932–3; his autobiography, *My Life*, appeared in 1930.

Venizelos, Eleutherios (1864–1936), Greek statesman, b. Crete. Studied law in Athens, led the Cretan revolt in 1905, and was Prime Minister of Greece in 1910–15, 1917–20, 1924, 1928–32, 1933. He promoted the Balkan League (1912) and, opposed by King Constantine, set up a rival government at Salonika 1916–17, forcing the King's abdication. In 1935, foreseeing a royalist coup, he joined a Cretan revolt, which failed; he fled to Paris and was condemned to death in his absence.

Victor Emmanuel II (1820–78), son of Charles Albert of Sardinia, became King of Sardinia in 1849. He was proclaimed first King of Italy in 1861 at Turin after the Austrians had been defeated and Garibaldi had succeeded in the south. Known as the 'honest king', he reigned as a strictly constitutional monarch.

Victoria, Queen (1819–1901), Queen of England, was grand-daughter of George III, and succeeded her uncle, William IV, in 1837. In 1840 she married Prince Albert of Saxe-Coburg-Gotha, and bore him four sons and five daughters before his death in 1861. Conscientious, hard-working and of strict moral standards, she had by the end of a long life (Jubilees 1887 and 1897) won the affection and respect of her subjects.

Wilberforce, William (1759–1833), English philanthropist. He was the parliamentary leader of the campaign against the slave trade, abolished in 1807. He then worked against slavery itself, but declining health compelled him in 1825 to retire from Parliament, where he had remained independent of party.

William I of Germany (1797–1888), King of Prussia and first German Emperor. He succeeded to the throne in 1861 and continued resistance to reform, appointing Bismarck as chief minister, and supporting him through the Austro-Prussian and Franco-Prussian wars. He was proclaimed German Emperor at Versailles in 1871.

William II of Germany, (1859–1941), King of Prussia and German Emperor from 1888, was grandson of William I and of Queen Victoria. He dismissed Bismarck and, a man of great energy and impetuosity, helped to precipitate the First World War. Forced to abdicate in 1918, he lived in exile at Doorn in Holland until his death.

Wilson, Thomas Woodrow (1856–1924), Democratic President of the USA 1913–21. He brought America into the First World War and advocated the League of Nations: his administration, ending in tragic failure and physical breakdown, introduced prohibition and women's suffrage.

2

Science and Technology

Summary of Chapter

Introduction

It was the sixteenth and seventeenth centuries that saw the dawn of a new age of human civilization: the age of science. Since then, science and technology have advanced faster and faster. With their help, man has gained such control over the world that there is simply no aspect of life left untouched. And so close now is the relationship between science and technology, on the one hand, and the society we live in, on the other, that it is not easy to understand the complex ways in which they affect one another.

It is certainly not enough to take a narrow view of science and say it is simply a growing body of knowledge about such things as quarks, quasers and chromosomes. We should not regard technology as just a means of making our lives more convenient or more pleasurable with supertankers and satellites, computers and colour television, atomic power and aerosols. We have to think how all these inventions and discoveries have affected the societies we live in. What was the reason why this or that scientific or technological development went ahead? What is the impact of any particular development on the way that you and I and our fellow men live together? These are the important questions: and if we are to answer them, there are many things we have to take into account.

There is, for instance, a philosophy behind the growth of scientific knowledge – we ought to know about that. We ought to understand how scientists behave as a group. What do they think they are doing, and why do they think they are doing it? We need to understand something about the importance of science and technology to a nation's economic and military strength – something which, because it determines the way governments spend their money on science, has a lot to do with the way science is organized. It also has much to do with the way that governments decide we should be educated. It becomes more and more necessary that we should know *how* science and technology work – because only by doing so can we square up to the tremendous problems with which society is faced.

The fact is that the modern world is apparently a prosperous one and this prosperity is to a great extent founded on science and technology. But at the same time it is a world of increasing violence, an unjust world with the rich greedy for more material possessions while the majority of the world's soaring population live in miserable poverty. It is a world in which pollution threatens the health of the environment. We must consider therefore to what extent science and technology are also responsible for these evils. And most important of all – is the future that science and technology is accelerating us towards sufficiently under our control that we can look forward optimistically to the further progress of the human race?

The Scientific Revolution

If we are to understand the way modern science and technology have developed, we must begin with the scientific revolution that occurred in Europe during the sixteenth and seventeenth centuries. It was then that the idea first grew up that scientific knowledge was practical and useful: an idea that now binds science and technology closely together. The philosophers Francis Bacon (1561–1626) and René Descartes (1596–1650) were among the first prophets of the Age of Science. They recognized that knowledge of the physical world – based on observation and deduction – could be a powerful force for advancing civilization. Descartes thought that through the use of science men could become 'the masters and possessors of nature'. That idea has become the chief justification for the preoccupation of the modern world with science and technology.

Before the scientific revolution, science was not often regarded as a way of securing a more comfortable future. More usually it was employed to provide intellectual support for fixed religious or philosophical beliefs, and it was

The Great Equatorial Telescope in the Dome, Greenwich Observatory. Mansell Collection.

encouraged only so long as it did not challenge those beliefs. But from the fifteenth century onwards, the old, traditional ideas about the motion of the heavenly bodies, the human body and man's place in nature began to crumble under the attack of men like Copernicus (1473–1543), Galileo (1564–1642), Kepler (1571–1630) and Harvey (1578–1657). The ideas introduced by these men were all based on systematic evidence obtained from experiments, and the Church was not long able to suppress those ideas. With the help of mathematical advances such as logarithms and the calculus, and new instruments such as the telescope, microscope and air pump, experimental science made rapid progress. The study of mechanics, begun by Kepler and Galileo, led to the formulation by Isaac Newton (1642–1727) of his laws of motion and gravitation, which made possible a unified treatment of all celestial and terrestrial motion. Although these laws have been superseded in the twentieth century by Einstein's relativistic mechanics, they are classic examples of the way science tries to understand natural phenomena. Simply in the way they are expressed, they are tremendously far-reaching in their power to explain observable events as well as to predict new phenomena.

But a great reason for the rapid progress of natural philosophy – as physical science was then called – was the realization that scientific knowledge was not only intellectually satisfying, but useful. The old, medieval picture of the world had been a rigid, religious one. This new picture was open and non-religious, and it appealed to practical men like merchants and politicians who had an interest (an economic one) in a better understanding of the material world. King Charles II of England, for example, responded to the demand for improved techniques of navigation (which were needed for exploration and trade) by founding the Royal Observatory at Greenwich in 1675, with the aim of 'finding the longitude of places for perfecting navigation and astronomy'. Greenwich was one of the first research institutions sponsored by a government: as well as being an early example of the way in which the difference between pure research (scientific inquiry for its own sake) and applied research (inquiry with a practical purpose in mind) can be blurred.

Science in the Eighteenth Century

The eighteenth century did not see the kind of outstanding scientific achievements of the century before: it was, in fact, a necessary period of consolidation before the next wave of advance in the century to come. The principles established by Isaac Newton were applied to every possible problem in mechanics, and in the process Newton's clumsy geometrical methods were replaced by a more powerful form of mathematics – the analytical mathematics worked out by men like Euler, Laplace and Lagrange, without which nineteenth-century physics could not have developed. Important observations were made in the field of electricity, though often the stimulus to do so came from the wish to amuse fashionable society. Science was very much the province of the wealthy amateur, and the Royal Society of London (founded in 1662) became more like a gentlemen's club than the centre of intellectual excitement it had been in Newton's time. Part of the reason for the lull in scientific activity was simply that science still promised much more for the progress of civilization than, in practice, it could give. In the fields of navigation, clockmaking and optics, it had proved its worth. But technical advances in mining, agriculture, textile manufacture and marine engineering owed much less to scientific knowledge than to the practical inventiveness of craftsmen, millwrights and instrument-makers. But for all that, science began to gather new force in Britain towards the end of the century, particularly in the growing industrial centres of the north and Midlands: Glasgow, Newcastle, Manchester and Birmingham. In these towns scientists, doctors, engineers, businessmen and industrialists, often radical in their political and religious opinions, met in newly-founded philosophical societies. The best known is perhaps the Lunar Society of Birmingham. Among its members and associates were the Scottish engineer, James Watt (1736–1819); his patron and later business partner, Matthew Boulton; the founder of the modern pottery industry, Josiah Wedgwood; the Nonconformist minister and discoverer of oxygen (in 1774), Joseph Priestley (1733–1804); and the doctor, botanist, scientific propagandist and poet, Erasmus Darwin, grandfather of Charles Darwin. The spirit of the activities of the Lunar Society was one of scientific rationalism and individual enterprise – an essential ingredient in the tremendous upheaval of this period, the Industrial Revolution.

The Industrial Revolution

The Industrial Revolution is the name given to the period between about 1760 and 1830 when Great Britain, followed by other European countries and America, underwent an immense change from an economy based on agriculture and handicrafts to one based on large-scale, mechanized industry. There were revolutionary changes in the means of production, and these launched Britain into an age of self-sustaining economic growth – too easily thought to be the same thing as progress. The results of industrialization were far-reaching social and political changes, and society is still trying to adapt to these today.

   What was the drive behind industrial development in the eighteenth century? It was a growing demand for manufactured goods – particularly textiles, hardware and pottery. This was the result of the steady increase in living standards, which in its turn was a consequence of increased colonial and slave trading, improved banking and business practices, and technical developments in traditional manufacturing and agricultural methods. For example, manufacturers found they could not satisfy the demand for cotton goods inside the old framework of the industry, which was that of a cottage industry – goods were made not in a single factory but in people's own homes, which were of course widely dispersed. It was natural for the manufacturers to turn to new, more efficient and profitable production methods. Hargreaves' spinning jenny (1746), Ark-

Arkwright's original spinning machine, 1769.
(Photo: Crown copyright. Science Museum, London)

wright's water frame (1769) and Crompton's mule (1779) were the first in a series of simple but very effective textile machines that were invented to meet the new needs. Together with James Watt's improved steam engine of 1781, they heralded an age of mechanization, steam power and production concentrated in factories. These changes were highly successful – they increased production, reduced costs and yielded immense profits, and so led to a very rapid growth of industrialization. The demand for steam engines and machinery forced the coal and iron industries to expand. The increased need for dyes, bleaches and soaps in the textile industry caused the development of large-scale chemical processes, which used mineral raw materials instead of the traditional (and limited) animal and vegetable sources. All this created a need for improved transport, both for the raw materials and the finished products, which resulted first in a boom in canal- and road-building, and later in the development of railways and steamships. Workers were beginning to drift from the land to the swelling factory towns, but new machines and methods in agriculture to some extent made up for this loss of labour. So change in one industry brought about change in others; and where it was no longer possible to progress by adapting existing methods, science was called on to point new ways forward.

Science in the Nineteenth Century

The Political and Economic Background

To the wealthy owners of industry, the steam engine was symbolic of an age of science, rationalism and enterprise. To the new class of factory workers it looked quite different – a symbol of oppression. It committed them to an appalling life, stripped of dignity and independence, and controlled by the monotonous rhythm of the machine. There was widespread resistance to mechanization – there were strikes, and machines were attacked and smashed. But the effect was often to make the manufacturers even more determined to mechanize their factories. Andrew Ure, an outstanding defender of the factory system, explained why in a book published in 1835: 'When capital enlists science in her service', he notes, 'the refractory hand of labour will always be taught docility.' In other words, science itself could be used to defeat the rebellious worker. In some cases the mere threat to introduce machinery, and so to throw men out of work, was enough to keep down wages; while other inventions such as Roberts' self-acting mule (patented in 1830) were commissioned by factory owners with the deliberate aim of undermining the authority of the skilled spinners, and simplifying the spinning process in such a way that women and children could be employed – at much lower wages.

At the beginning of the Industrial Revolution the general belief among those who had reason to think about what was happening was that all these changes were bound to be beneficial. This belief was encouraged by a very important book published in 1776 by the Scottish economist Adam Smith, *Wealth of Nations*. Adam Smith believed that a society which was freely competitive and acted on the basis of what was called enlightened self-interest (if everyone looked after his own needs, the total effect would be good for everyone) could not help developing in a way that would be of benefit to all. But experience of the misery and gross inequality created by 'laissez-faire' capitalism soon tempered this view. ('Laissez-faire' means, roughly, 'Don't interfere.' The idea was that capitalism should be allowed to operate and develop without interference from government.) Thomas Malthus, in his *Essay on the Principle of Population* (1798 and 1803), went so far as to say that poverty was not a temporary misfortune; it was the natural condition of all but a privileged handful of people, since population would always grow more quickly than the necessities of life could be provided. This was an approach just as unrealistic as Adam Smith's, but it was given an air of respectability by its claim to describe human affairs by means of inevitable scientific laws. Its harshness was later to be echoed by Charles Darwin's theory of natural selection, with its phrase about 'the survival of the fittest'.

Throughout the first half of the nineteenth century there was great social discontent, and attitudes like that of Malthus only added to it. There were many who agitated against the brutal so-called laws that were appealed to by Malthus' followers and others: calls for change were made by Chartists, trade unionists, Utopian socialists, and middle-class followers of the utili-

Casting a cylinder for HM frigate *Agincourt* (armour-plated) at Maudslay's foundry. Mansell Collection.

tarians Jeremy Bentham and John Stuart Mill. (The utilitarians believed that an act was good insofar as it led to the greatest good of the greatest number of people.) It was through this agitation for change, and this resistance to the more cruel practices of free competition, that Britain managed to banish the 'spectre of communism' which Karl Marx and Friedrich Engels saw haunting Europe during 1847 and 1848, when revolution swept across the Continent. At the Great Exhibition of 1851 Britain celebrated her position as the leading industrial and technological power in the world. But that position was bought at a heavy price – the widespread social squalor and misery of smoke-blackened industrial cities that is so vividly portrayed by the novelist Charles Dickens.

But capitalism was not without its problems. Apart from labour trouble, there was the question of how to invest profitably the enormous surplus wealth accumulated by the owners of industry. With the aim of opening up ever larger markets, money was poured into colonial expansion; and the phenomenal rise of the railways between 1830 and 1850 was financed from this surplus wealth. But from 1850 onwards, and increasingly, Britain felt the economic competition of the rising industrial powers – Germany, France and America: a challenge that was an important contributing factor to the outbreak of the First World War in 1914.

The Organization of Science

This is the background – economic, social and political – against which we must consider the development of science and technology. Here was a quick-growing industrial economy, driven along by its desire for a high return on invested capital, able certainly to encourage technical invention – but able also to hinder it.

An example of encouragement is the rapid growth of the railways and the boost this gave to the coal and iron industries. But for much of the century, Britain was economically so far ahead of her rivals that neither government nor industry paid much attention to the need to invest in scientific and industrial research. Some scientists (such as Charles Babbage, who in 1831 founded the British Association for the Advancement of Science) kept trying to persuade the government that it ought to give organized support to science. They also complained that there were too few jobs for scientists, and that the salaries offered were too low. But these complaints took effect only very slowly. Britain lagged a long way behind France and Germany in providing scientific education and creating close links between science and industry. And science itself continued to be largely an activity for the middle class. At the beginning of the century it had been immensely popular with the fashionable gentry, who flocked to hear Humphrey Davy's lectures at the Royal Institution, founded in 1799. (Though the Royal Institution was, on the whole, for the top people of the time, its well-equipped laboratory was the scene of some very fine research work by Davy (1778–1829) and his brilliant protégé Michael Faraday (1791–1867)). There was a great need for skilled workers; and men like Henry Brougham, founder of the 'Society for the diffusion of useful knowledge', and Thomas Hodgskin, who founded the London Mechanics Institute, fought to have scientific and technical training extended to the working classes. But it was an uphill struggle. The fear was a very simple one – that if the mass of the people were educated, especially in science, it would lead to revolution. One magistrate summed it up when he said that 'science and learning, if universally diffused, would speedily overturn the best-constituted government on earth.' Many scientists and inventors were, in fact, self-educated, and had to find the money for their own research.

The scientific community *was* steadily becoming more professional. Many specialist scientific societies were founded. In all fields, Britain had an impressive number of first-class scientists; though, as T. H. Huxley pointed out in 1881, 'The peculiarity of English science has been that the army has been all officers.' But by the end of the century, the German education system was producing nearly ten times as many graduate scientists and engineers as the British system. It was because there were so few competent technicians and technologically-minded industrialists that British discoveries – such as synthetic aniline dyes (Perkin, 1856) and the open hearth steel process (Siemens, 1867) – were exploited so slowly. It needed the shock of the First World War before the government began to think seriously about its role in organizing and providing money for scientific research and education.

The Main Streams of Scientific Thought

During the nineteenth century the fields of physical science that were linked most strongly with industry were chemistry, metallurgy and, in physics, the study of heat and energy, and electricity and magnetism. Geology, which was given a great stimulus by the canal-cutting of the Industrial Revolution (to cut a canal you had to understand the structure of the land it went through), was also of great practical importance for the exploitation of mineral resources. The study of the geological evolution of the earth and of the way that different fossils were found in successive layers of rock was one of the many contributions that led to Darwin's theory of biological evolution. The other main advances in biology – the theory of cells, the germ theory of disease and the application of physical and chemical concepts to life processes (see *Medicine*) – were leading by the second half of the century to major improvements in medicine and public health.

Chemistry

By the end of the nineteenth century chemistry emerged as a science that was quantitative (that is, concerned with measurement) and experimental. A leader of the chemical revolution was the Frenchman Antoine Lavoisier (1743–94). His careful experiments on gases and combustion led him to appreciate that what happened when a substance was burned was that it combined with the newly discovered oxygen, rather than that (as had been widely believed) burning was caused by the release of a substance called phlogiston. In his *Elementary Treatise on Chemistry* (published in 1789), Lavoisier was the first to state the law of conservation of mass during chemical reactions; he also reintroduced the idea of 'elements' as the basic chemical building blocks from which, by combination, all other compounds are made. Earlier he had devised a new system of naming chemical compounds, designed to make it clear from which elements the compound was formed. This was an important step towards simplifying the understanding of chemistry, and it was followed by the use of symbols for the elements. Dalton first used pictorial symbols for this purpose, but they were superseded by the now familiar alphabetic abbreviations, introduced by Berzelius.

In 1803 John Dalton (1766–1844) introduced his atomic theory of matter. He extended an idea that had been successful in explaining the properties of gases, and proposed that the smallest particles of an element were tiny, identical and indestructible 'atoms', different elements having atoms of different mass. This theory, too, was successful in practice – it explained the whole number ratios by which elements were observed to combine – but it was many years before it was generally accepted. Some scientists found it hard to believe that particles could be too small to be seen: or they tried to argue that, since space was apparently continuous, it made no sense to suppose that matter existed only as particles of discrete (that is, discontinuous) size. There was also, at first, great confusion over the correct way of determining atomic weights.

From the beginning of the nineteenth century, the study of chemistry branched out into a number of different fields. Davy, and later Faraday, studied electrolysis – the effect of passing an electric current through chemical solutions and molten compounds. A Frenchman, Haüy, took up the study of crystallography (that is, the science of the structure, forms and properties of crystals).

The great Swedish chemist Berzelius (1779–1848) prepared, purified and analysed most of the mineral compounds that were then known, as well as introducing the terms isomer, catalysis and polymer. An isomer is a compound containing the same number and type of atoms as another substance but differing in the spatial arrangement of these atoms. Catalysis is the speeding up of a chemical reaction by the presence of a substance, the catalyst, which itself is not permanently changed. A polymer is a large molecule formed by the linking together of many, often identical, smaller molecules. Von Liebig, Dumas and Wöhler explored the vast new area of organic chemistry (the chemistry of carbon compounds). In 1828 Wöhler synthesized urea, an organic substance known to be produced by animals. This suggested for the first time that substances made by living things are fundamentally the same as all other chemical compounds – which was contrary to the view, widely-held at the time, that they required a special vital force for their manufacture.

Gradually, from the study of isomers and the occurrence of series of similar organic compounds (eg the alcohols), it began to be realized that the particular spatial arrangement of the atoms within a molecule was as important as the identity of the atoms of which it was composed. Kekulé (1829–96), in developing this idea of molecular structure, introduced also the idea of the chemical bond: different elements being characterized by the number of such bonds or 'valencies' that their atoms can make with other atoms. Thus, on the basis that hydrogen (H) is univalent and oxygen (O) is divalent, the water molecule, long since set down as H_2O, was now represented as H—O—H, indicating the two bonds made by the oxygen atom, one with each hydrogen atom. It soon became clear that the central feature of organic chemistry was the tetravalency of carbon. (The suffix 'tetra' comes from a Greek word meaning 'four'.) This, combined with the ability of carbon atoms to make strong bonds with each other (thus forming chains or rings of carbon atoms), enabled scientists to make much greater sense of the diversity of organic compounds. The possibility of a six-atom carbon ring was a particularly brilliant insight of Kekulé's (in 1865), and provided the solution to the long-standing problem of the structure of the benzene molecule (C_6H_6). But understanding of the exact nature of the chemical bond had to wait till the discovery of the electron, in 1897, and the development of the modern theory of atomic structure in the early twentieth century.

The Growth of the Chemical Industry

Alongside this progress in chemistry there was a steady growth of the chemical industry. An important branch of this was the 'alkali trade', which was under continuous stimulation from the expansion of textile manufacture to develop large-scale processes for making bleaches (bleaching powder was first introduced in 1784), soda (made from common salt first by the Leblanc process, 1790, and later by the Solvay process, 1861), and sulphuric acid. The emission of corrosive fumes from alkali works created one of the early problems of atmospheric pollution, and it was not until 1864 that some limited control was imposed by means of the Alkali Works Regulation Act.

Another important sector of the chemical industry was based on coal as a source of raw materials. From the early nineteenth century coal gas began to be widely used for lighting, following successful pilot schemes by Murdock (an associate of Boulton and Watt) and Windsor. Coal gas is one of the products obtained from the distillation of coal. The liquid product from this process, coal tar, was found to be a complex mixture from which organic chemicals such as benzene, naphthalene, phenol and aniline could be extracted. Almost by chance, in 1856, Perkin discovered that aniline could be used to make aniline dyes: and that was the basis of the coal tar colour industry – which, as it happened, flourished much more in Germany than in Britain. Increasing skill in the manipulation of organic compounds soon led to the use of coal tar as the starting point for the manufacture of a wide variety of solvents, food additives (saccharine, 1885), antiseptics, drugs (aspirin, 1899) and explosives. The first synthetic fibre was rayon (commercially available in the 1880s as 'artificial silk'); and two of the earliest plastics were celluloid (1860s) and bakelite (1909). In 1844, artificial fertilizers were first manufactured as a result of the study by von Liebig and others of the nutritional requirements of plants.

Heat and Energy

Many aspects of physics and chemistry were linked during the first half of the nineteenth century by questions about the nature of heat. By 1850 the answer to those questions had become clear with the formulation of the fundamental laws of thermodynamics. The first of these laws, the law of conservation of energy, recognizes that energy can exist in a number of interchangeable forms (such as kinetic energy of motion, potential energy as stored in an extended spring, and electrical energy), though in any closed system the total energy is constant. Heat is to be understood as a form of energy which a substance can possess by virtue of the random motion of its constituent particles. The second law is rather more subtle: but by recognizing the tendency for all forms of energy to be degraded to heat, it sets strict limits on the efficiency with which engines can convert heat into useful mechanical work.

The idea of heat as motion had been familiar during the seventeenth century; but at the end of the eighteenth century the view generally held was that heat was a material substance which could be added to an object, or removed from it, to make the object hotter or colder. The French chemist Lavoisier even included 'caloric', his name for the matter of heat, in his list of chemical elements in 1789. In fact the theory was quite adequate to explain many contemporary observations on specific heat, latent heat and the generation of heat by chemical reactions. The caloric theory was so well established, indeed, that it was unshaken by Count Rumford's demonstration in 1798 that, to account for the vast generation of heat during the boring of cannons, an *unlimited* quantity of caloric must be present in a *limited* amount of matter.

The first serious study of the steam engine as a device for developing mechanical power from heat was made by the French engineer Sadi Carnot (1796–1832) in 1823. He gave an ideal account of the operation of a heat engine: it was a cyclical process in which caloric entering the high-temperature boiler is later expelled into the cooler condenser, producing mechanical motion in the same way that water falling from a higher level to a lower level will drive a water wheel. Although this picture of the process was incorrect – insisting on the conservation of caloric rather than total energy – it was an important step towards the second law of thermodynamics. During the 1840s the scientific community slowly became converted to the idea of the interchangeability of different forms of energy. James Joule (1818–89) worked out the formula relating electric current to heat generation in a resistor, and carried out impressively accurate experiments to determine the mechanical equivalent of heat: work that was complemented in Germany by a doctor, Robert Mayer. By 1851, two Germans, Helmholtz and Clausius, and William Thomson (later Lord Kelvin) in Britain, had put thermodynamics on a firm mathematical footing.

Engineering

Society was growing more and more dependent on mechanical power, and this did much to stimulate scientific interest in heat and energy; although the principles involved are so basic that it could only have been a matter of time before they were grasped. The steam engine itself benefited very little from a better theoretical understanding of its working. It was advances in the design of high-pressure boilers, valves and pistons, through the skill of engineers such as Richard Trevithick and George Stephenson, that were responsible for its evolution and its successful adaptation for use on railways and in steamships. And it was similar practical considerations, and later the availability of the new liquid fuel, petrol, that played the biggest part in the development of the internal combustion engine by Lenoir, Otto, Daimler and Diesel. But theory did have its effects. The application of thermodynamics to the liquefaction of gases by Kelvin, Pictet and Linde had important consequences for the growth of refrigeration and the preservation of goods; and from work done by Gibbs and Le Chatelier on the thermodynamics of chemical reactions sprang advances in chemical engineering.

Throughout the nineteenth century, the increased demand for machines, railways, ships, bridges and armaments led to rapid progress in engineering skill and accuracy; and this depended very much on the availability of new or improved materials, particularly from the metal industry. Lathes, the micrometer and slide rest, milling machines and standard screw threads were introduced by a series of inventors, notably Maudslay, Whitworth, Nasmyth and Clement; and the new precision in engineering made possible the mass production of standardized and interchangeable parts. The elegant bridges and tunnels of Thomas Telford, Isambard Kingdom Brunel and Robert Stephenson; Brunel's enormous steamship, the *Great Eastern*, launched in 1858; and the capacious iron and glass Crystal Palace designed by Joseph Paxton to house the Great Exhibition of 1851, are classic examples of the scale and grandeur of nineteenth-century engineering and architectural projects. These were made possible by advances in heavy engineering such as Nasmyth's steam hammer (1838), and by the increasing use of mathematics for the analysis of stress in beams and structures.

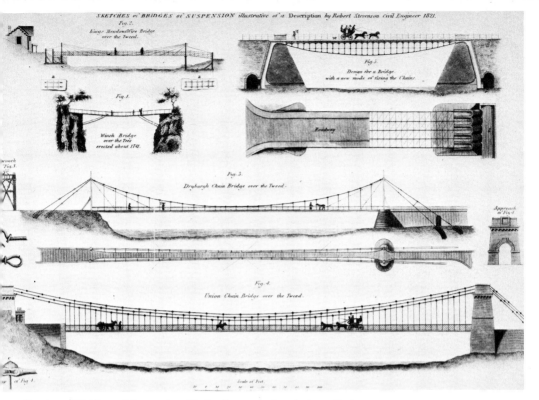

Sketches of Bridges of Suspension (R. Stephenson's description, 1821).
(*Photo: Science Museum, London*)

Iron and Steel

It is surprising that it was not until the 1850s that the first cheap and reliable
method of steelmaking was invented. Iron production had soared under the
stimulus of the Industrial Revolution; but steel, though far superior both for
construction and for working parts to the more brittle cast iron and the softer
wrought iron, was still very much a luxury metal. It was left to Henry Bessemer
(1813–98), an outsider to the traditionally minded iron industry, to undertake
a series of large-scale experiments in steel production, financing himself from
a successful previous invention. In 1856 he unveiled his famous converter in
which hot air was blown through molten pig iron, burning out the excess
carbon and raising the temperature sufficiently to keep the resulting steel
molten without need of fuel. An alternative method was developed during the
1860s by the Martin brothers, in France, and William Siemens, English representative of the influential German family of industrialists. Using the general
principle of regeneration, whereby incoming fuel is preheated by outgoing
waste gases, steel could be produced on a vast scale in an open hearth furnace.
In the end this method became preferred to the Bessemer converter – particularly after Thomas, through careful scientific research, had shown (in 1879)
that even high-phosphorus ores could be used, provided the furnace had a basic
lining of limestone. Towards the end of the century, cheap steel and electricity,
with potentialities far exceeding those of iron and steam power, marked the
beginning of a period of human history in which mankind would have tremendous power to change the face of the earth.

Electricity and Magnetism

While engineering and metallurgy had a considerable non-scientific tradition, and advances, as we have seen, were largely a matter of inventors setting out to meet practical demands, the electricity industry was science-based from the start. In fact, useful applications of electricity were far from the minds of the eighteenth-century experimenters such as Gray, Dufay and Franklin, who were mainly concerned with static electricity which manifested itself in the attractive and repulsive forces between bodies charged by friction. Coulomb and Cavendish established that the force between electric charges is proportional to the inverse square of the distance between them; and this, because of its similarity to Newton's law of gravitational attraction between masses, allowed much already existing mathematics to be applied. A major advance was made in the 1790s by the Italian Volta (1745–1827); following up the work of his compatriot Galvani on electricity and animal tissues, he constructed the first battery capable of producing a steady, low-voltage electric current. Chemists in particular eagerly exploited this new discovery, and in 1807–8, at the Royal Institution, Humphry Davy used the world's most powerful battery to isolate, for the first time, the metals sodium, potassium, magnesium and calcium by electrolysis of molten salts.

In 1820 the Danish physicist Oersted (1777–1851) accidentally made the crucial observation that an electric current would deflect a magnetic needle. The complementary effect, that an electric current could be generated in a conductor by a moving magnet, was discovered by Faraday in 1831, and finally demonstrated the intimate connection between magnetism and electricity. Faraday had a deeply intuitive and visual understanding of electromagnetic phenomena, and it was left to James Clerk Maxwell (1831–79) to reduce all previous work in this field to a concise mathematical form, first published in 1862. Maxwell's equations were found to contain within them the description of electromagnetic disturbances propagating as waves at high speed, and it soon became clear that this description could be fitted to light. Furthermore, waves similar to visible light but of a lower frequency were predicted. In 1888 these were demonstrated to exist by Hertz; they have become the basis of twentieth-century radio communications. Electromagnetic theory was the crowning achievement of nineteenth-century physics; but the discovery in 1897 by J. J. Thomson (1856–1940) of the fundamental particle of electricity, the electron, and the fruitless search for the lumeniferous ether (the medium through which light was supposed to propagate), were death to much of classical physics. However, Maxwell's equations have managed to survive, intact, the twentieth-century revolution in physics.

The Electrical Industry

The first major application of electricity was the telegraph, which grew up alongside the railways as a convenient means of communication, speeding up commercial transactions and breaking down geographical barriers. The pioneering work was done in the 1830s by Henry, Wheatstone and Morse, whose dot-and-dash alphabetic code was devised in 1832 for the purpose of

The Great Telegraphing Room at the new offices of the Electric and International Telegraph Company, Moorgate Street, London, 1859. Mansell Collection.

telegraphy. In 1866, after a number of false starts, a Transatlantic cable was laid; and in 1876 the Scottish-American inventor, Alexander Bell, patented the telephone, the logical successor of the telegraph. Telegraphy required only a light electric current available from batteries; but other applications of electricity such as electroplating, lighting, and driving electric motors required a heavy current. The design of generators, however, made slow progress from their theoretical start in 1831, though Wilde and Siemens in 1867 made the first dynamo using an electromagnet energized by another generator rather than a permanent magnet. Dynamos began to be used increasingly in conjunction with arc lights for outside lighting, but the widespread use of electricity had to wait for the development by Swan and Edison of the evacuated, carbon (later metal) filament light bulb (1880). This opened up the huge domestic market and made the building of power stations and mains distribution systems a profitable enterprise. With the opening of the Pearl Street Station of the Edison Illuminating Company in New York in 1882, a period began of intensive exploitation of electric power. Hydro-electric power stations, the high-tension AC grid-system, electric trams and trains, and a host of electric appliances were quickly introduced, and powerful companies such as Westinghouse and General Electric took their place among the steel empires of Krupps, Carnegie and Vickers at the foundations of modern industry.

Science and Technology in the Twentieth Century

And so, having built up a picture of the nineteenth-century achievements of science and its growing importance to industry and to economic development, we approach our own times.

During the twentieth century, the continual increase in the scale and scope of scientific and technical activity has become an essential feature of society. One major reason for this is that social progress – through the reduction of poverty, the improvement of health and public services and increased opportunity for leading a full life – is widely held to depend on economic growth and high industrial productivity. Their past record has shown that science and technology are well suited to the achievement of these economic ends; and they have therefore developed to serve the needs of a rapidly growing industrial economy.

Certainly for the fortunate populations of western Europe, America, and, later, Russia and Japan, the result has been a period of affluence beyond the dreams of our fairly recent ancestors. The benefits of modern science and technology are obvious, even if they are not accessible, to everyone. But it is unfortunately true that, often, what may appear to be benefits, also pose a potential or actual threat to the quality of life. As an example, the private car has enormously increased the power of human beings to move about – but it has also produced congestion and pollution by noise and fumes. Modern medicines can cure many diseases – but their use can lead to the evolution of more virulent germs capable of resisting drugs. Electronic computers have

Inhaling oxygen supplies to combat the polluted air of Tokyo. (*Photo: Camera Press, London*)

immensely increased our capacity to handle information – but they also pose new threats to individual privacy. So there is a growing body of opinion that questions whether more and more sophisticated science and technology are really continuing to produce social progress. And such a view (we shall look at it more closely later) runs right across much of the conventional wisdom that has guided the development of science and technology in modern society.

Some Developments and Trends in Modern Science

In the modern world, science and technology might be compared to two climbing plants – vines, perhaps – each of which supports the other in an upward spiral of growth. Every time there is an advance in scientific understanding of the natural world, it leads inevitably to increased ability to control and manipulate the environment. On the other hand, science now has at its disposal an impressive range of sophisticated machines, instruments and techniques with which to examine the natural world. Because of this, modern research is vastly different in practice from that of the nineteenth century. No longer can individuals working with home-made apparatus in private laboratories expect to make significant contributions – though this does still occasionally happen. Today much research is carried out by large teams of scientists with extensive technical back-up and data-processing facilities. The ever-increasing precision with which scientists study apparently obscure details often gives the impression that modern science is a vast collection of very small fragments of knowledge. It is true that scientists find it very difficult to keep up with all the latest publications, even in their own speciality; but it is also true that the overall unity of science is maintained by the common use of basic techniques and concepts in a wide range of different disciplines. For example, modern analytical techniques such as electron microscopy and X-ray diffraction (for the determination of microscopic spatial structure), paper chromatography and mass spectrometry (for the determination of chemical composition), and the use of radioactive isotopes to monitor groups of atoms, are all exploited in every kind of scientific work. In the same way, mathematics is no longer an essential tool only for physicists and chemists. New powerful techniques, such as numerical and statistical analysis combined with high-speed computers, have made it possible to formulate and analyse more sophisticated mathematical models of all kinds of systems. This often leads to a blurring of the distinction between the traditional divisions of science; subjects have grown up which cut across those divisions – biophysics, molecular biology and geochemistry are examples – requiring combinations of physicists, chemists, biologists, geologists and mathematicians to work together on the same research project.

Physics

The scope of modern physics extends from one extreme to its opposite: from elucidating the structure and evolution of the universe with the help of giant radio telescopes, to the study of tiny subatomic particles by means of powerful particle accelerators. There are cosmologists and astrophysicists who work in terms of the age of the universe (thought to be about 10^{10} years) and with distances of the order of millions of light years. There are also high-energy

Model of an aluminium atom.
(*Photo: Science Museum, London. By courtesy of Sir Lawrence Bragg.*)

physicists concerned with 'elementary' particles (such as mesons, positrons and anti-protons) whose lifetime may be as short as 10^{22} seconds (just enough time to cross an atomic nucleus if travelling at the speed of light). Each field is as esoteric – that is, difficult for outsiders to understand – as the other. Astrophysicists have predicted the existence of mysterious 'black holes' (stars of such high density that their powerful gravitational attraction prevents even light from leaving their surface); and high-energy physicists have introduced such qualities as 'strangeness', 'charm' and 'colour' in an attempt to classify the continually proliferating number of subatomic particles. But, surprisingly, recent theories are attempts to understand *on the same basis* both the gravitational forces that operate on a universal scale, and the nuclear forces that dominate the behaviour of elementary particles. The underlying ideas that unite these extremes are based, to a large extent, on the new conceptions of space and time that are contained in the revolutionary theories of Albert Einstein (1879–1955): the *Special Theory of Relativity* (1905) and the *General Theory of Relativity* (1915). Like much in modern physics, the ideas embodied in these theories often run counter to common sense. All the same, they are now accepted as giving a more complete description of motion and gravitation than Newton's laws (though these remain sufficiently accurate for most everyday applications).

The other major new physical theory that revolutionized twentieth century physics, quantum theory, also seems very strange at first, and it gives rise to fascinating philosophical questions. It was developed during the 1920s and

1930s, notably by Schrödinger, Bohr, Heisenberg and Dirac, and it arose from the realization that many properties of atoms, electrons and even light could be explained only by attributing to them both wave-like and particle-like properties. The conclusion from this is that the behaviour of matter on the atomic scale can only be described by probabilistic laws. This means therefore that the behaviour of a single system cannot be predicted exactly, but only the average behaviour of a large number of similar systems. So, for example, the exact moment of decay of a particular radioactive nucleus is impossible to predict: all that can be said is how many similar nuclei will on average decay in a given time interval. A further feature of the wave-particle duality inherent in quantum theory is that certain properties of particles (for instance, the position of an electron and its velocity) cannot both be known exactly: the smaller the error in the measurement of the position (say), the larger must be the error in the measurement of velocity. This is a simple expression of Heisenberg's famous Uncertainty Principle.

Quantum theory is now the basis for understanding not just atomic and nuclear structure and the properties of elementary particles, but also the large-scale properties of matter. From detailed knowledge of the behaviour of atoms and electrons it is now possible to give fundamental reasons why some materials are metallic and conduct electricity well, while others are electrical insulators; why iron is one of the few elements that are magnetic; and why some metals and alloys exhibit the remarkable low-temperature phenomenon of superconductivity (that is, the sudden and complete loss of electrical resistivity below a certain temperature, usually within about $20°$ of absolute zero, $-273°C$). Similarly, chemistry makes considerable use of quantum theory to understand chemical bonding (see p. 102), the structure of molecules and the mechanisms of chemical reactions.

There is a very fine distinction between 'pure' physics and chemistry, and the more applied sciences of metallurgy, materials and electronics. Both fundamental knowledge and careful trial and error have contributed to our present ability to create plastics, metal alloys, glasses and ceramics that have almost any combination we desire of such properties as heat resistance, strength, flexibility and conductivity. Detailed knowledge of the behaviour of electrons in different materials is at the basis of the modern electronics industry, which over the last few decades has had such an enormous impact on society. The invention of the transistor in 1948, followed by the development of reliable microelectronic circuits, has given rise to faster computers, better telecommunications and audio equipment and innumerable black-box gadgets for use in every conceivable situation.

Molecular Biology

It is tempting for us now to imagine that we might in the end be able to understand living systems on the same fundamental level as we understand inanimate, non-living chemical and physical systems. Over the last few decades molecular biology has had great success in demonstrating the value of using modern physical techniques to analyse biochemical processes occurring within individual cells. The best-known achievement in this field is the explanation of the molecular basis of heredity – that is to say, the mechanism by which certain characteristics of an organism are passed on from one generation to the next. Rapid progress followed a major breakthrough in 1953, when Watson and Crick suggested the famous double-helix structure of DNA (deoxyribonucleic acid). Watson described this in his book *The Double Helix*, which is also a fascinating and important study of scientists at work. DNA is a large biopolymer now known to be the principal carrier of genetic information in living organisms. In plants and animals it is largely found in the chromosomes in cell nuclei. The DNA molecule is divided into many sections, called genes, each of which is a blueprint for the production of a particular protein essential to the correct functioning of the cell. The cell's characteristics are therefore determined by the structure of its DNA by means of a genetic code (which appears to be universal to all forms of life). During cell division, an exact replica of the parent cell's DNA is acquired by the daughter cells; in this way all the characteristics of the original cell are passed on to the new generation. But biologists still do not know how individual cells manage to maintain a perfect balance between the multitudes of different processes that occur within them. On still another level of complexity is the understanding of how individual cells interact in an integrated manner in multicellular organisms. One of the great challenges to modern science lies in the unravelling of the complex physical and chemical mechanisms of the brain and nervous system of man. One most intriguing aspect of this problem is how to bridge the gap between the physical description of brain activity (in terms of nerve impulses, neural networks and chemical hormones), and the corresponding psychological or mental description (in terms of thinking, learning, memory and consciousness).

Recent advances in molecular biology have raised the possibility of genetic engineering. This involves the modification of the genetic material (that is, the DNA) within bacteria, plants or animals so that the organism acquires new characteristics. Experiments in genetic engineering are now progressing with speed. Probably, in the not too distant future a number of potentially beneficial applications may become possible. For example, the genes responsible for the nitrogen-fixing ability of certain bacteria could be transferred directly into the DNA of crops such as wheat: that would eliminate the need for large-scale feeding of these crops with nitrogenous fertilizers. Another possibility is to incorporate the gene responsible for the synthesis of insulin into suitable bacteria and so provide a much more convenient source of this protein (which is essential to the survival of millions of people suffering from diabetes). Indeed as a remarkable example of the speed of scientific advance, the first reports of success in this venture were already being made by 1978.

On the other hand, the possible misuses of the techniques of genetic engineering are horrific. They range from the creation of totally new and virulent microorganisms (perhaps by accident, perhaps deliberately for military purposes) to the (thankfully) more fantastic vision of a 'brave new world' in which people would be tailor-made by genetic surgeons, who would give them predetermined qualities. Clearly the future direction of experiments in genetic engineering is a matter of general public concern and should not be decided only by single-minded scientists or economic interests eager to exploit any commercial possibilities. Following widespread public debate, within and outside the scientific community, many countries have in fact now introduced strict regulations controlling such experiments. It remains to be seen whether the correct balance has been achieved in protecting society at large while not stifling exciting scientific research.

The Exploration of Space

Whatever the more controversial motives behind the superpower space programmes (that is, whatever political and military aims may lie behind them), knowledge of the universe and the earth has been greatly increased by the exploration of space. Satellites give a unique opportunity for studying radiation from outer space that does not normally penetrate as far as the earth's surface, as well as providing meteorological and geophysical information about the earth and its atmosphere. In recent years a combination of satellite pictures of the earth's surface, seismic and magnetic surveys, ocean studies and bore holes into and through the earth's crust have not only yielded rewards in terms of valuable mineral resources; they are also giving a more complete picture of the dynamic evolution of the earth in terms of plate tectonics (which is the term now preferred to the older term of 'continental drift') and long term climatic changes. Similarly space probes that have been organized to the moon, Mars and Venus have extended our knowledge of the solar system and the resolution of the perennial question of the existence of life on other planets is now tantalizingly close.

If the more traditional sciences are growing, there are also entirely new fields of study that are beginning to be investigated. One example is cybernetics, which analyses methods of communication and control in complex systems. It grew up parallel with the development of electronic computers, and is now much concerned with the use of computers and robots to simulate human intelligence and human sense perception. An important branch of cybernetics is information theory, which deals with the efficient storage and communication of information. Another new field is operational research: like information theory, this has stimulated the study of new mathematical methods in, for instance, statistics and optimization theory. First successfully used during the Second World War in connection with military strategy, operational research uses scientific methods to help with the organization and planning of complicated operations such as space missions, disaster relief, industrial production runs or mountaineering.

The extension of scientific methods into psychology, the social sciences and economic and social planning is an increasing tendency in the modern world: but this, too, is not without its dangers. Attempts to analyse scientifically and to quantify human behaviour and motivation are often impossible without the observer introducing a significant bias. Too easily the results of such research can be used to manipulate people and human decisions. Among human desires there are many that are perhaps illogical but are still humanly important, and these might be overruled on the basis of unrealistic but, allegedly, objective and scientific simulations and predictions. They might make scientific sense, but no human sense at all.

Science Policies and the Social Functions of Science

Ever-increasing demands are being made on both material and human resources; and science and technology are having a far-reaching impact on all aspects of society. These facts have made it necessary for governments to assume increasing responsibility for their control. It is obvious that a comprehensive policy for science should begin by working out the goals that society wishes to reach in its support of science and technology. These would then form a basis for (among other things) planning educational facilities for scientists and engineers: deciding on priorities in the way money is spent on fundamental research and more applied research, directed to particular practical ends; and ensuring the most fruitful use of research by co-ordinating work done in different fields. But in fact scientific organization has grown in a very day-to-day fashion, the result of historical and political reasons as well as the fact that science fulfils within society a number of different functions. It helps to create wealth and to make more direct contributions to human health and welfare; but science and technology are also involved in the maintenance of national defence and the promotion of national prestige. The motivation behind the work of many scientists remains a genuine desire to advance knowledge (though often to advance their careers as well); and art, philosophy and literature are all stimulated by the intellectual contribution of science to culture. (See p. 298.)

The Marxist scientist, J. D. Bernal, in a controversial book, *The Social Function of Science* (1939), was one of the first people to argue that science should not be regarded as a self-governing activity, shut off from the rest of human affairs and unfolding according to an inner logic of its own. On the contrary, he argued, science interacts dynamically with the rest of society, and so it should be actively controlled to ensure that society receives the fullest benefit from it. This view was regarded as heretical by many scientists who feared that it would lead to interference with their freedom of research. But the Second World War cut short this debate by providing, in the need to win the war, a goal which everyone accepted, and to which the efforts of science could be directed without argument. In the First World War science was applied in a haphazard fashion, but in the Second World War scientific resources were fully mobilized. The effectiveness of this was demonstrated in the rapid development of radar, jet aircraft, operational research and the atom bomb. The success of well organized science in wartime convinced governments that a vigorous science policy was vital to the maintenance of national security and to the rebuilding of a new and prosperous world.

Science and Politics since the Second World War

In the years immediately after the Second World War there was a rapid expansion of the universities and the scientific civil service and large sums of money were spent on research and development (known as R and D). This was a time when the status and political influence of scientists had never been higher. The public, preferring to associate the war with the development of nylon and penicillin rather than the atom bomb, looked to science as the hope for the future. But the dropping of the two atom bombs on Japan in August 1945 had tremendous effects inside the scientific community that penetrated far deeper than the arguments about this particular use of the bomb. The question of the moral responsibility of scientists was raised. This was a very real question for many physicists, chemists and engineers who had the opportunity of working on the peacetime nuclear armaments programme. Since then, many other issues (such as chemical and biological warfare, genetic engineering and experiments using live animals) have deepened the dilemma of the scientist. For all that, the Cold War background of the 1950s meant that a large proportion (nearly three quarters in 1958–9) of R and D expenditure by the British government was on defence.

The science boom continued under the assumption, which was hardly questioned, that no amount of science was too much. But by the early 1960s ideas began to change. It was seen that the open commitment to science was unrealistic in the light of the economic situation, which was getting worse, and of other demands on government money. There was a drop in the proportion of R and D spent on defence, partly because the Cold War turned to a

Britain's second nuclear test explosion on 31 May 1957. (*Photo: Crown copyright reserved*)

thaw. But expensive military and space research was now justified in terms of the 'spin off' that it generated: that is, the discoveries and developments of which peaceful use could be made. And certainly the incentive given by this research to the development of sophisticated aircraft, computers, micro-electronics and new materials was enormous. But the public has never been convinced that the same benefits might not have been achieved if the same resources had been available, not to the military but to the civilian sector.

In fact, early in the development of space technology, Britain, by cancelling the Blue Streak missile in 1960, took the sensible decision to opt out of the space race. This left America, with its ambitious programme to put a man on the moon by 1970, to challenge the apparent Russian lead in the field. The American space programme had tremendous prestige and great sums of money were made available for it, which led to the 'brain drain' of highly qualified scientists across the Atlantic to work in the United States. This caused great concern in Britain in 1964–5, but the harmful effect was exaggerated; those who deplored the 'brain drain' failed to appreciate that there are strong international links among the scientific community, and also that Britain made up for her loss to some extent by recruiting from countries poorer than herself, such as India. It also became clearer, from closer studies of the way in which new technological advances are made, that many other factors besides high expenditure on R and D are involved when it comes to applying science and technology to the improvement of a country's economy. Britain has probably suffered from the higher prestige that is traditionally attached to pure rather than applied research, and from the reluctance of industry to take the necessary risks in developing new inventions. On the other hand, the technological success of Japan at this time owed much to the way in which she exploited innovations that originated in other countries. In 1964 Harold Wilson, about to become Prime Minister, promised Britain a 'white-hot technological revolution'. But what went wrong there was that people believed that all that was needed was more and better technology; so that a lot of money was wasted in investment in industries where the real problems were bad management and poor industrial relations. The insistence on carrying on with the Anglo-French Concorde project to produce a supersonic airliner, despite soaring costs and heavy criticism on environmental grounds, is another example of the obsession with high technology which aims more at maintaining the prestige of the aero-space industry than at satisfying any real, urgent social need.

That sort of conspicuous waste of scientific and technical resources – together with the association, in many people's minds, of science with war and the deterioration of the environment – has led to what we now have: disenchantment with science and technology – even distrust of them. While the whole world marvelled at the split-second precision with which the Americans first landed a man on the moon on 21 July 1969, the joint American-Russian Apollo/Soyuz link-up in space in July 1975 was cynically regarded as the most expensive handshake in history.

But there has been an ironical consequence of the exploration of space. It has done much to stimulate public concern about the wellbeing of 'spaceship earth' and her delicate life-support system. It is from a global viewpoint that

Concorde G-BOAC, the fourth production aircraft, leaves London's Heathrow Airport. (*Photo: British Aircraft Corporation*)

the problems of congested cities, over-population and pollution must be tackled. To meet these problems we shall have to work out a very different kind of science policy, much more concerned with the health of society and the quality of the environment. This is one of the greatest challenges facing society today. (See pp. 122–4.)

Scientific Education, and the Organization of Research and Development

The scientific activity for which the government is responsible can be separated into five divisions: education, fundamental research, research carried out on behalf of public utilities, defence, and the encouragement of industrial research.

Education, of course, is a must for anyone who wants to keep afloat in today's complicated, rapidly changing world; and science and mathematics have long been accepted as important subjects. (As we have seen, it was not always so: there was a time when they had to fight for a place in the school curriculum.) Some sort of education in science is valuable even to those who are not going on to be scientists or technologists. Science, after all, is a very important ingredient in our culture – it helps if we understand it; and we all need the basic grasp of numbers (numeracy, as it is called) and some elementary knowledge if we are to cope with the science that we come up against in everyday life.

The universities are places where scientists and engineers are trained for the work they are to do; they are also centres for the advancement of learning, where a great deal of fundamental research is carried on. As part of their tradition, the universities have clung to the idea of academic freedom, which means that research workers have the right to follow their inspiration. They should be free, in fact, to work on new and untried ideas – and it is to be hoped that some funds will always be made available for such work. But more and more, scientists are having to base their claims for research grants on pragmatic grounds: that is, on the argument that the work they do will have practical advantages. British universities now contract with government departments or industry to do much scientific R and D work; they also receive grants from the Medical, Agricultural, Natural Environment, Science and Social Science Research Councils.

The range of scientific work carried out at the universities is enormous. It covers the whole spectrum of science – from obscure speculations about the origin of the universe, to possible links between lead pollution from cars and anti-social behaviour. But much 'mission-orientated' research, as it is called (that means it has a specific practical end in view) is carried out in special government institutions. Examples are the Meteorological Office, the Transport and Road Safety Laboratory, the Sea Fisheries Research Laboratory and the Cancer Research Institute.

'Big' science needs its own separate establishments. This is the name given to fields such as nuclear and high energy physics, space exploration and radio astronomy, all calling for extremely large installations that need elaborate maintenance. This kind of research is so costly that it is often carried out by international teams – as, for instance, at the highly successful European Centre for Nuclear Research (CERN) at Geneva, or the European Space Research Organization (ESRO). And there are many other fields of research which, because they have nothing to do with defence or economic competition, can be covered by international teamwork. This is of great help to developing countries that cannot afford to carry out their own research or do not have the trained manpower to do it. Such work – for instance, research into climate, tropical diseases, agriculture in semi-arid regions and the control of pests such as locusts – is often sponsored or co-ordinated by agencies of the United Nations. Other subjects (oceanography, meteorology and geophysics are examples) cannot be confined within national boundaries: they encompass whole oceans, global patterns of weather and so on. However, the Law of the Sea Conference of 1975 was unable to reach any conclusions, the reason being that every nation taking part was anxious to preserve its own interests – an example of the difficulties that may lie in the way of international co-operation. The fact is that we now recognize that the ocean has vast potential as a source of energy, food and minerals: and the desire each nation has to stake its own claim has hindered co-operation in oceanographic research.

Defence and Military Technology

A great deal of the R and D money spent by a government goes – and is likely to continue to go – to defence. Because of its secrecy, much military research is undertaken in special institutions (such as, in Britain, the Admiralty Underwater Weapons Establishment and the Atomic Weapons Research Laboratory). The links that these establishments have with research groups in universities have become more and more controversial. In America, the Vietnam War exposed the extent to which research in universities was carried out for military purposes. Why does this sort of thing cause controversy? The answer is that, however the scientists involved may justify their work as fundamental research, it is almost certain that top priority in the further development of any discovery will be given to its military use. Examples are the perversion of research on plant hormones and crop diseases to produce defoliants (which destroy plant life) and more virulent strains of bacteria; the rapid application of lasers to the accurate guidance of bombs and missiles; and, of course, the development of the atomic bomb.

The world has been overshadowed by the threat of mass destruction by nuclear weapons since 1945; but, despite attempts at control (for instance in the Partial Nuclear Test Ban Treaty of 1963, the Non-Proliferation Treaty of 1970 and the American-Russian Strategic Arms Limitation Talks), nuclear technology is advancing relentlessly. More and more countries are acquiring the ability to explode nuclear devices. The political problem of limiting the spread of nuclear weapons is made more difficult because the same sort of technology is required for the peaceful production of electricity from nuclear power. The major powers may seem to be reducing their commitment to the horrific weapons of chemical and biological warfare; but America and Russia are certainly looking further into the possibilities of environmental warfare, which might involve such things as the control of weather (the seeding of clouds to produce disruptive, torrential rain has already been used in Vietnam) and the triggering of tidal waves, earthquakes and cyclones. The increasing sophistication of conventional weapons has, unfortunately, been only too apparent in the many wars and terrorist operations that continue to trouble the world. Matters are made worse by the exploitation by many countries of the lucrative international arms trade as a source of profit and political influence. (That is to say, one country can affect the policies of another by the promise, perhaps, to sell military aeroplanes or tanks.) Spy satellites that are devised to monitor army manœuvres and military installations, over-the-horizon early warning systems, vertical take-off and landing 'jump-jets' and heat-seeking missiles designed to home on enemy aircraft – these are only a few examples of the military hardware that has been made possible by modern science and technology. And the use of computers for remote control (as in, for instance, pilotless aircraft) presents mankind with a specially uncanny possibility – a battlefield in which no human beings play a part, except as victims.

Science and Industry

Private industry is the only other source apart from government that has sufficient resources, together with the motive, to undertake R and D programmes which are risky and expensive. Since the end of the nineteenth century, industrial research has been regarded by many firms as an essential investment; and the government, because it is concerned with the well-being of industry, gives both encouragement and financial support. In Britain this aid from the government is often administered through research associations: there are about forty of these, covering various industries or groups of industries (for example, the Electrical Research Association and the Production Engineering Research Association). But the government also undertakes such research itself in the nationalized industries such as coal mining, the Post Office and atomic energy.

What motive does private industry have in its spending on R and D? Largely it aims rather at devising new products and processes which reduce costs, improve competitiveness and increase profits, than at providing goods that satisfy a real need or are likely to last. Many firms feel they have to invent a new and improved product before some competitor makes their old one out-of-date. The result for the public is bewildering. They are faced with a dizzy choice of goods, each of which is advertised as being, in some new way, better or more fashionable than the same thing made by someone else. Technology and even fundamental science have certainly been stimulated by market forces in competition with one another, but those forces also bring about a distortion of priorities that many people find depressing and frustrating. For example, more money is spent on cosmetics research than on cancer research; and many products are made deliberately obsolescent (that is, in a short time they will break down or decay or become out-of-date) so that the public has to go on spending on replacements. (For some of the consequences of planned obsolescence, see page 228.) And another of the less desirable characteristics of a society in which the consumer is encouraged to throw things away after brief use only is the failure to incorporate safety features and to carry out rigorous testing until it is demanded by law.

But it is too simple to put all the blame on the powerful vested interests of private industry for the way science and technology have been developed for economic ends. High-pressure advertising certainly manipulates the demand for consumer goods. But the process by which the luxuries of yesterday become the necessities of today has become so ingrained that people regard it as their right to increase their standard of living every year. Not so long ago, such an idea would have seemed nonsense. Under this pressure from the never-satisfied consumer, it is no wonder that governments have tended to judge their success in managing the economy by crude measures of material wealth – with too little regard for the social and environmental costs, which become increasingly obvious. (See *The Environment*.)

Some Features of Modern Technology and Methods of Production and Organization

Many of the important features of modern technology and of methods of production and organization are developments of trends that began with the Industrial Revolution. They include automation and mass production; the use of 'scientific management' techniques; the growth of world-wide communications; the high consumption of energy and raw materials; and the use of synthetic substitutes for natural products.

Automation and Mass Production

Andrew Ure, the Victorian philosopher quoted on page 98, regarded a factory in which there was no human work force as an ideal. And today, advances in production and control engineering (again relying heavily on electronics and computers) have made the automation of many processes a reality. What Ure had in mind was that you could increase profitability if you could somehow discover how to do without costly – and unruly – labour. This desire – to cut out the cost and the human cussedness of labour – remains one of the reasons for automation. But it causes workers to become redundant or un-employed – results that are often justified as unfortunate evils arising from the necessary rationalization of production. The answer, it is argued, lies in schemes for retraining workers and equipping them for work in other fields. Another argument is that automation saves men and women from doing mono-tonous, heavy or dangerous work, and leads to shorter working hours. But, even given wider educational opportunities that are designed to encourage the fuller use of greater leisure, still the possibility that machines might do every-thing threatens to rob many people of the enjoyment they get from using their own hands in productive and creative work.

The first step towards full automation was the introduction of the assembly line in 1913 by the American car manufacturer, Henry Ford. By keeping workers and machinery stationary, and moving the partly completed car from stage to stage, Ford was able to increase efficiency and reduce costs, and so to produce much cheaper cars. Of course, mass production makes sense only if you are producing large numbers of identical items. Often, the price of cheap-ness and convenience is loss of individuality – and of choice. The fact remains that this is the means by which consumer products have become widely avail-able, and that it is being constantly extended: for instance, into the building industry (with the prefabrication of standardized constructional units) and into agriculture (with the intensive factory farming of animals).

Science and the Management of Organizations

An important contribution that science makes to the way modern organiza-tions are run takes the form of what is called 'scientific management'. This involves the use, for example, of operational research, data processing machines and industrial and social psychology. The scope of operational re-search as a basis for decision-making has been enormously increased by the arrival of the electronic computer (first used for commercial purposes in 1954). Scientific methods of analysis are used, such as statistical sampling, simulations and projections; the danger being that those who employ these methods will lose sight of their limitations, and fail to realize that though the methods may be scientific, the interpretation of the results they lead to is usually not. (The element of human judgment, right or wrong, cannot be removed.) Psycho-logists are widely employed in public relations and advertising; they are expected to give advice on the best and most appealing way of devising a pub-licity campaign. Psychology is also resorted to in factories, where the modern approach is to use industrial psychologists to help create working conditions that will lead to harmony between workers and management, and encourage maximum efficiency – an approach pioneered in the 1880s by an American, Frederick Taylor. But in many cases the use of computers, surveys and photo-copying machines has only increased the amount of information-sifting, form-filling and general paperwork that has to be done. And the defrauding of organizations by tampering with computer programs is fast becoming a major problem.

Scientific management can, in theory, lead only to greater efficiency. In fact, it often leads to less, and to a worsening service to the public. Added to the increasing size and complexity of organizations, this has given rise to a complaint often expressed: that businesses and organizations of all kinds are becoming faceless bureaucracies to whom their customers and clients are little more than statistics on wall charts.

Communications

Obviously enough, rapid and efficient communications are of the first importance in the modern world. Many of the resources of science and technology are devoted to providing them. Modern telecommunications networks, often using satellite linkages, can beam almost instant transmission of news and entertainment, commercial information, political propaganda and military intelligence to any spot on the earth's surface. This is one way in which the world, in the last few decades, has shrunk; it has also got very much smaller, so far as the transport of passengers and goods is concerned, with the invention of jumbo jets, high-speed trains and hovercraft, motorway systems, juggernauts and supertankers.

One result of all this is that the world has become a sort of 'global village' in which ideas, news, fashions – even outbreaks of influenza – spread rapidly to all countries. This does mean, of course, that increasingly Moscow looks like London, and London like Tokyo, and that all over the world we tend to wear similar clothes, and drive similar cars, and watch the same films; some people regard this increasing sameness as a threat to the separate identities of nations or races. On the other hand, easy communication is a necessary step towards the abolition of prejudice, which thrives on ignorance, and an essential basis for co-operation between nations.

Modern Technology and the Environment

Advanced technology, and the high standard of living that it makes possible, both depend on a cheap, abundant supply of energy and raw materials. The point has been proved very painfully, of late: for example, by the paralysis brought about in Britain by strikes in the coal-mining and electricity industries, and by the panic that followed when the world price of oil was quadrupled after the Arab–Israeli war of October 1973. Rapid transport, automation, home comforts, abundant consumer goods – they all rely on an almost unlimited supply of energy, capable of being turned on by the flick of a switch.

The extravagance with which society has become accustomed to use energy and natural resources is matched only by the wastefulness with which it disposes of rubbish and effluent. The resulting damage to the environment has been a subject of much debate in recent years – though in fact the problems have been present, and growing, ever since the Industrial Revolution. The increasingly rapid extraction of the world's limited stock of non-renewable resources (for example, oil, coal and metal ores) is visibly scarring the face of the earth. And pollution of the environment by industrial, agricultural and domestic waste is made much worse by the use of man-made substitutes for natural substances. Many of the detergents, pesticides and plastics produced by chemical technology and materials science are not readily degradable in the environment (that is, capable of being broken down) by chemical or biological action. So they accumulate in the soil, in the atmosphere or in waterways – at best becoming eyesores, at worst a threat to human health, wildlife and the stability of the ecosystem (that is, to the intricate network of relationships between living things and their environment). The disastrous effects of chlorinated hydrocarbon pesticides (for example, DDT) on animal life are well known (see page 223), but a new hazard has recently been discovered: this lies in the possible damage to the protective ozone layer in the upper atmosphere that might result from the widespread use of aerosol sprays. Nature is pretty tough and resilient, and can do much to neutralize pollution, but there have been many signs in recent years that pollution may have gone too far for this natural capacity for recovery to operate. One of the worst features of the situation is that we simply know too little about such matters.

The common approach to these problems is to look to advanced technology for answers to the damage it has helped to cause. So there is talk of pollution control and the recycling of raw materials. These are certainly measures that ought to be taken. But will they work unless they are part of much more radical changes in modern industry and the affluent society that it serves? It has been suggested that modern technology is an economic success only because it is an ecological failure. Others argue that the key to the problem is cheap and abundant supplies of energy, because this would allow the economic extraction of raw materials even from the lowest-grade ores, as well as the efficient control of pollution. But there is quite certainly an upper limit to the amount of power the world can generate. That limit is set by the catastrophic results that would follow if the earth's surface temperature were raised so that too much waste heat was released into the environment and the polar ice-caps melted.

In the short term, as has been shown by the energy crisis, what is needed is energy conservation and new ideas for supplying our future requirements. Goethermal power, wave power, tidal power, wind power, nuclear power, solar power, as well as the traditional fossil fuels – all these are possibilities that deserve attention. Many people have particular faith in nuclear power, generated either in fast-breeder reactors (fission reactors which produce new nuclear fuel during the course of operation), or eventually in fusion reactors (though it is still far from being a practical proposition to control the extremely high-temperature plasmas in which fusion occurs). But whether a method is technologically feasible or not is only one consideration when it comes to plan-

Prototype Fast Nuclear Reactor, Caithness, Scotland. The reactor top showing the fuel handling machine console. (*Photo: United Kingdom Atomic Energy Authority*)

ning the future. More and more people are suspicious of the constant appeal to more sophisticated technology.

But the argument goes much deeper than this, and involves more than the impact of advanced technology on the environment.

Some Criticisms of Modern Science and Technology

To many people it seems the height of folly to rely on nuclear power to supply man's future energy needs. The nuclear fuel plutonium −239 is not only the core material for nuclear bombs, but also one of the most poisonous substances known. Yet it would be necessary to transport and process vast quantities of it; and that would present enormous problems of safety and security. Then the safe disposal of long-lived radioactive waste is a tremendous burden to lay on the shoulders of future generations. But governments throughout the world are committed, both by actual construction projects and expensive research programmes, to set out on this course of action.

All of this illustrates an important point about modern science and technology. Because of the expertise and the massive resources involved, the power that is tapped through science and technology is necessarily controlled by centralized, technocratic organizations – industrial or governmental. If these organizations persuade us that the problems of technological planning are non-political matters, to be decided by experts, it is possible for them to take far-reaching, irreversible decisions without sufficient consultation with the public. In the same way the aloof, intellectual image that is cultivated by many scientists prevents them from helping the public to make informed judgments – for example, about the desirability of heart transplants, experiments in genetic engineering or the building of a new high-energy particle accelerator. So science and technology can become the instruments of what is much more like totalitarian social control than democratic social planning – a nightmarish possibility that was foreseen by George Orwell in his novel *1984*. As an example, the choice of which kind of nuclear power station to build is certainly the concern of experts – but underlying it is another kind of choice. Would it not be better, given the risks of nuclear power, to meet the energy crisis by reorganizing society so that each individual consumes far less energy? Alas, in the interests of short-term political and economic ends, proper consideration of the implications of that kind of choice is likely to be overlooked.

The great gap in standards of living between the rich and poor countries of the world is an example of the way in which technological power is used to increase rather than to lessen the unequal distribution of wealth – which in its turn increases many social tensions. In 1966, the richest third of the world's population had a fuel consumption per head about fourteen times larger than the poorer two-thirds. The plundering of the world's resources by the wealthy nations – apart from producing political conflicts over the security of supplies – has distorted world trade *against* the interests of the poorer nations which are trying to catch up. What is more, technological progress in the industrialized nations often has a damaging effect on the economies of the developing countries – for instance, in the declining demand (because synthetic products are used instead) for raw materials like jute and rubber on whose export those countries depend heavily for their income. So it is not simply a question of the have-nots demanding what is possessed by the haves: it is rather a question of the haves making it impossible for the have-nots to enjoy the same benefits. The incidental costs of modern science and technology – the deterioration of the environment, noise, the mental stresses that result from the breathless pace of modern life – are paid for by everybody, but the benefits are often available only to the few.

Some people in their criticism of modern science and technology point the accusing finger at science itself. In encouraging a detached, objective viewpoint, science seeks only to analyse, categorize and quantify everything; in so doing, it ignores the personal and spiritual qualities of life. Science, these critics say, reduces man's position in nature to that of an insignificant collection of atoms; it substitutes despair and uncertainty for the hope, security and meaning that were found in religion and mythology. Whether or not the argument is taken as far as this, it is obviously true that the idea that purely technological solutions exist to fundamental human problems has, in the light of recent experience, become very difficult to believe. Optimists who saw in the contraceptive pill the solution to the population explosion – or in high-yield crops, fertilizers and irrigation, the Green Revolution that would eliminate world hunger – have become disillusioned. Success in controlling populations, in providing the world with the food it needs, depends at least as much on social and political changes. It depends on deep-rooted attitudes to the morality of birth control, or to the desirability of large families in poor communities; it depends on patterns of land ownership, and all the questions that arise from the domination of the world economy by the rich nations.

The truth is that, when it comes to facing many of the enormous problems that confront the developing countries of the Third World, modern sophisticated technology, for all its power, seems a thoroughly unsuitable instrument. The long-term problems of poverty, overpopulation and lack of education are simply not to be solved by imposing on the developing countries Western capital-intensive technology, or levels of consumption and educational methods that are suited to the Western way of life. Where that is done, rural unemployment is increased, people flock to the overcrowded cities, and a split economy is created – one in which a rich minority prospers at the expense of the poor majority. In any case, in countries where manual labour is the most abundant resource, production by the masses is a far more sensible policy than automated mass production.

Alternative Technology and Intermediate Technology

There is one constructive aspect to all these criticisms. It lies in ideas or concepts which are called Alternative Technology (AT) and Intermediate Technology (IT). The first, which is sometimes also referred to as radical technology or people's technology, is an attempted answer to the failures of advanced technology within the rich nations. The second, also known as appropriate technology, is more concerned with the problems of developing countries; it aims at introducing a kind of technology that, in scale, complexity and the way it consumes resources, is more suitable for the limited skill and capital of these countries. Both ideas or concepts have, however, the same goal – to devise technologies that would disrupt the environment and social harmony as little as possible, and are simple enough to be available to virtually everyone without the need for centralized and expert control. Neither AT nor IT refuses to recognize the value of a scientific understanding of the natural world – though the priority given to high-energy physics, for example, might be very low. On the contrary, accurate knowledge of the physical world is regarded as crucial, not so that we can realize the arrogant vision of Descartes of becoming 'the masters and possessors of nature', but so that technologies may be chosen that are in harmony with nature. AT therefore lays great emphasis on ecology, the study of the relationships between living things and their environment. It recommends the use of non-polluting and renewable sources of energy such as wind, sunlight, moving water and methane gas produced from decaying organic waste; the development of organic farming methods that do not rely on vast inputs of inorganic fertilizer; and the return to non-polluting, and therefore slower, forms of transport, such as bicycles, canal barges and airships – with a much higher priority given to public than to private transport. AT is not primitive technology – in its approach to the environment and human needs it is highly sophisticated. Many recent, but 'low-impact', technological innovations could be adapted to its ends; for instance solar heating panels, aeronautically designed windmills, geodesic domes, the bacterial production of edible protein from organic wastes, and even electronics.

But a vital principle of both AT and IT is to make technology work for man, rather than making man a slave to technology. Because something is technologically possible, it is not necessarily desirable. This is particularly true since the more technological a society becomes and the more it bases its life on machines, the more control passes from individuals to professional experts, with less value attached to personal judgments. Those who advocate AT and IT suggest that these undesirable effects may be prevented by the giving of power to smaller, more self-governing organizational units, employing simpler technology, so that individuals have greater opportunities to assume responsibility and to take part in the making of decisions. Only in some such way can people continue to have the personal involvement in activities affecting them that is necessary if they are to be fully committed and to feel the satisfactions vital to healthy human lives.

Small is beautiful is the title of a book by E. F. Schumacher on the philosophy behind IT. Opposed to the traditional slogan, 'the bigger the better', this is a phrase that is now widely heard. It points to a new vision: of small, local communities using small-scale technology and aiming as much as possible at self-sufficiency, in contrast to ever more sophistication, complexity and interdependence – which rapidly becomes difficult to understand, let alone to manage.

The Future

In the light of what is actually happening around us, many people, with some justification, regard AT as a Utopian dream. Certainly, the creation of a Fourth World of decentralized, small communities employing AT would need revolutionary political and social changes and a wholly new outlook on the aims of technology. Many of the trends that have been apparent since the Industrial Revolution would have to be reversed. People would have to return to working on the land; they would have to be satisfied, in terms of material well-being, with less than what is possible. The whole idea of 'science for its own sake' would have to be transformed. It is difficult for people in the rich nations even to contemplate such changes in their thinking and their way of life. But in many countries, small communes are putting the principles of AT to the test. This view of the future is at least as feasible, and perhaps a great deal more desirable, than the view presented by the optimists of the Age of Science. Science fiction writers and futurologists have for years dreamed of space travel to the stars, vast under-ocean cities, robot slaves and push-button satisfaction; but even if these were possible, they would offer no guarantee of human happiness.

There can be no disagreement that the modern world has reached a period of crisis. But whether one is a pessimist, predicting the doom of civilization, or an idealist planning a new post-industrial society to be set up after the collapse; or whether one confidently looks forward to the renewed march of progress after temporary setbacks; still the responsibility of science and technology as contributors to the crisis has to be seriously assessed. Only by way of such an assessment can we hope to ensure that the future development of science and technology serves not to deepen the crisis, but to create a better world for everyone.

Prominent People

Abel, Sir Frederick (1826–1902), English military chemist who devoted himself to the science of explosives.

Adams, John Couch (1819–92), English mathematician and astronomer. He shared equal honours awarded by the Astronomical Society for the discovery of the planet Neptune (1846) with the French astronomer Leverrier, working independently.

Adrian, 1st Baron (Edgar Douglas Adrian) (1889–1977), English physiologist. He shared with C. Sherrington the 1932 Nobel Prize for medicine for their discovery of the functions of the neurons.

Agassiz, Louis (1807–73), Swiss–American embryologist, author of *Lectures on Comparative Embryology*, *Researches on the Fossil Fishes*, and *Studies on Glaciers*. He was an opponent of Darwinian evolution.

Airy, Sir George Biddell (1801–92), English mathematician who was Astronomer Royal from 1836 until his retirement in 1881. He set up a magnetic observatory at Greenwich.

Ampère, André Marie (1775–1836), French mathematician and physicist who propounded the theory that magnetism is the result of molecular electric currents. The unit of electric current is named after him.

Ångström, Anders Jöns (1814–74), Swedish physicist who studied heat, magnetism, and especially optics; the angström unit, used for measuring the wavelength of light, is named after him.

Appert, Nicholas (1752–1841), Frenchman who invented the method of preserving animal and vegetable foods. He designed a preserving jar in 1795 and canning techniques in 1810.

Appleton, Sir Edward Victor (1892–1965), English physicist, discoverer of the ionized region of the upper atmosphere which became known as the Appleton layer. He discovered that sun spots emit radio waves and his researches led to the development of radar. Nobel Prize winner 1947.

Arago, Dominique François Jean (1786–1853), French astronomer and physicist, best known for his discoveries in astronomy, electromagnetism and optics.

Argand, Aimé (1755–1803), Swiss physician and chemist, inventor in about 1782 of the Argand lamp. It has a cylindrical wick, which allows air to pass to both inner and outer surfaces of the flame, thus increasing its power.

Arrhenius, Svante August (1859–1927), Swedish chemist, one of the founders of modern physical chemistry. A director of the Nobel Institute, he originated the dissociation theory of electrolysis, and won the Nobel Prize for chemistry in 1903.

Austin, Herbert (1886–1941), English motor-manufacturer, pioneer of the small car – 7 horsepower – which he put on the market in 1921.

Avogadro, Amedeo (1776–1856), Italian physicist who in 1811 formulated his hypothesis of the molecular composition of gases, since known as Avogadro's Law.

Ayrton, William Edward (1847–1908), English electrical engineer, inventor of a number of electrical measuring instruments.

Baird, John Logie (1888–1946), Scottish television pioneer, manufacturer of boot polish and (in Trinidad) jam. He invented the televisor and the noctovisor.

Banks, Sir Joseph (1743–1820), rich English amateur scientist and naturalist who accompanied Captain Cook on his expedition to the Pacific, 1768–71. Through him the breadfruit was transferred from Tahiti to the West Indies, and the mango from Bengal.

Beaufort, Sir Francis (1774–1857), hydrographer of the navy. He introduced the wind scale (1805) which bears his name.

Becquerel, Antoine Henri (1852–1908), distinguished French physicist who in 1896 discovered radioactivity in uranium. He shared with the Curies the 1903 Nobel Prize for physics.

Bell, Alexander Graham (1847–1922), Scottish inventor, later an American citizen, who taught deaf mutes and spread his father's system of 'Visible Speech'. His inventions of the articulating telephone (1872–6), the photophone (1880), and the graphophone (1887) made him famous and rich.

Benz, Karl (1844–1929), German engineer. The motor car he produced in 1885 was one of the first to be driven by an internal combustion engine.

Bernal, John Desmond (1901–71), Irish physicist, author of *The Social Functions of Science*, *Science in History*, and *The Freedom of Necessity*. Lenin peace prize 1953.

Berthelot, Marcellin Pierre Eugène (1827–1907), French chemist and politician, was one of the founders of thermochemistry and the first to produce organic compounds synthetically.

Berzelius, Jöns Jakob (1779–1848), Swedish chemist, founder of electrochemical theory and devisor of the system of chemical symbols.

Bessemer, Sir Henry (1813–98), English inventor and engineer. For his process of converting cast iron direct into steel (patented 1856) he was knighted in 1879.

Blackett, Baron (Patrick Maynard Stuart Blackett) (1897–1974), British physicist whose work on nuclear and cosmic ray physics gained him a Nobel Prize in 1948. The year before, he had advanced the theory that, 'All massive rotating bodies are magnetic'.

Bode, Johann Ehlert (1747–1826), German astronomer remembered for his theoretical calculation (Bode's Law) of the proportionate distances of the planets from the sun.

Bohr, Niels Henrik David (1885–1962), Danish nuclear physicist who won the Nobel Prize for chemistry in 1922 for investigations into atomic structure and radiation. With others, he applied the quantum theory to atomic processes.

Bondi, Sir Hermann (b. 1919), British mathematician and astronomer, b. Vienna, who is associated with the steady state theory of the universe.

Boulton, Matthew (1728–1809), English engineer who, with James Watt, manufactured steam engines at his Soho works near Birmingham. He also improved coining machinery, and a Boulton press was used at the Royal Mint until 1882.

Bragg, Sir William Henry (1862–1942), English physicist who won the Nobel Prize in 1915 with his son for their work on radio-activity, X-rays and crystal structure.

Bragg, Sir William Lawrence (1890–1971), son of the above. He succeeded Rutherford at the Cavendish Laboratory in Cambridge, 1938–53.

Bramah, Joseph (1748–1814), English inventor of the safety lock (1788), the hydraulic press (1796), and a machine for printing serial numbers on bank notes (1806).

Brennan, Louis (1853–1932), Irish inventor whose inventions included a monorail locomotive on the gyroscope principle and a gyro-directed torpedo.

Brewster, Sir David (1781–1868), Scottish physicist, noted for his research into the polarization of light. He invented the kaleidoscope in 1816 and helped to found the British Association for the Advancement of Science.

Bright, Sir Charles Tilston (1832–88), English telegraph engineer who supervised the laying of the British telegraph network and the Atlantic cables (1856–8).

Brunel, Isambard Kingdom (1806–59), English civil engineer, helped his father in building the Thames (Rotherhithe) tunnel. He was the engineer of the Great Western Railway and designed the *Great Western* (1838), the first steamship built to cross the Atlantic, the *Great Britain* (1845), the first ocean screw-steamer, and the *Great Eastern*, at the time the largest vessel ever built. He also designed the Clifton Suspension Bridge and the Royal Albert Bridge over the River Tamar at Saltash.

Brunel, Sir Marc Isambard (1769–1849), father of the above, b. France, was chief engineer for New York before settling in England. His most remarkable undertaking was the Thames Tunnel (1825–43).

Buchner, Eduard (1860–1917), German chemist, famous for his work on the chemistry of fermentation: a Nobel Prize winner in 1907.

Bunsen, Robert Wilhelm (1811–99), German chemist and physicist, discoverer of the metals caesium and rubidium, and inventor of the charcoal pile, the Bunsen burner, and magnesium light. With Kirchhoff he originated spectrum analysis.

Buys Ballot, Christoph Henrich Diedrich (1817–90), Dutch meteorologist who invented the aeroklinoscope and a system of weather signals.

Cannizzaro, Stanislao (1826–1910), Italian chemist who developed the work of Avogadro in distinguishing between molecular and atomic weights.

Carnot, Sadi (1796–1832), French engineer and physicist: the founder of the science of thermodynamics, establishing the principle that heat and work are reversible conditions.

Cartwright, Edmund (1743–1823), English inventor of the power loom, and of a wool-combing machine (1790).

Carver, George Washington (1864-1943), black American agricultural chemist who founded the Tuskegee Institute.

Cavendish, Henry (1731–1810), English scientist, famous for his investigations into the nature of gases. In 1760 he discovered the extreme levity of inflammable air, now known as hydrogen gas, and later, the chemical composition of water.

Chadwick, Sir James (1891–1974), English physicist, one of Rutherford's collaborators in atomic research. In 1932 Chadwick discovered the neutron.

Chapman, Sydney (1888–1970), English mathematician and geophysicist, famous for his work on the kinetic theory of gases, geomagnetism, and solar and ionospheric physics. An upper layer of the atmosphere and a crater on the far side of the moon are named after him.

Charles, Jacques Alexandre César (1746–1823), French physicist, the first to use hydrogen gas in balloons.

Cierva, Juan de la (1895–1936), Spanish engineer who, in 1923, developed the basic principle of the autogiro, a type of flying machine that can descend vertically by means of a windmill revolving freely on its own shaft.

Cockcroft, Sir John Douglas (1897–1967), Cambridge nuclear physicist who shared the 1951 Nobel Prize with E. T. S. Walton. They had worked together in the historic 'atom-splitting' experiments. In 1931 Cockcroft developed high-voltage apparatus for atomic transmutations.

Cockerell, Christopher (b. 1910), English inventor of the hovercraft.

Cohn, Ferdinand Julius (1828–98), German botanist, founder of the science of bacteriology.

Colt, Samuel (1814–62), American inventor who took out his first patent for a revolver in 1835 and played a major role in the development of small arms in the 1850s.

Compton, Arthur Holly (1892–1962), American physicist whose discovery that X-rays change in wavelength when scattered by matter is called the Compton effect (1923). He won the Nobel Prize for physics in 1927, and helped to develop the atomic bomb.

Compton, Karl Taylor (1887–1954), American scientist-administrator, brother of the above. President of Massachusetts Institute of Technology 1930–48.

Crompton, Samuel (1753–1827), English inventor of the spinning-mule (1779), which substituted machinery for hand work.

Crookes, Sir William (1832–1919), English physicist who discovered the element thallium (1861) and the sodium amalgamation process (1865). He invented the radiometer (1873–6) and the spinthariscope, and was a great authority on sanitation.

Curie, Marie Sklodowska (1867–1934), first great woman scientist, b. Poland. With her husband Pierre she discovered radium, and they shared the 1903 Nobel Prize for physics. After Pierre's death, Marie isolated polonium and radium in 1910, and received the Nobel Prize for chemistry in 1911.

Cuvier, Georges (1769–1832), French naturalist, noted for his classification of animals and his studies in comparative anatomy.

Daguerre, Louis Jacques Mandé (1789–1851), French photographic pioneer who invented the daguerreotype process. He also invented, with Bouton, the diorama – paintings illuminated in a dark room to give the illusion of reality.

Daimler, Gottlieb (1834–1900), German motor-builder who invented a petroleum motor for cars at Kannstatt in 1885.

Dalton, John (1766–1844), English chemist and mathematician who first described colour blindness ('Daltonism'). His atomic theory elevated chemistry to a science, demonstrating that the atoms of the chemical elements are qualitatively different from one another.

Darwin, Charles Robert (1809–82), English naturalist and one of the pioneers of experimental biology. After an important voyage around the world on the

Beagle (1831–6), he spent many years formulating his theory of evolution before publishing *The Origin of Species* (1859). His theory of natural selection and the important supplementary theory of sexual selection expressed in *The Descent of Man* (1871), were violently attacked and strongly defended but gained recognition from almost all biologists. His books are still banned in South Africa.

Davy, Sir Humphry (1778–1829), English chemist who invented the miners' safety lamp in 1815. His fame lies chiefly in the views originated in *On Some Chemical Agencies of Electricity* (1806); and his *Elements of Agricultural Chemistry* (1813) contains the first use in English of the word 'element'. He also discovered sodium, barium, strontium, calcium and magnesium.

De Forest, Lee (1873–1961), American electrical engineer and inventor of the vacuum tube: the first to use alternating-current transmission.

De Havilland, Sir Geoffrey (1882–1965), pioneer of civil and military aviation in Britain and designer of the famous Moth machines.

Dewar, Sir James (1842–1923), Scottish chemist and physicist, who liquefied and froze many gases, including hydrogen, invented the vacuum flask, and (with Sir Frederick Abel) invented the explosive cordite.

Diesel, Rudolf (1858–1913), German engineer who was born in Paris of German parentage, and invented an internal combustion engine which he patented in 1893.

Dirac, Paul Adrien Maurice (b. 1902), English physicist who shared with Erwin Schrödinger of Austria the 1933 Nobel Prize for physics for their work in developing Heisenberg's theory of quantum mechanics.

Draper, John William (1811–82), American chemist, born near Liverpool. Professor of chemistry at New York University, he was the first, using Daguerre's process, to take a successful photograph of the human face (1840) and of the moon.

Dyson, Sir Frank Watson (1868–1939), English astronomer who was Astronomer Royal 1910–33, and Astronomer Royal for Scotland 1905–10.

Eastman, George (1854–1932), American inventor who produced a successful roll film (1884), the Kodak camera (1888), and joined with Edison in experiments which made possible the moving-picture industry. In 1928 he exhibited the first colour motion pictures in Rochester, New York.

Eddington, Sir Arthur Stanley (1882–1944), English astronomer (Greenwich observatory 1906–13; Cambridge observatory 1914–44) who wrote on relativity and gravitation, and on the philosophical bearing of new developments in physics.

Edison, Thomas Alva (1847–1931), American inventor of the transmitter and receiver for the automatic telegraph; the phonograph (1877); the first practical incandescent lamp (1880); the first hydroelectric plant (1882); and many devices for the electrical distribution of light and power.

Eiffel, Alexandre Gustav (1832-1923), French engineer whose works include the 300 m-high Eiffel Tower (1887–9) at a cost of £260,000, and the Panama Canal locks.

Einstein, Albert (1879–1955), German mathematical physicist and astronomer. His theory of relativity superseded Newton's theory of gravitation and caused a revolution in conceptions of space, time and gravity. In 1921 he was awarded the Nobel Prize for physics for his work in quantum theory.

Fabre, Jean Henri Casimir (1823–1915), French naturalist whose study of the habits of insects were beautifully recorded in his *Souvenirs entomologiques*. He was known as the 'Insects' Homer'.

Fairbairn, Sir William (1789–1874), Scottish engineer. In Manchester (1817) he took a lead in making iron boats; and for the Menai tubular bridge (Robert Stephenson's idea) he invented the rectangular tube finally used. He erected a thousand bridges on this principle.

Falconer, Hugh (1808–65), Scottish botanist and palaeontologist who made the first experiments in growing tea in India.

Faraday, Michael (1791–1867), English experimental physicist, founder of the science of electromagnetism. He succeeded Sir Humphrey Davy as Professor of chemistry at the Royal Institution in 1833 and went on to make vital discoveries in electricity, heat, light and magnetism.

Fermi, Enrico (1901–54), Italian nuclear physicist whose research contributed to the development of the atomic bomb. Nobel Prize winner 1938.

Finsen, Niels Ryberg (1860–1904), Danish physician who established an institute for light therapy and founded phototherapy. Nobel Prize winner 1903.

Fisher, Sir Ronald Aymer (1890–1962), British scientist who revolutionized both genetics and the philosophy of experimentation by founding the modern corpus of mathematical statistics.

Fitzroy, Robert (1805–65), British meteorologist and admiral, who travelled with Darwin on the *Beagle* and published with him a *Narrative of the Voyages* in 1839. The Fitzroy barometer was invented by him and he instituted the storm warnings that developed into daily weather forecasts.

Fleming, Sir Ambrose (1849–1945), British scientist whose invention of the thermionic radio valve in 1904 revolutionized radio telegraphy.

Fokker, Anthony (1890–1939), Dutch aircraft engineer, b. Java.

Fourier, Jean Baptiste Joseph (1768–1830), French mathematical physicist. Although actively involved in politics – he accompanied Napoleon to Egypt in 1798 – he found time for research, especially on the flow of heat along a conductor. His chief work is the *Theorie analytique de la chaleur* (*The Analytical Theory of Heat*) (1882).

Fraunhofer, Joseph von (1787–1826), German optician who founded an optical institute at Munich. He discovered the dark lines in the sun's spectrum, called Fraunhofer's Lines.

Friese-Greene, William (1855–1921), English inventor of the cinematograph, whose first film was shown in 1890.

Fulton, Robert (1765–1815), American engineer who was the first to experiment successfully with steam navigation. He produced the first submarine (*Nautilus*) at Brest in 1801, invented torpedoes in New York in 1806, and in 1807 launched a paddle steamer, *Clermont*, on the Hudson River.

Galton, Sir Francis (1822–1911), English founder of eugenics, cousin of Darwin. His investigations in meteorology are recorded in *Meteorographica* (1863), and contain the basis of the modern weather chart. In 1885 he proved the individuality of fingerprints, and devised fingerprint identification in 1893.

Galvani, Luigi (1737–98), Italian physician and physiologist who, as Professor of anatomy at Bologna, made important discoveries in animal electricity.

Gauss, Karl Friedrich (1777–1855), German mathematician and astronomer who set up the first special observatory for terrestrial magnetism at Göttingen. He made major contributions to astronomy, mathematics and physics; in 1833 he devised the electromagnetic telegraph which functioned over a distance of 9,000 feet.

Gay-Lussac, Joseph Louis (1778–1850), French chemist and physicist who did research on gases, temperature and terrestrial magnetism. In 1808 he made the important discovery of the law of volumes.

Geikie, Sir Archibald (1835–1924), Scottish geologist who was director-general of the Survey of the United Kingdom (1882–1901), and head of the Geological Museum, London.

Goodyear, Charles (1800–60), American inventor whose experiments led, in 1844, to the invention of vulcanized rubber. This made possible the commercial use of rubber, and a brand of motor car tyres still bears his name today.

Hahn, Otto (1879–1968), German chemist and physicist, chief discoverer of uranium fission. With Strassmann he obtained barium isotopes by bombarding uranium with neutrons in 1939. Two years before his death he was awarded the Enrico Fermi Prize.

Haldane, John Burton Sanderson (1892–1964), English biologist and geneticist, noted for his work in mathematical evolutionary theory.

Hale, George Ellery (1868–1935), American astronomer who earned fame by his researches in solar and stellar spectroscopy. The 200-inch reflecting telescope on Mount Palomar is named after him.

Helmholtz, Hermann von (1821–94), German physicist and physiologist, equally distinguished in physiology, mathematics, and experimental and mathematical physics. In physical science he is known by his paper on *Conservation of Energy* (1847).

Henry, Joseph (1797–1878), American physicist who made discoveries in electromagnetism, electrical induction, meteorology and acoustics.

Herschel, Sir John (1792–1871), British astronomer who continued his father's researches and also pioneered photography, a term introduced by him.

Herschel, Sir William (1738–1822), German astronomer, father of the above. He made a reflecting telescope (1774) with which in 1781 he discovered the planet Uranus. He added greatly to knowledge of the solar system and the Milky Way; his *Catalogue of Nebulae* (1786) revealed that some of the nebulae he could see were separate star systems outside our own.

Hertz, Heinrich Rudolf (1857–95), German physicist who, in 1888, identified radio waves as belonging to the same family as light waves.

Hinshelwood, Sir Cyril Norman (1897–1967), English chemist. He shared with Professor Semenov of Russia the 1956 Nobel Prize for chemistry for researches into the mechanism of chemical reactions.

Hodgkin, Dorothy Crowfoot (b. 1910), the third woman to win the Nobel Prize for chemistry, awarded in 1964 for her X-ray analysis to elucidate the structure of complex molecules, notably penicillin and vitamin B_{12}.

Howe, Elias (1819–67), American inventor of the sewing-machine (1846).

Hubble, Edwin Powell (1889–1953), American astronomer who, in 1923, discovered a distance-indicating cepheid variable star in the Andromeda strain.

Huggins, Sir William (1824–1910), British astronomer, founder of the science of astro-physics, and pioneer of spectroscopic photography.

Huxley, Thomas Henry (1825–95), English biologist who, as assistant surgeon on HMS *Rattlesnake* (1846–50), studied marine organisms. His main work was in vertebrate morphology and palaeontology. He coined the word 'agnostic', and was a strong supporter of Darwinism.

Huxley, Julian Sorrell (1887–1975), English biologist and philosopher, grandson of the above and brother of novelist Aldous. Professor of zoology at King's College, London (1925–7) and secretary of the Zoological Society of London from 1935 and first director-general of UNESCO, 1946–8.

Joliot-Curie, Jean Frédéric (1900–58), and his wife Irène (1896–1956), French scientists who discovered artificial radioactivity. They won the Nobel Prize for chemistry in 1935 for the synthesis of new radioactive elements. In 1939 Frédéric demonstrated the possibility of splitting the atom. Irène was the daughter of Pierre and Marie Curie.

Jones, Sir Harold Spencer (1890–1960), British astronomer who determined that the mean distance of the earth from the sun is 93,004,000 miles.

Kapitsa, Pyotr (b. 1894), Russian physicist who worked on atomic research with Rutherford at the Cavendish Laboratory, Cambridge, returning to Russia in 1935. Awarded the 1978 Nobel Prize for his work in low temperature physics.

Kelvin, Lord (William Thompson) (1824–1907), British mathematician and physicist, known for his work on heat and thermodynamics, and contributions to electrical science and submarine telegraphy. He invented the syphon recorder (1867), and a machine by which ships can take accurate soundings while at sea (1872). He introduced the Kelvin or Absolute scale of temperature.

Kirchhoff, Gustav Robert (1824–87), German mathematical physicist who, with R. W. Bunsen, originated spectrum analysis and, with the aid of the spectroscope, discovered the elements caesium and rubidium in 1860.

Lamarck, Jean Baptiste Pierre Antoine de Monet de (1744–1829), French biologist and pre-Darwinian evolutionist whose conclusions were published in his famous *Philosophie Zoologique* (1809). Lamarck denied the unchangeableness of species and prepared the way for the new accepted theory of descent.

Lamb, Sir Horace (1849–1934), English mathematician, writer of a standard work on hydro-dynamics.

Lavoisier, Antoine Laurent (1743–94), French chemist who successfully applied chemistry to agriculture and was the first to establish that combustion is a form of chemical action. He gave us the word 'oxygen', and was guillotined during the French Revolution.

Lesseps, Ferdinand, Vicomte de (1805–94), French engineer who was granted a concession to build the Suez Canal in 1856, the work being completed in 1869. In 1881 work began on his scheme for a Panama Canal; but in 1892–3 five directors, Lesseps among them, were charged with breach of trust. Lesseps was sentenced to five years imprisonment, but was too ill to serve the sentence.

Leverrier, Urbain Jean Joseph (1811–77), French astronomer who suspected the existence of the planet Neptune.

Lippmann, Gabriel (1845–1921), French physicist who invented a capillary electrometer and was a pioneer in colour photography. Nobel Prize winner 1908.

Low, Archibald Montgomery (1888–1956), British scientist who worked in the fields of wireless, television, and anti-aircraft and anti-tank weapons.

Lyell, Sir Charles (1797–1875), Scottish geologist, whose *Principles of Geology* (1830–3) might be ranked after Darwin's *Origin of Species* among the books that had the profoundest influence on nineteenth-century scientific thought. In 1830 he divided the geological timescale into three periods, which he called eocene, miocene and pliocene.

Lysenko, Trofim (1898–1976), Russian biologist who maintained that environmental experiences can change heredity.

Macadam, John Loudon (1756–1836), Scottish inventor of the 'macadamizing' system of road-making. In 1827 he was appointed surveyor-general of metropolitan roads.

Marconi, Guglielmo, Marchese (1874–1937), Italian inventor and electrical engineer who developed the use of radio waves as a practical means of communication. In 1901 he received in Newfoundland the first transatlantic telegraphic radio signals sent out by his station in Cornwall, thus demonstrating that radio waves can bend round the spherically-shaped earth. In 1909 he won the Nobel Prize for physics; and in 1920 he opened the first public broadcasting station in Britain, at Writtle.

Maxim, Sir Hiram Stevens (1840–1916), American inventor whose machine gun was perfected in London in 1883. He also invented a pneumatic gun, a smokeless powder, and a flying machine (1894).

Maxwell, James Clerk (1831–79), Scottish physicist whose work revolutionized fundamental physics. His great work, *Electricity and Magnetism* (1873), gave physics a celebrated set of equations for the basic laws of electricity and magnetism. Also famous for his investigations on the kinetic theory of gases.

Medawar, Sir Peter Brian (b. 1915), British zoologist, author of *The Art of the Soluble* and *The Future of Man*; president of the British Association 1969. He shared the Nobel Prize for medicine and physiology with F. M. Burnet in 1960 for their discovery of acquired immunity against foreign tissue.

Meitner, Lise (1878–1969), Austrian scientist; she was a co-worker of Otto Hahn and interpreted his results (1939) as a fission process. With Hahn and Fritz Strassmann she was awarded the Enrico Fermi Prize in 1966.

Mendeleyev, Dmitri Ivanovich (1834–1907), Russian chemist who made important contributions to physical chemistry and chemical philosophy. The first to discover the critical temperatures, he also formulated the periodic law of atomic weights (1869) and drew up the periodic table, predicting the properties of elements which might fill the gaps.

Mesmer, Friedrich Anton (1733–1815), Austrian physician and the founder of mesmerism, or animal magnetism.

Michelson, Albert Abraham (1852–1931), American physicist, b. Poland. Collaborated with E. W. M. Morley in an experiment to determine ether drift. He won the Nobel Prize for physics in 1907.

Millikan, Robert Andrews (1868–1954), American physicist who won the 1923 Nobel Prize for physics for his work on the elementary electric charge and the photoelectric effect. In 1925 he discovered cosmic rays in the upper atmosphere and, while analysing them in 1933 with Anderson, discovered positrons (positive electrons).

Morse, Samuel Finley Breese (1791–1872), American pioneer in electromagnetic telegraphy and inventor of the dot-and-dash code that bears his name. In 1843 Congress granted him $30,000 to build the first telegraph line from Washington to Baltimore; it was first used the following year.

Müller, Sir Ferdinand (1825–96), German-born botanist who emigrated to Australia in 1847 and was director of Melbourne Botanical Gardens, 1857–73. He introduced the eucalyptus into Europe.

Murdock, William (1754–1839), Scottish engineer and inventor, the first to make practical use of coal gas as an illuminating agent.

Nasmyth, James (1808–90), Scottish inventor of the steam hammer in 1839, devised for forging an enormous wrought-iron paddle-shaft. He also invented a steam pile-driver.

Needham, Joseph (b. 1900), British biochemist, historian of science, orientalist, and author of the historical work *Science and Civilization in China*.

Nernst, Walther Hermann (1864–1941), German scientist who, in 1901, established the 'third law of thermodynamics' that dealt with the behaviour of matter at temperatures approaching absolute zero. He won the Nobel Prize for chemistry in 1920.

Nobel, Alfred Bernhard (1833–96), Swedish inventor and philanthropist. He discovered dynamite and invented blasting-jelly and several kinds of smokeless powder. Having made a fortune from the manufacture of explosives, he bequeathed a fund for annual prizes to those who make major contributions in the fields of physics, chemistry, physiology or medicine, literature and peace.

Nuffield, Lord (William Richard Morris) (1877–1963), British motor car manufacturer who, in 1943, established the Nuffield Foundation, endowing it with £10 million.

Oersted, Hans Christian (1777–1851), Danish physicist, Professor at the university of Copenhagen, who discovered electromagnetism in 1819.

Ohm, Georg Simon (1787–1854), German physicist, Professor at Munich, who in 1827 formulated the law defining electrical current, potential and resistance, one of the foundation stones of electrical science.

Otto, Nikolaus August (1832–91), German engineer and inventor of the four-stroke gas engine that bears his name.

Pauli, Wolfgang (1900–58), Austrian-born physicist who, in 1925, introduced his exclusion principle which helps to explain atomic structure statistically. In 1930 he gave the first theoretical prediction of the existence of neutrinos. Nobel Prize winner 1945.

Penney, Baron (William George) (b. 1909), British scientist. His nuclear research team developed the advanced gas-cooled reactor chosen for the power stations at Dungeness and Hinkley Point.

Piazzi, Giuseppe (1746–1826), Italian astronomer who, in 1801, discovered the minor planet Ceres, the first of the asteroids to be seen by man.

Planck, Max (1858–1947), German mathematical physicist, whose main work was on thermodynamics and was an important contribution to the development of quantum theory. In 1918 he won the Nobel Prize for physics.

Preece, Sir William Henry (1834–1913), Welsh electrical engineer, associated with the expansion of wireless telegraphy and telephony in Britain.

Priestley, Joseph (1733–1804), English chemist, a pioneer in the chemistry of gases, who shared with Scheele the discovery of oxygen. In 1775 he discovered hydrochloric and sulphuric acids.

Ramsay, Sir William (1852–1916), Scottish chemist, discoverer with Lord Rayleigh of argon in 1894. Later he discovered helium and other inert gases, which he called neon, krypton and xenon. He won the Nobel Prize for chemistry in 1904.

Rayleigh, Lord (John William Strutt) (1842–1919), English mathematician and physicist. He studied sound and the wave theory of light; with Sir W. Ramsay he discovered argon in 1894 and won the Nobel Prize for physics in 1904.

Rennie, John (1761–1821), Scottish civil engineer and famous bridge-builder. He built the old Waterloo and Southwark bridges and designed the granite London Bridge which stood until recently. He also designed many docks, including London, Hull, Liverpool and Dublin; constructed Plymouth breakwater; made canals and drained fens.

Richardson, Sir Owen Williams (1879–1959), English physicist who worked on thermionics, or emission of electricity from hot bodies. He won the Nobel Prize for physics in 1928.

Rutherford, Lord (Ernest Rutherford) (1871–1937), British physicist, b. New Zealand, famous in the field of atomic research. In 1899 he discovered the emission of alpha and beta rays from radioactive atoms; in 1904 he postulated, with Soddy, the general theory of radioactivity. He won the Nobel Prize for chemistry in 1908, and three years later announced his nuclear theory of the atom. In 1918 he succeeded in splitting the atom.

Sachs, Julius von (1832–97), German botanist, founder of experimental plant physiology. His experiments were concerned with the influence of light and heat upon plants, and the organic activities of vegetable growth.

Sanger, Frederick (b. 1918), British scientist who, in 1955, determined the molecular structure of the protein insulin. Nobel Prize winner 1958.

Scheele, Carl Wilhelm (1742–86), Swedish chemist, discoverer of many chemical substances, including oxygen; he also discovered chlorine and baryta (1774) and the composition of the tungsten-containing mineral, scheelite (1881).

Scott-Paine, Hubert (1891–1954), pioneer in the design and construction of aircraft and seacraft.

Senefelder, Alois (1772–1834), Bavarian inventor of lithography about 1796.

Siemens, Sir William (1823–83), German-born electrical engineer who settled in England and constructed many overland and submarine telegraphs. He designed the steamship *Faraday* for cable-laying and constructed the Portrush Electric Tramway, as well as inventing a water-meter, pyrometer, and bathometer.

Singer, Isaac Merritt (1811–75), American mechanical engineer who improved early forms of the sewing machine and, in 1852, patented his single-thread chain-stitch sewing machine.

Smeaton, John (1724–92), English engineer who built the third great Eddystone Lighthouse (1756–9), which stood till 1882. His other main works were Ramsgate harbour (1774), the Forth and Clyde Canal, and many bridges. He also invented an improved blowing apparatus for iron-smelting.

Smith, William (1769–1839), English surveyor and canal-builder who, as engineer to the Somerset Coal Canal, began a study of the strata of England. His epoch-making *Geological Map of England* (1815) was followed by twenty-one geologically-coloured maps of English counties (1819–24). Known as 'the Father of English Geology', he was the first to map the rock strata of England and to identify the fossils peculiar to each layer.

Soddy, Frederick (1877–1956), English chemist who, in Glasgow in 1913, laid the foundation of the isotope theory, coining the word 'isotope'. He won the Nobel Prize for chemistry in 1921.

Stephenson, George (1781–1848), English engineer and locomotive designer. In 1814 he constructed his first locomotive, *My Lord*, to haul coals for the colliery tram-roads at 6 mph. He and his son Robert built the *Locomotion* for the Stockton and Darlington Railway (1825), the first locomotive for a public railway. In 1829 his *Rocket* won at a speed of 30 mph the prize of £500 offered by the Liverpool and Manchester Railway, whose chief engineer he was.

Stephenson, Robert (1803–59), English engineer, son of the above, who engineered railway lines in England and Colombia and designed many bridges, including the Menai and Conway tubular bridges.

Stokes, Sir George Gabriel (1819–1903), Irish mathematician and physicist, pioneer of the modern theory of viscous fluids, who made important contributions to the theory of light.

Talbot, William Henry Fox (1800–77), English pioneer of photography which he developed independently of Daguerre. In 1835 he took the earliest negative photograph, 'Lacock Abbey, Wiltshire'. He was also one of the first decipherers of the Ninevite cuneiform inscriptions.

Telford, Thomas (1757–1834), Scottish engineer who built bridges (two over the Severn and the Menai suspension bridge), canals, more than 1,000 miles of road, and 1,200 bridges, as well as churches, docks and harbours.

Thompson, Sir D'Arcy Wentworth (1860-1948), Scottish zoologist whose *On Growth and Form* (1917) has influenced biological science.

Thomson, Sir George Paget (b. 1892), English physicist, son of Sir J. J. Thomson. He won the Nobel Prize for physics in 1937.

Thomson, Sir Joseph John (1856–1940), English physicist and mathematician, father of the above. In 1897 he discovered electrons and in 1906 won the Nobel Prize for physics. His study of deflection of 'positive rays' in the magnetic field led to the discovery of isotopes.

Thorpe, Sir Thomas Edward (1845–1925), English chemist who researched in inorganic chemistry and, with his friend Arthur Rücker, made a magnetic survey of the British Isles.

Tizard, Sir Henry Thomas (1885–1959), English scientist and administrator who was chairman of the Scientific Survey of Air Defence and chief scientific adviser to the British Government, 1947–52.

Todd, Lord (Alexander Robertus) (b. 1907), Scottish biochemist, noted for his work on the structure of nucleic acids. Nobel Prize winner 1957.

Trevithick, Richard (1771–1833), English mining engineer and inventor. The development of the high-pressure steam engine was largely due to him.

Volta, Alessandro (1745–1827), Italian physicist who invented the voltaic pile, producing electricity from a cell. He also discovered the electric decomposition of water and made investigations into heat and gases. His name was given to the volt, the unit of electrical potential difference.

Wallace, Alfred Russell (1823–1913), British naturalist and joint author with Darwin of the theory of natural selection, although he did not use the phrase. Wallace and Darwin, coming independently to the theory, read a joint paper to the Linnean Society in 1858.

Wallis, Sir Barnes Neville (b. 1887), British scientist and inventor who designed the Wellington bomber, the swing-wing aircraft, and the 'bouncing bomb'.

Watson-Watt, Sir Robert (b. 1892), Scottish physicist who in 1935 first built radar equipment to detect aircraft.

Watt, James (1736–1819), Scottish engineer and inventor who made important improvements to Newcomen's steam engine by inventing a separate condenser in 1764. He entered into partnership with Matthew Boulton of Soho, Birmingham. The watt as a unit of power is named after him.

Weismann, August (1834–1914), German biologist who worked on the question of individual variability in evolution and rejected the idea of the inheritance of acquired characteristics.

Wheatstone, Sir Charles (1802–75), English physicist who, with W. F. Cooke, patented an electric telegraph in 1837, thus becoming for the Old World what Morse was for the New. He also introduced the microphone and, in 1829, patented the concertina.

Whittle, Sir Frank (b. 1907), British inventor and aviator, a pioneer in the field of jet propulsion. He built the first jet engine in 1937 which led to the first flight of Gloster jet-propelled planes in May 1941.

Willcocks, Sir William (1852–1932), British engineer, b. India: planned and carried out great irrigation works for Egypt (the Aswan Dam, 1898–1902), India, South Africa and Iraq (Hindiya Barrage).

Young, James (1811–83), Scottish chemist whose experiments (1847–50) led to the manufacture of paraffin oil and solid paraffin on a large scale.

Young, Thomas (1773–1829), English physicist, physician and egyptologist who established the undulatory, or wave, theory of light and its essential principle of interference, and was the first to describe astigmatism of the eye.

Zeppelin, Ferdinand Count von (1838–1917), German inventor of the first airship or dirigible balloon of rigid type (1897–1900). Zeppelins were constructed at Constance, their inventor's birthplace, and used in the First World War.

3

The Exploration of Space

Summary of Chapter

Why Explore Space?

That morning in October 1957 when the world awoke to hear over the radio the 'bleep bleep' of the Russian satellite Sputnik 1, a centuries-old dream that man would one day venture into space began to come true. Great explorers in years gone by had opened up the finite world and man's need for new challenges to exercise his inborn desire for discovery was subject to practical limitation. Flying made the world seem to shrink in size still further. Confined to his tiny planet, it was inevitable that man should look out into space for new areas of exploration.

Space presented man with an unlimited new frontier. More than anything previously attempted in the history of man's efforts to explore his environment, the journey into space requires far more than guts and physical determination. It demands vast expenditure, far beyond the means of most nations.

Only two nations so far have been able to afford to put man into space— the United States of America and the Soviet Union. It is questionable whether they would have succeeded as they have, had it not been for the political motivation of competing against each other in the space race. By the mid-1970s, communications satellites would surely have been developed to satisfy the commercial pressures of television and telecommunications; but it seems unlikely that journeys to the moon or probes to Mars and Venus would have been possible yet, had it not been for the dictates of military strongarmsmanship.

The very valid claim is made that there are vast spin-off benefits for mankind from the space programme. No longer, for example, need food stick to the frying pan, which can now be coated with the same material used to prevent spacecraft re-entry vehicles burning up when coming back into the dense atmosphere of the earth. But many people will argue that more useful ideas could have been developed—experiments in cancer research perhaps—had the money spent on space been otherwise employed. The ethics of expenditure on space research will be debated for many years to come, but as space travel becomes more commonplace the public will tend to accept its existence more readily and begin to appreciate the advantages it brings to the human race.

The Space Race

It was an enormous military intercontinental ballistic missile (ICBM), developed and tested in Russia, which in August 1957 gave the Soviet Union a vehicle capable of putting a small piece of 'hardware' into orbit round the earth. To do this the rocket had to be able to accelerate itself and its payload to a speed of about 18,000 mph, and this at a time when few men had flown faster than sound (660 mph) in an aeroplane. Looking back twenty years to those early days – now that men have walked fairly frequently on the surface of the moon – it is difficult to appreciate how incredible the achievement of the first Sputnik seemed.

A period of almost feverish activity was precipitated by the Soviet triumph. The United States found it hard to swallow the humiliation of being second into space and the US Air Force hurriedly prepared a Thor-Able rocket based on the Thor military intermediate-range ballistic missile (IRBM) to put a tiny Pioneer space probe, weighing only 84 lb, and carrying a little TV camera, into orbit round the moon. It was launched on 17 August 1958, but seventy-seven seconds into the flight the Thor booster rocket exploded and the upper stages together with the Pioneer crashed into the sea.

Another attempt, Pioneer 1B, launched in October 1958, reached an altitude of nearly 71,000 miles but was 128 mph too slow to escape from the earth, and it fell back to burn up over the Pacific Ocean. Pioneer 2, launched the following month, was even less successful. The US Army then prepared a four-stage launcher based on the Jupiter military IRBM to launch Pioneers 3 and 4 (only 13 lb) so that they would pass close to the moon. Pioneer 3 left Cape Canaveral on 6 December 1958 but failed to achieve the escape velocity of 25,000 mph needed for it to overcome the gravitational pull of the earth.

Meanwhile the Russians were very much more successful. Lunik 1 (or Luna 1) became the first successful moon probe, in January 1959. Using the same basic ICBM as had put the first Sputnik into orbit, together with a second stage rocket, Lunik 1 was launched from the cosmodrome at Baikonur and passed within 3,700 miles of the surface of the moon. Lunik 2, launched in September 1959, did even better and its 860-lb payload, packed with instruments which had monitored the flight, crashed on to the lunar surface. But the Americans suffered the ultimate in humiliation when Lunik 3, launched by the Russians a month later, actually succeeded in passing round behind the moon and photographing the far side of it, a sight which had never before been seen by man.

The US Army programme had continued and in March 1959 Pioneer 4 was launched, but its second-stage rocket burned for ten seconds instead of nine and the probe shot off out towards the sun, missing the moon by 10,000 miles. The obvious need for a co-ordinated programme resulted in the creation of the National Aeronautics and Space Administration (NASA), and a new series of Pioneer space probes was planned using a three-stage Atlas-Able launcher based on the military Atlas ICBM. The new probes weighed 387 lb and carried paddle-like blades containing solar cells to generate electricity from the sun's rays.

Unfortunately, Atlas-Able 1 caught fire and exploded at Cape Canaveral in September 1959, and a second one launched in November the same year blew up over West Africa. Atlas-Able 3 failed in September 1960 to achieve escape velocity and plunged back to the earth, while in December Atlas-Able 4 exploded at 40,000 ft. The remainder of the Pioneer programme was devoted to probing beyond the moon, further into deep space.

Although these Soviet successes and American failures set the scene, in the late 1950s and early 1960s, for man himself to embark on space exploration, the American effort was not all fruitless, nor was the Soviet effort necessarily more scientifically effective. The Russian achievement was based on the availability of their enormous ICBM, whose 'brute force' enabled them to put their space probe payloads out beyond the gravitational pull of the earth without much difficulty. However, the sophistication of the Russian instrumentation and telemetering for these early probes was open to some doubt. The Americans, nevertheless, were bringing back masses of information on the nature of space flight, even if their probes were failing to achieve their primary objectives.

Manned Space Flight

The Western World had to wait until manned space flight became possible in 1961 before the United States began to have successes which could match those of the Soviet Union, and even in this sensational respect the Russians were first by nearly a month when the late Yuri Gagarin became the first man to venture into space, on 12 April 1961, in his spacecraft Vostok 1. Astronaut Alan Shepard was the first American in space on 5 May 1961 in his spacecraft Mercury 3.

The Russians laid themselves open to criticism from animal-lovers when they first sent dogs into space in preparation for Yuri Gagarin's flight. The first space dog, Laika, was put into orbit in November 1957 and its medical condition was carefully monitored during the flight. No attempt, however, was made to recover the dog or its space vehicle, Sputnik 2. In May 1960 Sputnik 4 was launched, but an attempt at recovery was a failure. Sputnik 5 in August 1960 carried two dogs, Belka and Strelka, both of which were recovered alive by parachute after eighteen orbits. Re-entry failure again spoiled the mission of Sputnik 6 (the third trial flight of the Vostok spaceship) but two more Vostoks were successful in March 1961 and their dogs were brought back alive.

The Russians must have been well satisfied with the results of their space flights with dogs because Yuri Gagarin was launched in Vostok 1 only days after the last of these missions had been brought to a successful conclusion. They had been able to put to the practical test the survival of a living creature in the alien environment of very high acceleration and deceleration during lift-off and re-entry, weightlessness in space, and a long period breathing only oxygen. The animals were also found to be little the worse for the then unknown effects of cosmic ray bombardment.

Gagarin's spacecraft was only 7 ft 6½ ins in diameter and weighed only 10,400 lb, but at the time it was a far bigger piece of hardware than the Americans could hope to accelerate to orbital velocity. Together with its instrumentation cylinder the spacecraft was 24 ft 1¼ ins long. Inside, Gagarin was strapped on a couch in a reclining position to survive the accelerations on his body. TV cameras monitored his facial expressions throughout the flight, the single elliptical orbit of which lasted only 1 hour 48 minutes. During the flight he reached an apogee (his furthest distance from the earth) of 203 miles and

Vostok 1. (*Photo: Novosti Press Agency*)

a perigee (minimum distance) of 112½ miles. Although the Russians are still reluctant to issue full details of their early space flights, it appears that Gagarin stayed trapped inside his spacecraft for the landing. In all five subsequent Vostok missions the cosmonauts were ejected from their capsules at about 23,000 ft to avoid the danger of a heavy landing, and hopefully came down gently by parachute.

Meanwhile the Americans were preparing Project Mercury with the objective of putting a one-man spaceship into orbit and recovering the astronaut safely back to earth. They, too, first tried out putting an animal into space, and Ham, a chimpanzee, was launched in Mercury 2 on 31 January 1961. Despite a number of unpredicted changes in the planned orbit of his capsule, Ham was brought back safely to enjoy an apple on his release. It was soon after this success that Alan Shepard became the first US spaceman, when on 5 May he was launched from Cape Canaveral in Mercury 3 and flew in his capsule Freedom 7 for 15 minutes 22 seconds. This flight was described as sub-orbital; nevertheless Shepard experienced weightlessness for five minutes, achieved a speed of 5,180 mph and reached an altitude of 116.5 miles. Instruments recorded that he was subjected to 11 g (eleven times the force of gravity at the earth's surface) during his re-entry into the atmosphere, but his recovery was faultless.

Redstone rockets with a thrust of 78,000 lb were used to launch the Mercury spacecraft on the sub-orbital flights but more powerful Atlas rockets boosted the others on orbital missions. The spacecraft were bell-shaped to allow for a large-diameter (6 ft 2½ ins) heat shield to protect the capsule during re-entry. Within the bell the pilot, his life-support system, electrics, controls and instru-

Marine helicopter picks up Virgil Grissom from the Atlantic after his spaceride in Mercury Capsule 'Liberty Bell 7'. (*Photo: National Aeronautics and Space Administration (NASA), reproduced here by courtesy of the Royal Aeronautical Society*)

ment displays were accommodated. An upper cylindrical section contained the recovery parachutes and radio aerials. The astronaut lay prone on a couch tailored closely to his body shape which ensured that the effects of g forces during lift-off and re-entry were minimized.

During re-entry the capsule was subjected to temperatures as high as 3,000°F, so very careful design was needed to ensure that the astronaut came to no harm during this critical stage of his flight. The ablative shield was formed of glass fibre and resin and the resin was allowed to vapourize and burn away during the deceleration. Other parts of the capsule were not subjected to such high temperatures but were also insulated from the hot exterior. Control of the capsule was by eighteen rockets burning hydrogen peroxide, each giving up to 24 lb thrust. They were operated either automatically, or under ground control, or as part of the astronaut's 'fly-by-wire' remote control system. The three retro-rockets used a solid chemical propellant fuel, and each developed 1,160 lb thrust. Their purpose was to reduce the speed of the capsule from 17,500 mph orbital speed by about 350 mph in order to initiate the re-entry sequence.

Next to go was Virgil 'Gus' Grissom on 21 July 1961 in spacecraft Liberty Bell 7. His sub-orbital flight was similar to Alan Shepard's, and all went well until he splashed down in the ocean awaiting recovery by helicopter. A redesigned hatch cover blew off prematurely and Liberty Bell sank, but Grissom managed to swim away from it in time.

The Russians stole the next march in space progress by keeping cosmonaut Herman Titov in space for 25 hours 18 minutes, during which time he completed seventeen orbits of the earth. His spacecraft Vostok 2 was launched on 6 August 1961. Only a long time afterwards was it learned that Titov had been badly disorientated during the flight and had suffered ear damage. Nevertheless he had a hero's welcome in Red Square, Moscow, on his return.

Like all the Vostok flights, Titov's achieved an apogee of 115.5 miles, a perigee of 113.5 miles and an inclination of 65°. The capsule was a sphere surrounded by a heat shield, with a cylindrical instrumentation section and a re-entry rocket engine. Like Mercury it had three modes of control – automatic, manual by the cosmonaut, or from the ground. The life-support system maintained sea-level pressure in an atmosphere of nitrogen and oxygen closely similar to air.

A chimpanzee named Enos flew two very successful orbits in November 1961 aboard Mercury 5, but the United States had to wait until 20 February 1962 before John Glenn became the first American to go into orbit. His spacecraft Mercury 6 had its problems, especially as the final minutes before lift-off were reached. But all was well and the orbit was established with an apogee of 162 miles and a perigee of 100 miles. During his 4 hour 55 minute flight, during which he was weightless most of the time, he commented on the 'fireflies'– brilliant particles which seemed to surround the capsule at the sunrise of each orbit.

Among the faults that developed was an indication that the heat shield had become unlocked from the capsule. In order to help make sure that it was retained in position, Mission Control told Glenn not to jettison his retro-rockets before re-entry. As a result the retro-pack burned up and Glenn could see red-hot pieces flying off. His historic comment was, 'That's a real fireball outside!' Friendship 7 was successfully recovered in the Atlantic but it actually splashed down forty miles short of the predicted area.

Mercury 7 followed on 24 May 1962, and Scott Carpenter in his spacecraft Aurora 7 became the second American in orbit. He carried out a number of scientific experiments during his flight, which lasted 4 hours 56 minutes. He tried manœuvring the spacecraft and used up rather a lot of fuel. One or two other mistakes led to the spacecraft overshooting the splashdown area in the Atlantic by 250 miles. Carpenter was forced to take to the safety of his liferaft.

Next it was the turn of the Russians again. They managed to get two Vostoks into orbit at the same time and although they were only about three miles apart at one stage, it is believed that no actual attempt was being made to manœuvre them closer together. First to go was Andrian Nikolayev who was launched in Vostok 3 on 11 August 1962. The following day Pavel Popovich followed in Vostok 4. Nikolayev was in orbit for 94 hours 27 minutes, going sixty-four times round the earth, while Popovich stayed up for 70 hours 29 minutes and completed forty-eight orbits. Live TV transmissions from space for the first time, showed the cosmonauts in weightless condition.

One of the most successful American shots followed with Mercury 8.

John H. Glenn boarding Mercury capsule 'Friendship 7'. (*Photo: by courtesy of the Royal Aeronautical Society*)

Astronaut Walter Schirra was launched in spacecraft Sigma 7 on 3 October, and after correcting some problems with his spacesuit temperature control managed to complete six orbits in what was described as a 'textbook flight'. His splashdown was particularly impressive–only four and a half miles from his recovery ship, and the TV cameras took full advantage of their grandstand view. Schirra's flight lasted 9 hours 13 minutes and he suffered some blood circulation problems for a few hours after he returned to earth.

Mercury 8 had proved successful enough for the Americans to authorize the final Mercury mission to last for more than twenty-four hours. Astronaut Gordon Cooper was launched in spacecraft Faith 7 on 15 May 1963 atop the Mercury 9 rocket, and he went on to achieve twenty-two orbits in a flight lasting 34 hours 20 minutes. As in the case of all the Mercury shots he was weightless for all but a few minutes of his flight. He ejected a 6-in. spherical beacon from his spacecraft and confirmed that he could clearly see its flashing light as it drifted away to be lost in space. Other experiments included some work on the guidance system for the forthcoming Apollo programme. Cooper had to control his re-entry manually, owing to a short circuit, but he splashed down successfully within four miles of the aircraft carrier awaiting him. It is said that the total Project Mercury programme, when it came to an end with Mercury 9, had cost more than £163 million.

In June the Russians sent up their second paired Vostok mission, which was particularly famous because it carried Valentina Tereshkova, the world's first woman to venture into space. Valeri Bykovsky was first away in Vostok 5 on 14 June, followed two days later by Valentina in Vostok 6. Bykovsky set up a record 119 hours 6 minutes (nearly five days) in eighty-one orbits, while

The cabin of Voskhod 2. (*Photo: Novosti Press Agency*)

Valentina Tereshkova achieved forty-eight orbits in 70 hours 50 minutes. She suffered a little from disorientation and space sickness but came to no harm. She married cosmonaut Nikolayev five months afterwards, and a baby daughter born later to the couple was perfectly normal; this did much to dispel fears of damage by radiation to women in space.

The excitement generated by Valentina Tereshkova's flight heralded a lull in both Soviet and American space activity. Both the Mercury and Vostok programmes had come to an end. Nearly two years were to elapse before the Americans attempted another manned flight in Gemini 3, but the Gemini spacecraft were much more advanced than Mercury, being twice as heavy and much more versatile. Above all, each spacecraft, as indicated by the name Gemini (the Latin for 'twins'), was to have a crew of two astronauts. The Russians, of course, knew all about the Gemini plans, and it was probably because of this that they decided to mount the two Voskhod missions–the first with three cosmonauts and the second with two–before Gemini could begin.

The Russians were reluctant to release pictures of the Voskhod spacecraft, probably because they used the basic Vostok craft, lashed up somewhat precariously to carry the extra crew members. It is said that in Voskhod 1 there was so little room that the cosmonauts were required to fly without spacesuits. The crew, Vladimir Komarov, the pilot, Konstantin Feoktistov, a scientist, and Boris Yegorov, a doctor, were launched on 12 October 1964 and completed sixteen orbits in 24 hours 17 minutes. The doctor was able to watch at close quarters his companions' reactions to the flight.

The First Spacewalk

The Voskhod 2 mission starting on 18 March 1965 was probably even more significant. Cosmonauts Pavel Belyayev and Alexei Leonov went higher than any previous manned flight, reaching an apogee of 308 miles. They made seventeen orbits and the flight lasted 26 hours 2 minutes. It was Leonov, however, who really made history on this mission by taking the first spacewalk. He was outside the capsule for about ten minutes, attached to it by a lifeline, and his movements were monitored by TV. On their sixteenth orbit the automatic re-entry system failed and Belyayev had to fly the craft manually back to earth. They came down in a cushion of deep snow and it was several hours before searching helicopters found them, but all was well.

Not to allow themselves to fall too far behind, the Americans decided that preparations should be made for a similar spacewalk early in the Gemini programme, although it had been intended that all the astronaut should do was open the hatch and put his head and shoulders outside. Leonov's brave achievement had proved that such a feat was not particularly dangerous. But no more Russians were to go into space for a period of two years. During 1965 and 1966 they rested on their well-earned laurels, while America got the Gemini programme going extremely successfully and quickly, putting another twenty astronauts into space during the period.

The Gemini spacecraft consisted of two main sections, the re-entry module and an adapter module. The crew compartment, with 55 cu. ft of space, was in the re-entry module and had side-by-side ejection seats. There were sixteen thrust rockets for re-entry control and most of the systems were housed outside the pressure cell, making more room for the crew. The adapter module connected the re-entry capsule to the launcher rocket and contained the life-support and electrical systems. British-developed fuel cells were used for the first time to develop electrical power, and as a spin-off benefit these produced a by-product—a pint of drinking water every hour. Another sixteen thrust rockets mounted on the adapter module gave the craft altitude and manoeuvring control. The Gemini flights were launched by Titan 2 rockets and, in conjunction with the final five shots, Agena rockets were placed in orbit at the same time to act as docking targets.

Gemini 3 was the first manned flight of the series. Virgil Grissom and John Young were launched on 23 March 1965 and made three orbits in a 4 hour 53 minute flight. They took with them a 50-lb miniaturized computer with which Grissom was able to calculate a change in his orbit. It was the computer which failed on the Gemini 4 flight and the crew had to revert to making a manually controlled re-entry. James McDivitt and Edward White were the astronauts on this mission, which was launched on 3 June 1965 and achieved sixty-two orbits in four days. White completed the long awaited first American spacewalk, manoeuvring himself around for twenty-one minutes by bursts from an oxygen-powered space gun. During the manual re-entry McDivitt was late firing his retro-rockets, and as a result he and White came down forty miles from their recovery vessel.

Astronaut White sets his camera while spacewalking outside Gemini 4. (*Photo: NASA*)

The Gemini 5 mission was to be a long one, designed to prove that men could survive weightlessness long enough to get to the moon, pay a short visit to the surface and return. Gordon Cooper and Charles Conrad were launched on 21 August and achieved 120 orbits in 7 days 22 hours 56 minutes. The Gemini 6 mission, planned for October, was postponed when the Agena rocket it was to use as a target was lost, so Gemini 7 was the next away on 4 December and this eventually served as a target for Gemini 6. Frank Borman and James Lovell were the astronauts aboard Gemini 7 and they stayed up for nearly two weeks, achieving 206 orbits. The delayed Gemini 6 mission finally got away on 15 December and lasted just over a day, during which Walter Schirra and Thomas Stafford brought it to within 6 ft of the other spacecraft.

Docking in Space

The first space docking was achieved by the crew of Gemini 8 when they linked up their spacecraft with an Agena target which had been launched 101 minutes ahead of them. Astronauts Neil Armstrong and David Scott went into orbit on 16 March 1966 and, unfortunately, soon after the successful docking operation a faulty thruster rocket threw them out of control. This was the first real space emergency, and they managed to escape by firing their retro-rockets after only six orbits and survived an emergency splashdown two days earlier than intended. News media all over the world reported the details of this adventure in space, but most failed to appreciate the significance of the docking–the first major advancement in space technology demonstrated by the Americans ahead of the Soviet Union.

Somehow Gemini 9 was fated with bad luck. The original crew was killed in a jet fighter accident. Then the Agena target was lost and a reserve target got away all right, but the Gemini mission aborted because it was just too late to fit into its window (that is, its launching-time slot). Eventually Thomas Stafford and Eugene Cernan went into orbit on 3 June, and later Cernan managed a two-hour spacewalk. In just over three days they made forty-five orbits, and the very successful recovery was made from a splashdown less than half a mile off target. On 18 July John Young and Michael Collins went off in Gemini 10 for a three-day mission and docked easily with their Agena target rocket. They fired its rocket engine to place them into a higher orbit, and later homed on to another Agena which had been left behind by Gemini 8 so that Collins could spacewalk out to it and retrieve a package which had been collecting space dust for four months.

The next crew up were Charles Conrad and Richard Gordon in Gemini 11 on 12 September. They went straight up and rendezvoused with their Agena target while still on their first orbit. Gordon spacewalked for forty-four minutes and later the spacecraft was spun to produce an artificial gravity. Re-entry was this time completely automatic. The last Gemini shot, no. 12, took place on 11 November with astronauts James Lovell and Edwin Aldrin. Aldrin spacewalked no less than three times during the flight and was outside the capsule for a total of five and a half hours. They, too, managed to create a gravitational force by spinning the capsule, and their re-entry was automatic. The Gemini project had cost well over £500 million at its conclusion, but it did achieve ten flights without any casualties.

As 1966 came to an end, both the United States and Russia were poised to launch their respective Apollo and Soyuz manned-flight programmes on an incredulous world. Vladimir Komarov was first away in Soyuz 1 which was launched on 23 April 1967. It is thought his spacecraft may have suffered difficulties because re-entry began ahead of schedule on the eighteenth orbit. All was not well during the return to earth; the parachute lines supporting the spacecraft became tangled and Komarov was killed in the resulting crash. Remarkably, perhaps, this was the first flight fatality in the first six years of space exploration.

Apollo started in 1964 when a command module (CM) was placed unmanned into orbit. An eighteen-month delay in the start of manned flights followed the electrical fire on the launch pad in which astronauts Grissom, White and Chaffee lost their lives. The first unmanned test of the Apollo and its Saturn 5 launcher took place in November 1967, and Apollo 7 became the first manned flight when Walter Schirra, Donn Eisele and Walter Cunningham were launched on 11 October 1968. They were up for nearly eleven days and completed 163 orbits, during which they checked out the command and service modules and simulated the extraction of a lunar module (LM), which on this mission was not actually carried.

Soyuz 2, launched on 25 October, was an unmanned target for Soyuz 3, which, with cosmonaut Giorgi Beregovoi aboard, was launched the following day. An automatic approach for docking was made, followed by a manual approach, but Beregovoi never actually docked Soyuz 3 to Soyuz 2. His sixty-four-orbit flight lasted 94 hours 51 minutes.

Frank Borman, James Lovell and William Anders became, at Christmas 1968, the first men to fly right round the moon. Their Apollo 8 mission began on 21 December when they went thundering out into space atop a 3,000-ton Saturn 5 rocket. They spent twenty hours going ten times round the moon taking pictures and filming, and it was on Christmas morning that Borman thrilled the world by reading an extract from the Book of Genesis over the radio. They splashed down in the Pacific just eleven seconds ahead of schedule.

The Russians achieved their first manned docking in January 1969. Soyuz 4, with cosmonaut Vladimir Shatalov, was launched on 14 January, and Boris Volynov, Yevgeny Khrunov and Alexei Yeliseyev went off in Soyuz 5 the following day. The two spacecraft were brought to within 350 ft of one another automatically, but the actual docking was manual, steered by Shatalov.

Russell Schweikart leaving the Apollo 9 command module for extravehicular activities. (*Photo: NASA*)

Khrunov and Yeliseyev transferred to Soyuz 4 and the two craft undocked after four hours. Soyuz 4 landed after 71 hours 14 minutes and Soyuz 5, with Volynov now alone, landed after 72 hours 46 minutes in space.

The first of the Apollo manned flights carrying a lunar module began on 3 March 1969 when James McDivitt, David Scott and Russell Schweickart went up in Apollo 9. They had to separate the command module from the S4B third-stage rocket after establishment in orbit, then turn the CM round and dock on to the LM, housed in the S4B, and withdraw it. McDivitt and Schweickart went through the interconnecting tunnel into the LM, test-fired its rocket engine and later separated from the CM, going out 113 miles before jettisoning the descent stage and docking the ascent stage alone back on to the CM. During ten days they made 151 orbits of the earth. All the elaborate equipment for the ultimate moon landing had been checked out and had been found to work perfectly.

A Giant Leap for Mankind

Apollo 10 was to be the final rehearsal before man stepped on to the moon. Thomas Stafford, Eugene Cernan and John Young were launched on 18 May and their flight plan was similar to that being worked out for Apollo 11. While Young in the CM remained in lunar orbit, the two other astronauts took the LM down twice to within nine miles of the lunar surface. Something nearly went wrong when they finally jettisoned their descent stage, the ascent stage going into a violent pitching motion, but despite this, docking was successful. Altogether eight hours had been spent away from the CM. Some remarkable TV pictures were obtained on this flight.

It was Apollo 11, however, launched only two months later on 16 July, that was to be one of the most historic missions of all time. Neil Armstrong, Edwin Aldrin and Michael Collins went into lunar orbit on Saturday 19 July. Collins remained in the CM *Columbia* and Armstrong and Aldrin took the LM *Eagle* down towards the moon. Armstrong manually controlled the landing onto an area of the moon known as the Sea of Tranquillity and told Mission Control back at Houston 'The Eagle has landed.' The time was 2117 hours BST on 20 July. At 0356 hours the following day Armstrong became the first man to step on to the surface of the moon, making his famous remark, 'That's one small step for a man; one giant leap for Mankind.' The two astronauts erected a US flag and tried walking in the strange conditions of one-sixth gravity. They unveiled a plaque, received a telephone call from President Nixon, collected soil samples and left behind a scientific package. The ascent and docking with *Columbia* and the return journey were uneventful, and splashdown on 24 July was only thirty seconds later than predicted. These three lucky astronauts had visited a new land that no earlier adventurer had even had the opportunity to discover; remote from the earth on a heavenly body that man had longed to explore from the beginning of time.

Before the next Apollo mission it was the turn of the Russians to send up three spacecraft and to have them all in orbit at the same time. They were Soyuz 6, 7 and 8. The first away, on 11 October 1969, was Soyuz 6, with cos-

Charles Conrad and Alan Bean, the Apollo 12 crew, on the moon; here the photographer is reflected in his companion's visor, worn to counteract the strength of the sun's rays on the moon. (*Photo: NASA*)

monauts Georgi Shonin and Valeri Kubasov as crew. Soyuz 7, a day later, carried three–Anatoli Filipchenko, Viktor Gorbatko and Vladislav Volkov. Finally, Soyuz 8 went off on 13 October with Vladimir Shatalov and Alexei Yeliseyev. No attempt was made at docking one craft to another, but the Russians claimed that docking was no part of the plan for this mission. Soyuz 6 was famous for the successful experiments in welding metal structures together, which took place in its workshop in preparation for the assembly of space stations in space. All three craft returned after eighty orbits and about 118 hours had been completed.

The second lunar landing trip began on 14 November 1969, not without excitement. The Saturn 5 rocket was struck by lightning on the pad and after lift-off Mission Control briefly lost contact with Apollo 12 and its crew, Charles Conrad, Richard Gordon and Alan Bean. The mission went ahead, however, and the lunar module *Intrepid* touched down as planned, only 600 ft from the unmanned Surveyor 3 spacecraft which had soft-landed in the Ocean of Storms region in April 1967. Conrad and Bean stayed on the moon thirty-one and a half hours and walked out on the surface twice, collecting soil and rock samples and placing a package of scientific instruments in position. They also rescued the TV camera from Surveyor 3. The total mission lasted ten days and the only real snag was the accidental damage to the colour TV camera in *Intrepid* which had spoiled any chance of watching their activities from earth.

The superstitious will say that it was inevitable that Apollo 13 would have problems. It very nearly came to disaster with an explosion in the service module when the spacecraft was 205,000 miles from earth. The first problem, before launching, was a warning of possible infection of the crew from German measles, as a result of which the reserve command pilot, Jack Swigert, replaced a colleague. Jim Lovell, Fred Haise and Swigert were launched on 11 April 1970, and inaccuracies in the burn time of the rockets made this a far from perfect launch. When, after fifty-five hours of the flight, an explosion occurred, the mission was inevitably aborted, and all efforts were then made to recover the crew. The spacecraft had to pass behind the moon and a real-life science fiction story began to unfold. Possible damage to the heat shield was the final fear; but the sight of three parachutes lowering Apollo 13 gently towards the sea was one of the most heartening and dramatic sights ever to have been shown live on the world's television screens.

After a long break, Soyuz 9 was the next to go, on 1 June 1970. Cosmonauts Andrian Nikolayev and Vitali Sevatyanov were the first men to be launched at night, and their mission was remarkable as a new long-duration record. They spent nearly eighteen days in space and suffered some rather uncomfortable physical effects from their prolonged weightlessness when they landed. Their final descent back to earth was the first ever televised by the Russians.

Apollo 12 splashdown. (*Photo: NASA*)

Another long gap was to occur before Apollo 14 set off on 31 January 1971, en route for the third moon landing. The crew were veteran commander Alan Shepard, CM pilot Stuart Roosa and LM pilot Edgar Mitchell. The launch was delayed for forty minutes to avoid further trouble from thunderstorms such as had beset Apollo 12, and a serious problem occurred when Roosa tried to make the docking manœuvre with the lunar module when 7,200 miles from earth. The lunar landing of the LM *Antares* went ahead satisfactorily, however, and the touchdown on 5 February was only 87 ft from target. During two EVAs (periods of extra-vehicular activity) during which they spent a total of nine and a half hours on the moon, Shepard and Mitchell became quite tired and fell behind schedule in their tasks, especially when they tried to climb to the rim of Cone Crater. Mission Control back on earth monitored Shepard's heart-beat at 150, and finally the two explorers were told to turn back without reaching their goal. The return to the command module and the journey back to earth were routine, and the crew were the last to be required to spend three weeks in quarantine after their return.

The First Space Station

In the spring of 1971 the world was poised ready for another major Soviet advance in space technology–the first scientific space station in near-terrestrial space, called Salyut. Plans for the American Skylab were not to reach fruition for another two years. Salyut was designed to stay in the earth's orbit and to be visited by Soyuz spacecraft sent up at intervals from the USSR. The Soyuz craft, when docked, completed the Salyut space station system, which as a whole then weighed about 18 tons. Inside, the cosmonauts and their equipment were housed in a chamber with roughly 15-ft sides. Originally three crewmen were to be carried, but after the disaster to Soyuz 11 this was reduced to two.

Salyut 1 thundered out into space on 19 April, unmanned and under remote control. Because three-man Soyuz vehicles had to be got up to it–which must have been close to the upper weight limit for the Soviet launcher rockets–Salyut was established in a low orbit and needed rocket boost firings to maintain its orbit and prevent premature re-entry. Four days later Vladimir Shatalov, Alexei Yeliseyev and Nikolai Rukavishnikov left earth in Soyuz 10 and the rendezvous with Salyut was carried out automatically, bringing it to within 600 ft. Shatalov then took over manually and docked during Soyuz 10's twelfth orbit. There is some mystery still about the cosmonauts' failure actually to enter the space station, although it was reported that Rukavishnikov became ill during weightlessness. They were docked to Salyut for five and a half hours, then completed thirty orbits and returned to earth.

The ill-fated Soyuz 11 was launched on 6 June carrying Georgi Dobrovolsky, Vladislav Volkov and Victor Patsayev. Once again the approach to Salyut was automatic to 328 ft, after which the crew completed the docking. Preparations were made in Salyut to 'continue comprehensive scientific and technical studies in joint flight' with the orbital scientific station, and the cosmonauts achieved a record of nearly twenty-four days in space. On 30 June, after undocking, a perfectly normal firing of the re-entry braking rocket was completed, but

The Salyut orbital station in the workshop. (*Photo: Novosti Press Agency*)

communication with the crew was lost. Re-entry and the release of the parachutes were automatic, but a helicopter crew found the cosmonauts all dead
inside their capsule. Later it was revealed that a faulty valve had caused a fatal
decompression in the re-entry vehicle.

By July 1971 the Apollo programme was drawing to a close, with just three
more moon landings to go. All three were incredibly successful. Apollo 15
blasted off from Cape Canaveral on 26 July, carrying David Scott, Alfred
Worden and James Irwin. Their colossal Saturn 5 rocket, the most powerful
yet launched, produced 3,500 tons of thrust. One or two things went wrong;
there was a warning of a short circuit, broken glass on an altimeter in the
lunar module *Falcon* and a trace of a water leak, but the lunar landing was
authorized by Mission Control and took place on 30 July a few hundred feet
from the planned position in a valley near Hadley Rille. Scott and Irwin had
eighteen and a half hours on the surface in the course of three EVAs. They
were the first to use a lunar rover, an electrically-driven wheeled vehicle, and
were said to be delighted with it though it was like riding a 'real bucking
bronco'. Beautiful TV pictures of the 1,200-ft deep chasm, Hadley Rille, two
and a half miles from the *Falcon*, were transmitted back to earth from the
lunar rover.

On the second EVA they found a piece of crystal rock, believed to be part
of the original moon which is, of course, normally covered with a layer of
space dust, and this became famous as the 'Genesis Rock'. The rover, which
had carried them faithfully a total of seventeen and a half miles, was left behind

on the moon and was used to televise by remote control their lift-off from the surface. There was doubt about the sealing of the hatch of the CM *Endeavour*, which delayed the jettison of *Falcon* for one orbit; then Worden made a nineteen-minute spacewalk to recover film from a scientific instrument bay, and finally a successful splashdown was made despite the failure of one of the three recovery parachutes to open. Scott, Irwin and Worden had been in space for just over twelve days, two days longer than any previous Apollo mission.

Apollo 16 did not blast off until 16 April the following year and the mission lasted a day less. The crew, John Young, Thomas Mattingly and Charles Duke, had a number of snags to clear on the way up but the big problem came after the LM *Orion* had separated from the CM *Casper* and Mattingly announced his doubt that *Casper* could be placed in its required circular waiting orbit. Emergency redocking was considered and premature return to earth was for a time quite likely, but the problem was resolved and *Orion* went on, six hours late, to touch down on the Cayley Plains of the Descartes landing site. Young and Duke ended up only 10 ft from a deep crater. During their first EVA Young drove the lunar rover round in circles as on a skid pan to check out wheel adhesion, and in the second they drove out two and a half miles to Stone Mountain. A TV camera was set up which could be operated remotely by Mission Control to enable geologists to make their own independent inspection of rocks and other features. In the third EVA the astronauts explored North Ray Crater and competed with one another to see who could jump the highest under the conditions of one-sixth gravity. Lift-off and redocking were uneventful, but a snag developed in *Orion* which made it necessary to leave it in lunar orbit instead of crashing it back on to the moon's surface. The journey home ended with full deployment of the parachutes and the crew was the first to return without any trouble from irregular pulse rate.

After all the experience that had been gained it was fitting perhaps that Apollo 17, the final moon-landing mission, should be rated the most successful of them all. But Eugene Cernan, Ronald Evans and Harrison Schmitt were all set to go on 6 December 1972 when the countdown came to an abrupt halt thirty seconds before blast-off. Finally, 2 hours 40 minutes late, they got away just in time to achieve the planned landing on the edge of the Sea of Serenity. There was a problem when three of the twelve hatches failed to fasten during the docking manoeuvre, but this was resolved. The LM *Challenger* separated from the CM *America* on the twelfth lunar orbit, and Cernan and Schmitt went down to a landing between the Taurus Mountains and the Littrow Crater. They set up the fifth ALSEP experiment and, despite the accidental loss of a 'mudguard', drove their lunar rover out to Steno Crater to collect samples. In their second EVA they drove more than four miles to the foot of the mountains and on the way back, at Crater Shorty, Cernan disturbed the celebrated 'orange soil', thought at first to have been volcanic but later proved to be orange-coloured glass beads formed by meteor impact. During the third EVA they found some huge boulders which provided remarkable TV pictures.

A plaque, signed by President Nixon and all three astronauts, was left behind on the moon; it read: 'Here Man completed his first exploration of the Moon,

December 1972. May the spirit of peace in which we came be reflected in the lives of all Mankind.' Their time on the surface was practically seventy-five hours. Docking back on the CM *America* was a little troublesome and took twenty minutes, and the crew spent two more days in orbit mapping the far side of the moon. Finally a copybook splashdown was made only four miles from the recovery ship. The mission had lasted some twelve and a half days. During the total Apollo programme nearly 850 lb of lunar material was brought back to earth, and during the course of the missions it was established that there is a sizeable flow of heat from the lunar interior, indicating that the core, 620 miles deep, is partially molten rock. Scientists now tend to believe that the moon came originally from outer space and was captured by the earth's gravitational field. Total costs of Apollo are put at some £10,000 million.

With the Apollo programme virtually completed, the United States got down to the job of catching up with the USSR by putting the Skylab space station into orbit around the earth. On 14 May 1973, the unmanned Skylab Workshop blasted off atop a mighty Saturn 5 rocket, but serious vibrations which occurred during the launching ripped away one of the solar wing panels and caused the other to jam partially open. The thermal shield was also lost and temperatures within the laboratory began to climb. The launch of the first crew, Charles Conrad, Joseph Kerwin and Paul Weitz, was postponed for five days, but they finally got away on 25 May using a Saturn 1B launcher. Docking with Skylab for a time seemed impossible, but it was achieved and Conrad and Kerwin, in an eight-hour spacewalk, managed to lever the reluctant 'wing' into place and erect a 24-ft 'sunshade' to protect the workshop. Their pioneering work ensured an adequate supply of electricity and salvaged practically the whole Skylab programme from what otherwise could have been a com-

Gene Cernan test-drives the lunar rover vehicle at the Taurus-Littrow landing site on the moon. (*Photo: NASA/IPS*)

pletely abortive mission. Their splashdown took place on 22 June and they left Skylab still in orbit to await further visitors.

Skylab 3, the second manned mission, went off on 28 July. A faulty thruster caused trouble but a docking with Skylab was easily achieved. The crew, Alan Bean, Owen Garriott and Jack Lousma, all suffered from space sickness. A gas leak in another thruster made necessary the preparation of a rescue mission, but in the end it was not needed. In the course of an EVA another parasol sunshade was erected, and the crew were then able to work for long periods in the laboratory. They stayed in orbit for fifty-nine days and on splashdown found themselves upside-down in their capsule in a very rough sea off San Diego. Skylab 4 eventually got away on 16 November 1973 carrying Gerald Carr, Edward Gibson and William Pogue, their aim being to stay in orbit for eighty-four days. One of their tasks was to photograph the comet Kahoutek, but they also settled down to a steady routine of scientific investigations. EVAs accounted for more than three days in space. When they undocked they were completing their 1,213th orbit and the Skylab itself was on its 3,898th. Skylab was left behind dead and depressurized by this last crew. All three were in much better physical shape on splashdown than their predecessors, thanks to the one and a half hour programme of exercises they had undertaken each day.

Meanwhile the Russians had launched Soyuz 12 on 27 September, carrying Vasili Lazarev and Oleg Makarov, to test structural modifications and improved systems designed to overcome the circumstances of the Soyuz 11 disaster. They were in space for nearly forty-eight hours. In fact Soyuz 13 was in orbit at one and the same time as Skylab 4, having been launched on 18 December. However, no contact was possible since they had different radio frequencies. It may be that cosmonauts Pyotr Klimuk and Valentin Lebedev were supposed to have docked with a Salyut space station (which became known as Cosmos 613); but officially they continued work to develop a 'universal spaceship' and re-entered the earth's atmosphere on 26 December. Salyut 3 went into orbit on 25 June 1974 and Soyuz 14 and Soyuz 15 stood by to dock with it. Cosmonauts Pavel Popovich and Yuri Artyukhin followed it up in Soyuz 14 on 3 July, caught it up twenty-six hours later, and successfully docked with it. Their work included watching for mineral deposits and possibly a military reconnaissance function, and they returned to earth on the sixteenth day. Soyuz 15, launched on 26 August and crewed by Gennady Sarafanov and Lev Demin, was a failure. After thirty-six orbits it had to make an emergency re-entry and never achieved a docking with Salyut.

The Apollo-Soyuz Link-up in Space

Soyuz 16 was a dress rehearsal for the Apollo-Soyuz test project in which US and Soviet spacecraft were to link up in orbit. Cosmonauts Anatoli Filipchenko and Nikolai Rukavishnikov were launched on 2 December and proceeded to make a number of simulated docking runs with an 'imitating ring' target. After a routine landing on 8 December it was announced that the whole complex of new systems had been checked out and no further rehearsals for the ASTP were required. The Russians then put up their Salyut 4 space station on 26 December, but it was not until 10 January 1975 that cosmonauts Alexei Gubarev and Georgii Grechko were sent up in Soyuz 17 for docking to take place on 12 January. Scientific work and, no doubt, military reconnaissance occupied them for thirty days until their return on 9 February, after the longest Soviet space flight.

Another ferry flight was attempted on 5 April when cosmonauts Vasili Lazarev and Oleg Makarov left earth in what should have been the Soyuz 18 mission. However their third-stage rocket developed a fault and their space-craft was promptly recovered, successfully. Another Soyuz replaced it and re-ceived the designation Soyuz 18. This was to be the long expected sixty-day mission. In fact cosmonauts Pyotr Klimuk and Vitali Sevastyanov stayed up for sixty-three days; they were launched on 24 May and docked with Salyut 4 two days later. They landed back successfully on 26 July, five days after the Apollo-Soyuz test project was all over.

The ASTP, conceived originally in 1972 as a joint peaceful exploration of outer space and signed by President Nixon and Prime Minister Kosygin, was to be the last manned space mission of the 1970s launched by the United States and the last of Russia's Soyuz flights for some while. Preparations lasted three years, with technicians visiting each other's countries, to ensure that the critical

Alexei Leonov and Valery Kubasov about to board Soyuz 19 for the Apollo-Soyuz link-up. (*Photo: Novosti Press Agency*)

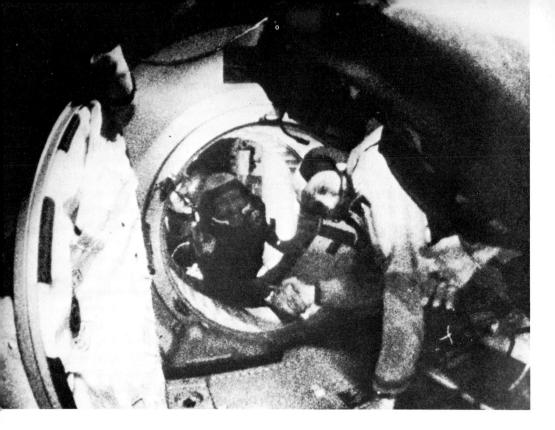

A historic handshake between the commanders of the joint US–Soviet space mission following the link-up of the Apollo and Soyuz spaceships. (*Photo: NASA*)

docking of a Soyuz with an Apollo could proceed without difficulty. Not the least of the problems to be overcome was that of language. In the event, both Soyuz 19 and Apollo 18 made faultless lift-offs from their respective launch pads on 15 July 1975 and came smoothly together on 17 July. The Russian crew were Alexei Leonov, the first spacewalker, and Valeri Kubashov, and the Americans were Thomas Stafford, Vance Brand and Donald Slayton. The ensuing handshakes in space were duly recorded by TV cameras. Soyuz 19 returned to earth after six days in orbit on 21 July, while Apollo stayed on until 24 July to complete a scientific programme. Both re-entries were completely successful.

Will the Apollo–Soyuz link-up point the way to greater unity among the nations of the world? There is precious little sign of this happening so far. But one dream of protagonists of space exploration has always been the creation of a spirit of comradeship among all races, who, in the context of space, see themselves as members of an earth-based brotherhood, with their potential adversaries beyond the confines of this planet. If East can meet West and work together as successfully as they did in the ASTP, perhaps the realization of this utopia is yet within the realms of possibility.

Only the Russians have continued manned spaceflight activity since the ASTP link-up in 1975. Their Salyut 5 space station was sent up on 22 June

1976 and was occupied by two crews for a total of 65 days before it was destroyed when it re-entered the Earth's atmosphere on 8 August 1977 over the Pacific Ocean. Soyuz 21 was launched on 6 July and a day later docked with Salyut 5. Unfortunately the full flight was not completed, due it is said to fumes from the environmental system, and Soyuz 21 returned after 48 days linked to the space station. Soyuz 24 was the second to go and with Victor Gorbatko and Lt Col. Yuri Glazkov as crew was launched on 7 February 1977 and docked a day later. The crew's first job was to recondition the environmental system. Some scientific experiments were performed but the flight was not a long one and Soyuz 24 was brought back to Earth on 25 February.

Meanwhile Soyuz 22, which was launched on 15 September 1976 with Valery Bykovsky and Vladimir Aksenov as crew, is thought to have been the first manned spy satellite and spent a lot of time watching a large scale NATO exercise. Soyuz 22 was up for nearly eight days.

Following the demise of Salyut 5, the next Soviet space station, Salyut 6, was launched unmanned on 20 September 1977. Soyuz 25 was the first to try to dock with it, and was launched on 9 October with Lt Col. Vladimir Kovalonok and Valeri Ryumin as crew, but it returned after two days. Soyuz 26 and Soyuz 27, however, were soon to make history as the first double docking. The crews exchanged spacecraft for their returns to Earth. Soyuz 26 with Yuri Romanenko and Georgi Grechko set a new duration record of 96 days from its launch on 10 December 1977. Soyuz 27 was initially crewed by Vladimir Dzhanibekov and Oleg Makarov and was in orbit for six days from 10 January 1978.

Soyuz 28, launched on 2 March 1978, had the first 'international' crew with Alexei Gubarev as Commander and a Czech, Vladimir Remek, as his colleague. They docked with Salyut 6 and stayed in orbit for nearly eight days, meeting the Soyuz 26 crew on their arrival. Soyuz 29 was launched on 15 June and docked with Salyut 6 two days later. It carried Vladimir Kovalyonok and Alexander Ivanchenkov, who later made news with a spacewalk of 2 hours 5 min on 29 July to test a new spacesuit outside the space station. They had previously unloaded supplies from two Progress unmanned supply ships which had been sent up to them.

A third 'international' crew was Valery Bykovsky and Sigmund Jähn, an East German, aboard Soyuz 31 launched on 26 August. They spent seven days at the space station with Ivanchenkov and Kovalyonok (who remained on board) and returned on Soyuz 29. By 20 September the original Soyuz 29 cosmonauts had exceeded the 96-day record set up by the Soyuz 26 crew earlier in the year. A few days earlier they had achieved another 'first' when they backed off Soyuz 31 from the space station and redocked it at another docking port. This was the craft they used to return to earth, after 140 days in orbit, on 2 November 1978.

The space station, Salyut 6, completed its first year in orbit on 29 September 1978, and in this time it was visited by no less than six manned spacecraft and two Progress supply ships. A third, Progress 4, arrived on 6 October.

The Russian Lunar Programme

While the Americans were striving to achieve their manned expeditions to the moon, the Russians had decided that they would not risk human life on such hazardous missions. Their lunar programme was designed to develop a fully automatic probe which would do all that the Apollo programme set out to achieve, scientific experiments, TV and photographic coverage and even the return of soil samples to earth. Was this space exploration in the true sense of the word? As a very significant part of the total story it is worthy of some outline of its achievements. The Russian work had begun with Lunik 1 in 1959 and by the end of that year Lunik 3 had provided the first pictures of the rear face of the moon. Then came a gap of three years, broken on 2 April 1963 by Luna 4 which missed the Moon by 6,000 miles. Luna 5, 7 and 8, all in 1965, crashed rather unsuccessfully on to the lunar surface, while things went badly wrong with Luna 6 which missed it by 100,000 miles.

By the end of January 1966, however, Soviet luck began to change and Luna 9 placed the first man-made object reasonably gently on to the moon. The capsule had a small TV camera, which began to send still pictures back to earth. With this success behind them, the Russians put three satellites, Luna 10, 11 and 12, into lunar orbit in March, August and October 1966, and the last of these sent back some remarkable TV pictures of the craters on the moon. Luna 13 was a triumph for the Soviet programme. After its landing in the Ocean of Storms in December, extensible arms dug up lunar soil and the radioactive level on the surface proved to be very small.

Luna 13 on the moon. (*Photo: Novosti Press Agency*)

Russia's Zond probes should have led to cosmonauts circumnavigating the moon; in fact, some tortoises in Zond 5 did just this in 1968, but Proton launcher mishaps reported in January, April and June 1969 probably confirmed that the anticipated manned missions would have been too dangerous. Luna 15 in July 1969 coincided with America's Apollo 11 mission which put the first men on the moon. It crashed to destruction in the Sea of Crises, but had Apollo 11 failed and Luna 15 been successful the public might have been excused if they had reacted unfavourably to further manned flights. Luna 16 in September 1970 drilled holes in the moon and brought back 4 oz of soil samples – but the advantages of a manned mission were readily apparent because the Apollo 11 astronauts brought back 46 lb.

Luna 17, however, was to be another Soviet spectacular. Launched on 10 November 1970, it soft-landed in the Sea of Rains and disgorged an eight-wheel robot vehicle called Lunokhod 1. This was controlled by TV/radio link with the USSR and it operated from time to time on the surface for nearly a year, covering a distance of almost 35,000 ft by October 1971. It had TV relay facilities and was largely engaged on soil analysis.

Luna 18, launched on 2 September 1971, was fated to crash-land in the Sea of Fertility; the Russians had had high hopes of it being another soil-sampler. This was quickly followed by Luna 19, which went into lunar orbit and conducted useful experiments on radiation. Luna 20 made a perfect lift-off on 14 February 1972, and later a landing was made successfully between the Sea of Fertility and the Sea of Crises and a core sample was brought back to earth.

On 8 January 1973, the Russians launched Luna 21, carrying their second lunar rover, and a successful touchdown was made in the Sea of Serenity. Lunokhod 2 was heavier than the first one, and was said to be twice as fast. After each lunar night it was reactivated by remote control from earth, and by the time it was shut down on 3 June it had travelled a total of twenty-three miles on the lunar surface. The Russian exploration of the moon was concluded by Luna 22, launched into lunar orbit on 29 May 1974, and by Luna 23 which was launched on 28 October 1974, only to crash-land in the Sea of Crises on 6 November. Luna 23 had been intended to obtain a further soil sample.

The Future and Assessment of the Past

Alongside all their lunar and earth-orbiting activity, both the United States and Russia were looking out beyond near-terrestrial space to the other planets of the solar system. Mars and Venus have been the primary targets, although Jupiter and Mercury have also received attention. In terms of exploration, the probes that have gone off on these missions represent very early and relatively crude attempts to establish the nature of these neighbouring worlds. Man, no doubt, will want in time to follow them; but the idea of manned flights to other planets of our solar system remains a dream unlikely to be realized for many years. The difficulty, of course, is in the recovery of the explorers and the tremendous length of time such journeys could take, which creates enormous problems of provisioning and life support. Nevertheless, the unmanned probes are certainly charting the way into deep space and sending back to earth masses of scientific information.

What of the future? Russia has the stage for a few years to match US orbital experience and to develop the huge modular space station which is the goal of Russian long-term space planning. The United States looks forward to the first launch of the Space Shuttle in the early 1980s.

What has been achieved in the first twenty years of space flight? Against a background of the continuous development of the earth satellite programmes, in which Russia has launched far more vehicles than the United States and in which many other nations of the world are now participating, as much for international prestige as for pure scientific knowledge, the manned satellite and lunar programmes have persisted throughout the 1960s and the first half of the 1970s. But there has followed a lull in manned space flight activity. International tension has perhaps eased enough to allow East and West to pause in their competition, and to come together to chart the course of further exploration. The Americans have been to the moon, the Russians have not. But the Russians have put sophisticated machinery on the moon and have achieved almost as much as the Americans, without risk to human life. Both the United States and the Soviet Union have launched, and later manned, earth-orbiting space stations, and the Americans have been able to link up with and dock their craft against a Russian space craft with the result that American astronauts and Soviet cosmonauts were seen, in relayed colour television, shaking hands in space.

Further development of the US Skylab and Soviet Salyut space stations is leading to earth-orbiting laboratories like the European Spacelab, which should be operational in the early 1980s. Access to Spacelab will be by way of the US Space Shuttle which will be launched vertically like a rocket, will orbit as a spaceship and will land back on earth like an aeroplane, ready for re-use on another mission. It is expected that such a system will enable manned space exploration to continue at reduced cost and with much less wastage.

One day, perhaps, the twenty-first century space colony will exist as foreseen by artists – a huge structure, twenty miles long and four miles in diameter, which will be provided with the same gravity as on earth and even its own internal weather conditions.

Though man has begun the conquest of the universe, he has not yet conquered the infirmities of his own body. Thousands of years ago, in Egypt and Babylon, the ancients gave their attention to the heavens, worked out ideas about the movement of the stars (some of which have stood the test of time), and laid the foundations for those astonishing adventures that had their climax in the landing on the moon. But it was then also that they turned to the conquest of disease. To understand what medicine has achieved in our time, we must go back to the beginning.

4

The Development of Modern Medicine

Summary of Chapter

The Roots of Medicine

In the Western world, ideas about medicine derive from those of Ancient Greece rather than from the magical practices of primitive tribes. No rational theory or treatment is possible so long as disease and its cure are regarded as being supernatural in origin. The first suggestion of a natural or rational theory can be found in the doctrine of the four elements, ascribed to Thales of Miletus about 600 BC. A century later Empedocles of Sicily built this doctrine into a philosophy of medicine by suggesting that health depended on a balance of those four elements and that disease resulted when they were out of balance. His theory suggested the first system of medicine. The four elements, he argued – earth, air, fire and water – generated four qualities, and mingling of the four qualities produced four humours (a humour was thought to be a basic fluid in the body that influenced human health and character) – blood, phlegm, yellow bile, black bile. In the fourth century BC Hippocrates, a physician (or possibly a band of physicians) of Cos, a Greek island, developed the four humours into a humoral pathology (that is, a study of disease based on the humours), and this was a basis of reasoning on which both the theory and the practice of medicine could be founded and carried further.

Hippocratic teaching formed the ground plan of a number of writings ascribed to Galen, a Graeco-Roman physician born at Pergamos in AD 131. Galen's writings are of the greatest importance; it was through them that Greek theory and practice were assimilated, many centuries later, by medieval Europe. Greek medicine travelled by two separate channels – first, through monastic medicine, which is the name given to the medical practice of Byzantium and of small Christian communities scattered throughout Europe during the Dark Ages (roughly AD 476–768); the second channel was Arabian medicine, which branched off from the Byzantine. In AD 431 the Patriarch of Constantinople, Nestorius, fled with his followers to Mesopotamia after being accused of heresy. These Christians later settled in Persia, and in the seventh century they were swallowed up by the Moslem empire. The Moslems encouraged science and tolerated Christian physicians. Their Empire spread west into southern Spain, where they founded a number of centres of learning, of which Cordova became famous for its medical teaching.

In the ninth century these two branches of medicine – the monastic and the Arabian – were fused together to some extent in the school of Salerno, which was non-sectarian (that is to say, it was not confined to any religious faith) and international. Students from Salerno spread through western Europe and into Britain, bringing with them some knowledge of Arabian medicine. Teaching centres were set up in the universities of Padua and Bologna in Italy, at Montpellier in France, and at Oxford and Cambridge in Britain.

Medicine in northern Europe was now firmly in the hands of the Church, and it had become an educational discipline – something learned for its own sake – rather than a practical art to be applied at the bedsides of the sick. As

The laboratory of an alchemist in the sixteenth century. Mansell Collection.

Moslem power diminished, so Christians moved into southern Spain. Adventurous scholars searched in the old Moslem centres for the source of writings from Salerno, and with the help of Jews and Moslems they translated Arabic manuscripts. These manuscripts were themselves translations of Greek texts, and were full of errors, additions and emendations, so that the new Latin versions were not very much like the Greek originals. The Church did not favour new and creative thought, but its power grew steadily weaker during the fourteenth century. There was no longer much confidence in the authority of ancient teaching and texts, and as a result, in the fourteenth and fifteenth centuries quack doctors and weird theories abounded. This was the age of alchemy (a semi-magical chemistry that aimed to turn base metals into gold) and astrology (a system of predicting the future and casting horoscopes by observing the position of the planets, the moon and the stars); both of these are pseudo-sciences or false sciences that derived from Arabia, and strongly influenced the practice of medicine. The treatment of a disease, for example, might depend on the horoscope cast for a patient by an astrologer.

The Renaissance

In 1453, Christian Byzantium fell to the Ottoman Turks and Italy was flooded with refugees who brought with them many of the priceless manuscripts which had been stored in that city. Latin had been the language of the Middle Ages.

Scholars now flung aside the Latin texts and turned instead to writings in Greek. And so it was that, at last, physicians were able to examine the older texts of the great Greek philosophers – Hippocrates, Dioscorides, Aristotle and Galen. At once they discovered how full of errors were the versions used by their predecessors. The voyages pioneered by Prince Henry the Navigator, Sebastian Cabot and Christopher Columbus widened the horizons of Europeans; the invention of printing increased the scope of their reading. This was the beginning of the Renaissance, which brought not only a revival of classical learning and art, but also a new freedom of thought and a questioning of tradi-

An amputation, by an unknown artist. (*Photo: from an engraving in the Mansell Collection*)

tional teaching. So no sooner had the theories and practice of the ancients been restored in their original form, through the rediscovery of those older texts, than men began to object that the old ideas themselves were full of errors. Galen's ideas and theories about human anatomy had been based on the anatomy of the pig and the ape. Now, inspired by the new spirit of discovery and inquiry, artists (Leonardo da Vinci among them) dissected human bodies and discovered how wrong Galen had been. And in 1543 the first great anatomical textbook was produced – by Andreas Vesalius, who called his work *De Humanis Corporis Fabrica* (*Concerning the Design of the Human Body*).

Anatomy is the basic science of surgery, but the Church forbade clerks to shed blood, and Arabian physicians held surgery to be unclean and unholy. So the trade passed into the hands of quacks and barbers. The great French surgeon Ambroise Paré, who was active in the middle of the sixteenth century, did much to raise the standard of treatment and to introduce a more humane and scientific approach. English surgeons achieved a better standing when in 1540 Thomas Vicary secured from Henry VIII a charter which gathered many small, scattered trade-guilds into a United Company of Barber-Surgeons – although the barber did not entirely disappear from the scene until 200 years later. Medicine benefited from the work of Jean François Fernel, who tried to discover the cause of disease from a study of normal physiology, but perhaps even more from the theories and practice of Aureolus Theophrastus Bombastus von Hohenheim, commonly known as Paracelsus. This extraordinary Swiss physician made a number of discoveries, including the observation that lung diseases are associated with mining; but the importance of his influence lies in his rebellion against accepted ideas.

In 1553 Michael Servetus, a Spaniard who had studied medicine in France, dared to question Galen's ideas about the movement of the blood. Galen had held that the blood ebbs and flows; Servetus suggested that it circulates round the lesser (or pulmonary) system. Servetus was burned at the stake in October that year, and is usually claimed as a martyr of science, but he was burned for other reasons as well as this one – the book he wrote contained a number of religious heresies. Seventy years later, in 1628, the Englishman William Harvey published *De Motu Cordis et Sanguinis* (*Concerning the Movement of the Heart and the Blood*), in which he showed that Galen's ebb-and-flow theory was entirely wrong, and proved that blood circulates. Harvey's work, remarkable in itself, is even more notable as being one of the very first medical discoveries to be based on inductive reasoning from deliberate experiment. Harvey did not use a microscope and could only guess how blood passed from the arterial to the venous system at the periphery. Marcello Malpighi discovered the capillary network (the system of tiny, hair's breadth blood vessels) in 1660. Using an improved microscope of his own design, Antoni van Leeuwenhoek confirmed Malpighi's finding and showed that capillaries form an anastomosis (that is, a network of communications) between the arteries and the veins. Robert Boyle, Robert Hooke and Richard Lower showed that the function of circulating blood was connected with the respiration of air. John Mayow found the 'fire air' part of ordinary air to be what was essential for both combustion and the maintenance of life. This work of the 1670s, con-

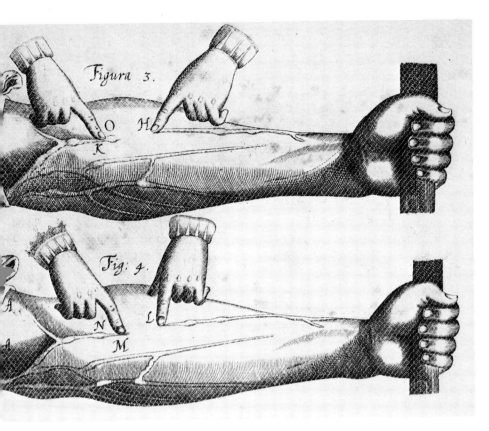

Ligatures and circulation of the blood, from Harvey's *Anatomica*. Mansell Collection.

firmed and developed by Edmund Goodwyn, Joseph Priestley and Antoine Laurent Lavoisier in the eighteenth century, established the basic elements of circulatory and respiratory physiology – the science of the circulation of the blood and of breathing.

The Discovery of Cells

At the end of the seventeenth century Isaac Newton and Carl Linné (Linnaeus) introduced orderly thought and classification into natural science. Linnaeus' botanical system – he arranged plants in classes – suggested that diseases might be classified in a similar manner. For centuries medical philosophers had sought the *cause of disease* – that is, one single cause. At the beginning of the eighteenth century they began to search instead for the *causes of diseases* – that is, a variety of causes. This gradually led to new ideas about the body. The anatomy of Vesalius had represented the body as a collection of organs that could be demonstrated by dissection – by cutting up the body. In 1800 Marie François Xavier Bichat put forward a theory of tissues or membranes –

structures out of which the organs were composed, and which were individu-
ally capable of acquiring disease. The work of Jean Cruvelhier and Karl Roki-
tansky suggested subdivision of the tissues into smaller units. Then, in 1831,
by means of an improved microscope, Mathias Jacob Schleiden observed the
cell nucleus in vegetable tissue. Shortly afterwards Theodor Schwann, an anatomist and physiologist, discovered nucleated cells in animal tissue (that is,
cells forming round a nucleus). The two men discussed their findings and,
in 1839, Schwann drew attention to an important fact about all living organisms – that they essentially resemble one another because they are all composed
of a cell structure. In 1858 Rudolf Virchow described the body as a 'cell-state
in which every cell is a citizen'. Cells had individual life and the power of creating new cells, but they could themselves grow only from cells that already
existed. This cell theory completely changed old ideas about the disease process.

The Discovery of Germs

Many early writers explained the spread of a disease by the theory of con-
tagion – illness was supposed to come from the direct contact of one person
with another. According to a later theory, 'stink' or bad air was the cause –
an example of this theory being the use of the term 'malaria' (or 'bad air')
for an illness that was thought to be caused by poisonous vapours given off
by marshes. In the eighteenth century this simple idea of bad air became more
complex, developing into the theory of miasma or pythogenic theory. (A
miasma is an unhealthy vapour, and 'pythogenic' means 'produced by filth'.)
Miasma was not air itself but a product of sewers, cesspits or infected wounds,
carried to human beings, and from one human to another, by air currents.
The discovery of gases by Joseph Black and others in the second half of the
eighteenth century suggested that carbon dioxide might be the agent to blame.
But no evidence could be produced that gases were responsible; and so solid
matter, such as suspended soot, came under suspicion. One of his students
reported that in 1860 Joseph Lister, the great surgeon, taught that the cause
of infection might prove to be a fine, pollen-like dust.
   About 1857 Louis Pasteur, Professor of chemistry at the University of Lille,
started to investigate the nature of souring. He showed that particular yeasts
or ferments are responsible for particular forms of fermentation – that is, that
the yeast which ferments grape juice into wine will not also produce cheese
from milk. He proved that ferments are living organisms, which can reproduce
themselves and are easily killed by heat. Pasteur went on to demonstrate that
yeasts are carried by air but are not part of the air itself. If boiled milk was
introduced into a glass tube and the ends of the tube drawn out to a fine capil-

lary and bent at an angle, the milk did not sour. The milk was in contact with air through the bore of the capillary, but yeasts from outside could not pass the stagnant column of air in the bend of the tube. It was on the basis of this work that, in 1864, Louis Pasteur propounded his germ theory. Twelve years later Robert Koch isolated the organism responsible for causing anthrax, an infectious disease in sheep and cattle, and successfully grew it on a culture medium. In 1882, having grown a number of micro-organisms in pure culture, Koch showed that a given organism is found constantly in a given disease, that the organism can be grown outside the host body for several generations, and that the isolated and cultured organism is capable of reproducing the original disease in any animal that is susceptible to it. Koch's postulates, as these discoveries of his are called, prove the truth of Pasteur's germ theory. And if we wish to locate a dividing line between ancient and modern medicine, we can say it is marked by the germ theory and Virchow's cell theory.

The History of Infectious Disease

Because of their limited knowledge, ancient physicians were quite unable to deal with infection, so that some diseases have had a profound effect on human development. Indeed, the early history of disease in western Europe is (with the exception of leprosy and tuberculosis) the history of acute infection. Acute infections are diseases of the crowd. There are records of great epidemics in Greek and Roman times, when cities were large and contact with older urban communities in the Middle East was often made by land and sea. What was called famine sickness is the most commonly recorded illness between the time of the Roman occupation of western Europe and the fourteenth century. This is in fact typhus fever, which often breaks out in the conditions created by poverty and lack of proper food. Typhus was present in all European prisons, in the industrial slums of the nineteenth century, during the Irish potato famines of the 1840s, and in the Civil War years that followed the Russian Revolution of 1917. But leprosy, a chronic, slowly killing infection, aroused much greater terror in medieval Europe. This horribly disfiguring disease is known to have occurred in Norway and Sweden before the tenth century AD, but appears to have become more common and widespread during the twelfth and thirteenth centuries, perhaps because Crusaders returning from the Near East introduced a more deadly strain. Fear of leprosy led to the making of laws. The statute *De Leproso Amovendo* (*Concerning the Banishment of Lepers*) aimed at segregating lepers in special places; and a number of cities drew up regulations to prevent infected persons entering their gates. The French King Philip the Fair proposed to burn all lepers alive, thus purging both their infection and their sin – a reminder that disease was thought to be inflicted on man by God as a punishment. It was sheer fear of leprosy, and not the existence of a great many lepers, that gave rise to these measures. It has been calculated that, even in the worst years, the number of British lepers never rose above between four and six per 1,000 of the population.

The same is not true of plague. Bubonic plague, a disease of rodents transmitted to humans by fleas which infest rats and people, caused a high death rate in Europe during the Plague of Justinian in AD 540–90. There is no record of another pandemic for 800 years. Then, in 1346, plague broke out of its ancient fastness in Manchuria, probably carried by a Tartar horde who besieged a company of Genoese merchants in the fortified trading post of Caffa, now Theodosia, on the Black Sea coast. The merchants escaped, carrying the plague with them to Genoa, from where it quickly travelled all over Europe, reaching the port of Melcombe, now part of Weymouth, Dorset, in June 1348. This explosive pandemic, known in Britain as the Black Death, caused an immense loss of life and social upheaval in most European countries. It is impossible to estimate even roughly how many people died. There has recently been a tendency among historians to underestimate the death roll; but available evidence suggests that at least a quarter, and probably more, of the European population perished. The Italian poet Petrarch foresaw that people in time to come would not believe that so many had died. Writing of the plague at Avignon, in France, in 1348, he asked if posterity was likely to believe the accounts written at the time, when those who had actually lived through the disaster could themselves hardly credit the magnitude of it.

Europe was never wholly free from plague during the next three centuries, and from time to time it erupted into large pandemics. The best-known English visitation is that of 1664–5. More attention has been paid to this than it deserves because of first-hand accounts in the diaries of Samuel Pepys and John Evelyn, and because it was the last of the British epidemics. In fact, the Great Plague of London was by no means the most deadly outbreak in the capital; and it affected the out-parishes and suburbs more severely than the city itself. This fact is quite important since it disproves the widely held theory that the Great Fire of 1666 put an end to plague; although it is true that bubonic plague did disappear rather suddenly from Britain and most of Europe after 1666. The last certain British deaths are two at Redruth, Cornwall, in 1671. The last major Western outbreak was in the south of France, 1720–2, but plague continued in Eastern Europe for many years, one of the worst epidemics being in Moscow in 1770. European plague then became an exotic and unusual disease, very occasional cases occurring in the nineteenth and twentieth centuries. This sudden dying out of an infection that had been widely prevalent in Europe is as mysterious as its absence during the 800 years which separate the Plague of Justinian from the Black Death. No credit can be given to medical discoveries or to social legislation.

Leprosy and syphilis can both cause changes in bone structure. Medieval skeletons showing signs of leprosy have been found in Europe; but no bones have been discovered that show syphilitic changes. It is therefore safe to assume, as accounts written at the time suggest, that syphilis appeared as an entirely new disease about the year 1497, and was an import from either Africa or the West Indies. Since Europeans had never experienced the infection, they possessed no resistance. Syphilis became widespread during the early sixteenth century and there is evidence that it occurred in a more acute form than it does today, and was transmitted by other means than sexual intercourse. The case histories of such famous sufferers as Ivan the Terrible in Russia and Henry VIII in England suggest that syphilis may have had a considerable effect on sixteenth-century politics. The history of the offspring of those two rulers, the idiot Fedor and the weakling Edward VI, together with the record of many stillbirths and miscarriages in both families, support the theory that congenital syphilis, inherited by a child from its parents, had a great effect on the growth of the population. Mass resistance to the disease gradually increased over a period of seventy years until, by the beginning of the seventeenth century, syphilis had assumed a more chronic form and had become largely a venereal infection – that is, one caused by sexual intercourse.

The common name given to syphilis, the Great Pox, is a reminder that the Small Pox already existed in sixteenth-century Europe. The early terms used for diseases can be misleading. For instance, 'mezel' is a thirteenth-century name for leprosy, while 'smallpoxe and mesles' is a fairly common sixteenth-century term for a single illness. 'Small Pox' probably covered a number of fevers characterized by a rash – true smallpox, chicken pox, measles and German measles. The early form of smallpox in Europe was probably the mild *Variola minor* or alastrim, which became replaced during the sixteenth century by virulent smallpox, *Variola major*, an import from Africa, the West Indies or Central America. By the end of the seventeenth century smallpox was the most common disease of childhood, but infants and young children often developed the mild form, the death rate being higher among older children and adults. The pattern of infection then changed; from being a common but mild childish illness, smallpox became the most deadly disease of the young. Throughout the eighteenth century it destroyed more children in their first ten years of life than any other infection, with the possible exception of infantile diarrhoea. Mortality in London began to lessen about 1790, but the death rate had begun to fall generally in country districts some forty years earlier. It is reasonable to suppose that the death of so many children before the age of puberty was a check on population growth, and that the removal of this check is partly responsible for the rapid rise in European population from the middle of the eighteenth century.

Tuberculosis is probably the oldest of all known diseases; it affects animals and birds as well as men. The two most important strains of tubercle bacillus (the organism which causes the disease) are the bovine, primarily affecting cattle but capable of being transmitted to man through infected milk; and the human, which is spread directly from one individual to another. Bovine tuberculosis commonly affects glands, bones and joints. It was often known as King's Evil because in many countries, including Britain, the Royal Touch – being actually touched by the ruling king or queen – was supposed to effect a cure. Human tuberculosis more usually attacked the lungs, and was known as phthisis or consumption. Evidence of tuberculosis has been found in Egyptian mummies, and in American Indian skeletons dating from the pre-Columbian era (that is, before 1492). There are recognizable descriptions of the disease in the Hippocratic texts. The disease must therefore have existed in Europe for centuries, but it became much more common in the crowded, insanitary conditions of industrial towns. The pulmonary form, which is spread directly from person to person by droplet infection, was one of the most deadly of all diseases from 1750 until the Second World War. This disease alone caused an average of over 60,000 deaths a year in England and Wales during the first five years in which deaths were required to be registered, from 1838 to 1843. Tuberculosis was probably the worst social scourge of the Industrial Age because it kills slowly and was more commonly a disease of the young adult. All too often the sufferer had a family which, prevented from working, he could not support; and on his death his dependants were left without a breadwinner and unable to fend for themselves. The number of deaths began to fall slowly after 1850 and had reached 27,754 in 1937. From then on, the decrease became more rapid until deaths in 1966 were less than a tenth of the 1937 figure. No single medical advance caused this dramatic decline. The victory over tuberculosis was won by a combination of medical and scientific discoveries, social legislation and improved living conditions. Better housing, adequate nourishment, opportunity for relaxation, and good working conditions all played a part, helping to change tuberculosis into a disease less deadly and less prevalent than what we now consider the 'trivial' illness of influenza.

The Fight Against Infection

Not one of the infections we have been discussing could have been cured during the time when it was at its worst. The reason is that early doctors treated the symptoms rather than the disease. They relieved pain by means of opium, constipation by a purgative and coughs with a linctus, and they encouraged the patient's natural resistance. As late as 1800, drugs in common use still included a number of semi-magic remedies, in part derived from the supposedly curative power of sacrificial meats. Many physicians and many more of their patients regarded prevention – but prevention of a mystical kind – as more hopeful than cure. Talismans, charms and amulets were carried to ward off disease. The idea is still to be found in the occasional habit of carrying a potato to prevent rheumatism. An example of the doctrine of signatures, based on the theory that like cures or prevents like, is the wearing of a tooth-shaped stone against toothache. The 'hair of the dog', nowadays meaning an alcoholic drink to cure an alcoholic hangover, originated in the swallowing of hair from a rabid dog to prevent hydrophobia, or rabies.

The hair of the dog suggested the first rational method of preventing disease. About AD 1000, Chinese physicians collected the dried scales of smallpox pustules, ground them to powder, and blew a few grains into the nostrils of the person they wished to protect. In the seventeenth century it became a common

European practice to put uninfected children into the same bed as a child suffering from a mild attack of smallpox so that they could 'get it over' before reaching the more dangerous age of puberty and adult life. A combination of these two ideas suggested the technique of variolation (from the French *verole*, a pustule), the deliberate inoculation of pustular matter from a mild case of smallpox. Variolation was introduced at the beginning of the eighteenth century. Seven years after it was described in the Journal of the Royal Society in London, Lady Mary Wortley Montagu – the English traveller and eccentric – strongly advocated the method, having seen it successfully used in Constantinople. Variolation did not become popular until, as a result of experience gained in the American colonies, Dr James Kilpatrick, introduced an improved method, which chiefly consisted of making a superficial scratch instead of a deep cut. Recent research suggests that variolation was far more widely employed than used to be imagined, and that it was responsible for a drop in deaths from smallpox during the second half of the eighteenth century.

Variolation, however, means inoculation with smallpox; and it must have been risky, and probably helped to spread infection, although perhaps in a mild form. About 1771 a milkmaid told Edward Jenner, then apprenticed to a surgeon in Sodbury, Gloucestershire, that she could not catch smallpox because she had already suffered from cowpox, a related disease of cattle. After a long investigation, Jenner started to experiment with humans. He published his findings in 1798 and, despite some opposition, over 100,000 people had been vaccinated in Britain alone before 1801. (The term derives from *vacca*, the Latin for a cow.) It required much ingenuity to make sure that vaccinia lymph remained effective when it was sent long distances. In 1803 twenty-two children, two of them freshly vaccinated, were despatched across the Atlantic from Spain to the port of Caracas, a new pair being vaccinated from the previous pair every ten days. At Caracas twenty-six children were enlisted and so carried the chain round the world to the Philippines, Macao and Canton. British and American missionaries took lymph from Macao and Canton into the Chinese interior. Many countries introduced compulsory vaccination – the first real attempt to eradicate disease on a national scale. More recently an international campaign of vaccination has been successfully launched. In 1975 Bangladesh was declared free of infection, leaving only Ethiopia as a focus of smallpox in the world.

Jenner was not aware that micro-organisms existed. After propounding the germ theory, Louis Pasteur turned his attention to the possibility of other 'vaccines' and went on to produce vaccines that were effective against anthrax and rabies. His pupil, Emile Roux, discovered that the blood serum of an infected animal could be filtered to remove organisms, yet still keep the antibodies that fight against infection. In this way he produced diphtheria antitoxin, first used in 1891, which reduced diphtheria deaths in London fever hospitals from 63 per cent of cases in 1894 to under 12 per cent in 1910.

In 1865 Joseph Lister applied Pasteur's discovery of living micro-organisms to surgery, evolving an antiseptic technique. Lister used carbolic acid, which is effective – but dangerous. The danger of carbolic led to a search for the 'perfect antiseptic', a selective agent that was capable of destroying harmful bacteria without damaging body tissue. In 1910 Paul Ehrlich, after a long series of experiments, succeeded in synthesizing salvarsan or '606', which he called his magic bullet, believing it to be effective against most bacteria. Trials showed that only the *spirochaete* (*treponema*), which causes syphilis, was sensitive to this arsenical preparation. But salvarsan killed the organism when injected into an infected animal or human, and is the first drug that can be truly said to cure an infection. Early in 1935 Gerhard Domagk discovered that a dyestuff, called prontosil rubrum, cured mice infected with streptococci. The active principle proved to be sulfanilamide, the first of the 'sulfa' drugs which can be taken by mouth or by injection and which reduce the invading organism to a feeble state so that the body defences can act more efficiently.

In 1877 Louis Pasteur and Jules Joubert observed that the large anthrax bacillus is sometimes destroyed by smaller bacteria. This led them to suppose that one micro-organism might be set to make war upon another – the theory of antibiosis. In 1876 John Tyndall had reported that a mould, *Penicillium glaucum*, caused the death of bacteria grown in mutton broth. Tyndall supposed that the thick layer of mould deprived the bacteria of oxygen. In 1928 Alexander Fleming noticed that a culture dish, impregnated with staphylococci, had become contaminated by a *Penicillium* mould and that colonies near the mould were dying. He grew the mould in broth, filtered it, and found that the filtrate, when injected into animals, destroyed a wide range of pathogenic organisms (that is, organisms that cause disease) without harming the body tissues. He published his findings in 1929, giving the name Penicillin to his mould broth filtrate. But Fleming, primarily a laboratory scientist, failed to appreciate the potential importance of his work.

Alexander Fleming. (*Photo: St Mary's Hospital Medical School, University of London*)

Penicillin lay forgotten until 1939 when Ernst Chain, Howard Florey and others started an investigation. The first trial of crude penicillin in a human patient began on 12 February 1941. By 1943 enough had been produced to allow its limited use, under strict control, by the medical personnel of the Allied military forces. Penicillin proved so effective that, in 1958, more than 440 tons of the pure crystalline form were produced by the USA alone. Other antibiotics followed, notably streptomycin, which kills the tubercle bacillus. But antibiotics are not the final answer to the cure of infections. Bacteria can develop resistance, since antibiotics are not true germicides which kill by direct contact. Strains of micro-organisms that are resistant to antibiotics have already developed, and this is one of the reasons why syphilis, which had been almost defeated by penicillin in 1958, has become more prevalent in recent years.

The History of Hospitals and Medical Care

Early hospitals existed for the care of the sick rather than for their cure. The first were temples dedicated to Aesculapius, the son of Apollo, chief god of healing in the Greek pantheon. Treatment took the form of a temple sleep (called incubation), during which the god appeared in a dream and gave advice. At a later date, incubation was backed up by a regimen which might include bathing, massage, diet and exercise. The Romans founded the *valetudinaria*, which may have been hospitals or rest houses for crippled soldiers. Christians inherited traditional responsibility for the sick from the Romans and, more particularly, from the Jews. The famous Hôtel Dieu in Paris is believed to date from the seventh century AD, although the first indisputable record is not until 829. The earliest known British 'hospital' is identified by a grant of land from Athelstan in 937 to an already established Saxon hospital at York.

A great age of hospital-building started in 1198, initiated by Pope Innocent III, who in 1204 founded Santo Spirito in Sassia in Rome. Thirteenth-century hospitals derived from three sources. First, every episcopal see (the diocese of a bishop) maintained one or more. Second, most trade and professional guilds established houses for their aged, sick and distressed members. Third, generous patrons founded a number of refuges, usually in conjunction with a chantry where an endowed priest sang masses for the repose of the founder's soul. About 750 'hospitals', most of them very small, have been traced in Britain alone. It is difficult to be sure in any particular case of the purposes of these foundations. Some were for the care of the sick; some were orphanages, almshouses, or resting places for pilgrims; many served all these purposes. The most common type of medieval hospital was the lazar house, an asylum for the segregation of lepers, of which there were some 220 in Britain and over 2,000 in France. Medicine was firmly in the hands of the Church, and all hos-

pitals were religious in character. Churchmen regarded disease as a supernatural visitation and believed that it could only be cured by a miracle – an
idea that persists to this day in faith-healing and pilgrimages to Lourdes. The
hospital building itself followed the plan of a church, with a large main ward
leading up to the altar and side wards or chapels dedicated to various healing
saints. Doctors were clerics, although not necessarily priests. Nursing was performed by religious orders, although it seems to have been customary for
patients who were less ill to act as nurses.

Many hospitals, particularly lazar houses, fell out of use after the Black
Death. Their endowments proved a temptation to both Church and Crown,
a number being suppressed and their revenues impounded during the fifteenth
century. On the European continent hospitals tended to pass, by friendly agreement, into the control of municipal authorities. In France this transfer was
completed in 1544 when Francis I instituted the Grand Bureau Général de l'Au-
mone des Pauvres. The Hôtel Dieu in Paris had the reputation, under the
Bureau's administration, of being the finest hospital in the world. Similar institutions on a smaller scale were founded in French Canada at Quebec in 1637–
9 and at Montreal in 1644. Both acquired a good reputation. Events took a
different turn in Britain, where many smaller foundations had been closed
down and their revenues confiscated in the fifteenth century. It is clear from
contemporary accounts that such hospitals as remained were badly run and
failed to care for the large numbers of sick and poor who faced only a miserable
death. The decision of Henry VIII and Edward VI to suppress the religious
foundations might therefore have led to improvements, if the revenues had
been diverted to education and to the care of the sick. But most of the money
was impounded. The so-called Royal Foundation consisted of the reopening,
after petitions from the citizens of London, of a few suppressed monastic
houses. A very few provincial hospitals escaped suppression; a survey made
in 1719 revealed that twenty-three English counties lacked hospital accommo-
dation of any kind.

No fewer than 154 hospitals were founded in the British Isles between 1720
and 1825. National prosperity, the Enlightenment (the eighteenth-century
movement that questioned traditional beliefs and prejudices, and laid a stress
on strict scientific method), the miserable plight of the sick poor in the rapidly
growing industrial towns, combined to produce a unique British institution,
the 'Voluntary Hospital'. These hospitals owed their foundation, maintenance
and medical attention to the voluntary payments and services, freely given,
of individuals. The earliest attempt to found a voluntary hospital seems to
have been not in Britain itself but in the American colonies. In 1620 the small
community of Henricopolis, Virginia, started to build a hospital but the project
failed for lack of support. (The first American hospital of any size was the
Pennsylvania, founded by Thomas Bond and Benjamin Franklin in 1751; but
this was not a true voluntary hospital because half the cost was provided by
the legislature.) In 1715 the banker Henry Hoare and a group of friends
founded a charitable institution which, in 1723, became the Westminster Hospital, London. Many more followed, not only in London but in the provinces.
By the end of the eighteenth century every county and many large towns in

Britain had their own hospitals founded and maintained by private benefactors.

Although the eighteenth century was an age when hospitals were founded, it was not a time of good hospital treatment. In 1788 Jacob René Tenon published some notes on the hospitals of Paris. The Hôtel Dieu housed about 1,680 beds, but nearly 1,200 of these contained four to six patients at one time. Tenon saw some wards in which the patients had no other bedding than heaps of straw. People suffering from dangerous fevers were herded together with those who were only mildly ill. The number of deaths averaged 20 per cent of admissions. The same was true of the large Allgemeines Krankenhaus in Vienna and the 1,300-bedded Moscow Hospital, in Russia. Some reform followed Tenon's reports and another survey begun by John Howard in 1777. But hospitals remained notoriously dirty and dangerous to life until the middle of the nineteenth century, when the work and theories of Florence Nightingale led to a better type of building, insistence upon cleanliness, and a high standard of nursing. Sick care in Germany was greatly improved by the Lutheran Order of Deaconesses at Kaiserswerth, founded by Pastor Theodor Fliedner and his wife in 1836. Elizabeth Fry, the English Quaker, visited Kaiserswerth but failed to introduce a similar system into Britain. The reform of British nursing is usually regarded as resulting from the endeavours of Miss Nightingale and her school at St Thomas' Hospital; but some credit should be given to the Anglican Nursing Sisterhoods, founded on a scheme similar to that of Kaiserswerth. The earliest, the Sisterhood of St John the Evangelist or St John's House, started work in 1848 and instituted a school for probationers at King's College Hospital, London, in 1857, three years before the Nightingale School at St

A French hospital in the late eighteenth century. Mansell Collection.

Thomas'. The Orthodox Nursing Sisterhoods are said to have been initiated by a report on the work of St John's House made to Tsar Alexander II. Orthodox Sisterhoods achieved a high standard of patient care in Russia until the 1917 revolution.

The Treatment of the Mentally Ill

If ordinary hospitals were bad, madhouses were worse, and it is fortunate that not many existed. The oldest and one of the best known is St Mary of Bethlehem, London, founded by Simon FitzMary in 1247. 'Bedlam' seems to have specialized in the care of the insane from about 1450. Other early madhouses are Juliusspital at Würzburg, Germany, and the notorious Narrenthurm or Lunatics' Tower in Vienna. The Philadelphia Almshouse, founded by the Society of Friends in 1713, had a short life as a madhouse before becoming the Philadelphia General Hospital in 1785, but the first American institution solely for lunatics opened at Williamsburg, Virginia, in 1773. In all countries insanity was regarded not only as incurable but as a disgrace, often as divine punishment for sin. Lunatics were commonly treated as criminals, chained, and confined to damp cells, lit only by a small grating. Any 'treatment' given was punitive – douches of cold water, purgatives, emetics and cauterizing plasters. It is horrible to think that lunatics provided an entertainment, especially at Bedlam and in Vienna, where the public paid a small entrance fee to see the keepers goad their charges into idiotic antics.

In 1793, at the height of the Terror in Paris, Philippe Pinel of the Bicêtre Hospital asked permission of the Commune to free selected lunatics from their chains. He had to abandon the experiment because of the suspicion that he was aiding wanted aristocrats. Pinel received permission from the National Assembly for a renewed attempt in 1798. He freed forty-nine patients and found that their condition quickly improved when they were no longer chained. Pinel published a description of his method in 1801. Meanwhile two English Quakers, Edward Long Fox and William Tuke, had taken charge of small asylums in England – Fox, a physician, at Cleeve Hill near Bristol, and Tuke, who was not medically qualified, at The Retreat, York. In the 1790s both these pioneers gave their patients as much freedom as possible, and encouraged them to be usefully active in the house and grounds. Dr John Conolly, appointed resident physician to the largest madhouse in England, the Middlesex Asylum at Hanwell, abolished all forms of mechanical restraint in 1839 but, despite his example and writings, the movement spread only slowly.

Pinel's work in France was continued by Jean Esquirol and Etienne Georget, who began to regard insanity as a disease that could be treated and cured. In the USA Dorothea Lynde Dix, a retired schoolteacher, drew the attention of Congress in 1848 to the plight of over 9,000 epileptics and insane persons

William Norris: confined in this manner in Bethlem Hospital. From an engraving after a drawing by G. Arnold, May 1814. Mansell Collection.

whom she had personally visited and observed to be chained, beaten and cruelly treated. She was responsible for the foundation of thirty-two new institutions and the improvement of some older ones. The idea of keeping people chained up was gradually replaced by the idea of keeping them apart from others; the old mad-doctor turned into the alienist who looked after people unfit to be at large. Treatment was of secondary importance. 'It must be remembered that we are an asylum rather than a hospital', wrote the chairman of Colney Hatch, in Middlesex, in 1859. Nineteenth-century discoveries in medicine and science tended to lay emphasis on physical causes of disease. So nineteenth-century alienists, responsible for the insane, concentrated on finding a physical or somatic reason for the patient's mental condition. ('Somatic' means relating to the body rather than to the soul or the mind.) Jean Martin Charcot of the Salpêtrière Hospital in Paris was not the first to recognize the existence of somatic disease of the nervous system, but he did more than anyone to distinguish somatic 'neurology' from animist 'psychology'. ('Animism' is the belief that souls have some sort of physical existence and indeed can exist outside the body; someone who believes in ghosts or reincarnation is an animist.) Sigmund Freud, who worked with Charcot, afterwards practised in Vienna and set out the principles on which psychiatry, the modern treatment of mental illness, is based.

Charcot separated patients into groups – the hysterical patients, and those who were organically ill – and he did this by means of hypnotism or mesmerism. This very old art takes the second of these names from Franz Anton Mesmer, who achieved an immense reputation with his 'animal magnetism' in Paris during the years preceding the Revolution. Experience led Freud to divide the brain into three levels – conscious, pre-conscious and sub-conscious. Without help, no one could recall events stored in the lowest level. Events subconsciously stored might be recalled under hypnosis, or a psychologist might be able to identify them by allowing the subject to talk at random. The skilled psychologist could then trace an association of ideas which might lead him to the underlying reason for the trouble. Thus Freud developed the technique of psychoanalysis which is, in essence, the release of repressed experience from the subconscious into the conscious mind. It then became possible to explain rationally the delusion which the patient had been unable to recognize. Two of Freud's pupils, Carl Gustav Jung and Alfred Adler, modified Freud's theories and extended his work. Adler is responsible for breaking away from the Freudian idea of sex as the driving force in personality. He substituted the need for power, and so introduced the inferiority complex. The views of Freud and his associates have met with opposition, but they may be regarded as the starting point of the modern psychiatric clinic.

Social Medicine and Public Health

As knowledge advanced, so the ideal of protecting whole communities from the inroads of disease began to be recognized. Social medicine depends upon action by village or town authorities which can be extended to national governments and finally to international organizations wielding the necessary authority. Lepers were segregated by local laws and by national statutes designed to prevent contamination of the uninfected. During the Black Death of 1348 the Venetian republic appointed three guardians of public health who, when there was another outbreak in 1374, were ordered to exclude infected ships.

Freud and his chow in his study at Berggasse 19. (*Photo: Mary Evans Picture Library*)

Likewise the town of Ragusa, in Dalmatia, ordered persons suspected of suffering from the disease to be detained for thirty days before they were allowed to enter the gates. (The houses in which they were detained, called the *lazaretti*, are still standing outside the gates of Ragusa, now known as Dubrovnik.) The port authorities of Marseilles extended the period to forty days in 1383, and in 1403 Venice made a law that travellers from the Levant (the land round the eastern Mediterranean) must be isolated in a detention hospital for the same period (in Italian, *quaranta giorni*, which is where the word 'quarantine' comes from). During the years of plague most large cities imposed regulations about burial, the burning of clothes and bedding, the destruction of domestic animals, the removal of refuse heaps and the isolation of infected houses. The notorious chalked cross and the words 'Lord have Mercy on us' were primarily a warning to passers-by not to loiter in the neighbourhood; watchmen had orders to move people on. Little real progress was made until the growth of industrial towns and the arrival of Asiatic cholera in Europe pointed to the need for efficient disposal of sewage and a pure water supply before city life could be regarded as safe.

The movement towards 'public health' was, for two reasons, more rapid in Britain than in other countries. First, greater industrialization combined with a generally rising population to produce overcrowded towns in which sewage could not be removed by the traditional village method of spreading it over fields; nor could adequate supplies of clean water be obtained from shallow wells or unpolluted streams. Second, government in Britain tended to be less centralized than in European countries. There existed a local machinery of parish officers elected to administer the rate levied on householders under the Elizabethan Poor Laws.

In 1804 an epidemic of yellow fever in Gibraltar aroused fear that this dreaded disease might invade Britain by ship. The government established a Board of Health under the Privy Council. The Board started work in May 1805 but the expected invasion did not occur and it was dissolved in August 1806. The Board not only set the pattern for future Boards but is usually regarded as the first parent of Britain's present Department of Health and Social Security.

In 1817–18 Asiatic cholera started to spread over the world from a focus in central India. Unlike plague, cholera travelled slowly, giving British authorities time to take action. A Central Board of Health was instituted in 1831. The members advised setting up Local Boards of Health composed of the chief magistrate and clergy of the district together with representatives of the medical profession and influential inhabitants. Cholera arrived in Britain (Sunderland) in October; twenty-five towns had formed Local Boards by mid-November. The Central Board was reconstituted to include members who had first-hand knowledge of cholera, and did excellent work. By February 1832 the Board employed forty-two inspectors and medical officers who advised 822 Local Boards in England and Wales, and about 400 in Scotland. During its term of office the Board issued a number of wise directives, requiring parish officers to abate nuisances, provide nurses and medicines, destroy bedding and clothing, and cleanse infected homes. This legislation, empowered by the Cholera Act of 1832, broke down in practice because parish officers did not possess the physical means of enforcing the law, and all costs had to be charged to the poor rate. But, by the time the epidemic ended and the Board had been dissolved in December 1832, there existed a primitive public health service throughout the country.

The 1831–2 cholera epidemic was one of the reasons for the appointment of a Royal Commission to inquire into the working of the Poor Laws. At this point Edwin Chadwick, a lawyer-journalist, produced a notorious scheme to strengthen local authority by the bringing together (or union) of parishes and the replacement of outdoor relief of the poor (which meant help given without the requirement that the poor person go into a workhouse) by confinement in institutions. It is not altogether Chadwick's fault that his proposals became translated into the workhouse or 'union' of hated memory. Appointed Secretary of the new Poor Law Commission, Chadwick investigated the causes of the high death rate in industrial towns, and in 1842 published his *Report of an Inquiry into the Sanitary Conditions of the Labouring Population of Great Britain*. The report shocked both the government and prosperous citizens. Chadwick was encouraged to turn to practical detail. What could be done to prevent so many deaths? He worked out plans for the disposal of sewage and the provision of clean water. His argument that such steps would help to keep disease at bay was greatly strengthened by the cholera epidemic of 1849, in which Dr John Snow and Dr William Budd showed that cholera and typhoid fever are diseases carried by water and that they are caused by the contamination of water supply by sewage. But perhaps Chadwick's chief legacy is the Medical Officer of Health – a doctor appointed by the local authority and given the power to deal with all matters affecting the health of the community. Chadwick's influence spread widely. His example was followed by Lemuel Shattuck, who initiated sanitary reform in the USA, and by sanitary reformers in Germany and Russia. John Simon succeeded Chadwick as the greatest exponent of public health in Britain. Appointed Chief Medical Officer of the Local Government Board in 1871, Simon was largely responsible for drafting the 'great' Public Health Act, that of 1875, which allowed implementation of a number of improvements during the next thirty years.

State-run Healthcare

Until late in the nineteenth century, a worker could call only upon his own savings, mutual benefit clubs, poor relief, or private charity for his treatment and maintenance when he was sick. In 1883 the German Chancellor Bismarck introduced a compulsory insurance scheme for workers, an example followed by Austria in 1888. Similar plans were initiated by Norway, Denmark and Sweden at the beginning of the twentieth century. In Britain Lloyd George introduced in 1911 his National Insurance Bill, which came into force in 1913. This Act provided free consultation, general practitioner treatment, and sickness benefit. It applied only to workers earning less than £150 a year, and did not cover dependants. Nor could the cost of hospital care be recovered. Some provision for dependants had already been made by the School Medical Service, started in 1907, and this was extended by the Maternity and Child Welfare Act of 1918. But National Insurance in Britain suffered from the disadvantage that consultation and minor attention lay in the hands of the doctor; preventive and social medicine in the hands of local authorities; and hospital treatment in the hands of voluntary hospitals or municipal infirmaries, which had their origins in the Poor Laws. In most European countries public hospitals were almost entirely the responsibility of the State, so that a patient did not suffer the stigma of charity or pauperism as in Britain. A comprehensive scheme to bring all aspects of medical care under one authority was first proposed in 1917, and in 1919 the Ministry of Health was inaugurated. A Council on Medical and Administrative Services was set up which issued a preliminary report in 1920, outlining a plan usually known as 'The Lost Opportunity' – a financial crisis made implementation impossible. Further schemes were suggested by the British Medical Association ('The Doctors' Plan') and by a committee of civil servants ('The Beveridge Plan') in 1944.

All comprehensive health services then existing had arisen to meet the special needs of small communities scattered over wide areas. The oldest is that of Russia, dating back to 1862. It was inefficient, depending largely upon the *feldsher*, a semi-trained medical orderly rather similar to the 'barefoot doctors' of present-day China. The Russian service improved over the years; by 1917 hardly a single village lay more than twenty miles from the nearest cottage hospital, and districts were regularly visited by 'flying squads' of specialists. These cottage hospitals, usually staffed by only one qualified doctor, carried out all branches of medicine, the work being done by a number of *feldshers* and nurses under medical supervision. This is an obvious way of economizing in trained personnel when they are in short supply, when settlements are widely scattered and there are long distances to travel. The Soviet government continued the scheme, which has now developed into the Health Centre, the basic unit of the present Health Service in the USSR.

Norway, a large and mountainous country with a small, scattered population, is said to have appointed, some centuries ago, government-paid men, not necessarily doctors, whose job was to administer public health as well as care for the sick. The service developed as an insurance scheme with free hospital treatment. If a patient consulted a private doctor, his fee must be paid but could be partly recovered from insurance. Sweden, often studied as the 'ideal' health service, depended upon municipal hospitals, in the planning of which the Swedes have been pioneers. Their health service, as the term is understood today, dates from the end of the nineteenth century when a National Board of Health appointed provincial physicians to act as a combination of general practitioner and public health officer. The service is based upon insurance and regulated fees are paid by the patient to the doctor, 70 per cent of the fee being recoverable by the insured patient.

The Australian service owes its beginning to private enterprise and not to laws passed by the government. In 1912 the Revd John Flynn, distressed by the plight of sick people in remote stations, started to found in isolated outposts small hospitals, each staffed by two trained nurses. Flynn conceived the idea of doctors established at central bases, linked by wireless telegraphy, and serving the outposts by aeroplane. Before 1914 both wireless and the aeroplane were too primitive for such use. But an efficient receiving and transmitting set was developed by A. H. Traegar in 1926 and the first aerial medical service was established at Cloncurry, Queensland, in 1928. So began the famous Royal Flying Doctor Service. Depending upon direct payment and donations as well as state grants, the success of this remarkable service has been largely due to voluntary effort.

Britain did not have the Russian and Australian problem of great distances and scattered communities, nor the long history of state-employed medical officers that resulted from the difficult terrain of Norway; nor the combined general practitioners and public health officers of Sweden. The British National Health Service Act of 1946, which was implemented in 1948, set out to provide comprehensive care for all sections of the population and for all purposes, without payment at the time of use. In effect, the Act extended insurance to everyone; but it retained two principles – that payment should be compulsory but that it should be up to anyone to decide whether or not he would accept benefit. It transferred all hospitals, voluntary or municipal, to the trusteeship of the Ministry of Health and of Parliament, costs being met out of general taxation. Can the structure which emerged from the Act be accurately described as a comprehensive National Health Service? Perhaps not, for the Act did nothing to bring together and indeed did something to separate the three branches of curative, preventive and social medicine. A Green Paper and Consultative Document of 1972 had greater integration as its purpose; but the proposals, as implemented in 1974, seem at present only to have more widely separated the administration from the working doctor.

International Healthcare

International control of disease started with a conference on quarantine regulations in Paris in 1856. The first Red Cross agreement was signed at the Geneva conference in 1864. Further conferences on the way cholera and plague were passed on were held in 1892–4 and 1897. The first global organization for world health, the Office International d'Hygiène Publique, was established in Paris in 1907. The League of Nations continued and enlarged the work by means of a Health Organization set up in 1923. The United Nations Relief and Rehabilitation Administration (UNRRA), created in 1943, acted as an international health organization for just over two years. In 1946 an International Health Conference, held in New York and attended by representatives of more than sixty nations, took over the functions of UNRRA and formed the permanent World Health Organization (WHO) in 1948. A multitude of problems have been attacked including malaria, venereal disease and tuberculosis. Embracing as it does all medical functions, curative, preventive and social, WHO may be regarded as a supra-National Health Service.

Modern Developments in Medicine

Maintenance of health on a national and international scale, rather than by individual effort, was largely dictated by the immense forward strides made in the last century. Modern medicine is not only more complex but more expensive.

Radiotherapy

Radiotherapy is one instance. X-rays were discovered in 1895 by Wilhelm Konrad Röntgen of Würzburg in Germany, and quickly came into use for diagnosing fractures or tracking down metal objects embedded in the tissues. In 1897

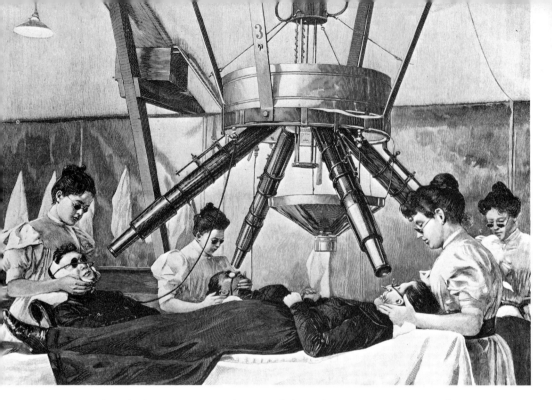

Early radiotherapy: treatment by Jinsen light at the Jinsen Institute, Copenhagen, 1901. From a print in the Mansell Collection.

Walter Cannon of Harvard introduced the bismuth meal, later replaced by barium, used by E. J. Beck of Chicago to reveal lesions in the human stomach and intestines in 1906. (A lesion is a marked change in the texture or function of an organ.) Use of X-rays started in 1897 to bring about a cure for the form of skin tuberculosis known as lupus. Marie Curie, a Pole by birth, and her French husband Pierre began to investigate the phenomenon of radioactivity in 1898, and in 1902 they isolated radium from pitchblende. Radium emanation 'radon' was introduced for the treatment of cancers in 1921. Radioactive isotopes followed in 1946–50. Treatment by X-rays beamed to a limited area ('Röntgen therapy') had been started by Henri Coutard of Paris in 1921. His method, when combined with powerfully radioactive isotopes, led to the radium, cobalt and caesium 'bombs' for localized treatment of cancers.

Glandular diseases

Some treatment is expensive because it is prolonged. This is particularly true of the endocrine disorders (diseases of glands) which may be corrected by supplying a secretion which is missing. Cretins were thought to be incurable idiots until they were given an extract of thyroid gland. Pernicious anaemia or Addison's disease was first treated with raw liver by G. R. Minot and W. P. Murphy in 1926. Then it was found that the adrenal cortex secretes steroids and these revolutionized treatment. The most notable example is diabetes which had been recognized as an incurable disease in very early times. J. von Mering and Oscar Minkowski discovered in 1890 diabetes could be produced by cutting out the pancreas. Eleven years later E. L. Opie of Staunton, Virginia, showed that it was due to a particular part of the pancreas, and in 1921 F. G. Banting and C. H. Best of Toronto isolated the essential secretion, insulin.

Surgery

The recent history of surgery demonstrates very well this combination of successful effort with increased complexity and expense. For years surgery had been destructive, almost confined to the amputation of limbs and the removal of stones, growths and foreign bodies. The art began to become constructive, in the sense of mending organs rather than simply cutting them out, at the end of the eighteenth century, and was given a scientific basis by the work of John Hunter.

But although the techniques of operating made considerable advances in those years, the pain caused by a surgeon inevitably set a time limit to his operations, and so hampered progress. In 1800 the twenty-year-old Humphry Davy suggested the first practicable means of anaesthesia, nitrous oxide, which was used in dentistry by Horace Wells of Hartford, Connecticut, in 1844. Nitrous oxide proved too uncertain, and a one-time partner of Wells, William Thomas Green Morton of Boston, experimented with ether. On 16 October 1846 Morton gave a successful demonstration at the Massachusetts General Hospital. In November 1847 James Young Simpson of Edinburgh introduced chloroform, a more powerful agent than nitrous oxide or ether, which remained the preferred anaesthetic for more than half a century.

Anaesthesia permitted rapid advance in surgical techniques; but surgery remained dangerous because so many wounds became infected. The risk of sepsis has, however, been greatly exaggerated. Overall deaths from operative surgery stood at 9 per cent in 1860, two-thirds of these deaths being caused by wound infection. A figure of 45 per cent is often quoted, but this applies only to emergency amputations made necessary by a compound fracture. The

Morton's apparatus for inhaling ether. Mary Evans Picture Library.

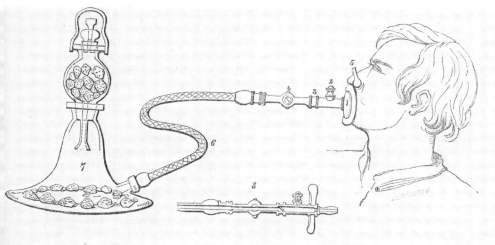

THE APPARATUS FOR RENDERING SURGICAL OPERATIONS PAINLESS.

antiseptic method introduced by Joseph Lister in 1865 proved its worth when it was used by Prussian army surgeons during the Franco-Prussian War of 1870–1. Civilian surgeons, particularly in America, England and France, were slower to understand the great benefit which antisepsis had conferred. It is for this reason that surgeons of the Germanic nations pioneered operative surgery in the last quarter of the nineteenth century. Notable among them is Theodor Billroth of Vienna. William MacEwan in Scotland and Just Lucas-Championnière in France were also early exponents of Lister's technique who made notable advances. Many thought the new operations were simply experimental, of no practical value, and so unjustified. Sir John Erichsen of University College Hospital, London, remarked in 1874: 'The brain, the thorax, and the abdomen will forever remain closed to the hands of the wise and humane surgeon.' But all these areas had been explored before 1900. The danger of carbolic, recognized by Lister himself, led to a search for better means of preventing infection. Antisepsis imposed a germ-killing barrier between a source of infection and the open wound. Asepsis ensures that no source of infection is allowed near the wound. It is achieved by sterilizing all instruments, dressings, and everything else used in an operation. Asepsis began to replace antisepsis in the 1880s, the leading early advocate being Ernst von Bergmann of Berlin.

Modern surgery of the brain, lungs and heart depends largely on experience gained in the two World Wars and on control of circulation and respiration. In 1935 Harold King isolated d-tubocurarine, the active principle of the arrow-poison curare. It was introduced as a muscle relaxant or paralysing agent in

A patient with kidney failure, and his artificial kidney machine. (*Photo: OBS/Camera Press, London*)

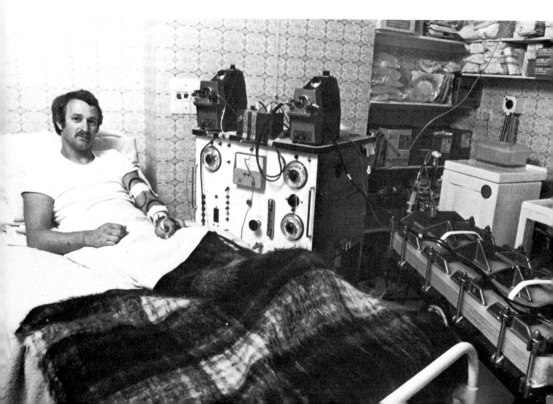

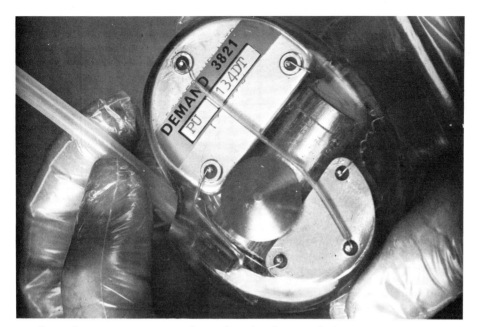

Another replacement: Heart pacemaker with nuclear battery which uses heat from the radioactive decay of a small amount of plutonium-238 to generate electricity in a tiny semi-conductor thermopile. (*Photo: United Kingdom Atomic Energy Authority*)

1942 by H. E. Griffiths and G. E. Johnson of Montreal. Paralysis of the respiratory muscles made possible mechanical control of respiration, the first machine for the purpose having been devized by Clarence Crafoord of Stockholm in 1938. Control of circulation began in 1950 when W. G. Bigelow and others in Toronto began to investigate methods of cooling the bodies of animals. This led to hypothermia, a state of semi-hibernation, in which the patient can be kept alive but with a motionless heart. Obviously hypothermia by itself imposed a time limit; if it went on too long irreversible brain damage would result. Need for prolonged operation suggested 'cutting the heart out of circuit' by use of a method of circulation outside the body. Two Russian workers, Brukhonenko and Tchetchilin, invented a primitive heart-lung machine in 1926, but it was not until 1953 that the first 'pump' was used on a human patient by John Gibbon of Philadelphia. There are now a variety of models, but the underlying principle of all of them is the same. Blood is saturated with oxygen and pumped through the patient's vessels. Thus there is no need for either heartbeat or natural respiration. The immobile heart can be opened and a defect repaired.

Transplants

An apparently obvious development is to replace a defective heart or other organ with a new structure. This is, in fact, a very old idea, although alleged early successes belong more to mythology than to history. Replacements can be by mechanical contrivances, of which dentures and the very successful metal hip-joint prostheses are examples. The heart-lung machine is an instance of an artificial organ, and so is the artificial kidney or dialyser. Autotransplants, parts of the patient's own body transferred to a new site, have been used for centuries in the form of skin grafts, and the method can be applied to cartilage, tendon and bone. Homotransplants are tissues transplanted from one human individual to another. Heterotransplants are from one species to another i.e. from a monkey to a man; it is reported that O. M. Lannelongue of France successfully transplanted a sheep's thyroid into the human as a cure for myxoedema in 1890.

Autotransplantation of skin was practised by early Hindu and Chinese surgeons. The delayed pedicle graft, in which a flap of skin is partially separated from one area, attached to another, and wholly freed from the original site at a later date, was used by Gasparo Tagliacozzi of Bologna in 1597 and became known as the Tagliocotian operation. This method formed the basic technique of Harold Delf Gillies, a New Zealand-born surgeon, at Queen Mary's Hospital, Sidcup, in the First World War. Very extensive repairs, particularly of burned areas, were undertaken by another New Zealander, Archibald McIndoe, in the Second World War. An important form of homotransplant is the transfusion of blood donated by one person to meet the deficiency of another. Attempts to transfuse blood have been made at least since 1664 and probably earlier, but the operation was dangerous until 1901 when Karl Landsteiner of Vienna divided human blood into four groups, of which any one might not be compatible with another. The first blood transfusion service started in south-east London in 1921 through the enthusiasm of Percy Lane Oliver, local secretary of the Red Cross. The first 'blood bank' for storage of donated blood was set up at Cook County Hospital by Bernard Fantus of Chicago in 1937.

Corneal grafting is another important form of homotransplant. When it was suggested, just over a century ago, that blindness caused by an opaque cornea might be cured by replacement, the idea was dismissed as 'one of the most audacious fantasies'. The first human attempt was probably made by a German surgeon named Sellerbeck in 1878, but the operation was very seldom performed until after 1905 when E. K. Zirm of Czechoslovakia achieved a limited success. Two surgeons, Magitot and Morax, used the cornea of an enucleated eye which had been stored for eight days in 1912. New techniques and storage methods made corneal grafting a very successful operation after the Second World War and led to the British Corneal Grafting Act of 1952, which permitted the removal of eyes from dead persons unless objection had been lodged. This was incorporated in the Human Tissue Act of 1961 which permitted individuals to bequeath their bodies, or selected organs, for transplantation into others. In 1979 the method was applicable even to patients in their nineties, who were often able to return to their normal activities within a week. Replacement was successful in more than 70 per cent of cases.

This legislation had been made necessary by work done on the actual transplantation of organs. Practical interest in this type of surgery was aroused by a Frenchman, Alexis Carrel, who published the results of many experiments in 1908. In 1923–6 C. S. Williamson succeeded in transplanting kidneys from one animal to another, but the method could not be applied to the human because of the risk of renal failure (failure of the kidney). In 1944 W. J. Kolff of Holland built the first artificial kidney or dialyser. Attempts to transplant kidneys from human to human were undertaken on several occasions between 1945 and 1953, but all failed because the problem of tissue rejection had not been appreciated. In 1954 J. P. Merrill and J. E. Murray of the Peter Bent Brigham Hospital, USA, transplanted a healthy kidney from an identical twin into the body of his twin brother who suffered from renal insufficiency. The operation was successful and, since identical twins can from the point of view of blood and tissue typing be regarded as one individual, served to underline the fact that the main barrier to successful homotransplantation is the natural refusal of the body to accept foreign material. Research showed that this immune or rejection response can be partially damped down by irradiation and the use of certain drugs (immunosuppression), and a number of kidney transplants were then carried out. A measure of success with the kidney suggested attempts at grafting other organs such as the heart, lungs and liver.

In 1963 Thomas E. Starzl of Denver, Colorado, transplanted the liver of a young child into the body of a three-year-old boy who suffered from a congenital defect, but his patient died from haemorrhage before the operation was completed. By 1968 Starzl had performed five transplants on patients who survived for some months. It must be remembered that all these patients would have died within a matter of days had an operation not been attempted. A great number of such operations have now been performed throughout the world, and the survival rate is now years rather than months. The operation has been assisted and, to some extent, supplanted by the elaboration of an 'artificial liver'.

In January 1964 J. D. Hardy and W. R. Webb of Jackson, Missouri, removed the heart of a man dying of cardiac failure and prepared to replace it with that from a patient suffering irrecoverable brain damage. The donor's death was too long delayed and the surgeons used the heart of a chimpanzee instead. The operation was unsuccessful but this heterotransplant was the first attempt to replace the heart of a human being. In 1964 Professor Christian Barnard of Cape Town had had ten years experience of open heart surgery and for four years had been studying the problems of organ transplantation. Barnard decided in November 1967 to attempt transplantation of the human heart. In December he transplanted the heart of a girl into the body of Louis Washkansky at the Groote Schuur Hospital, Cape Town. Washkansky lived for only eighteen days, but even this short period showed that transplantation of the heart might prove to be a feasible operation of the future.

Work continues on other replacement techniques. The present opinion is that, during the next twenty years, development of mechanical 'cardiac assist' devices may prove more hopeful that actual replacement of the heart, which has not met with great success.

In the same way, development of compact dialysers (artificial kidneys) which can be conveniently carried, may help the patient with renal failure. But the problem here is a little different. Dialysis is unlikely ever to be perfect because it does not replace the metabolic function of the kidney. Only transplantation of the actual organ can restore full renal function. This is dependent upon availability of a suitable donor with the correct type of tissue, which remains a problem in all transplantation techniques. At present, immunosuppression therapy, required to prevent rejection, is unsatisfactory because all immunoresponses are suppressed, thus rendering the patient vulnerable to infections.

It is probable that a new approach, aimed at diminishing the immune response to the graft without impairing that to micro-organisms, may be hopeful.

The advances made in medicine, in public health and in the general standard of living have changed the pattern of death. The great killers of the past were bubonic plague, smallpox, tuberculosis and acute infections. Death from many of those came early. The killers of today are arteriosclerosis, coronary infarctions, (that is obstructions) and the cancers. Much of this type of disease was regarded as the natural termination of old age only a century ago. But old age then began in the middle forties because the average age at death was forty-five. Now the average expectation of life is seventy-two years. The question is whether this type of death is avoidable; for instance, there is an undoubted statistical relationship between heavy cigarette smoking and death from lung cancer. Or is there a gene for long life, one of those genes or hereditary factors first postulated by the Austrian Gregor Mendel in 1865?

Advance can bring harm as well as benefit. Iatrogenic diseases are illnesses caused by medicine itself. The most terrible example is the apparently harmless drug thalidomide, introduced as a safe sleeping pill in 1956. Five years later it had been discovered that expectant mothers who took thalidomide during the early months of pregnancy had produced children suffering from crippling deformities. Experience gained with blood transfusion, heart-lung machines, surgical and other techniques enable the survival of people whose death would have been inevitable before the Second World War. But these advances pose ethical problems which have yet to be answered. Transplantation of a heart requires a skilled team and costly apparatus. Is the money better spent on less dramatic but more useful operations? Such surgery is still largely experimental. Is it justified to make a patient the subject of experiment? Is it ever right to transplant a piece of one human into another? Many would answer no; the religious sect known as Jehovah's Witnesses will not even permit transfusion of blood. This entails another difficulty. Is it permissible for a parent to refuse a child something which may save its life even though, in the parent's opinion, it may damn its soul? In the eyes of many people, life is sacrosanct. Is it ever justifiable to abort the life of a foetus in the mother's uterus?

So we reach the greatest medical and ethical problem of today. When does life begin and at what point does it end? Until the eighteenth century, death was regarded as the cessation of respiration. New methods showed that many people apparently dead could be restored by artificial respiration. A hundred years ago death was defined as the absence of both respiration and heartbeat. Doctors subsequently found that there can still be recovery after the heart has stopped. Then death became 'a flat EEG', absence of brain function as recorded by the electroencephalogram; but patients who have taken overdoses of barbiturate drugs have been restored when brain, cardiac and respiratory function have all apparently ceased. A Cambridge professor bought a joint of meat, cultured the muscle tissue, and demonstrated that the cells were still living. So there is intellectual death when the brain function has ceased; physiological death when pulse and respiration have stopped; cytological death (cytology is the study of the living cells) when the body cells have ceased to live. What is true death and at what point do we 'switch off the pump'?

Prominent People

Adler, Alfred (1870–1937), Austrian psychiatrist, founder of the school of individual psychology. A former pupil of Freud, he rejected Freud's emphasis on sex, suggesting that man's problem is a struggle for power to compensate for feelings of inferiority.

Anderson, Elizabeth Garrett (1836–1917), one of the first Englishwomen to enter the medical profession. Overcoming great opposition, she became visiting physician to the East London Hospital; was later elected the first woman mayor in England.

Banting, Sir Frederick Grant (1891–1941), Canadian physician; with C. H. Best and MacLeod, discovered insulin.

Behring, Emil von (1854–1917), German bacteriologist, founder of the science of immunology; discovered diphtheria and tetanus anti-toxins. Nobel Prize winner 1901.

Best, Charles Herbert (b. 1899), Canadian physiologist: with F. G. Banting and MacLeod, discovered the use of insulin in the treatment of diabetes, first administered in 1922.

Bichat, Marie François Xavier (1771–1802), French physiologist whose study of tissues founded modern histology. He was the first to simplify anatomy and physiology by reducing the complex structures of the organs to the simple or elementary tissues.

Blackwell, Elizabeth (1821–1910), British-born, the first woman to obtain a medical diploma in the United States. Like E. G. Anderson she faced great opposition, but was admitted into hospitals in Paris and London and had a successful practice in New York.

Braille, Louis (1809–52), French educationist who invented a system of reading and writing in relief for the blind. As the result of an accident, Braille himself was blind from the age of three.

Calmette, Albert (1863–1933), French bacteriologist; with Camille Guérin, developed the BCG tuberculosis vaccine in 1921.

Carrel, Alexis (1873–1944), born in France, but worked as a surgeon in America. Nobel Prize in 1912 for his success in suturing blood vessels in transfusion, and organ transplants. Discovered white corpuscles in 1922, developed artificial heart in 1936.

Chain, Ernst Boris (b. 1906), biochemist of Russian origin, b. Berlin, who was awarded the Nobel Prize for physiology and medicine in 1945, jointly with Sir Alexander Fleming and H. W. Florey, for his prominent part in researches on penicillin.

Cooper, Sir Astley Paston (1768–1841), British surgeon and author of medical textbooks. Surgery, hitherto 'frightful alternatives or hazardous compromises', was raised by him to a science.

Curie, Pierre (1859–1906), Professor of physics at the Sorbonne. Worked jointly with Marie Curie at Paris on magnetism and radioactivity. He was run over and killed by a car in Paris.

Dale, Sir Henry Hallett (1875–1968), English physiologist. He shared the 1936 Nobel Prize for medicine for his work on the chemical transmission of nerve impulses.

Ehrlich, Paul (1854–1915), German bacteriologist who was a pioneer in haematology and discovered salvarsan for the treatment of syphilis. Nobel Prize winner 1908.

Ellis, Havelock (1859–1939), Englishman who gave up medicine for literary and scientific studies. His *Studies in the Psychology of Sex* was influential in changing public attitudes.

Fleming, Sir Alexander (1881–1955), Scottish bacteriologist; discovered the antibacterial enzyme lysozyme in 1922 and penicillin in 1928. Awarded the Nobel Prize for medicine jointly with Florey and Chain, 1945.

Florey, Howard Walter, (1898–1968), British pathologist, b. Australia. Shared 1945 Nobel Price with Fleming and Chain for work on penicillin.

Freud, Sigmund (1856–1939), b. Moravia, Austrian psychiatrist and founder of psychoanalysis. Professor of neuropathology at Vienna, he evolved theories of the mind and of the sexual drive in humans that had great influence on modern thinking.

Hahnemann, Samuel Christian Friedrich (1755–1843), German physician who founded homeopathy (the treatment of disease by small doses of drugs that in health produce similar symptoms).

Haldane, John Scott (1860–1936), British reformer; he studied the effect of industrial occupations upon health.

Hunter, John (1728–93) and **William** (1718–83), British doctors, most distinguished and influential of medical teachers and practitioners. William raised obstetrics to the rank of a respected medical discipline and John established the principles of surgery soundly on a broad biological basis.

Jenner, Edward, (1749–1823), British physician, whose discovery of vaccination against smallpox (1796) helped to lay the foundations of modern immunology.

Jung, Carl Gustav (1875–1961), Swiss physician and psychologist. A former pupil of Freud, he developed the theory of 'complexes', and became leader of the Zurich school of psychoanalysis.

Koch, Robert (1834–1910), German bacteriologist who discovered the bacillus of tuberculosis. He also worked on cholera and cattle diseases and was awarded the Nobel Prize for medicine in 1905.

Landsteiner, Karl (1868–1943), Austrian scientist, discoverer of the four primary human blood groups and Nobel Prize winner for medicine, 1930. A naturalized US citizen, he died in New York.

Lister, Baron (Joseph) (1827–1912), British surgeon whose great work was the introduction in 1865 of the antiseptic system which revolutionized modern surgery and greatly reduced hospital mortalities.

Manson, Sir Patrick (1844–1922), British physician, known as 'Mosquito Manson' from his pioneer work with Ross in malaria research. He helped to found the London School of Tropical Medicine.

Mechnikov, Ilya Ilyich (1845–1916), Russian physiologist, famous for his theory of phagocytes (1884). He won the Nobel Prize for medicine in 1908.

Mendel, Gregor Johann (1822–84), Austrian botanist. As abbot of an Augustinian cloister in Brünn, he carried out researches on hybridity in plants, and his detailed observations of the common garden pea established the principles of heredity which bear his name.

Minot, George Richards (1885–1950), an American who, with W. P. Murphy, discovered in 1926 the curative properties of liver extract in pernicious anaemia. He shared the Nobel Prize for medicine in 1934 with Murphy and G. H. Whipple.

Morton, William Thomas Greene (1819–68), American dentist; in 1846 was the first to demonstrate surgical anaesthesia by means of sulphuric ether.

Osler, Sir William (1849–1919), Canadian physician and medical historian, Professor of medicine in Canada, America, and Oxford, England. An authority on diseases of the blood and spleen.

Pasteur, Louis (1822–95), French chemist whose researches into fermentation led to the science of bacteriology, while his work on infectious diseases and their prevention led to the science of immunology. In 1864 he invented pasteurization (for wine) and in 1885 devised a rabies vaccine to cure hydrophobia.

Pavlov, Ivan Petrovich (1849–1936), Russian physiologist who worked at the physiology of circulation and digestion; is best known for his study of animal behaviour, particularly conditioned reflexes and the relation between psychological stress and brain function. Nobel Prize winner 1904.

Pinel, Philippe (1745–1826), French physician, famous for his work in reforming the old and barbarous methods of treating the insane.

Röntgen, Wilhelm Konrad von (1845–1923), German physicist who discovered X-rays in 1895. He won the Nobel Prize for physics in 1901.

Ross, Sir Ronald (1857–1932), British physician, b. India, who discovered the malaria parasite (1895–8). He won the Nobel Prize for medicine in 1902.

Sauerbruch, Ernst Ferdinand (1875–1951), German scientist who was a pioneer in tuberculosis surgery.

Semmelweis, Ignaz Philipp (1818–65), Hungarian obstetrician, a pioneer in the use of antiseptic methods which greatly reduced puerperal fever following childbirth.

Sherrington, Sir Charles Scott (1875–1952), British scientist, an authority on the physiology of the nervous system and reflex action. Shared with E. D. Adrian the 1932 Nobel Prize for medicine.

Simpson, Sir James Young (1811–70), British obstetrician who introduced the use of chloroform in childbirth (1847).

Smith, Sir Grafton Elliot (1871–1937), Australian anatomist, an authority on brain anatomy and human evolution.

Stopes, Marie Carmichael (1880–1958), British pioneer advocate of birth control and birth control clinics.

Sydenham, Thomas (1624–89), London physician, often named 'the English Hippocrates'. Emphasized that medical theories alone are of little value to the practitioner who must rely upon his powers of observation.

Syme, James (1799–1870), Edinburgh surgeon, first to show that excision of a diseased joint is usually preferable to amputation of the limb (conservative as opposed to destructive surgery). Father-in-law of Joseph Lister.

Trousseau, Armand (1801–67), Professor of medicine in the Paris Faculty. A masterly clinician who did much work on tuberculosis and other diseases of the chest. An excellent teacher, many of his pupils became well-known.

Vesalius, Andreas (1514–64), of Padua. The most commanding figure in European medicine after Galen and until William Harvey. Father of anatomy. Published *De Fabrica Humani Corporis* 1543. Derided in his lifetime, Vesalius burned his manuscripts, left Padua, and gave up the study of anatomy.

Virchow, Rudolf (1821–1902), Professor of pathology, Berlin. Published *Cellular-Pathologie* 1858, in which he described the body as 'a cell-state in which every cell is an equal citizen', thus altering the old concept of diseased organs to that of diseased cells, the basis of modern pathology.

Wells, Sir Thomas Spencer (1818–97), London gynaecologist, became famous as an outstandingly successful exponent of ovariotomy, the only abdominal operation performed before Lister's introduction of antisepsis. The Wells' haemostat ('Spencers') invented by him is the most commonly used surgical instrument.

Withering, William (1741–99), Birmingham physician. His *Account of the Foxglove* 1785 is a pharmacological classic which drew attention to the fact that traditional folk-remedies might be useful in scientific medicine.

Yersin, Alexandre (1863–1943), surgeon in the French Colonial Army. In 1894 at Canton discovered *Pasteurella pestis*, the causative organism of bubonic plague, the disease known as the Black Death (1348) and the Great Plague of London (1665). The organism was discovered independently in 1894 by a Japanese bacteriologist, Shibasaburo Kitasato (1852–1931).

5

The Environment

Summary of Chapter

Population

In all the efforts made internationally during the 1960s to solve the problems of world poverty and underdevelopment, the main issue was one of population. Because we now have greater control over major epidemics – smallpox, plague, yellow fever and malaria (see *Medicine*) – people throughout the world are living longer. In Sri Lanka, as just one example, the death rate dropped by half in twenty years – and in the same period, the population doubled. Food and other resources, however, have not increased at a similar rate. Experts came to two conclusions. The poor were poor because there were too many of them; and conditions would improve only when it became the general practice for people to control the size of their families.

So massive programmes of family planning were set up. But the population in most parts of the world, and especially in the Third World (the poorest, least developed nations), is still rising in the 1970s. In mid-1975 there were 3,967 million people in the world. This figure increases by 2.5 per cent every year, which means that, if there is no change either of policy or in the way we live, there could be 14,000 million of us by 2020 and 28,000 million by 2050.

This population, of course, is not evenly spread across the globe, and it is not growing everywhere at the same speed. In the developed world, where about one billion (1,000,000,000) people live, birth rates are generally lower – 1 per cent in the USSR and the USA, only 0.5 per cent in Britain. (But in some of these areas, population densities are very high already: in England and Wales there are 323 people to a square kilometre, as compared with 93 for Europe as a whole and 10 for North America.) What will happen in the future? One way of answering that question is to look at the growth of population in Europe, and then see what it might tell us about the problems of India and China.

The great population expansion occurred in Europe in the early nineteenth century, with the Industrial Revolution. In Britain in 1800, the population was growing at the rate of about 1.8 per cent every year, and that continued to a peak in 1820. Modern medicine meant that not only were people living longer, but more children survived beyond the first year of life. Improvements in industry and farming made it possible for this larger population to enjoy a gradually improving standard of living.

At first more land was cleared to produce more food, but in time this was no longer possible. The proportion of people living in towns increased; and when pressures became too great, the surplus population began to emigrate. In 1820 the British government gave grants to people to help them to settle in South Africa; the potato blight in Ireland in 1845 and the years following resulted not only in the death of a million people from starvation, but the emigration of 3 million to the United States.

Apart from helping some to emigrate, the European countries were able to support their growing populations by importing food and raw materials from

other parts of the world. They paid for these imports by exporting manufactured goods from the ever-growing number of factories.

So, by emigration and world trade, European countries were able to cope
with the population explosion until the birth rate began to fall. A general improvement in social and economic conditions meant that parents began to see
the value of producing only a small family. The former need to have large
families no longer existed – not only because more children survived, but also
because their parents were better cared for by the state when they became old,
ill or disabled. Compulsory state education meant that children cost their

'Bustee' dwellers in appalling living conditions at Dacca (*Photo: by courtesy of Oxfam*)

parents more, because they were becoming breadwinners at a later age; and depression and unemployment in the years following the First World War made smaller families necessary. In many parts of Europe since the Second World War the birth rate has stabilized, and the wish for a high standard of living has limited family size to two or three children.

In India, however, this process has not taken place. The population here has grown from 248 million in 1921 to 609 million in 1976, and it continues to grow at one million a month. This means that in a single year the equivalent of the total population of Australia is being added. The chief reason for this growth is a decline in the death rate – although life expectancy is still only 42 years for men and 40.5 years for women (compared with 67 for men and 74 for women in the USA). Since half of the population is under 15 it is easy to see why the population grows so fast, especially when you appreciate that the average age for marriage in India is 15.6 years.

Another problem is that the population is becoming increasingly urban – more and more people are trying to find work in the towns and cities. In Europe, employment was able to keep pace with the growing movement away from the countryside and into the towns, but it is not so in India. Since 1962 the population of Calcutta has grown from 3,400,000 to 7 million; of this population, three out of every four people are living in slums, and many sleep on the pavements.

At first sight it would seem that the obvious solution to India's problem is a strong family planning policy. Such a policy was already under way in 1950. But surveys have shown that family planning has not worked. One survey, carried out in the Khanna area, makes the big, central problem clear. Its findings were that: 'An overwhelming majority of the people have a large number of children because they want large families. More important, they want them because they need them.'

Why do the people of India want and need large families? First, because children are economically valuable. In a rural community (and in India 70 per cent of the population still lives outside the towns), a child makes a vital contribution from an early age. Children help in the fields; they care for animals; they help with household tasks and, unlike children in the West, they cost their families little compared with the contribution they make. Second, as the child becomes older it is his responsibility to care for his parents when they fall ill or grow old. With no welfare state, parents need children simply for security. In many rural communities, children are sent to the city to earn money, which is then sent home to help the family. In Khanna as many as a quarter of the families were receiving money in this way. Then again, fertility is still regarded as a good thing, and a son is prized. Many children still die young, so that to be sure of grown-up children in the future parents need to give birth to a large number. Also, in a society where pleasures are few, a family is one of the satisfactions life has to offer.

How then can the people of India reach the position where they no longer want or need large families, but instead see the benefits of small ones? It has been suggested that social and political change may prove to be the only key to solving the population problem, and this point was made again at the 1974

World Population Conference in Bucharest. Health, education, employment, reduced birth and death rates – they are all intimately connected.

When people in India can see that it is no longer necessary to have a child every year to make sure that three or four children survive into adulthood; when employment outside agriculture, or better working methods, have minimized the need for child labour; when children become an economic liability rather than a necessity; when welfare schemes provide security in old age, sickness and unemployment; when women are free to pursue careers outside the home, and when family life is no longer the chief source of entertainment – only then will people turn naturally to family planning. In fact, if the developed world wants to help reduce population pressure, it should be working with more determination to create an international order that makes it easier to get rid of poverty.

Sixty out of every hundred people in the world live on only 15 per cent of the world's land – in Europe, India, Pakistan and Bangladesh, and in China. The last of these areas provides interesting contrasts. In China, steps to limit population have been linked with overall development programmes. The huge population (estimated at 800 million) has been used in mammoth public works schemes and in agriculture, which in China is labour-intensive – that is, it uses a great deal of labour rather than machinery. Economic growth has occurred side by side with the development of better education services, and these conditions have been widely shared by a large part of the population.

At what cost to individual freedom, we might ask, has this been achieved? China has an authoritarian government which can order people to take up specific forms of employment. But the same relationships between development, and better conditions for a large part of the population, have resulted in a decline in birth rates in countries with other kinds of government – in Costa Rica, Sri Lanka, South Korea, Taiwan and Malaysia. On the other hand, where economic growth has been highly concentrated in a few hands, as in Brazil, Mexico, the Philippines and Thailand, big families are still customary for large sections of the population.

World population, its size and growth, is certainly one of the main problems now facing the world community. We simply cannot allow population to continue to increase at the present rate because the pressure on world resources, and the scale of pollution created, will become too great. But we should not think that this is a problem only for the Third World. In many senses, population in the affluent world presents the world community with problems that grow more worrying all the time. A child born today in the USA will consume twenty times as much of the world's resources as an Indian child, and will contribute fifty times as much pollution. It is impossible for the rest of the world's people to reach such living standards; and indeed, if the population of the USA continues to increase, the strain on the world's resources will become intolerable. It is to these matters that we must now turn – the pressure on world resources of food, raw materials and energy, the enormous problem of pollution that the massive world population is causing, and the measures that are being taken to conserve what remains of the natural environment.

Resources and Energy

The question of world resources and energy supply – whether the world has enough food to feed its people, enough minerals to sustain industrial development, enough water for industrial, agricultural and domestic use and enough energy to keep everything going – is occupying the attention of numerous experts throughout the world, and the conclusions they draw are almost as many as the experts. It is impossible here to cover the whole field or to draw many conclusions. We will simply try to look at the scale of the problem and to examine some of the solutions being put forward.

Of course the answer to the question: How long will the resources of the world last? depends very much on the standard of living we demand. A high standard of living such as Americans enjoy depends on a continued supply of necessary resources. It is certain, as we have already seen, that the whole population of the world cannot hope to enjoy such a standard of living.

The USA, containing only 6 per cent of the world's people, uses at present 25 per cent of the world's steel, 25 per cent of its fertilizer and 40 per cent of its wood pulp. Americans own 40 per cent of the telephones, 47 per cent of the cars and 33 per cent of the TV sets. If everyone in the world were to have as many cars as the Americans, world steel production would have to increase fivefold – an impossibility. Of course, it is not only the Americans who use a disproportionate share of the world's resources – North America, Japan and western Europe, which contain only one sixth of the world's people, together use 80 per cent of the world's raw materials.

Food

When we come to the world's food supply, this contrast is even more marked. While two thirds of the world starves, the other third is obsessed with slimming and suffers illness through overweight. The United Nations estimates that 300 million children in developing countries lack protein to such an extent that their physical growth and development are greatly retarded. The fact of the matter is that the world is hungry because the more affluent nations demand a standard of living only made possible by using and exploiting the resources of less fortunate parts of the world.

What can be done about the world food problem? Many solutions have been put forward and tried – the so-called Green Revolution, for example, whose aim is to produce new strains of basic crops that give an increased yield per acre and are more resistant to disease. A new strain of rice, IR8, developed at the International Rice Research Institute in the Philippines, was a cross between a tall rice from Indonesia and a dwarf rice from Taiwan. Yields have been increased fourfold in the Philippines by the use of this strain, while work at the International Maize and Wheat Improvement Centre in Mexico has resulted in yields of wheat trebling between 1955 and 1969. But the excitement that was once felt about these methods – seeing in them a universal solution to food shortages – has evaporated. Such high yields require enormous amounts of water and fertilizer; and to these must be added the initial cost of seed. The farmer in the developing world often does not have the money, the skill or the incentive. Unless the price he can obtain for his surplus crop is high, he will see no point in producing more than he needs for himself. Two other problems may arise. First, his soil may become exhausted faster; and second, he may use the money from the sale of his crop to buy machinery, which will merely cause more unemployment. In the words of Norman E. Borlaug, who was awarded the 1970 Nobel Peace Prize for bringing about this Green Revolution: 'It has given man a breathing space ... but the frightening power of human reproduction must be curbed: otherwise the success of the Green Revolution will be ephemeral only.'

We have already touched on a second method of increasing food production – the use of fertilizer. It is possible by this method to multiply yields by four; however, fertilizer not only causes pollution problems (see page 222), but in recent years its cost has risen so fast that it is out of reach for those who need it most. The whole of Africa uses the same amount of fertilizer as Italy; while the $7\frac{1}{2}$ million people of Sweden use as much as the 609 million Indians. Twenty-five per cent of the world uses 75 per cent of the fertilizer, and in countries like Britain its effectiveness is decreasing. Between 1949 and 1968 use of fertilizer increased 800 per cent, but yields increased by only 35 per cent.

Not only is the price of fertilizer very high – at the Medak Agricultural Centre, South India, the cost of a bag rose from £4 in June 1973 to £8 in October 1974 – but many fertilizers are themselves in short supply. So the question is whether countries like Britain are prepared to use less so that precious supplies can be used where increased yields are essential.

Another solution would be to increase the amount of land under cultivation by clearing and irrigating. In eastern Asia there is little good agricultural land left for cultivation, but there is undoubtedly room for opening up new areas in Latin America and Africa. There are considerable difficulties here – erosion (the wearing away of the land surface) easily results, and continuous irrigation can make the soil salty because the water dries in the sun and leaves mineral salts. The UN Food and Agricultural Organization considers that most of the fertile land in the world is already farmed and that the marginal land needs high capital investment, engineering skill and agricultural research to ensure that the cost of preparing it is not greater than the profit to be gained from it.

A change in eating habits could help to ease the world's food problem. In Kenya, work is proceeding in the domestication of native animals such as the eland and other antelope. These animals are better suited to the local conditions than cattle; they are more resistant to disease and have a higher ratio of flesh to body weight. The dugong or manatee, the river cow of South America and Africa, converts river vegetation to meat; and this not only produces food but keeps the river clean. And if people could be persuaded to eat the hippo, this animal would provide as much meat as sixty sheep.

In the developed world we are being encouraged to eat new synthetic (man-made) foods. Protein can be produced by growing yeast on oil or even on vegetable waste. Toprina is being produced in this way at Grangemouth in Scotland, while another synthetic source of protein, protoveg, is obtained from soya beans. A similar substance, kesp, is prepared from a type of field bean in East Anglia and the West Country. 'Meat' produced in this way costs only one sixth as much as red meat, and is already used in catering and in some convenience foods.

In fact, to consume meat at all is a very wasteful way of obtaining protein, and 90 per cent of the diet of the human race is vegetarian. Twenty-two lb of protein in animal feed produces only one lb of protein in beef. A plate of steak and chips represents enough cereal to feed a family for a week in a drought situation, or enough vegetable protein to supply the full needs of an adult for a fortnight. Fifty per cent of the world fish catch is converted into fish meal to feed pigs and poultry in developed countries. Of the remainder, more than 33 per cent is eaten by the already well-fed. If more fish was used directly as protein for human consumption, it would make an enormous contribution to the world's food supply.

Food supplies could also be increased simply by preventing waste. It is estimated that rats and other pests, together with disease, consume between 30 and 50 per cent of the crops in developing countries and 10 per cent in the rich world, either in the fields or in storage. Rats can be controlled by a chemical called Warfarin, but in Britain Warfarin-resistant strains are developing, while in India religious custom makes control difficult. A swarm of locusts can eat about 3,000 tons of food crops every day. They, too, can be controlled by insecticides; but as we shall see later, this creates further problems.

The answer to the world's food problem has been seen by some as simply a problem of redistribution. You move the food to where it is wanted. This is what is done in times of drought and disaster under the World Food Programme set up in 1963 by the United Nation's Food and Agricultural Organization (FAO). But the cost of transport and handling charges makes this uneconomic as well as inefficient. It may solve problems in the short term; but in the long term, the Third World has to be helped to produce its own food. This needs techniques like the Green Revolution; but it also requires a more realistic world economic system, which will enable the people of the Third World to earn high wages and so to buy the food and the agricultural equipment they need. This in turn may well mean that the rich world needs not only to eat less and to eat different things, but also to be prepared to pay more for raw materials so that the Third World can buy more. President Nyerere of Tanzania has said: 'In 1963 we had to produce 5 tons of sisal to buy a tractor. In 1970 we had to produce 10 tons of sisal to buy the same tractor.' Thus the very conditions of world trade act against the Third World in its struggle to raise living standards. In 1950 the developing countries had 30 per cent of world trade, but by 1970 this had sunk to less than 20 per cent.

Water

The world's most precious and most widely used resource is water. Seventy-five per cent of the earth's surface is covered by it; it is used in agriculture, for domestic purposes, for transport, in the production of energy and in nearly every industrial process. The consumption of water is increasing all the time. In Britain, use increases by 3 per cent every year. In 1938 the British used 651 million gallons a day; by 1948 the figure was 778 million gallons; it is now 5,000 million gallons.

How then can world water supplies be safeguarded? The hydrological cycle is the name given to the process in which water from the earth's surface in rivers, lakes and oceans is taken up by the wind and by plants which release water vapour into the atmosphere. This water vapour rises into the air, cools and condenses into water droplets; these form clouds and eventually rain, hail or snow, which fall back to earth and start the cycle all over again. The rate at which we can use water depends on how fast the hydrological cycle returns it to earth. At present Europeans are using underground water supplies at three times and Americans at twice the rate at which the cycle can return it to earth. In India 90,000 wells dug in the Ganges Plain are making serious inroads into underground water supplies. So if we are not to suffer from a critical world water shortage we shall not only have to try to reduce demand, but also to prevent losses from evaporation during irrigation and storage, to move water to where it is needed, and to investigate schemes for desalination – the removal of salt from sea water.

Reservoirs not only store water, but together with pipelines make it possible to transport water to other places. In California a lake was formed behind the Parker Dam and water was carried 242 miles to Los Angeles through mountains and deserts. In Wales many reservoirs, such as Lake Vrynwy, store water for towns and cities in England, against much local opposition. In developing countries, problems arise not only through the evaporation of water while it is being moved about, but because irrigation channels provide breeding grounds for the water snail, the carrier of the flatworm called bilharzia which causes chronic disease. A United Nations report in 1962 said that, '70 per cent of the urban population of the developing countries either have an inadequate supply with no mains, or dangerous water, or both. This rate rises to 90 per cent outside the larger towns.'

It is argued that desalination could solve many of the world's water problems, since 97 per cent of the world's water is salt. But this requires vast applications of energy, which is in itself expensive and in short supply. Desalinated water costs somewhere between three and four times a gallon as much as reservoir water, and the initial installation costs are high. At Eilat in Israel 250,000 gallons a day are produced, while in Kuwait 6 million gallons are produced in a plant powered by local oil and natural gas. This is a viable solution for wealthy countries such as Kuwait, made rich by its oil, but it is hardly a practical proposition for irrigation projects in the Third World.

Other projects such as melting icebergs, building barrages across estuaries or making rain by releasing frozen carbon dioxide into clouds are being researched. But what might be the effect on the environment? The melting of icebergs could lead to widespread flooding, while the rain-makers have little control over where the rain falls.

However water supplies are maintained in the future, water will un-doubtedly cost more and will come to be regarded as a precious commodity. Of course, dry areas of the world already look on it as such; but in areas of high rainfall it is still used wastefully. In the drought in Britain in the summer of 1976 we were forced to restrict our use of water. Have we however learnt the lesson? Today we see few signs of the moderation in water use we were then forced to adopt. To ensure sufficient world supplies for the future, industry will have to recycle water for use over and over again, while research into plants that can resist drought would help in agriculture. Domestic users, too, will have to demand less of it, and, in the end, pay more for it.

Minerals

World resources of materials from plant and animal sources are renewable – that is, they can be replaced indefinitely. But mineral resources are not. They occur on the earth's surface in fixed quantities, and though, while man continues his search for new sources, we do not know exactly how long supplies will last, we do know quite certainly that one day supplies will be exhausted.

When will that happen? The answer depends, of course, on how rapidly we use them. As one example, the use of iron ore has increased by four times since 1950, and if this rate of increase were to continue, supplies would be exhausted by 2050. But it is likely that, as reserves run down, prices will rise; it will then become worthwhile to use ores with a lower percentage of iron. This alone would increase potential reserves. New exploration is also likely to take place, more scrap will be recycled, and other materials may well be substituted.

This sort of possibility of extending the length of time before reserves run out exists in the case of many other minerals. Developments in technology are making it possible to use less material in manufacture. For example, computer components which in 1945 were a couple of feet long are now only the size of a pinhead. Comparison of the Forth rail and road bridges, built in 1890 and 1964, shows how bridges can now be built using very much less material. In Cornwall, Britain, tin is now being mined again from the waste tips of old mines; while in South Africa, gold waste tips are being mined for uranium. Later we shall be looking more closely at the possibilities of recycling from scrap. In Britain, 56 per cent of the lead used is recycled, but enormous quantities of materials are still being wasted. We continue to use more and more steel in the car industry and for domestic goods. We are victims of the practice of built-in obsolescence – cars, refrigerators and similar products could be built to last longer and so save steel; but manufacturers prefer to make sure that they can go on selling these things by designing them so that they wear out and have to be replaced. Optimists believe that, as minerals run out, man's ingenuity will find substitutes either among the renewable resources, like plants and animals, or by using new minerals. It has been suggested, for example, that metals could be extracted from granite, but this would involve immense quantities of energy as well as creating vast areas of derelict land.

Energy

In everything we say about the use of man's resources, we keep coming back to the need for energy. For many years mankind has been dependent on irreplaceable stores of energy, all derived from past radiation. These reserves of coal, oil and natural gas are not renewable, and today we are realizing that we cannot continue to use these resources at an ever-increasing rate.

Between the two World Wars, the use of energy rose by $1\frac{1}{2}$ per cent a year, in the 1950s by nearly 5 per cent, in the 1960s by 5.5 per cent. In recent years, the demand for oil alone has grown by 7 per cent a year. The USA uses twice as much energy per head of the population as any other developed country.

Let us look first at the conventional sources of energy and their future prospects, and then at some alternative sources and at ways of conserving energy.

Coal

Until 1920, coal provided at least 80 per cent of the world's energy. This figure dropped to 60 per cent by 1950 and in 1970 was only 35 per cent. World coal reserves are high and it is estimated that at worst they could last another century. Eighty-eight per cent of these reserves are in the USA, the USSR and China. Coal is likely to remain a major source of power for generating electricity. But the use of coal is costly in its effects on the environment – it pollutes the air, it causes danger and ill-health to those who mine it, and it devastates the landscape.

Natural gas

Natural gas, or methane, is another source of energy. Generally found in oil fields, its use was limited at first by transport problems. The USA now has pipelines that take methane direct from the Texan oilfields to the north-east coast, and tankers can now carry it as a refrigerated liquid. Between 1965 and 1970 large fields of natural gas were discovered off the English coast. By the end of 1977 all consumers in Britain had been converted to natural gas. But how long will it last? The US Petroleum Institute suggested in March 1973 that the USA had only ten years' supply. A renewable source of methane is sewage, and much research is needed into this possibility.

Oil

Oil, of course, is *the* energy source today, meeting 52 per cent of the world's needs. In recent years we have seen the devastating effect on the world economy of, first, oil shortages, and then of vastly increased prices. Oil is used not only for electricity and transport, but also as a lubricant and as a raw material in a whole range of petrochemical industries; it forms the basis of fertilizers, plastics, and synthetic fibres such as rayon and nylon. The very fact that oil comes largely from a region whose political situation is unstable – more than half the world's reserves are in the Persian Gulf – has led consumer countries to look urgently for other sources of energy and for economies in use.

The discovery of oil in the North Sea has been of tremendous importance to Britain. Capital development costs are very high. North Sea oil supplies from the Forties, Argyll and Auk fields were inaugurated on 3 November 1975 and it is hoped that Britain may be self-sufficient in oil by 1980.

The union of oil-producing countries to form OPEC (Oil Producing and Exporting Countries) has shown very clearly that the countries which hold the resources needed by the rest of the world wield enormous power. When in 1973 OPEC announced price increases of almost 200 per cent the Shah of Iran (one of the main oil-producing states) suggested that coal might be used for heating homes and generating electricity. If oil continued to be used at the present rate, he said, it would all be gone in thirty years. Oil should be reserved for the petrochemical and medical industries.

Everyone agrees, in fact, that if demand goes on increasing, oil reserves will last only until the early years of the next century. It is easy to understand why Middle East countries with few other resources want to make as much money as they can, while they can; and why also they hope to slow down the demand for oil (and so make their advantage last longer) by raising prices. In 1977 the world demand for oil did show signs of slackening and hence a meeting of OPEC in December did not recommend a general price increase.

Shortages and high prices have made it more economic to look elsewhere for oil. The USA has vast deposits of oil shale in Colorado, Wyoming and Utah. A pilot plant is being set up, but costs are high; much energy is needed and an enormous amount of water, and the environment would be destroyed. A more suitable source is the Canadian Athabasca tar sands, from which oil can be processed. It has been estimated that, at the present rate of consumption, these sands could supply the needs of the USA and Canada for about sixty years.

Nuclear energy

But what about nuclear energy? In 1974, 280 nuclear power stations were either operating or being constructed throughout the world. In the core of a fast breeder reactor is a ton of plutonium that can produce as much energy as 3 million tons of coal. As a source of energy, this is undoubtedly a solution for the future. Almost limitless energy can be made available from nuclear fission.

But the use of nuclear energy poses some frightening problems, which arise from the operation of nuclear power stations and reactors and from the difficulties of disposing of radioactive waste. The storage tanks for this waste have to be constructed of very strong, leak-proof material. Places have to be found where they can be safely buried. Some radioactive elements have a half-life of 100 years, some of 1,000 or more. (The half-life is a measure of the time it takes for the materials to decay and disappear.) The power stations themselves have only a limited life and when they fall out of use, they will remain radioactive.

If we are to rely more and more on nuclear power, we will have to solve, in a responsible fashion, all the vast problems it creates.

Solar energy

In cloudless regions, solar power – energy taken from the sun – might provide

Above: Solar panels on roof of solar heated house in Milton Keynes. *Below:* Diagram of the heating system. (*Photos: Milton Keynes Development Corporation*)

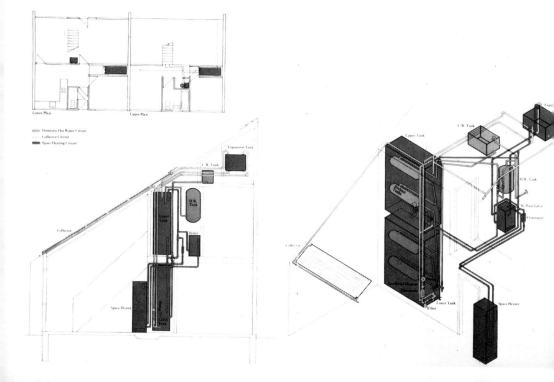

an answer to shortages. Research is still at an early stage; at the moment, to produce a reasonable amount of power requires a very large concentration of solar energy. For example, a single car driven by solar power would need a collection area of 600 square metres. The Russians have a scheme for trapping and concentrating the sun's rays with a series of moving mirrors. At present the most immediate use is for local units in individual houses or schools. Such schemes in Britain on Merseyside, at Milton Keynes and more recently in South London are being watched with much interest.

Geothermal power

Another possibility is geothermal power – that is, heat from the interior of the earth. A plant using this power at Landerello in Italy generates enough electricity for half of Italy's railway system. The Wairakei plant in New Zealand provides 20 per cent of North Island's power. There have been proposals for the use of geothermal energy in parts of Britain.

Tidal power

The power created by tides at sea may be used to generate electricity if the tide is strong and the tidal range great. A scheme is successfully operating at La Rance in France, and studies have been carried out in the Severn estuary in Britain.

Water power

Water has long been a source of power for operating water mills. Hydro-electric power schemes exist in many parts of the world, but they supply only 2 per cent of the world's energy. These schemes are very expensive to initiate, but they are cheap to run. The Snowy Mountains scheme in Australia diverted water to flow in a different direction by means of sixteen reservoirs linked

Aerial view of Geothermal Valley, Auckland, New Zealand. (*Photo: High Commissioner for New Zealand*)

Above: artist's impressions of a series of Cockrell rafts whose motion, caused by that of the waves, would generate electricity. *Below:* experimental raft at one tenth scale in the Solent. (*Photos: Natural Energy Centre*)

by tunnels. In Brazil, 80 per cent of the total generating capacity in 1970 was from water power; and in Africa, ambitious projects have involved the formation of huge island lakes – the Kariba in Zambia, completed in 1960, and the Volta in Ghana, completed five years later. Latin America and Africa still contain large, untapped sources of hydro-electric power.

All these are possible sources of energy for the future; but for the present, the urgent need is to investigate ways of saving energy. This is happening nationally and internationally. The British 'Save It' campaign suggests ways in which domestic consumers can use less. Schemes for district heating, for using waste heat from power stations to heat buildings, for providing better public transport, for carrying more freight by rail, for better insulation, and so on, are all being proposed and developed in Britain and elsewhere. We are beginning to understand that we cannot go on consuming more and more food, water, minerals and energy without looking ahead (how long will they last?) and at the effects on the environment (are we making the world an impossible place to live in?).

In recent years, people have begun to realize that limited resources can become a matter of politics. That happened when the OPEC countries got together. It also occurred when the leading producers of phosphates formed a similar union – they were able to treble their prices. Producers of cotton in Latin America threatened to stop sales to Japan unless the Japanese agreed to pay double the price – which they had to do. As a world community, we have to realize that we all depend on one another, and that sometimes it might be the poorer countries which hold the trump cards.

A country like the USA, which imports an enormous percentage of the raw materials it needs – for example, 95 per cent of its bauxite and 85 per cent of its nickel – has come to understand that it must keep the goodwill of the producer countries. In a particularly strong position are those countries that hold a large proportion of known resources – Thailand, for example, which has a third of the world's tin, and Zaire, with a half of the world's cobalt. On the other hand, the developed countries have to appreciate the problems of a country that is dependent on a single commodity – Zambia, 95 per cent dependent on copper; Liberia, 89 per cent dependent on iron ore; Mauritius, 93 per cent dependent on sugar; Ghana, 65 per cent dependent on cocoa. Conditions of world trade have made it more and more difficult for such countries to survive. We have already seen the Tanzanian predicament where more sisal production buys fewer tractors. Can the rest of the world grumble if the sisal producers demand to be paid more for their sisal so that they can go on existing?

Pollution and Waste

An ever-increasing world population using an ever-increasing quantity of the world's resources has naturally caused enormous problems in two particular fields – the pollution of the environment and the creation of waste.

Agricultural Pollution

The constant need for more and more food has led to the destruction of forests and the erosion of soil. Erosion takes place when farmers cultivate the same land for too long with the same crop and with inadequate fertilizers. In the 1930s drought on the prairies of North America, where wheat had been grown year after year, turned the soil to dust, which was then blown away by winds. Farmers have to learn to avoid such erosion – by contour-ploughing (ploughing across the slope and not up and down it); by terracing land to prevent soil being washed away; by strip-cropping (sowing with different crops in alternate strips) to prevent water from draining away down slopes; or by planting trees to anchor the soil and protect it from winds.

Man the farmer has also harmed his environment by his use of chemicals, both to make plants grow better and to protect them from pests, diseases and weeds. We have seen that fertilizers can certainly produce dramatic improvements in crop yields. But more and more now needs to be used, with less and less effect. In the USA, the use of nitrogen fertilizer has risen fourteen-fold in twenty-five years; this has produced changes in the structure of the soil, and every year more fertilizer must be applied to achieve the same results. Much of it is not absorbed by the plants, and on some farms 45 per cent of the nitrates used end up in rivers and lakes, causing pollution.

Lake Erie is a gloomy example of what happens. The run-off from fertilizers, combined with factory waste and sewage, has caused an excess of the process known as eutrophication. This occurs when the enrichment of the water causes too great a growth of algae (the simple plants that form the green scum on ponds), which use up all the oxygen in the water and so cause the death of

Erosion of the soil near Benson, Oxfordshire. (*Photo: Radio Times Hulton Library*)

other creatures who have too little oxygen. Lake Erie no longer contains sturgeon, whitefish and pike, but only carp, catfish and sludge worms. The whitefish industry, which used to produce about 2 million lb of fish every year, was producing only 13,000 lb by 1962. Some species of algae actually give off poisonous substances; and at Stone Lake, Iowa, blue-green algae have caused the death of 8,000 wild birds and animals.

Farmers are using more and more pesticides to prevent pests and diseases. We can see the justification for this, too – in Ethiopia in 1958 locusts ate grain worth a million pounds; and as we have seen, developing countries lose between 30 and 50 per cent of their crops through the ravages of disease and pests. But the use of pesticides has serious side-effects on the environment. DDT sprayed on crops seemed at first a perfect insecticide – it killed effectively over a long period and could be applied in low doses. But after some years it became obvious that it was affecting the environment in ways no one had foreseen. It was entering what is known as the food chain. Surplus DDT drained into the nearest river, where it was absorbed by weeds. The weed was eaten by fish, and they in turn were eaten by larger fish. Then these, too, were eaten – by birds. At each stage the DDT is consumed with the food, and more and more builds up. If at any stage man eats any of the creatures concerned, he too absorbs DDT. As we shall see later, the peregrine has become almost extinct as a result of DDT. Not only does the DDT build up in the adult bird, but it results in thin-shelled eggs which break, so that the young are not hatched. The effect of the indiscriminate use of chemicals for one purpose in one place can affect the environment and people miles away. In some areas, human milk is found to have a dangerously high concentration of DDT, and DDT has been found in the bodies of penguins living miles from where DDT is used.

Another unforeseen result of using DDT is that it has upset the delicate balance of nature. DDT used in orchards killed the codlin moth – but that led to an increase in the red mite previously eaten by the moth. In the Cañeta Valley, Peru, DDT killed pests on the cotton crop, but it also killed the creatures that normally preyed on the pests. In time the pests developed resistance to DDT; but by then their old enemies, who did not develop resistance, had been wiped out, so the pests multiplied even more rapidly.

We have to be careful not to over-react to these dangers. The use of DDT as a killer of pests causing typhus, malaria and yellow fever has transformed life for many people in the tropics. For example, in Georgetown, Guyana, following the use of DDT, the death rate among babies fell from 250 to 67 per 1,000 between 1945 and 1948. What we must realize is that the use of chemicals needs to be carefully controlled.

Air Pollution

The pollution of the environment by modern farming is small compared with the effects on air, water and land of factories, mines and the activities of urban man. Pollutants of the air include chemicals such as mercury, asbestos and lead, gases such as carbon monoxide and sulphur dioxide which are both by-products of burning coal, and grit and dust. Smog is the result of the combination of smoke and fog, and like other forms of air pollution can be dangerous to health. In one district of Osaka, Japan, half the population suffers from asthma brought on by air pollution.

The dangers of air pollution had been recognized in Britain for centuries, but it was only in 1956 that the Clean Air Act came into force. This Act was a direct result of a disastrous smog in 1952. On Thursday, 4 December, cold air over London trapped a layer of smoke and fumes. There was no wind to remove it, and by the time it dispersed over 4,000 people had died. The Clean Air Act, banning other than smokeless fuels, has virtually eliminated smog. Although the population has risen by 10 per cent and energy consumption by 17 per cent, amounts of smoke and sulphur dioxide in the air have steadily gone down.

Smog is still a great problem in Los Angeles, in the USA. The city lies in a hollow and cold air flows in from the sea at night to become trapped below an area of warmer air. Pollution, largely from 4 million cars releasing carbon monoxide and lead, becomes trapped under this warmer area, and the result is smog.

Other examples of air pollution causing environmental problems have occurred in Florida, USA, where pollutants of gaseous fluorides from phosphate factories have killed and crippled livestock; and in the Sacramento Valley, California, where sulphur dioxide pollution has caused the destruction of plant life over 67,000 acres.

Another alarming result of air pollution could be a change in the climate. An increase in carbon dioxide in the atmosphere could lead to an increase in world temperatures which in turn might cause the melting of the great ice caps and disastrous flooding of low-lying coastal areas. Alternatively, dust pollution in the atmosphere could result in the reflection of the sun's rays back into space, which would cause a drop in world temperatures. In Washington State, USA, atmospheric dustiness has increased by 57 per cent in recent years, and over Switzerland by 88 per cent. An increase in dust in the atmosphere can also cause increased rainfall. Records kept in Rochdale, Lancashire, between 1898 and 1927 not only showed a steady annual increase in rainfall, but also consistently lower rainfall at weekends when factories were closed and there was therefore less dust. Here again the lesson to be learned is that man tampers with his environment at the risk of causing results he has not foreseen and that are unwelcome to him.

Water Pollution

We have seen how farmers pollute water by allowing chemical wastes to flow into it. Even worse pollution is caused by factories. Factory wastes include many poisonous substances such as cyanide, mercury and lead, which are often discharged untreated into rivers and so into the sea. In Sweden the town of Växjö discharges sewage into Lake Thummen, which is also polluted by effluent from a textile factory. The pollutants cause excessive growths of algae,

The results of pollution: thousands of dead fish caught in the reeds at the edge of Coate Water in Wiltshire. (*Photo: Richard Slade, Camera Press, London*)

which in turn cause a lack of oxygen and eutrophication (see page 222). Work to rectify this situation is costly – it involves pumping off the upper layers and spraying the lake with aluminium sulphate. The River Damodar in India is full of pollutants such as cyanide from factories, two thirds of which have no treatment system at all. Waste from pulp- and paper-making in the city of Fuiji, Japan, has overloaded all the surrounding rivers' supplies of dissolved oxygen, and they have become little more than dead and stinking sewers. In Britain the River Trent, which in 1887 carried 3,000 salmon, now has no salmon and is seriously polluted.

As well as chemicals, many factories discharge hot water which causes thermal pollution (pollution by heat) and again kills whatever life is in the water. Detergents cause masses of foam which bacteria are unable to break down. And accidents, too, can have disastrous results. The accidental release of several gallons of insecticide into the Rhine caused the death of 40 million fish along 250 miles of river.

In the end this polluted water reaches the sea, where it combines with sewage and poisonous wastes for which the sea is a dump. The sea is also polluted by plastics and other items discharged by ships. The explorer Thor Heyerdahl has given a horrifying description of the water of the mid-Atlantic:

> ... there were far more oil lumps than fish. In the afternoon the smooth surface of the sea was covered with enormous quantities of brown and black clots of asphalt, floating in something which looked like soapsuds, and here and there the surface shimmered in all colours as if covered with petrol ... scarcely a day passed without some form of plastic container, beer can, bottle or more perishable materials such as packing cases, cork and other rubbish drifting closer ... .

Guillemot rescued after Torrey Canyon disaster by PDSA volunteers. (*Photo: Ken Young, PDSA Photographic Library*)

In 1969 over 10,000 seabirds died in the Irish Sea, and it is thought that their deaths were caused by the dumping of waste chemicals. When mercury is discharged into water, bacteria convert it to highly poisonous methyl mercury. In 1953, people in the Minamata Bay area of Japan began to show signs of numbness, anxiety and irritability, often followed by mental derangement and death. It was found that shellfish in the bay had consumed methyl mercury from a vinyl chloride factory and this had reached the brains of those who ate the shellfish.

The episode of the *Torrey Canyon* shows the dangers of oil pollution. The ship was wrecked on the Seven Stones Reef off Cornwall in March 1967. In one night it spilled 3,000 tons of crude oil and produced a slick which menaced seventy miles of coastline and resulted in the death of between 50,000 and 250,000 seabirds. Nor is this an isolated occurrence. In March 1978 the super-tanker *Amoco Cadiz* went aground off Brittany and the colossal amount of oil released into the sea had similarly disastrous results both on the birds and animals of the coast, and on the tourism of the area.

Water, as we saw earlier, is one of our most precious commodities, and steps need to be taken urgently to prevent dangerous levels of pollution which can result in ill-health or death – not only in animals, fish and plants, but also in man. What is needed is integrated treatment of rivers and lakes (that is, every-body agreeing what is to be done and working together), and international agreements on the levels of dumping at sea that can be safely allowed.

Blight

Industrial society not only pollutes our atmosphere and water; it also destroys and blights large areas of land. Until planning controls became tighter, factories could be built in places where they not only destroyed the beauty of the environment but also caused severe health problems. Man's need for coal still results in disease among miners, who develop silicosis and other chest complaints (silicosis is a lung disease caused by inhaling gritty dust), while children living near certain factories have been shown to have dangerously high concentrations of lead in their systems. In future we must think harder about the siting of factories.

Mining often has unexpected or undesirable effects on the environment. When a new deposit of minerals is found, man moves in; he clears forest, builds roads and railways and houses, diverts and dams rivers. Great holes are dug in the ground, and rock waste tips built up. Smelting and crushing operations often pollute air and water and destroy soil and plants. The mine then ceases to be productive, and the miners move on, leaving a derelict and broken landscape. At Ince, in Lancashire, twenty-three coal shafts cover 199 acres. There are also six acres of slag heaps, 250 acres under water or marsh owing to subsidence (the sinking of land), 150 acres liable to flooding and thirty-six disused shafts.

On the limestone island of Banaba in the central Pacific, mining for phosphates has removed or destroyed so much soil that agriculture has ceased. Vegetation cover was removed, with the result that water is no longer absorbed and conserved. Many of the inhabitants have been forced to leave their once-beautiful island.

It is sometimes possible to reclaim derelict land; but often the nature of the waste prevents animals and plants from returning. In a copper mine, for example, rock waste poisons plant life, and air pollution destroys vegetation and gets into the soil. As with London smog, it needed a disaster before action was taken to reclaim tips in South Wales. In October 1966 a tip suddenly collapsed, poured down a hillside and buried a school in Aberfan; 144 people were killed, including 116 children. The tips of Aberfan have now been levelled

The Aberfan disaster: hundreds of rescue workers struggle to clear Pantglas school from the engulfing sludge. (*Photo: Michael Charity, Camera Press, London*)

and landscaped and in other parts of South Wales, such as the lower Swansea valley, land that was once despoiled by industry is now returning to its former state. In the future, it may be necessary to look harder at ways of reclaiming land because land itself will be short; and a new awareness of environmental problems may produce more careful use of land for mining – for example, the removal of top soil and its replacement after mining is finished.

Waste

The problem of pollution of our environment is closely linked with the problem of waste disposal – not only waste from industry but also ever-increasing domestic waste. At a time when the world community needs to control and reduce its consumption of materials, we are throwing away more than ever before.

The increase of packaging in recent years has added considerably to the waste problem. We need packaging to protect, identify and draw attention to the goods inside; and it saves time in supermarkets. But things do seem to have gone too far when, as in the case of some aerosols, the can costs more to produce than the contents, and on top of that creates tremendous problems of how to dispose of it. Sometimes the weight of the packet is greater than the weight of what is inside. It has been estimated that, by 1980, packaging in Britain will form nearly 50 per cent of the weight and 75 per cent of the volume of refuse.

Collection of waste is in itself an enormous problem. In Britain, for every £1,000 spent on collecting rubbish, only 35p is spent on disposing of it – the rest is the cost of the actual collection. Disposal may be cheaper, but it also presents serious problems. Dumps can become the haunt of rats and insects and cause very unpleasant smells. And shortages of land make it more difficult to find suitable areas for dumping. Recent reports have shown the Greater London Council moving refuse by train to be dumped in distant rural areas.

But where rubbish is dumped in old gravel pits or mine shafts, land may be reclaimed. Near Chicago, rubbish is being dumped and then covered with impermeable clay or landscaped to form a new recreation area with a lake and ski slopes.

Unsorted rubbish can also be burnt. In Osaka, Japan, the incinerator not only produces electricity but also burns sewage sludge. Glass can be recovered from incinerator ash and used for road construction – in Kansas, USA, a surfacing material called Glassphalt has been developed, using glass instead of gravel as an aggregate. Plastic waste, one of the biggest items in today's rubbish, has a high calorific value, and can be used in district heating plants.

Obviously, rubbish that has been sorted is potentially of greater value both for re-use and for recycling. This sorting can be done either where the rubbish happens to be, as was the practice in Britain during the Second World War, or in plants run by local authorities where magnets can be used to extract iron goods and jets of air to blow out light materials, and mixing with water enables filtering to take place. But these methods are expensive. Customers have to be found for the various items that are sorted out in this way, and transport costs have to be met. Then, when it comes to using recycled materials, production techniques may need to be changed to incorporate them. Public attitudes also need to be changed; only when people realize that resources are not limitless will such schemes really get under way on the scale that is necessary. A scheme introduced by Oxfam in Huddersfield where households were issued with a series of sacks to sort rubbish has met with only limited success.

With some items, and in some places, recycling of refuse is already a reality. Many fibreboard packing cases are made from 40 per cent waste paper; and in Germany toilet paper is made in this way – though this means that it is grey in colour. Scrap iron and steel from old cars can be used to produce new steel – it is estimated that one ton of scrap saves $1\frac{1}{2}$ tons of ore, one ton of coke and $\frac{1}{2}$ ton of limestone. In Leicester, England, textile waste is shredded and used as padding. A quarter of the glass manufactured in Britain is made from glass scrap.

Glass bottles are an example of waste that can readily be re-used; but the cost of collecting, transporting and cleaning, together with the cheapness with which glass can be manufactured, means that bottles are more and more being used once only. The number of throwaway glass bottles in Britain increased from 180 million in 1968 to 446 million in 1971. If dairies stopped using the same bottles over and over again, there would be another 30 million bottles to dispose of every day. At present the average milk bottle makes twenty-five journeys, which means a great saving of resources. In many cases plastic bottles, which are a tenth of the weight and use less energy in production, are replacing glass ones. Plastics are at present difficult to recycle. That is because they are artificial compounds and cannot be broken down like other substances, by bacteria or micro-organisms. A technique called the pyrolysis process is being developed which would enable the plastic polymers to be broken down and converted back to their original raw materials. With the ever-increasing price of petroleum and natural gas, the raw materials for plastics, two things seem inevitable – it will be necessary to find some way of recycling plastic, and we shall have to think again about our whole use of plastics.

Despite the world shortage of food, those who live in the developed world waste incredible amounts of it. This organic waste, if separated from other rubbish, can be used as compost, because it decomposes naturally. Compost can not only be used as a fertilizer, but it also improves the structure of the soil. In the Netherlands, in the last forty years, at least 30 per cent of city waste has been returned to the land as compost. But again the consumer has to be convinced of the value or necessity of sorting – in this case, of separating organic waste from other kinds.

Other animal and plant products which are frequently treated as rubbish can be made use of. Animal fat, for example, can be used for candles or soap, and blood for fertilizer; and, as with sewage, organic waste can be converted into methane gas for use as a fuel.

One of the simplest ways of reducing the problem of waste would be for us to stop creating so much of it. For a start we could ask ourselves whether the amount of packaging we use today is really necessary. Consider a box of chocolates. Is it not over-packaged? Do we need the box, the fancy papers that separate layer from layer, and those that are used to wrap each individual chocolate? Second, we need to campaign against a practice we have already looked at: what is known as planned obsolescence. This is, remember, the term given to the situation in which manufacturers in search of a steady market for their goods make their products in such a way that the consumer simply has to replace them at regular intervals. Electric light bulbs *can* be made to last longer; car bodies and exhaust systems *could* have longer lives; and even nylon stockings *can* be made so that they will not ladder. In fact, making products shorter-lived than they need to be is not the only technique manufacturers use to ensure that the consumer never stops buying; they employ skilful advertising to persuade their customers to replace a still useful product with the latest 'improved' model, or constantly to re-stock their wardrobes with the latest fashion.

All this can be seen very clearly in the motor industry. The motor car is the symbol of the modern age and of modern attitudes towards the environment. It is, to begin with, an extremely wasteful machine. In its manufacture it swallows up 11 per cent of the world's aluminium, 50 per cent of its lead and 60 per cent of its rubber. It uses fuel inefficiently and in vast quantities – in Britain, 174 billion (174,000,000,000) gallons of petrol a year – and it ejects lead, carbon monoxide, rubber from tyres and asbestos from brake linings into the air. The lead, incidentally, is not only added to the fuel supply to improve performance, but also makes engines wear out more quickly.

The motor car also creates enormous problems of waste. In 1960, in the city of New York, 3,000 cars were abandoned as waste; by 1970, this number had risen to 70,000. The construction of roads to carry cars uses vast areas of land which could otherwise be used for housing or agriculture. It has been estimated that 25 per cent of the area of cities is devoted to cars, and road construction uses immense quantities of raw materials – for one typical traffic interchange, 26,000 tons of steel and 250,000 of concrete.

On top of all this, the consumer is encouraged to change his car before it is necessary, and the car, as we have seen, is deliberately made not to last. The British Consumers' Association has calculated that up to 1962 the average life of a car was fifteen years; since then it has dropped to ten years, and is still falling. For only a little extra cost the manufacturer could coat the steel in a car body with zinc and prolong the car's life by two or three times. If aluminized steel were used for exhaust systems, they would last longer than the present average of two years.

And there are alternatives to the throwaway car which is now the dominant form of transport. A railway can carry the same traffic on a quarter of the space, and uses far less concrete and steel. In Britain, only 23 per cent of goods are carried by rail compared with 40 per cent in West Germany. Everywhere, although the great railway networks already exist, we are cutting down on rail traffic and building new roads.

Here again the energy crisis and the increasing cost of fuel and raw materials is forcing us to think again. What is the most sensible way of using the motor car? Already more interest is being shown in a more basic car costing less and consuming less fuel. When we look at what the motor car costs us, in its use

Car dumps: the final legacy of the throwaway car. (*Photo: Gwen Patmore*)

of valuable resources of raw material and energy, its demand for more and more land for more and more roads, the waste and the pollution problems it causes, and add all that to the destruction of human life on the roads, the question becomes inevitable: Is it reasonable to continue making vehicles that, as things are going, will be even less efficient, and have even shorter lives?

Conservation

We have seen how man is now trying to clean up his environment and remedy some of the mistakes he has made in the past. But what effort is he making to preserve at least a part of his environment in as natural a state as possible? And how is he trying to prevent the further extinction of wild animals and plants?

Since 1600, thirty-six mammals and ninety-four types of birds have become extinct. Of these it has been estimated that 25 per cent died out naturally, but the other 75 per cent became extinct because of man's presence or his activities. Those activities are of two main kinds – the exploitation of animals and birds through hunting or sport, and the destruction of their habitats.

Indiscriminate hunting of animals and birds for food, skins, oil and bone, or purely for sport, leads to a great decline in numbers and even to extinction. The great auk, a duck-like seabird, became extinct in the nineteenth century after being ruthlessly hunted for the sake of its feathers. The whale is hunted by man as a source of raw material for pet food, margarine, cosmetics and fertilizers – nearly all needs that can be supplied by other, synthetic substances.

All species of whale are depleted in numbers. The population of fin whales, the largest still hunted, has decreased to a quarter or a fifth of what it was, and is still declining.

There has been a similar dramatic drop in the number of Bengal tigers; in 1930 there were 40,000, in 1939 30,000, but in 1970 there were only 1,500 in India, 200 each in Nepal and Bhutan, and 100 in Bangladesh. These survivors are scattered thinly in small groups. The Indian government is planning eight reserves to provide the tiger with the habitat and the prey he needs, and has passed laws to ban hunting. But there is still a demand for tiger skins, and illegal poaching continues.

The destruction of habitats is the other way in which animals become extinct or endangered. Where forests are cut down, hedges destroyed, wetlands drained or rivers polluted, animals and birds are no longer able to exist and must either move to other areas or die out. One of the rarest birds in the world, the Japanese crested ibis, now exists only on Sado Island in Japan. The cutting down of trees on a huge scale in the wetlands and virgin forests of northern China, Manchuria, Korea and Japan – the former range of its habitat – has reduced its numbers to eight. One of the rarest mammals, with only 400 survivors, is the golden lion marmoset of Brazil. Again the rapid cutting down of forests is to blame; it has meant that this creature is now limited to 400 square miles of coastal forest near Rio de Janeiro.

Pollution of rivers and the sea is a major cause of declining populations. The lung fish, an evolutionary link between fishes and reptiles, has existed for millions of years in lakes and rivers in Australia and Africa. Now its habitats are becoming polluted and its future is in doubt. The peregrine, a bird of prey, has survived persecution by gamekeepers, pigeon fanciers and egg collectors, only to decline rapidly from eating prey containing organochlorine pesticides. These pesticides, of which DDT is one, are now being used less; and there is evidence in Canada that, as a result, the number of peregrines is slightly on the increase.

A further danger to animals and birds results from the introduction to their territory of a foreign species. The dodo, which lived in Mauritius, was killed by sailors who hunted it for food and could easily catch it because it was a heavy, flightless bird. In the end, however, it was the pigs and monkeys introduced to the island by the sailors which brought about the dodo's extinction; they fed on dodo's eggs, and the last of these birds was observed in 1681.

In this century, the introduction of the grey squirrel into Britain from North America has resulted in the virtual elimination of the native red squirrel. The grey squirrel does much damage to trees and robs birds' nests, and because it is an introduced species has few natural predators. The goat, which was introduced to the Galapagos Islands, has resulted in the death of a large number of iguanas and giant tortoises – not because goats eat those species, but because they eat the plants which the iguanas and tortoises feed.

Does it really matter? With so many different types of animals and birds in the world, can't we manage quite easily without the Bengal tiger, the peregrine or the lung fish?

The answer is that every individual species has its importance; to understand

Above: the abundance of the tropical forest in the Congo; *Below:* the drastic effects of forest clearance in Malaysia. (*Photos: John Topham Picture Library*)

that, we need to understand something about food chains and what are called ecosystems. Every living thing depends on another living thing for its food – at its simplest, a fox eats rabbits and rabbits eat grass. When, in 1954, myxomatosis killed nearly all the rabbits in England, the food chain was upset in various ways. Foxes were driven to seek other types of food. The rabbits were no longer keeping the grass short, and the longer grass killed many flowers. The delicate balance of nature was disturbed. In Alaska the destruction of wolves led to an increase in the number of caribou, who were no longer preyed on. This in turn meant that the lichen was over-grazed by the caribou; and since lichen is very slow to grow, this resulted in a shortage of food which led to the starvation of many caribou.

Another example is the effect of the Aswan Dam in Egypt on the sardine fishermen of the Mediterranean. The silt which used to feed the plankton which in turn fattened the sardines now piles up behind the dam. Because it is no longer fed by so much fresh water from the Nile, the eastern Mediterranean is becoming saltier, and so the numbers of sardines have dropped dramatically. This kind of environmental backlash is happening all over the world, and man is at last beginning to realize that if he interferes with the delicate balance of nature he may produce quite unforeseen and unwelcome results.

Another reason for attempting to preserve all the existing species of plants and animals is for breeding purposes. Research in genetics (the study and science of heredity) shows the possibility of transferring genes from unrelated species to economically valuable plants. For example, common grasses have been used to improve the resistance of wheat to fungus diseases. Russian scientists have found wild potatoes growing high in the frosty Andes and are attempting to develop a strain which would survive the cold conditions in Russia. As we have already seen when discussing food resources, some wild African antelope are now being bred for meat. But once a species dies out, it can never be re-created.

If the poppy, cinchona and penicillin bacillus had been eradicated, we would have no morphine, quinine or penicillin. Curare, a poison with which South American Indians tip their blowpipe darts, is now used to treat tetanus. Digitalis, a drug used to treat heart disease, came from the English foxglove, but the margin between an effective and a poisonous dose was dangerously narrow. Now digoxin from the Spanish foxglove is used and is very much safer. Research suggests that the disease bilharzia may be combated by the soapberry plant, found in Ethiopia. Perhaps somewhere there is a plant which can be used to treat cancer. We have no idea what species may in the future be useful to man.

Again, plants and animals can be used as alternatives to pesticides for the control of plant and animal pests – this is known as biological control. An example of this is the control of prickly pear by the cactoblastis caterpillar. In California, at the end of the last century, the fruit crops were infested with the cottony cushion scale insect, which was accidentally introduced from Australia. The ladybird beetle and a fly whose larvae preyed on the scale insect were introduced, and in no time the scale insect was under control. Another example of biological control is the story of the American screw-worm fly, whose maggots burrowed their way harmfully into the hide and flesh of cattle. The female screw-worm fly mates once, and once only; so male screw-worm flies which were sterile were specially reared. They were released and mated with the females – result: a much smaller population of screw-worm flies, and a much reduced problem for the cattle ranchers.

We may agree that it is important to man for many reasons to preserve the variety of animal, bird and plant life. But how can this be achieved? One of the most striking ways of preserving natural habitats is by the development of national parks, nature reserves and game sanctuaries. The Yellowstone National Park, established in Wyoming, USA, in 1872 was the first in the world. There are now more than 1,000 national parks in eighty countries and 0.75 per cent of the earth's surface (excluding Antarctica) is devoted to this purpose. Of these parks, however, 35 per cent are in North America and 15 per cent in Africa, so there is plenty of scope for more.

National parks, however, create problems as well as solve them. Park officials have to cope with problems of overcrowding, pollution, traffic jams and so on. The Yellowstone Park had 2 million visitors in 1972; and Smoky Mountains in Tennessee, which had 15,000 visitors a year when it opened in 1934, had $3\frac{1}{2}$ million in 1974. Visitors have to be prevented from destroying animals by feeding them with the wrong food or leaving dangerous litter. Problems also arise when populations of protected animals grow too large. In Murchison Falls, Kenya, for example, elephants are breeding so rapidly that the park cannot support them, and they have begun to destroy their own habitat. They are now having to be culled – that is, from time to time an agreed number of surplus animals are killed.

In addition to national parks, naturalists are attempting to preserve key habitats which are fast disappearing. These include wetlands, lowland tropical rain forests, cloud forests, oceanic islands, coastal and estuarine zones, circumpolar regions, desert and semi-desert areas and high mountains. The World Wildlife Fund and the French government have bought areas of the Camargue, in southern France, and in Kenya attempts are being made to preserve the Lake Naharu area, one of the key areas for bird life. Over 400 species of birds, including at least $1\frac{1}{2}$ million flamingoes, form a part of this wonderfully balanced ecosystem now threatened by the growth of the nearby town of Naharu.

Another approach to conservation comes through national and international pressure groups. The International Union for the Conservation of Nature produces a Red Data Book of all mammals, birds and plants in danger of extinction. The Convention on International Trade in Endangered Species of Wild Flora and Fauna came into effect in 1975. Its aim is to protect species in danger of becoming extinct, but so far, only eleven countries have ratified the treaty. The World Wildlife Fund was set up in 1961 with the task of raising money to finance the work of conservation. It now has branches in eighteen countries and is seeking not only to conserve species that are threatened with extinction, but also to preserve habitats. Individual countries have societies dedicated to conservation, as well as all sorts of legal measures. In Britain about 1,000 square kilometres are protected in national nature reserves, and nearly all birds are protected by Act of Parliament. By contrast, in France all birds

The legendary wild horses of the Camargue which roam the countryside. (*Photo: E. Boubat, Camera Press, London*)

as large as, or larger than, a thrush are regarded as game birds.

What about the conservation of man himself, his customs, his buildings and his environment? In an age when Western technology and customs are spreading throughout the world, it is of the utmost importance that other ways of life should be preserved. Some tribes have already disappeared. The Yahi Indians used to live in California. Settlers attacked them and took their land, and the last of the tribe died in 1916. The building of the transcontinental highway in Brazil and the destruction of trees by prospectors and rubber planters is destroying the habitat of primitive Indian tribes, and already many have been wiped out.

And what of the architectural heritage of man? In Britain the National Trust administers not only areas of land that are particularly beautiful or interesting, but also more than 1,000 properties of historical importance. The Civic Trust has set up hundreds of schemes to improve the appearance of towns. Local amenity groups watch over buildings of special interest, try to save houses from destruction in the face of road development, and so on. People are becoming more and more aware that 'progress' is not everything: it is also important to keep the best of the buildings of the past, and a range of such buildings so that future generations can enjoy the variety and richness of the life of their ancestors.

So through this conservation movement – at international, national and local level – man is trying to preserve a reasonable environment for himself and for animals, birds and plants, and to ensure their survival into the twenty-first century.

6

Religion
in the
World Today

Summary of Chapter

There are three great religions in the West today – Judaism, Christianity and Islam – all understand the meaning of life as a response to God the creator, who reveals himself through his word, ie Holy Scripture. This response is one of trust, obedience and love by man towards God who made him. The modern secular West has replaced these with reason, freewill and love of family or community; or trust, obedience and love for the State.

The Indian religions, on the other hand, have always centred on man's search for God, for self-knowledge, for truth. The poem below was written by an Indian Christian, but it belongs to the tradition of eastern spirituality in which salvation, the Lord, the truth, lie within the heart of man and the way to discover it or him is through self-awareness.

> Lord,
> so eager was I for thy darsham
> that I donned the yellow robes of a samiyasi
> I walked the dusty, weary miles
> of the road from Dravida to the Himalayas
> in my bare feet.
>
> I endured the heat of noonday,
> the lash of monsoon tempests,
> the perils of tortuous jungle paths.
> Lonely forest shrines echoed to my kirtans
> when I offered juna with garlands of wild-flowers
> But nowhere did I find thee. . . .
>
> And then suddenly I met Thee
> met Thee walking the roads
> of my own heart.

From Morning Noon and Night,
Poems and Meditations from the Third World
edited by John Carden, published by the Highway Press.

These pictures which belong to Zen Buddhism might be interpreted by a psychologist as the search for the true self – the task of adolescence. When the self is known and mastered, the adult is then able to forget himself and go out to others.

In the West there has been a division in the past between religious people (who believed in a personal God) and atheists, who did not. The East is more used to atheist religions; one does not have to believe in a personal God to have a religious view of life. Today the West is encountering these atheist religions, and their influence is being felt among those who seek a meaning to life while rejecting traditional Western religion. On the other hand, some Westerners who practise yoga or meditational techniques will tell you that neither yoga nor meditation is a religion; when the truth is that yoga has a specific religious purpose, of arriving at union with God or the highest reality, and the meditational techniques are based on assumptions formed by a particular religious world-view. What such people mean by 'not religious' is that these techniques do not require a leap of faith to start with as Western religions do: though, in fact, the purpose of the meditations is to encounter one's true self and, in so doing, to become aware of the Other.

But throughout the whole range of religion today, atheist or otherwise, there are three discernible trends – the search for wholeness, the search for community, and the search for an authentic and meaningful lifestyle for this day and age. To be engaged in such a search may involve being in a state of constant flux; a dynamic, flexible, open reaching-out to the veritable kaleidoscope of people and events which make up today's rapidly changing world.

> Unlike men's frontiers
> God's frontiers may be crossed without permit or passport.
> There is a frontier I may cross
> deep within my own heart.
> There is a frontier I may cross
> as I reach out in loving concern to another man's need,
> Always I live on the Frontier.
>
> Prayer used by Congregational Prayer Fellowship

Christianity

Statistics show that the number of Christians is now growing at an unprecedented rate in different parts of the world. This expansion is in excess of the exploding birth rate, and represents large numbers of converts. Until recently, the Pentecostal churches in South America were growing faster than any in the world; now they have been overtaken in Africa. In Kenya alone there are, each year, eighty new congregations of Christians of all denominations.

The modern missionary movement began at the end of the eighteenth century. The nineteenth century was an era of Protestant advance as their missionaries went out in the wake of the colonizers. A renewal of Roman Catholic missions followed. Today, many former colonies have independent and indigenous churches which are centres of rapid growth. In Africa, the Roman Catholic Church is the strongest numerically – other Churches tend to splinter off into tiny sects. Statistics showing how many people subscribe to this religion or that are notoriously misleading; but the figures do indicate that Indonesia, until a short while ago a predominantly Moslem country, is now mainly Christian.

When we look at the traditional strongholds of Christianity, the picture is very different. In Western Europe, particularly, there is decay and a search for renewal. The Christian Church and its authority have been under attack in Europe throughout the past 200 years. The Protestant churches base their authority on the Bible as the word of God. Biblical criticism has undermined

Henry E. Clark expounding the seventh Chapter of Luke to the native teachers at Andavabato, in Madagascar. From an engraving in *Children's Missionary Paper*, page 1, vol 1, 1876. (*Photo: Library of Religious Society of Friends, London*)

not only the traditional view of how the Bible came to be written, but the interpretation of its contents. The authorship traditionally claimed for the various books is under question, and the Darwinian theory of evolution is at odds with the literal interpretation of Genesis. A complete re-evaluation of biblical material has been taking place. Archaeology has restored confidence in the accuracy of some of the Bible narrative, and a more positive understanding of the nature of the material is now possible; but this has not as yet had enough impact to counter the criticism which shreds the Bible to pieces in order to discover its nature – and is left with the pieces.

The authority of the Roman Catholic Church has also been under constant attack. Pope Pius IX (1846–78) tried to bring the Church up-to-date and introduce a relaxation of its unchanging rigidity; but the failure of his policies was decisive – the Church turned back to conservatism and then to rigid self-defence following a loss of temporal power and prestige. The Papal States, restored in 1815, straddled the centre of the Italian peninsula, standing in the way of Italian unification. The rising tide of the Italian *Risorgimento* swept them away, leaving only the Vatican City as a remnant of what had been. In 1870 the Pope's authority was re-affirmed at the Vatican Council, and the Church turned itself into a fortress in order, in an increasingly secular age, to withstand further encroachments. This reaction was to have a profound effect on the Church's development. A policy of retrenchment followed which covered all aspects of Church life, and any attempt to come to terms with the contemporary situation was seen as a threat to the faith. In 1910 the Catholic Modernists were condemned by Pope Pius X as heretics and conspirators, and

All Saints Church, Annesley, England. A symbol of the decay of Christianity in parts of the western world. (*Photo: National Monuments Record*)

liberal thought within the Church died or went underground. Like the Church in the Dark Ages after the collapse of the Roman Empire, Catholicism prepared itself to guard the eternal flame of truth among the pagan hordes until a more favourable time.

The Church in England meanwhile pursued a path of its own, insulated to some extent by the English Channel from events in the rest of Europe. The eighteenth-century Evangelical Revival hardened into a party, but it was due to Evangelical initiative that the modern missionary movement first got under way and slavery was abolished wherever British influence was strong. After Wesley's death, Methodism split apart but it remained the strongest and most influential of the Non-Conformist Churches. Non-Conformists were responsible for many of the reform measures passed through Parliament, and helped the passage of others, including the Catholic Emancipation Act.

The long overdue reform of the administration of the Church of England took place in the 1830s and opened the way for a revival of Anglicanism, but every effort at revival was mistrusted by the majority. The vigour which new movements brought into every facet of church life became frustrated and dissipated as time went on. The Evangelical party was too narrow in its outlook and its theology to have the influence that it might have had. The Oxford Movement, as it came to be known, was an academic and clerical movement which alienated many lay people. The reintroduction of altar candles, surpliced choirs, wafer bread, the reserved sacrament and such 'Poperies' aroused deep fears of a takeover by Rome. There was a Christian Socialist Movement in 1848–54 that failed in spite of devoted work by individuals. The Church of England, as a whole, never got to grips with the evils caused by the Industrial Revolution; and this resulted in the alienation from the Church of a great number of working-class people. After the First World War, Anglicanism went into decline.

All the Churches in Western Europe suffered to some extent from this increasingly Rip Van Winkle-type existence. The forces of conservatism which attempted to prevent the erosion of religion also prevented necessary change; but full understanding of what was happening was delayed until the 1950s. The Churches then woke to find themselves living amongst a generation which not only spoke an entirely different language, but lived in a different world of thought. In their anxiety to preserve the purity of the faith, Christians had lost the ability to communicate it, and the Churches were turning into museum pieces which seemed to have no relevance to modern life.

The Roman Catholic Church came to grips with the situation in 1959, when Pope John XXIII summoned the Second Vatican Council. At this council the missionary bishops, who were used to working in a variety of non-European cultures, persuaded their colleagues to dispense with the rigid Latin framework of the Church so that its appeal might become more truly universal. The process of sifting through what belonged to a particular time and place, and what belonged to eternity, began in earnest. Catholic dogmatic theology had collapsed, since it was founded on medieval scholastic assumptions about the world and its nature that could no longer be made. Did these assumptions belong to classical philosophy and not to Christianity, and should the basis for belief be moved back to a new understanding of the Bible? Did the social structure of the Church belong to the seventeenth century, and was the Pope the last surviving baroque monarch? Should the Church reflect modern society or should it have a unique structure of its own?

The immediate results of Vatican II were a new freedom of thought and behaviour for the faithful, the delegation of more power into the hands of bishops and to the heads of religious houses; a commitment to the Ecumenical Movement (the coming together of the Churches that had split apart) and the substitution of the vernacular instead of the Latin mass. This last change caused much distress among the faithful; indeed, the bewildering rapidity of change was disturbing and challenging to many who felt that cherished and well-tried traditions were being thrown out in the name of progress.

The academic theologians of all denominations have also become unpopular with faithful churchgoers. They are thought of as belonging to the Age of Reason, which regarded the mind as an unerring tool that could, if need be, objectively discover all truth. This cold rationality is repellent to those who are drawn to devotion by a sense of the mysterious otherness of God: only, they feel, to be rightly penetrated by reverence and love. The feeling after God and finding him in a mystical way is in tune with the modern desire for spiritual experience or a deeper reality; whereas the academics seem, to those who have that desire, to be wandering in a wasteland of barren intellectualism. The faithful would appear to have Karl Barth (1886–1968) on their side; though when he speaks of 'the secret of God that withstands the arrogance of religion', he does not imply that the secret can be arrived at by a mystical path, but rather the reverse: that 'God can only be known if he chooses of his goodness to reveal himself to us' (Karl Barth, *Commentary on the Epistle to the Romans*). The dangers of faith without reason, on the other hand, alarm intellectuals such as Francis Schaeffer (*Escape from Reason* Inter-Varsity Press, Illinois, USA; paperback (1968)). Schaeffer sees great dangers in the split which has been taking place between faith and reason.

The attempts of many scholars of all denominations to give an up-to-date rendering of the Bible have met, however, with more success. The Living Bible, which paraphrases the complete Bible in journalistic style, advertises itself on the cover as 'The Bible in everyday language for everyone'. This one version sold 12 million copies in two years, and in 1974 it was selling at the rate of 10,000 copies a day.

But it is from the United States of America that the main thrust of renewal in the historic Churches has begun to spread. America has been a country of revivals. In 1904, the Pentecostal movement started in New Orleans and spread throughout the world; but it was rejected by the strongholds of Christianity and split off into yet another denomination. The present renewal is called the charismatic movement – from *charismata*, the gifts (of the Holy Spirit). Unlike the Pentecostalists, those who belong to this movement are staying within their own Churches, helping to renew them from inside. It is unfortunate that the charismatic experience is described as 'baptism in the spirit', because this causes confusion with Christian initiation; it implies that those who have not had this experience are not really Christian, whereas 'renewal' is perhaps a better description. The effect of this experience is to bring a deeper commitment to, and living faith in, Christ, which means that there is often a change-over from passive to active Christianity; something the local church may find it hard to assimilate. Christian churches in the West have become more and more clericalized – that is, the clergy have taken over the functions of the whole church – so that, instead of being Christian communities, churches have tended to become one-man bands, in which anyone who takes a more than passive interest in religion is seen as a threat to the leader. 'You see, my dear,' said one Catholic priest to a protesting lady (but he might have been from any denomination), 'it's like a football match, and the lay people are there to cheer from the sidelines.' It is a feature of the charismatic movement that lay people come on to the pitch and start playing the game too. They also start to build communities, which are, primarily, extended families. This kind of group living is new in the recent history of the Church, where communities of this sort have traditionally been celibate. Another characteristic is that the coming together of Christians of all denominations, which has been worked and prayed for so hard elsewhere with marginal results, seems in charismatic circles to happen spontaneously and happily. It is too soon to measure the full impact this movement will have on the Church. At the moment it is growing fast, but its future will depend on how much of the new life the established Churches are willing to assimilate.

To be a Christian today is to experience bewilderment, excitement, frustration and difficulty. But in spite of the shocks and stagnation that the Church has gone through, there is a ferment of new life and new birth taking place.

Judaism

The word Jew, like the word Hindu, has an ethnic as well as a religious meaning – that is, it describes the race a man belongs to as well as a man's beliefs – but Orthodox Jews claim a unique place in the history of mankind as a 'holy nation', a whole people specially chosen and called out from the world to serve God. The Jewish way of life has traditionally been bound together with religious belief and custom, rigorously kept by the Orthodox, who stick to the letter of the law; reinterpreted by the Reformed, who wish to understand their faith in terms of modern knowledge. To become secular, or to change one's religion, was to lose one's identity and to cut oneself off from one's roots. Modern Christians, more sensitive to the Jewish position than in the past, are anxious to make a Jewish convert to Christianity feel a fulfilled Jew, one for whom God's promises to the Jews have been realized in Christ; but the Jewish family will reject such a convert much as the physical body rejects alien tissue. For 2,000 years, in the absence of a homeland, Orthodox Jewish groups clung together in alien environments, refusing to absorb or to be absorbed. In medieval Europe they were forced to live together in ghettoes; but even in free situations, they tended to form close, inward-looking groups. Not until this century has a secular way of belonging been possible – in the new State of Israel itself.

The secular nature of the State of Israel is a scandal to many Orthodox Jews, who, like their forefathers, had been devoutly praying for the return of their people to Palestine, and particularly to Jerusalem, as the centre of their religion. The very use of the word 'Israel', which means 'he who prevails with God', to describe a modern type of Western State is offensive to them. But Israel today is full of paradox – communism and capitalism, religion and secularism exist there side by side, united in the common cause of maintaining the existence of the new State in the face of Arab hostility. Nevertheless, in Israel the

Orthodox Jewish way of life is all-pervading. In some parts of the country for example, you would have stones thrown at you if you rode a bicycle on the Sabbath. When the Arabs launched their major attack on the most important day of the Jewish year, Yom Kippur, the Day of Atonement, which is given to fasting and prayer, the Israeli army was caught off its guard and suffered an initial defeat. After the disasters of the Yom Kippur war, posters appeared in all the towns bearing the slogan: 'Israel, trust in the Lord.'

The founding of the State of Israel was the climax of a momentous period in Jewish history. It was made necessary, in the eyes of Jewish leaders, by persecution on an unprecedented scale. The Jews have had to endure persecution off and on throughout their troubled existence; but never have they suffered as they have in the past hundred years.

The first large-scale persecutions began in Russia in 1870, as part of a wider campaign to force all the Tsar's subjects to belong to the Russian Orthodox Church – a policy aimed at bringing about greater political unity and stability throughout the country. Anti-semitism has been a continuing feature of Russian life, but in the 1870s alone, pogroms (organized massacres) increased to such an extent that over three quarters of a million Jews left Russia. Tsar Alexander III was convinced that his father's assassination was part of an international Jewish plot to bring down the monarchy, and he wrote in the margin of an official report sent to him: 'We must never forget that these are the people who crucified Christ.'

But this harsh treatment was to pale into insignificance alongside the systematic destruction of a whole people that was attempted by Nazi Germany. Many Jews realized what was happening and managed to escape; but millions did not. There are plenty of eye-witnesses still living who can testify to what happened; but already people find it hard to believe that modern 'civilized' men could practise genocide on this scale, or that such racial murder could succeed to the extent that it did. It is a fact that between 5 and 6 million Jews died under the Nazi regime. It is difficult to imagine suffering of these proportions; but it is with this tragedy in mind that we must try to understand modern Jewry, and the rise of Zionism – the movement that longed, prayed and worked for the return to Zion, the homeland, prophesied by Isaiah: '... The ransomed of the Lord shall return, and come to Zion with singing; everlasting joy shall be upon their heads; they shall obtain joy and gladness, and sorrow and sighing shall flee away.' (Isaiah 35:10 and 51:11.)

Not all Zionists are religious. With such a horrific background it is hardly surprising that there is a strong group in the new Israel that is atheist, left-wing, and highly aggressive in respect of any would-be invader. But what of the religious Jew? Sanctification of God's name in martyrdom, followed by the return to Zion, is at the heart of his faith, and it is due to his influence that the new Israeli State was settled in Palestine. Some Jews on arriving in South America wrote back enthusiastically to their relatives 'We have found Zion!' and atheist Jews could not in the nature of things, base their feeling on the biblical promise to give them possession of Palestine; but for the religious, no other homeland was acceptable. That fact, added to the difficulties Arab Jews were encountering in maintaining their faith in a Moslem environment, made the choice of Palestine, from the Jewish point of view, the only possible one.

Among the most significant developments in the State of Israel are the kibbutzim, the most left-wing of the agricultural communes set up by the first generation of new Israelis. The kibbutzim represent only about 4 per cent of the total population, but have an influence far outweighing their numbers. Their members play an active and leading part in Parliament and in the army, and atheist Jews claim that the kibbutz dream of a better society is all that now makes Israel, as a nation, unique. There are a small number of Orthodox religious kibbutzim; but these are a handful compared with the others, which belong to a socialist, atheist, back-to-the-land movement. The founders of the kibbutzim banded together to form pioneer settlements to cultivate land which, as often as not, was desert before they came. To do this they had not only to learn new skills, but also to change their style of living. The community life they have evolved during this experiment looks at first sight like a reaction against the close-knit, authoritarian family life and religious upbringing that the founders had experienced, particularly in the ghettoes of Europe. For example, the kibbutzim have reversed the role of women in their society. In strictly Orthodox families, a Jewish woman is given little purpose or outlet except to be a wonderful mother. Some kibbutzim have gone to the other extreme; they take children away from their mothers as soon as they are weaned, at six months, and communal baby care is organized in order to free mothers from all responsibility for their children. The women are encouraged to find satisfaction in the work of the commune and in the companionship of their peer group, rather than in their children. On the other hand, the puri-

Workers from a kibbutz in Israel making the desert bloom. (*Photo: Israel Information*)

tanical ethos of these communities is, in its way, just as demanding as the Orthodox religion. The community in a kibbutz has become an extended family whose influence is just as all-embracing and possessive as the nuclear (that is separate) Jewish families from which they came originally. Those who leave the kibbutz are treated in exactly the same way as the Orthodox who marry outside the Jewish faith or who are converted to another faith – they are completely rejected by the kibbutz family. A native mysticism, or communion with the land, appears to have taken the place of religious feeling. The agricultural communes can point with justifiable pride to what they have achieved by their concerted effort. To change their entire lifestyle, to make the desert not only bloom but bear fruit in the teeth of constant and active hostility, requires idealism and purpose; but it is still too early to gauge the effect of the revolution in upbringing on the next generation. Will this way of life continue to attract idealists seeking an alternative to modern society, or does it belong to the pioneering period of the new state? Whatever its future, the kibbutz is one of the most intriguing of modern attempts to found a new society.

Islam

If you wake at dawn in any Moslem city, in whatever part of the world you may be, whether in the heartlands of Islam – the Arab states of North Africa and the Middle East – or in Turkey, Iran, Afghanistan, Pakistan, Indonesia, Malaysia, Nigeria, East Africa, parts of Russia or China, you will hear the first call to prayer from the minarets of the mosques.

> God is great
> Come to prayer
> Prayer is better than sleep.

Today the age-old message will probably be broadcast through loudspeakers from a tape recorder – a symbol of what is happening in Islam as Western science and technology become absorbed into the mainstream of Islamic life.

This call to prayer (which takes place five times each day) is a reminder to the Moslem that his whole life is lived in the presence of God. Every aspect of life in society is dominated and circumscribed for the Moslem by the rule of life laid down in the Koran, the Moslem holy book, together with other traditions which have been handed down. There is no division between religious and secular life, and the Moslem therefore often judges Christianity by behaviour in Western secular life which is a denial of Christian belief, because the Moslem cannot conceive of the kind of separation between Church and State, religious and secular, which exists in the West. There is also no division as there is in the Christian Church, between clerical and lay people. The Imams who interpret the Koran are more like lawyers, and do not form a priestly class in the Western sense. Islam does not have missionaries as Christianity and Buddhism do, but spreads through trading routes as the ordinary Moslem carries out his business. In Africa, Islam is now spreading from the north as the desert people come south in search of a livelihood, and this is causing tension between the Moslem and the growing Christian communities. The same search for a living has taken Turks to West Germany and Pakistanis, Bengalis and Kenyan Asians to Britain. These are estimated at the moment (1979) to be over 5 million Moslems in Western Europe.

Islam has had a 'bad press' in Western circles. Ideas about the Moslem faith have been coloured by Western critics who have said that the backwardness of Moslem society is due to the inferior character of Islamic civilization. Moslems would say the opposite: that degeneration has been caused by a fall away from the purity of Islam. Up to around AD 1100, the civilization of Islam was in many ways more advanced than the Christian West; but a decline set in which showed itself in political weakness and economic and social decay. Moslems are very conscious of this, and there has been a series of reform movements that have sought to bring about a revival and resurgence of orthodox Islam. But, until recently, Islam has generally continued in decline, seemingly sick, and demoralized within itself. Now, with increasing prosperity within the heartlands of Islam there is new confidence and expansionism together with desire for reform – though the forces of conservatism are very strong. Islamic studies are being set up with the task of re-interpreting Islam. Exhibitions and educational efforts are being launched to make the West more aware of the rich cultural and religious heritage that Islam possesses.

The impact of the West on Islam has already been tremendous, yet in some ways it has only just begun. The shock of conquest by strangers of an alien religion has already been mentioned: but the new prosperity brought by Western technology, the Pan-Arab unity that has resulted from the common struggle against Israel, and the sense of Moslem identity being fostered in the United Nations, are some of the new factors in the situation. The outcome is unpredictable, but three main reactions can already be seen and could be described like this:

Westernism
Science
Technology
Freedom
Liberalism
Reason

Revivalism
Fundamentalism
Reform
Orthodoxy
Puritanism
Faith

Modernism
Science and reinterpretation of scripture.
Technology and reform.
Freedom comes from conforming to Islam.
Morality should be based on reinterpretation of scripture.
There is no division between reason and faith.

Most of the estimated 500 million adherents of Islam would probably wish to be identified with the Revivalists. They regard Western ideas as morally and spiritually inferior, an undermining influence on faith and society. Their opinion is well summed up in a poem by Sir Mohammed Iqbal (1876–1938) the Moslem philosopher – though Iqbal has taught that the modern Moslem needs to study what Europe has thought.

> Faith gives the strength to sit in fire like Abraham
> Faith is God, intoxication, self-expending
> Listen O dotard of the modern civilization
> Worse than slavery is the lack of Faith.

Those we have called Westerners by comparison represent only a tiny handful of the population, but they are a significant and influential part as they are mostly from the educated minority who supply the leaders. They regard the masses as being ignorant, backward, and superstitious, with a stereotyped world-view.

The Modernist is trying to re-evaluate Moslem principles in terms of modern society, and his position lies somewhat uneasily between the two other streams of thought, drawing on both. The essence of Modernism is expressed in this passage from *Letters on Islam* by Mohammed Fadhil Jamali, former Prime Minister of Iraq, written to his son from prison in 1961.

> Scholars must arise from amongst the Moslems who interpret Islam in a modern realistic way, taking into consideration modern science, modern philosophy and contemporary social trends. Some of those who deal with Islamic affairs indulge unduly in Western views and principles. Some others stagnate and hold fast to old moulds which do not belong to the essence of religion. What we want are scholars who study Islam from its pure original sources and who also know the new social and intellectual trends and so are able to apply the Islamic religion to the realities of modern life.

Dissatisfaction with traditional interpretations of the Shari'a is already apparent. Shari'a means, literally, the path leading to the water – that is, the way to the source of life. Public opinion is generally solidly behind the tradition, but the wearing of Western dress is itself a rebellion against the Shari'a, and there is controversy over the role of women in public life.

Egypt and Turkey have shown themselves to be particularly sensitive over this. Egyptian public opinion has swung against child marriage, and many throughout the Moslem world think that this practice is responsible for much of the degeneration in their society; they feel that women are forced into child-bearing before they are able to cope mentally or physically, and that the children suffer. But the practice of early marriage has strong backing from tradition, which says that Mohammed married A'isha while she was still playing with her dolls. Nevertheless, modern governments have tried to bring in reforms. Turkey has raised the minimum legal age at which marriage is allowed. Egypt has tackled the problem indirectly by not supporting early marriage with legal sanctions or redress in the courts. The position over divorce in Moslem countries is still overwhelmingly in favour of the man, though Turkey prides herself on treating women in law as favourably as any country in the West. In most Moslem countries a man can still divorce his wife for any reason whatever, whereas the woman can divorce the man only if he is impotent. Polygamy is also a matter for controversy. Though the Koran allows up to four wives, it stipulates that this is permitted only if each wife is treated with complete equality. Many today feel this is impossible. There is real perplexity about the position of women. Sir Mohammed Iqbal wrote:

> I too, am most sorrowful at the oppression of women,
> But the problem is intricate, no solution do I find possible.

Self-criticism is causing a repudiation of past attitudes of fatalism, blind obedience and low public morality as well as belief in the inferiority of women. The blame for all these ideas and practices is put squarely on the failure to live up to religious principles. Some critics assume that the East is spiritual, the West is materialistic. If the East retains its spirituality but learns the material skills of the West, all will be well. But can the Moslem world absorb Western materialism without becoming dominated by it? Words from a lecture given in 1934 by Dr Mohammed Fadhel Jumair are still topical:

> I wish the West had bequeathed us its inventive power, its sciences, and its organizations only. Then we would fear no danger. But the West challenged our moral and spiritual existence and began to undermine it as worms undermine the roots of a great tree, for it brought us cheap social customs, excessive sexual licence and a loosening of morals which warn of danger. The minds of our youth began to absorb sheer materialistic philosophies, accompanied by subversive Communist doctrines or agnosticism which make youth float as feathers in the wind with no faith and no principles, no clear direction and no positive high philosophy.
>
> Yes, the danger besetting the Moslems, and especially their youth, is very grave indeed, for they stand between stagnation which they inherited from previous dark centuries, and the sweeping flood of western civilizations. We have no saviour, brethren, in this critical situation except Mohammed, prayer and peace be upon him, and we have no positive philosophy except the philosophy of the Koran. This is what we should understand, and this is what I call for on this holy night.

For good or ill the Moslem world is assimilating these Western currents. Turkey took the conscious decision after the First World War to become a modern Western secular state under the leadership of Ataturk, and today the faith is strong and decisive in all aspects of Turkish national life. Will other Moslem states follow suit, and if so how can they harmonize secular Westernism with the Shari'a? Whatever the outcome, the tension between the two forces is already there, and at work creating a new society.

Hinduism

'Hindu' was the name originally given to the people living in India who were not converted to Islam. Hinduism today means the traditional religion of India which, during the centuries, has absorbed numerous creeds and ideas into its system, and covers a wide range of religious attitudes. From the earliest times

Painted scroll from west Bengal shows some of the multitude of Hindu gods and goddesses. The top two panels show Rama, Lakshmana and their *vanara* allies; in the bottom panel Hanuman leaping the straits of Lanka is almost caught by Sīmhikā. Victoria & Albert Museum. (*Photo: Victoria & Albert Museum*)

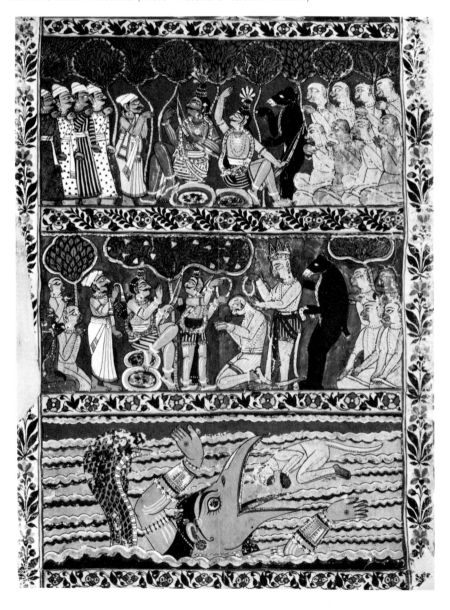

Eighteenth-century miniature painting from Jaipur of the infant Krishna, with his step-parents Yashoda and the cowherd Nanda. Victoria and Albert Museum. *(Photo: Victoria & Albert Museum)*

Hindu philosophy attempted to penetrate the meaning behind the multitude of Hindu gods and goddesses and the stories of the Vedas (the sacred scriptures); so there has always been a sophisticated body of thought alongside the popular religion. India has assimilated the religions of its conquerors without basically changing its own outlook – it still preserves traditions which go back 3,000 years and more. The concept of universalism, or a universal religion which in time will embrace all today's living faiths, is a Hindu one which springs from this experience of absorbing other viewpoints into its own idea of reality. Vivekananda (1863–1902) said in 1893:

> If there is ever to be a universal religion, it must be one which will hold no location in place or time; which will be infinite, like the god it will preach; whose sun shines upon the followers of Krishna or Christ, saints or sinners, alike; which will not be in the Brahmin, or Buddhist, Christian or Mohammedan, but the sum total of all these, and still have infinite space for development, which in its catholicity will embrace in its infinite arms, and find a place for, every human being.

More commonly the Hindu philosophers interpret the other religions as different ways of approach to the one God, or different paths up a mountain to the same summit. This attitude stems from the teaching of the Upanishad writings of the sixth century BC, which see a unified reality behind the universe – a reality hidden from men behind the illusion which is the world and life in it. Religion is seen as a search to discover this reality. It can be discovered through the use of yoga, which aims at self-control, clearness of mind, and concentration of purpose in order to pierce through the veil of illusion to the truth, by following a holy man who has already discovered the path and can help others to follow. This is the path of the ascetic few. Popular Hinduism follows the practice of Bhakti, devotion to a god who will help his (or her) worshipper to achieve salvation.

All these aspects of the Hindu religion are reflected by recent missionaries to the West. The Hari Krishna sect are a group of followers devoted to Krishna, the most recent incarnation of God in the Hindu system. They show their devotion to him by joy in worship, and can be seen dancing along the streets of Western cities in their yellow robes with partly shaven heads, shaking their tambourines in Krishna's honour. The Maharaj Ji, leader of the Divine Light movement, uses Raja Yoga techniques to help his followers in their search for reality. The Maharaj Ji claims to be a divine figure, leading men and women to a knowledge of truth through meditation, which seeks to bring the disciple to a constant awareness of the presence and reality of God. The disciples live together in a community called an ashram, following a Hindu pattern of life. The Maharishi Yoga, on the other hand, teaches transcendental meditation, a technique which he claims will bring to those who practise it regularly a deeper understanding and greater tranquillity, helpful in their daily lives to those active in the world. He does not emphasize the religious aspect of yoga, though he says that those who regularly practise TM, as it is called for short, will have a better understanding of their purpose in life.

These practices are part of everyday life in India; but in the West they have the appeal of the unusual and exotic, as well as attracting those who find this

Hari Krishna devotees in the streets of London. (*Photo: Sun News of the World*)

open-ended exploration of reality closer to the scientific approach to which they are accustomed.

Some Hindus who have received a Western type of secular education share the scepticism of the Western intellectual, but because of this similarity of approach there is for many educated Hindus no clash between scientific thinking and religious understanding. The whole of life is seen as being controlled by law, but this law is not understood as being a decree from God, to accept or rebel against, but rather as the way things are made: law as a scientist might understand the law of gravity, for example. We all, whether we understand it or not, take account of the law of gravity in the way we move, because as children we learned from the pain of falling over when we tried to walk. In the same fashion, the Hindu tries to take account of the way things are and the law by which they are made, in order to live harmoniously with himself and his environment. To do this successfully he must have the right knowledge, or put himself under the guidance of someone who has this knowledge; because the law, or dharma, is subtle and difficult to know, and he does not wish to go, as it were, against the grain and invite disaster in this life or the next by violating the law of his own being.

This concept of dharma, what one's duty in life is, causes conflict in Hindu society whenever there is need for change. Hindu philosophy teaches that nature consists of doing one's duty in the particular position in life to which one is called: which, in India, means according to one's caste. Each caste and sub-caste has a rigidly defined role, and it is considered right to keep to this role even if it is distasteful to do so. This makes social mobility, indeed social change of any sort, extremely difficult even when it is vitally necessary. One particular Hindu sect, the Lingayat, worshippers of Siva, who reject the caste system and are willing to marry across its barriers, have shown an ability to adapt to modern life which is impossible for many other Hindus.

The main impact of Westernization has been in this area of social change. The British during their occupation of India had a policy of religious toleration. Though the door has been wide open for Christian missionaries to work there, Christianity has made few new converts in India; but its influence has been considerable and has been exercised through education. Missionaries and government worked together to abolish the practise of Suttee – the suicide of a widow on her husband's funeral pyre – because this was felt to be too anti-social to be tolerated; but it was done with the help of the Brahma Samaj, a Hindu movement founded in 1828 by Raja Ram Mohun Roy (1772–1833) which was concerned with social reform.

The Arya Samaj, founded in 1875, was a strongly nationalistic reform movement within Hinduism based on the Vedic scriptures and was against idol worship and the caste system, but its base was confined to north and west India. Shri Ramakrishna (1836–86) was an outstanding spiritual leader who studied and practised Moslem and Christian as well as Hindu traditions, and taught the unity of all religions in their inwardness; the outward forms, he argued, were superficial. The Ramakrishna Mission was the first Hindu society to send missionaries to the West, and they brought back from the West the idea of social involvement which became an integral part of the Mission's work – they

The West takes up yoga. Yehudi Menuhin and his teacher Iyengar in Bombay. (*Photo: P. R. Shinde, Camera Press, London*)

built schools, hospitals and colleges.

Sarvepalli Radhakrishnan (1888–1975) is the most outstanding Hindu philosopher of our time and has been responsible for the publishing and interpreting of much Hindu sacred literature in the West. But the most well-known and influential figure of this century in both popular and reform Hinduism was undoubtedly 'Mahatma' Gandhi (1869–1948). He was both a religious and social reformer who used the full weight of his tremendous spiritual charisma to reform the Hindu attitude to the outcast, as well as leading the Indian struggle for freedom which he insisted must be a moral and religious struggle for self-mastery. Non-violence, self-discipline and adherence to the truth in spite of persecution were the three pillars by which his campaign was supported. He worked towards an India that would tolerate religious differences, and this brought him into conflict with orthodox Hindus, who suspected him of selling out to the British and wished to have no dealings with Moslems. His assassination by a right-wing orthodox Hindu stemmed from this distrust. But the attitude to untouchability has changed, and has been supported by new laws.

Other reformers have wished to abolish caste; but though caste differences are increasingly disregarded in public life, in private life they are still maintained and represent a powerful conservative force. Indeed, the loudest voices in Hindu society today are not those of the secularized Western kind of intellectuals, or of the moderates like Radnakrishnan, but of the conservative Hindus who wish to assert and maintain the special character of Hinduism.

In the past 200 years Hinduism has produced outstanding spiritual leaders who have reached international stature and have made progressive Hindu ideas known to a worldwide audience. The Westernized intellectuals have created the modern secular state. But the popular Hindu religion, largely unknown outside the borders of India, still commands the loyalty and devotion of the overwhelming majority of her people.

To appreciate what religion means to the ordinary Hindu one has to join the huge, swirling crowds of worshippers taking part in one of the Hindu festivals or making a pilgrimage to one of the holy places. This is a timeless, unchanging India seeking the presence of God in one of his many forms.

> As he worships before the Lord at Banaras, or Balaji the Lord at Tirupati, or the Great Mother at Conjeeveram, the pilgrim comes to see that all are equal before the Lord, in whatever form or place the deity may be worshipped. As the pilgrims from all over India mix together and worship at the great ancient sites, they come to know and cherish the fundamental unity of this land of Bharata [India], made sacred in so many places by the presence of the Lord.
>
> Swaprasad Bhattacharyya, *The Religion of the Hindus.*

Buddhism

Buddhism is the child of Hinduism, and shows its kinship in many ways. The belief in continual rebirth after death and the use of yoga-like techniques are two examples of ideas and practices they share. But Buddhism is very different in essence; so much so that Hindus find it difficult to know what to make of it. And in spite of obvious similarities it does not fit into the Hindu system. There is, for example, a complete denial of the existence of personality, going far beyond anything asserted by Hinduism. The Buddhist view is that there is no such thing as human personality, let alone a personal God. Not all Hindus believe in a personal God, but they would understand the notion of God as a person as a way of expressing a particular truth.

The original form of Buddhism – Hinayana – lost its foothold in India at the time of the Moslem invasion during the eleventh and twelfth centuries AD, and it has never regained the pre-eminence it once held there. All that remain are ruined stupas, or temples. A later form of Buddhism, Mahayana, which contains teachings and traditions belonging to followers of the Buddha as well as the Buddha himself, remains in Burma, Sri Lanka and Thailand. The Chinese form of Buddhism, Cha'an or Zen, which absorbed Chinese ideas about the religious aspect of work, existed in China and Japan until this century, when Buddhism came under attack from the Communist regime in China, and Japanese Zen began to decline.

Eighteenth-century Burmese sculpture of the Bodhisatta, Prince Siddhartha, leaving home in Kapilavastu at dead of night to renounce the world as the Buddha Gotama. Gods raise the horses' hooves so that the departure may be silent. Victoria & Albert Museum. (*Photo: Victoria & Albert Museum*)

Buddhist prophecies, composed between 200 BC and AD 400, foretold a gradual decline in Buddhism, ending in the disappearance of the pure Law within 2,000 years. And Buddhism has indeed declined in strength and influence since that date. By the twelfth century Ho-nen of Japan said that no one could understand the wisdom of the Buddha, and that a simple act of faith was all that people could then attempt. By this century the Japanese form of Buddhism, Zen, which lays great stress on meditation and rejects the use of images, had declined to a shadow of what it had been. Western interest, particularly the fashion for Zen that has grown up in the United States, has helped to renew this form of Buddhism in Japan itself. The number of books on Zen has increased 'like bamboo sprouts after a rain', according to a Japanese writer. The number of books on Zen written for Western readers is increasing at a similar rate. Scholars have been working to translate Buddhist scriptures and interpret them to the Western world, and others have been writing introductory books to popularize Buddhism, particularly Zen. This missionary effort bore little fruit until recently, when the gloomy world-view held by Buddhism, together with its scientific and psychological approach, has become more and more attractive to Western intellectuals. Buddhism is the most self-denying and life-denying of all the religions, and in its original form is unlikely to have any mass appeal in the West; but individuals have been attracted by the hard simplicity of its monastic life, others by its philosophical search for meaning and its strong emphasis on meditation. As Fredrick Franck says in his book, *The Zen of Seeing*: 'It is no accident that Zen is being discovered in the West at a time of realization that we are fast becoming strangers to our inner life, and that we are all too easily confused about what is real and authentic and what is phoney, about what we are truly like, and what we think we must like because it happens to be required.' What Westerners like Frederick Franck are looking for from Zen is well illustrated from the same book, in which Franck says of enlightenment: 'Seeing Things thus – I know what I am!'

Buddhism is strongest today in Sri Lanka, as the dominant religion; but elsewhere in the East it is fighting for survival in face of the Communist advance. It seems unlikely to survive in Communist China, where it has been under constant attack ever since Communism became established. Elsewhere it is being forced to become involved in politics, a strange outcome for a religion so little involved with wordly concerns. The most well-known political action

Eighteenth-century Tibetan *tanka* showing the Dhyani Buddha Amoghasiddhi. Victoria & Albert Museum. (*Photo: Victoria & Albert Museum*)

of recent times was the suicide of Buddhist monks who burnt themselves to death as a protest against the Vietnam war. Buddhists are becoming deeply involved in many ways as the tide of events bring them out of seclusion and contemplation into the fight for the values they believe in. Buddhism, of all religions, is the one most under threat from modern materialism; and of the major world religions, it is the one most in danger of extinction. Modern secular and materialistic societies, whether capitalist or Communist, are pursuing the goal of self-improvement. Buddhism pursues the opposite goal, that of complete self-denial; and this is attractive to those who find the pressures of modern society intolerable. This contrary way of life is difficult enough to sustain in a capitalist society, but nearly impossible in a Communist one, where any deviation from the Communist norm is seen as a threat to the corporate task of harnessing the energies of a whole people in an immense effort to reconstruct and renew their entire way of life for materialist ends.

Whether Buddhism can survive in the East depends a great deal on the scale and style of future Communist advance, and whether there is a widespread revolt against materialism and the ruthlessness with which both Communist and capitalist societies pursue their aims. It may survive in strongholds like Sri Lanka and Japan, and among scholars and intellectuals in the West. Buddhists themselves look forward to being born again in a future era when Maitreya, the next Buddha, appears on the earth with fresh enlightenment for the world.

Religion and Communism

In eighteenth-century Europe two great revolutions took place which were to influence the destiny of people all over the world – the Industrial Revolution and the French Revolution. Both signalled the breakdown of one kind of society, and the forming of something quite new. Religion tends to be a conservative element in society, and also an agent which binds people together; and those who felt threatened by the disintegration of the old society turned to Christianity as the stabilizing force that could protect their civilization from the destructive elements threatening to sweep it away. Tsar Alexander I was hailed as the saviour of Europe when, after defeating Napoleon in 1815, he used his power and prestige to engineer the so-called Holy Alliance – the banding together of the royal heads of Europe as Christian brothers in the common fight against the threat to their power and the stability and peace of Europe. Christianity, once famous for 'turning the world upside-down', became the buttress of the status quo; especially in Russia, where the immense and unwieldy nature of the country has made it difficult to govern except through a mixture of terror and idealism. The church in Russia was seen as a department of state, headed by a government official answerable only to the Tsar. Tsar, Church and State were an apparently inseparable trinity.

On the other hand, those who wished to change society were only too anxious to hasten the process of disintegration. Throughout the nineteenth century revolutionaries were at work in Europe fanning the flame of revolt. Karl Marx thought that revolution would occur only in societies which had reached a certain stage of maturity in their evolution; but from 1870 onwards it became clear that the countries of Western Europe were embarked on a course of peaceful progress, and Marx turned his attention to Russia, which he had previously considered too backward.

There the revolutionaries had met with failure and success – failure to convince the people themselves of the need for revolution, but success in the assassination of Tsar Alexander II before he could reform the constitution and take the country along the path of peaceful reconstruction. His son, Alexander III, clamped down on all attempts at change and improvement, and by so doing hastened the end of the old regime. The opportunity for revolution came in 1917, when the combination of famine and chaos caused by the 1914–18 War sparked off the long-awaited revolt. Under the Tsars, those who had strayed from the path of Christian Orthodoxy had been punished; now the position was reversed, and the Church, the pillar of the old regime, suffered persecution and harassment. There was no let-up until the 1939–45 War, when the Church was allowed to function again in order to comfort the people in their intense suffering. It is not always appreciated that Russian suffering in that war exceeded even what was endured by the Jews, certainly in terms of the number of lives lost.

Since then the Russian Church has been kept in a stranglehold of official permission. The number of churches allowed to function is strictly limited; worship conducted-elsewhere than in an 'official' church is illegal; church attendance penalizes a student or worker in his career; teaching religion to children is forbidden. In spite of all this, official Soviet figures show that a higher proportion of their people attend church worship than in most Western countries where there is no penalty or restriction.

Lenin described religion as the opium of the people, and it was supposed that in the forward march of Communism religion would wither away and be no longer needed. This certainly has not happened. To those engaged on a major reconstruction of a whole nation the immediate task and needs are overwhelming – more important than searching for a meaning to existence or the key to one's true identity. But it is from our understanding of the purpose of life that all action flows. In Boris Pasternak's novel *Dr Zhivago*, a woman is shocked to find Dr Zhivago writing poetry while Russia burns; she feels, as many Communists do, that with a whole country in need of saving, such an activity is mere self-indulgence. But Russian writers are the prophets of Russian society, the ones who hold up the truth of the situation as they see it and ask 'What does it mean?' and 'Where are we going?' It is they who are asking the perennial religious questions in terms of their own society. Writers like Solzhenitsyn are modern prophets calling their contemporaries to look again and ask 'What is really happening?' and 'Why?'

The need for prophesy as well as Marxist dogma seems to have been felt by Mao Tse Tung, the first leader of Communist China; in his published

Thoughts, he put himself forward as a philosopher-poet as well as a political leader. Communism has developed very differently in China from elsewhere – partly for historical reasons, partly because of the character of its people and because the nature of China's communal task is different from that of other countries. There are different brands of Marxism; but one thing is central to Marxist dogma, that the position of the worker in society is conditioned by his relationship to the means of production. Most Communist countries have understood this idea in the context of the Industrial Revolution and heavy industry; but in China, what was most needed was an agricultural revolution so that the country could fulfil the primary task of feeding its population. Chinese popular art today depicts beautiful fields full of growing crops with, very much in the foreground, agricultural machinery and workers busy improving irrigation or harvesting. When the Communist Party first took over in China they aimed at a broad Popular Front, and the different religious groupings were invited to take part; but as the Communist hold strengthened, these groups found themselves under intense pressure, turning to persecution as the full Communist programme got under way. Buddhism suffered most – surprisingly so on the surface, because the Chinese form of Buddhism incorporates the Chinese ideal of the spiritual aspect of manual labour, and most of the communities support themselves by agricultural work; unlike Buddhists elsewhere who rely on alms. But in practice the new regime felt threatened by any other form of ideology. The attack on Confucianism is easier to understand, since their religion represented the ideals of the hated middle classes. Christianity was also a victim, though there were few Christians in China in spite of much missionary effort. After being rejected at first, Taoism has been accepted officially as an allowable religion for Chinese Communists to hold, since it is said to enshrine the ideals of the peasants. But it also expresses the philosophy of Hegel, from whom Marx took much inspiration: that is, that truth does not reveal itself in one form but in the tension between two opposites. The Tao sign expressed the opposition and tension between light and darkness, symbolizing the whole of creation.

This synthesis between Marxism Chinese-style and religion is a fascinating development and one which could affect its whole future.

Both Russia and China are oriental societies which, both before and after Communism, have had little concept of the value of the individual; individuals are sacrificed with complete ruthlessness if it is considered to be in the interest of the community. Individualism, or the sense of the preciousness of the life of the individual human being, is something which belongs to Western Christianity and arose in the eleventh and twelfth centuries from the individual communing with Christ and meditating on the death of Christ for each and everyone. But if Russian Communism continues to divorce itself from any form of religious quest, even in its widest sense, because of an historical background which associated religion with the Tsarist regime, and Chinese Communism allows a religious element into the life of its community, it seems that Chinese Communism may in the long run emerge richer and stronger and more able to ask and answer the profoundest questions about human destiny.

7

The Arts

Summary of Chapter

Sometimes, I don't see how things that I call the arts can go on at all, but that's only at moments. I work within the limits of what I feel or know or have inherited. It is utterly impossible for people at the end of one culture phase and civilization to have the foggiest notion of what is going to emerge. A man at the end of the Roman Empire could no more envisage the Gothic world than my grandfather could have envisaged aeroplanes.

David Jones (1895–1974), poet and painter

Introduction

The way in which man's artistic creativity ties in with the rest of his history is complicated, and we can never talk about it as if it were something precise and readily comprehensible. Think round that quotation from David Jones. Among its meanings is this: that we are driven forward by life, from one experience to another, from one idea to the next; things change around us, bewilderingly; from whatever point we have reached, we look back and try to understand the path we have followed. There always has to be much guesswork, much theorizing, and there is always room for disagreement. The glory of it all is that there cannot be just one opinion, or one interpretation. In this section the story of the arts in modern times will be told as clearly as possible, so that, to take one example, we have some hope of understanding how the music of Haydn led, along an extraordinary 200-year-long twisting path, to the music of Stockhausen.

But if this has been the most exciting period in the history of man as an artist, it has also been the most confused one. To stay with music, it is a period when the orderliness of the eighteenth century gave way to the powerful disorder (as it sounded at first) of the nineteenth century; to the making, in fact, of a new kind of musical order – so that if we imagine Haydn being reborn, he might at first hearing have been astonished and puzzled by the music of Berlioz or Debussy (at different ends of the nineteenth century), and might feel wholly lost if he came fresh to the twentieth-century music of Webern. In the twentieth century, indeed, music has undergone yet more changes, rooted in those of the nineteenth century, but even deeper, more astonishing. The American John Cage's *Piano Concert* has a piano part whose elements can be played in any order the pianist chooses; and a part for orchestra, which can be played by any number of players – or none at all. The musical score consists of pages of which any number may be played – or, again, none at all. How did we travel from, say, the piano concertos of Mozart to John Cage's *Piano Concert*?

All the names mentioned so far have been European or American ones. But during the two centuries we are talking about, the world has become an infinitely smaller place, and European music has been influenced by that of Africa, Asia and elsewhere. And America being what it is – a great mix of people who have their origins all over the world – American music has been subject to all kinds of exotic influences from within, too – from Americans who came originally from Germany, or Italy, or the Pacific, or Russia, or Japan....

In painting and the visual arts in general, there have been similar huge transformations. What would the English artist John Constable (1776–1837), who was himself the instigator of major changes in the way people painted, make of the work of the modern American Jackson Pollock, whose pictures are whirls and splashes of wild colour? What would he make of some of the new theories of painting that follow one another in our time in such breathless succession? How would he react to those theories, for example, that attempt to allow chance and accident, rather than any sought-out intentions on the part of the artist, to determine the finished form of painting?

Again, in painting as in music, the whole world now exchanges ideas and influences. Somewhere along the road we shall follow, the work of European painters was deeply affected by Japanese art – discovered when Japan was opened up to the outside world in the mid-nineteenth century. Later, there was an even more remarkable turn of artistic events when the spirit and style of the art of Africans and other people who had been regarded as 'primitive' was absorbed into the painting and sculpture of artists in the West, so that the world had to have new thoughts about that very word 'primitive'. Perhaps the most decisive happening in the world of painting and the visual arts generally was the invention of photography. Until that moment, the visual artist had always been able to feel that one of his reasons for existence was that he alone could offer a faithful representation of the appearance of things. Now that element in his work was taken over by the camera. Not only did he have to reconsider the old value that was set on 'primitive' art (much of which had not been thought to be art at all), but he had to come to terms with a world in which a machine could very efficiently capture the appearance of objects, people and events. All sorts of questions are going to leap out at us when we consider matters like this.

Later, there were artistic movements whose adherents looked for subject matter in their dreams or nightmares – in a famous modern painting by Magritte a train is calmly puffing out of a fireplace, an event that certainly never occurred in waking life; or artists suddenly began to paint, with complete fidelity, such apparently boring everyday objects as cans of beans. Did such movements arise because the camera had taken over some of the artist's work? Or were other forces responsible – that interest in dreams and fantasies that we have had ever since the psychologist Sigmund Freud and his followers made us aware of the importance of our dreams and our fantasy life; or (in the case of the cans of beans) because we had come to believe that anything whatever was art, or that art was so exhausted that it could only pretend to be a camera? Or because artists in our time are rethinking the whole matter of what is a proper subject for art? Or simply because they want to thumb their noses at the world?

This is the sort of question we shall find ourselves asking. We shall have to dig around for explanations, too, when we look at the development of literature during those 200 years. When it comes to literature, in fact, we shall have to consider the influence on writing of an invention that is quite as profound as the influence of the camera on the visual arts. The perfection of cinematography – followed by that of television – has led to enormous changes in the work of writers all over the world. The development in literature in modern times has been as complicated and remarkable as in the other arts – and, as with them, it brings us to the brink of an age when every part of the world is likely to influence every other part. But the invention of cinema has certainly been the cause of some of the deepest changes in literature. It has made it possible to write in a swifter and more economical style than before. We can imagine, for example, that an early science fiction writer, like Jules Verne, would have difficulty in making his way through the work of a modern science fiction writer, like Kurt Vonnegut – not because Vonnegut writes obscurely, but because he writes for an audience who have picked up certain habits, when it comes to understanding a story, from the cinema.

Add to all this the impact of some of the very latest advances in technology. The invention of magnetic tape has begun to revolutionize music. Recording techniques have made huge areas of human experience available to us all, on tape or disc or film. Any one of us in a day may hear more music and see more paintings reproduced than our grandfathers could hope to hear or see in a year. And these changes have deepened our thinking about one of the great questions that have faced artists in modern times: the question of the relationship between the arts and the public – the mass of the people. During the last century or so there have been times when the artist seemed to be moving further and further out of touch with his fellow-men. And some of the most important artistic movements during the same period have been attempts to bridge that gap....

This is the scope of our story; these are the sorts of (often quite awkward) questions we must ask and attempt to answer. And we have to begin by looking at the first great change in the artistic atmosphere which coincided roughly with the beginning of the period we are interested in – that is, towards the end of the eighteenth century. We must look at the ideas behind two words without which the modern story of the arts cannot be discussed – Classical and Romantic.

The Birth of Romanticism

As a quick way of understanding what was meant by the classical view of art, look at the picture on page 268 of the Munich Glyptotek. Here is a great building in the Classical style, designed by von Klenze in the nineteenth century. It displays a fine, cool feeling for clean lines, for handsome geometry; for order (one little touch of untidiness anywhere along that façade would stand out as a horrible blot). It is in perfect control of itself, very thoughtful, strictly composed. Such a building represents perfectly the dominant spirit of thought and art during most of the eighteenth century. There was great respect for reason, and great distaste for what was called 'enthusiasm' – which meant any expression of feeling that was uncontrolled and passionate. (It is a fact that the word 'enthusiasm', which we use with approval, was then used scornfully.) Nature itself was regarded as potentially a dangerous force; left to itself it would quickly overwhelm the orderly human world and replace it with senseless chaos. Nature was tolerable only when it was trimmed into formal gardens and neat farms.

The Munich Glyptotek, designed by von Klenze in the early nineteenth century. (*Photo: Architectural Association*)

It was in a changing attitude to nature that Romanticism first made itself felt. Already in the middle of the eighteenth century a few English poets were beginning to write about natural scenery in a new spirit; they saw it not as a threat to human order, but as an embodiment of the Sublime. The Sublime (a word much used by the early Romantics) was the mysterious, the grand and awe-inspiring. It was behind the feeling you might have about a mountain, not fearing it as a raw piece of uncontrolled nature but responding to it as an example of the splendour, majesty – and, somehow, the meaning – of the natural world. To put it very briefly: while the Classical outlook was cool about mountains, the Romantic outlook was excited by them.

But this new feeling about nature was only the beginning. The Classical view of man himself was like the Classical view of natural scenery – man was best when he kept himself under control, mastered his emotions, set the highest value on his intellect and his reason. The Romantics saw man differently. They set greater store by feeling than by reasoning; they turned their attention from man as a social being, suppressing much of his inner life and the turmoil of his emotions and joining with his fellows to create rational, cool societies, to man as a stormy individual. Man was a force of nature, like a mountain. His feelings were all-important. The Romantic began to explore the inside of man, his heart and his imagination, just as the poets had begun to explore and celebrate, and find meaning in, the raw, wild world of nature.

Why was there this change which, beginning slowly in the middle of the eighteenth century, was complete by the century's end, and swept nearly everything before it in the first half of the nineteenth century? One obvious cause was the political break-up that found its fiercest expression in the French Revolution of 1789. The Classical world was orderly at a price; underneath its cool reasonableness seethed enormous discontent. It was all very well for those who ruled the countries of Europe to claim that only through the exercise of reason and self-control could tolerable societies be created. The great mass of people led lives to which we might apply the words of the philosopher Hobbes: they were 'poor, nasty, brutish and short'. At the end of the eighteenth century, the anger of people who had no share in the orderly, rational lives of their rulers boiled over. Now the fact is that artists – writers, painters, musicians – are sensitive to the changing feel of things inside the societies in which they live. The enormous political upsets of the time would alone have been enough to direct the artist's attention away from orderliness and the great Classical philosophy of self-control. The uncontrollable, impatient, strange and unpredictable in man was coming, politically, to the surface. Artists too began bringing those qualities to the surface in their work.

Looking back, we can see that certain writers in particular had immense influence in this matter of one general body of views about man and nature being replaced by another. The French philosopher Jean-Jacques Rousseau (1712–78) attacked the ideal of the civilized man, the man who tried to account for everything by the exercise of his reason; Rousseau sought to put in its place the ideal of the 'natural' man, who gave due weight to his emotions, however unruly. When Rousseau wrote his autobiography he called it his *Confessions*, and explored aspects of private experience that no writer in the Classical mould would have thought worthy of his attention. There you have it in a nutshell – the essence of this change was that artists were beginning to *confess* to feelings and desires and behaviour that had been methodically suppressed by their predecessors. The great German writer Goethe (1749–1832) wrote a novel, *Die Leiden des Jungen Werthers* (*The Sorrows of Young Werther*), in which his young hero was shown as being swept by storms of passion and feeling. It was a novel that spoke up for passion, and justified it. And in his great drama, *Faust*, Goethe made the case that man had a right to every kind of possible experience. Testing everything by the mind, the reason, was not enough; we ought to give equal value to the impulses of the heart and the imagination. To say such things was to set about overturning the Classical view with a vengeance. The Classical artist had been so suspicious of the heart, so wary of the imagination!

This huge explosion in the arts was nowhere greater than in music. In fact it has been said that, when Romanticism really took over, music was the most Romantic of the arts by far. It was felt to be this for a reason that is important for an understanding of the whole of this change. Among the marks of the new, Romantic outlook was a longing for what could hardly be expressed – for experience that could with difficulty be accounted for in words. Music was felt at this time to be the most expressive of the arts because it speaks to us without words, and so can take over (this was the argument) at the very point where language fails us. It is interesting, if you want to catch the very turning point between Classical and Romantic art, to study the music of Beethoven. He was, in many respects, a Classical artist: he used all the musical forms that in their nature are purely Classical. For example, all music based on the sonata is essentially Classical – the strict arrangement of musical ideas that is achieved by the sonata form springs obviously enough from the Classical desire for order and control. But within these forms Beethoven expressed ideas that are Romantic rather than Classical. His music is a penetrating exploration of human feeling and passion; much of it is not, in the Classical sense, in the least *cool*. Indeed, it might be said that the most completely Romantic composer was Hector Berlioz (1803–69), because he never composed a single sonata or quartet or concerto. He invented new forms for himself – musical structures that were designed to give full play to the imagination and to feeling, and were little restrained by older ideas of musical orderliness. 'Berlioz', wrote the French Romantic poet, Théophile Gautier, 'represents the Romantic musical idea, the breaking up of old moulds, the substitution of new forms for unvaried square rhythms.' And there again you have the essence of it – of this great change in artistic outlook. The Classical artist was interested in stability and order – so it could be said that under the most subtle and beautiful Classical music lay 'unvaried square rhythms'. Berlioz, and the other Romantic composers, introduced great variety of rhythm, and did not contain it within the square shape of Classical form.

In case any reader is annoyed by the word 'square', and argues, quite rightly, that it suggests that Classical music was mechanical and stiff and unsubtle, let it be said that Gautier was simply comparing a strict sense of rhythm, often very subtly used, with something much freer and more flexible. Listen to a piece of true Romantic music – almost anything by Chopin (1810–49), for example. It has form, all right, but it is a drifting, free form, taking us by surprise with variations of rhythm, and the last word you would use to describe it is 'square'. As an interesting technical matter, Chopin made much use of a device called 'rubato', which consists in taking some of the strict time from one note or phrase and adding it to another. A pupil of his once asked him to define 'rubato'. They were sitting at a piano lighted, as pianos used to be, with candles. Chopin blew gently on one of the candle flames. As it dipped and swayed under his breath and then stood up straight again, Chopin said: '*That* is rubato.' It is one more of the little points that enable us to understand the difference between Classical and Romantic. This subtle stealing of time in music ('rubato' means 'robbed') was not a common feature of the stricter (or squarer) world of Classical composition.

The first important point, then, to be made about the modern history of the arts, is that at the roots of that history lies this great change from the Classical outlook to the Romantic. It was not a simple matter. It did not replace a totally Classical world with a totally Romantic one. All the arts, in the last hundred years, have looked back at some point or other, through the gift of some particular painter or composer or poet, to the Classical tradition. Part of the work of one of the twentieth century's most remarkable musicians, Igor Stravinsky, can be called 'neo-Classical' (that is, a renewed form of Classical music). But the effect of that great change is still with us. It is often only by reference to it that we can begin to understand what the modern artist is attempting.

One way of accounting for what happened to the arts when the first energies of the Romantic movement had been exhausted – from about the middle of the nineteenth century – is to take the story of a single branch of the arts. If we look first at what has happened in the visual arts – in painting, especially – we shall not, of course, necessarily be discovering what happened in music or literature. We shall have to look separately at those other arts. But though each branch of art has its own history, and though it can be dangerous to discuss them as though they were simply variations of the same activity, nevertheless they do tend to follow the same waves of feeling, the same ideas.

The Visual Arts

Impressionism

Many streams of the nineteenth-century experience came together to make the new – and to many people, outrageous – art that had its origins in France and collected round the name of Impressionism. It was, to begin with, a name used scornfully and mockingly. In 1872 Claude Monet (1840–1826) painted a picture called *Impression, Sunrise*. The artist is looking straight into the sun, and what he is interested in is the play of light on water. Since that *is* his concern, and since the result is inevitably a brilliant vagueness and dazzle of colour, there is a complete absence of elements that it had always been thought painting could not do without. There is no strongly formal composition, no carefully thought-out arrangement of its various elements; there are no clear lines dividing one object from another. We are so accustomed now to paintings of this kind that we have to make a real effort of imagination to see Monet's painting, and all that early work of the Impressionists, as they appeared to most people in the 1870s. Most of those who saw that work felt very much as the English critic, John Ruskin, was to feel a little later when he looked at paintings of an Impressionist kind by James Whistler (1834–1903). Whistler, Ruskin wrote, was 'a coxcomb', who was 'flinging a pot of paint in the public's face'. Monet's painting seemed, to many, no better. And when, in 1874, the group of painters who were beginning to see things as Monet saw them – among them, Renoir, Cézanne, Degas, Sisley and Pisarro – held their first exhibition, this term, Impressionism, intended to be a very uncomplimentary term, was quickly applied to them. To say a picture was Impressionist was to say it was a daub, an incompetent and impudent mess. It was some time before the term became one, not of abuse, but of honour.

And what were those strands of the nineteenth-century experience that lay behind the work of the Impressionists? First, there was a purely scientific element. The painters were very much influenced by researches that had been carried out into the science of colour. A complex business: but you get some idea of the notions that had been picked up by the artists from such scientists when you realize that they included a quite revolutionary perception of the nature of shadow. A shadow had been thought of as a pure darkness; now it was understood to be a complementary of the colour of the object casting

Monet: Poplars on the Epte. Tate Gallery. (*Photo: Tate Gallery*)

the shadow. (For example, something that is yellow will cast a shadow that is predominantly violet.) If you are in Paris, go to the Musée de l' Impressionisme there; as well as offering a quite marvellous collection of Impressionist paintings, it sets out in fascinating detail these scientific ideas about the nature of human vision that lay solidly behind the works that, to those who hated them, seemed an abandonment of most of the traditions of painting. The human eye took some time to recognize that these pictures, with their dabs and streaks and explosions of bright colour, with one object dissolving into another, and with a general effect of quite hectic brilliance, were soundly – in fact, scientifically – based statements about the way we actually see things. It was probably only a century of new and revolutionary science that could produce such a new and revolutionary art, which began by causing offence and mocking laughter, and ended by persuading people that this, indeed, was a genuine reflection of the actual nature of human vision.

And the new, nineteenth-century view of the artist himself also lay behind this fresh approach to painting. We have seen that what the Romantic revolution did was to set great value on the individuality of the artists. As the American writer Tom Wolfe has said, in the eighteenth-century the artist was a gentleman; in the nineteenth-century, he became a genius. (Although the Oxford Dictionary tells us that the word 'genius' was first used in 1749 to mean a person of outstanding creative power, that usage is really a modern Romantic one.) In the Classical world, the artist had occupied his quite sober place in society; now he was an individual, often quite out of step with society. A new importance was placed on the special vision of the world that any particular artist might offer. So it was far easier than it had been a hundred years before for the artist to break new ground, to offer a view of things that represented a violent breach with tradition. It was easier, in the late nineteenth-century, to go off in a shockingly new direction, as Monet did.

One of the most interesting facts about the Impressionists is that they held together, as a group, far less firmly than is sometimes imagined. Indeed, the truth, when one looks at it, is that many artists were influenced by Impressionism, but then followed entirely individual paths of their own. There was Vincent Van Gogh (1853–90), for example, whose passionate and, in the end, totally original painting never became acceptable in his lifetime; though it was not long after his tragic death (he shot himself) that his stature as one of the greatest of painters was acknowledged. Van Gogh was deeply influenced by the Impressionists, and Impressionism certainly helped him to discover his own extraordinary style; but it will not do to think of him simply as an Impressionist. That would no more do than it would to describe Shakespeare as simply an Elizabethan dramatist. Both of them are great originals, who rose above the styles of their time. The same is true of Paul Gauguin (1848–1903) and Paul Cézanne (1839–1906), who again owed much to Impressionism and the new visual language it created, but have the size and exceptional individuality of men of special genius. What the careers of all three men illustrate is that increasing isolation of the artist from the public that was a fruit of the Romantic revolution. All of them led tempestuous lives, and found it necessary to break away very dramatically from the respectable world around them. Van Gogh, who had periods of positive madness, seemed to many to provide new evidence for the Romantic theory that a great artist was not, in any ordinary sense, sane. (Curiously, it is a seventeenth-century poet who best expressed this idea. John Dryden wrote, 'Great wits are to madness near allied.') Gauguin, who gave up a prosperous middle-class career and left his wife and family, fed the other Romantic view that an artist was a rootless creature, whose vision was bound to take him along paths that respectable people would regard as disgraceful, immoral and, in the last analysis, simply impossible to understand. Why could an artist not combine his pursuit of art with a perfectly ordinary and decent acceptance of a conventional social role?

This brings us to another aspect of nineteenth-century experience that lay behind this great artistic explosion. There was, of course, much conservative art being produced during the century, not breaking away in any new direction. There were portrait painters, landscape painters, and painters of the social

Van Gogh: Landscape at Auvers. Tate Gallery. (*Photo: Tate Gallery*)

scene who fed the appetite of increasingly prosperous industrial societies for untroubling art that they could buy and display in their homes. But the main trend of really original art was away from such polite ends. In England, the Pre-Raphaelite Brotherhood had begun as a protest against the conservative and complacent materialism of the nineteenth-century. Just as Charles Dickens in the novel had satirized the greedy acquisitiveness of the middle class, and the rich ugliness of the lives they led (read about the Veneerings in *Our Mutual Friend*, with their passion for whatever was 'bran new'), so the most lively artists looked for ways in which they might register their protest and point to other visions of the way in which men might best conduct their lives. The Pre-Raphaelites looked back to an idealized medieval world; they turned against the growing tendency for everyday objects to be machine-made, and they revived old crafts, emphasizing the importance and beauty and individuality of things made by hand. Alongside this went a strong socialist element – that is, they wanted to create a society in which work would have dignity, and men would enjoy their work, and where every object would be beautiful. The emphasis given by the Impressionists to the sheer loveliness of the visible world, and their rejection of the solid art of tradition, drew undoubtedly on similar feelings. It was about this time that the phrase '*épater les bourgeois*' began to be used–meaning to startle and scandalize the middle class. To give offence to the respectable world was becoming one of the accepted purposes of the artist. It can, from this standpoint, have been no surprise–or disappointment–to the Impressionists that they caused such anger to conventional critics. It was coming to be thought natural that true art should do this.

There was, of course, another impulse behind all this – photography had been invented in France by Niépce, and another Frenchman, Daguerre, began his important experiments in the use of silver iodide deposited on silver-plated copper about the year 1830. To all but the most conservative artists, photography seemed to remove the traditional basis of the artist's existence. He was no longer required to give – what, until then, only he could give – an exact image of the visible world. The camera had taken over that function. Now he was free to explore the other aspects of his skill. Monet could paint the shimmering dazzle of light on water all the more confidently because it was what photography could not do with the same truth to the dissolving vision of the moment, the magical ambiguity of natural colour. Van Gogh, painting a cornfield blown by the wind, could add to the golden agitation of that scene his own excitement, his own feeling for the way that what we see may be determined by what is going on in our heads as we watch it. His cornfield is certainly a cornfield – but it is also a statement about human anguish. The camera cannot capture such elements in a scene. From now on – and from this point we begin to understand what has happened to art in our time – the artist is deeply concerned with inner feelings, with ideas about life, and with ideas about the way we look at things, quite as much as he is concerned with the actual appearance of the world he lives in.

And many more human experiences begin to pour into the world of art. Let us follow one line of development from the Impressionists. Let us, in fact, follow Claude Monet himself, that very great Impressionist painter, whose early work gave the movement its name. His concern with light and colour never slackened. He painted certain famous series of pictures, all of the same scene at different times of the day. He sat, for example, at a window of the Savoy Hotel in London, and painted the scene down river, towards Westminster, in changing light – so you have a blue Westminster, a purple Westminster, a grey Westminster, a yellow Westminster. And towards the end of his very long life, half-blind, he painted immense pictures of the lily pond in his garden at home in France. In these paintings, the outline of things has quite disappeared; they are enormous patchworks of dissolving colour – except that patchworks is not really the word; since it suggests distinct sections of colour, whereas in these paintings all objects dissolve into other objects. They are pure spectacles of light and colour. And they certainly carry us towards some of the characteristic art of our own century. These great final paintings of Monet's were exhibited in 1960 in the Museum of Modern Art in New York, from where one could go a short distance to the Guggenheim Gallery, which has a great collection of action paintings.

Action Painting

Action painting developed after the Second World War. The most famous name associated with this is that of an American artist, Jackson Pollock (1915–66). Pollock would tack long stretches of canvas to the floor and brush paint on to it, apparently without taking thought as to the patterns the paint might make – for a period he simply poured the paint from tins. He said, however: 'When I am painting I have a general notion as to what I am about. I *can* control the flow of paint: there is no accident, just as there is no beginning and no end.' The paintings that resulted certainly look as if there was some 'general notion' behind them. They are not mere messes. A hostile critic might say they

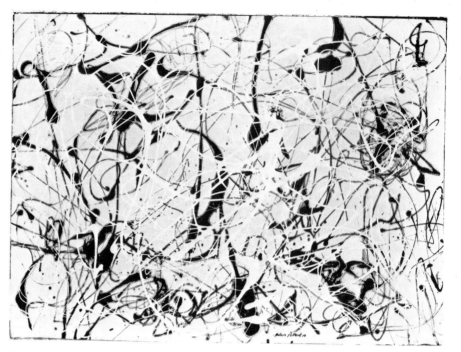

Pollock: Number 23. Tate Gallery. (*Photo: Tate Gallery*)

are the messes an artist might make; that is, they have a mysterious quality of design, and the colours seem related to one another in a way difficult to define. They seem (this is the point) not very far away from Monet's lily ponds; and one realizes that when Monet took Impressionism to its logical conclusion, and dissolved the visible world into shimmering patches of colour, he was preparing the way for art as dissolved, as far from the photographic representation of things, as action painting.

Dissolve is a word we ought to hang on to. Because it is a dissolving of the old, secure world of things set down as they obviously are, it is that kind of break-up of the visible world, that is the mark of the important art of our time. Behind it, as we have seen, lies a protest against the conventional view of things, because that is associated with middle-class respectability and the acceptance of industrial ugliness. There is growing concern with whatever it is that distinguishes an artist from a camera. If nothing had happened to affect the issue beyond the invention of photography, the artist would still be set, in our time, on this course. But much else has happened. To put it as simply as possible, that trend which followed from the scientific character of the nineteenth century, which threw up new ideas about the way we see things, has been sharpened by other developments. There are four obvious ones. The first is that change in man's view of himself that springs from the work of the great pioneer psychologist, Sigmund Freud (1856–1939). The second is the continuing struggle of man to make sense of his relationship to the machine, which, in the age of the computer and the space rocket, has become incredibly powerful. The third is the fact that our world has become very much smaller, that no part of it is now able to hide away from the twentieth century, and that forms of communication have immensely multiplied. And the fourth is the deeply disturbing character of the twentieth century itself.

The Influence of Freud

First, the great complex of consequences that followed from the work of Freud – what he did, to put it roughly, was to make us aware that our natures, our behaviour, our personalities, are founded on a profound unconscious life. What happens or is perceptible on the surface of our selves, everything we are conscious of, has its roots in the depths of our beings, in a great buried store of direct and indirect memory. In a sense, Freud's discoveries were a development of the Romantic interest in passion and emotion, in the furious complexity of being human. (Read, if you want to understand what a difference Freud made to the way we think of ourselves, the diaries of Francis Kilvert. Kilvert was an intelligent young parson who lived before Freud's work was published; it is quite astonishing to notice how innocently Kilvert wrote about acts and feelings of his that we could not now, any of us, describe without blushing. Even if we have not read Freud, we would still know, because Freud's ideas have reached us all, the hidden and perhaps shameful meaning of those acts and feelings; Kilvert, clever young man though he was, did not.) One of the pointers to what lies in our unconscious is to be found in our dreams. Freud discovered that in dreams we trace many clues to the way we behave consciously, on the surface of our lives. Much twentieth-century art draws upon this understanding. This is especially true of Surrealism, a school of art which was founded in the 1920s, though it had roots that went further back. The Surrealists set out to tap, as it were, their unconscious. They did this in two ways: by abandoning themselves to pure fantasy – they gave their imaginations complete freedom – and by painting a world like the world we know in our dreams. The fantasists included Paul Klee (1879–1940), who produced very

Klee: Comedy. Tate Gallery. (*Photo: Tate Gallery*) Copyright 1979, COSMOPRESS, Geneva, and SPADEM, Paris.

Magritte: La Lumière du Pôle (The Polar Light). Private Collection. (*Photo: Tate Gallery*) Copyright by ADAGP Paris 1979.

beautiful, weird, subtly coloured paintings and drawings with strange titles – such as *Twittering Machine*. The Italian Giorgio de Chirico (1888–1978) explored that oddity of dreams that sets us alone among great empty buildings, or in enormous city squares. The Spaniard Salvador Dali (b. 1904) made much of that lack of respect that dreams have for the known quality of things, so that a watch may be found draped like a circle of pastry over a fence. The Belgian René Magritte (1898–1967) painted men made of stone, a pair of boots with human toes. It was, as you see, all part of this dissolving of things. After Freud, we are no longer sure that we know what is real and what is not. It is easy enough to see how this chimed in with the artist's feeling that he was not now primarily concerned to set down the actual appearance of the world. Freud has led us to look inside ourselves for important truths about human reality. Surrealism is simply one of the most obvious consequences in art of the work of Freud and his followers. It is fair to say that all twentieth-century art in some way or other reflects the great and sometimes extremely disturbed view of ourselves and of the world for which he was responsible.

Art and Machinery

The art that springs from man's struggle to relate to machinery has some of its roots in the work of the Pre-Raphaelite Brotherhood that we have already looked at. They rejected the machine, and tried to point back to a world of handicrafts. In the 1890s there was a movement called Art Nouveau, the new art, which attempted to influence architecture and interior decoration. It produced designs of writhing plant forms – a style that did, in fact, add some gaiety to European cities: the original entrances to the Underground in Paris, the Métro, were in this style, and represented a small triumph for the movement, introducing notions of fine art into everyday industrial products. The best and most influential attempt to influence design in this way came with the founding, in 1919 in Germany, of the Bauhaus – a school of architects, painters, designers and craftsmen that fully accepted the existence of the machine, and set out to humanize its use. In Russia, shortly after the Revolution

Métro entrance, Station Cité, Paris 1900. (*Photo: Architectural Association*)

of 1917, a movement called Constructivism developed, another and very promising attempt to come to terms with machinery – to absorb, as it were, industrial techniques, and notions of design and construction springing naturally out of the use of modern materials, into the language of art. The work of the Russian founders of Constructivism was brought to a brutal halt as the hopeful and experimental post-Revolutionary atmosphere turned to something different, totally opposed to experiment. But the movement continues to have considerable influence on modern art.

It is easy, looking back over our century, to forget that such very positive movements among artists have existed, and continue to exist in many forms; attempts to apply art and design to our daily lives, to narrow the gap between art and everyday existence, and to realize the dream of William Morris, who came late to the Pre-Raphaelite Brotherhood, of a world in which our cities should be 'small and white and clean'. Much of the modern development of architecture belongs to such movements, though architecture has run into serious difficulties. The story of architecture in our time is a complicated one: but the fact is that many of the ideas on which it has been based – the idea, for example, of building upwards rather than sideways, so that free space might be preserved for public gardens and parks – have come into conflict with human nature. Most people do not like living in the sky, cut off from the ground; and tall buildings, with their apparatus of lifts and balconies and corridors, can be forbidding to live in, as well as being easily vandalized. In this field, ideas that seem fine in theory tend to be disastrous in practice, and we are a long way from realising the vision of men like William Morris or the founder of Constructivism, Vladimir Tatlin, who was born in 1885 and sank into such obscurity that the date of his death is uncertain.

The Shrinking World

The effect of the simple dwindling of the world in our century, brought about by revolutionary advances in transport and communications, has been to carry into the mainstream of European art many influences from outside. It all began in the middle of the nineteenth century with the opening up of Japan to European and American travellers and traders. Until then, Japan had been almost totally cut off from the rest of the world. Its art, quite unlike European art – economical, reducing the visible world often to the sparest lines and to a startlingly simple though subtle range of colours – had an enormous effect on the work of many artists in the West. Van Gogh and Whistler are only two among the more famous of those who absorbed into their work something of the style of Japanese art. In our century, the arts of Africa and South America, among other parts of the world, have had this kind of influence on Western painting and sculpture.

Picasso and Cubism

The most famous and remarkable of all twentieth-century artists, Pablo Picasso (1881–1973), drew on the art of Africa for many of his images. If a figure in one of his paintings has both eyes on one side of the nose, instead of dividing them between profiles as happens in reality, it is partly because

Picasso: The Three Dancers. Tate Gallery. (*Photo: Tate Gallery*) Copyright by SPADEM, Paris 1979.

this is a feature of much African art. One has to say 'partly' because Picasso was one of the painters involved in a great movement of the early part of the century, called Cubism. In essence, Cubism looks at all the aspects of an object simultaneously, so that front views, back views and side views are represented together in a painting. Usually the object was reduced at the same time to its geometrical elements – so that a face might become a triangle. The influence on Cubism of Negro art, much of which represents many aspects of a subject together in a single painting or carving, was considerable: but Cubism also developed out of some of the work of the Impressionists, especially Paul Cézanne, who said that the painter ought to look in Nature for the cone, the sphere and the cylinder. There are works by Henry Moore (b. 1898), the

Kwakiutl mask of Komokwa (North America). John H. Hauberg Collection, Seattle.

English sculptor, that take the form they do because he saw and studied examples of ancient South American sculpture – little known in the West until this century's great expansion of travel and communication.

What was happening was not a simple matter of imitation. Artists in the West were not pretending to be African, South American or Japanese artists. What they gained from this opening up of the world, and the consequent discovery of the art of distant places, was a new vision of the form that art might take. It was all part of an enormous change in men's way of thinking about the very nature of art. It had been believed that the paintings and carvings of Africans, the paintings of the Japanese, the great stone sculpture of, say, the Aztecs – in so far as anything was known about them – could be dismissed with the word 'primitive'. They represented a stage of art that Western man had grown out of. And the change in feeling amounted to this: that European artists discovered that all these distant arts, far from being the crude products of undeveloped skills and imaginations, were, by any standard, superb and powerful, and often filled with a force and strength that had disappeared from

European art itself. What is more, by being 'primitive', they were closer to the human unconscious, which Freud, as we have seen, had shown to be a source of important information about our human nature. The work of anthropologists in our century, who have found in the study of remote cultures many clues to the working of Western societies, has also helped to bring about this great change of attitude, and to increase the interest of Western artists in the work of people once believed to have nothing to teach the West. We are, it is obvious, only at the beginning of the great general changes in art that will follow, not only from this new respect for so-called 'primitive' art, but also from the entry into the mainstream of world art of living artists from every corner of the earth, bringing with them their own styles and traditions, and marrying them – now that art travels so easily across the face of the earth – to the styles and traditions of other peoples.

Change and Disorder

Many changes in modern art have been brought about by the disturbing character of the twentieth century. Global warfare, the fantastic speed of technological change, the barely credible expansion of human enterprise – have we even now adjusted to the very unlikely fact that men have landed on the moon? – have necessarily made art reflect the great agitation and disorder of the human spirit that have followed from such developments. It could hardly be a century of art calmly evolving.

One effect has been that art itself has been under fire, as it were, from some artists. Surrealism, which we have looked at, grew out of a movement called Dada, which was founded in the First World War, and lasted from 1915 to about 1922. It was a reaction to the shock of that first of the awful wars of our century. It set out, in its turn, to shock. One of its techniques was collage – the sticking of pieces of coloured paper at random on canvas. A leading Dadaist (the word 'Dada' is French and means 'hobbyhorse', but the name of the movement was intended to be irrelevant) was Marcel Duchamp (1887–1968), who in 1917 exhibited a lavatory basin with the title Fountains, (he signed it 'R. Mutt'), and on another occasion a reproduction of Leonardo da Vinci's painting, the Mona Lisa, with a moustache added to that famous face. The Dadaists called their work 'anti-art', and their purpose was to make nonsense of the whole business of art – the making, exhibition and sale of paintings and sculpture. Closer to the present day, we can trace some of the intentions of the Dadaists in the work, for example, of the school of Pop Art which emerged in Britain in the late 1950s and later in America. What the Pop artists did was to take photographs, advertisements, strip cartoons from comics, blow them up (sometimes to enormous size), and paint them in a technique known as 'hard edge' (the outlines violently rendered) and in crude, bright colour. In part, Pop Art was intended to suggest the banality and emptiness of many of the images by which we are surrounded, but it also derives clearly enough from that revolt of the Dadaists against most of the assumptions on which artists had always based their work – including assumptions about the subject matter with which art should be involved. In very recent years it has been succeeded by Minimal-

Oldenburg: *Lipsticks in Piccadilly*. Tate Gallery. (*Photo: Tate Gallery*)

ism, which reduces art to the smallest possible gesture an artist can make – a tiny scribble, perhaps, at the very edge of a blank canvas: or the arrangement of a number of common bricks into an oblong. There have been movements which produced self-destructive art – work which was specially made not to last. (An American artist sank several bags filled with gas into the ocean – that was, he claimed, a work – though an almost instantly disappearing work – of art.) There has been art which consists of digging a trench across a desert, or wrapping a part of a mountain in cellophane.

It is true that in our own day the tendency has been for theories of art to follow one another with bewildering speed. In a sense this may be a reflection of the present character of our civilization, with its dizzy succession of fashions – in clothes, in popular music, in domestic objects. But in a deeper sense it is certainly connected with the disturbed quality of our century – mankind is bewildered by over-rapid change, and by the violence and destructiveness that have marked our history since 1914. We have, therefore, alongside calmer work, a bewildered art, which asks questions about the use of art itself, and about its very definition. Draw a line along a street, and ask why it should not be regarded as art. It cannot be exhibited, it cannot be framed, like a painting, or placed on a plinth, like a work of sculpture. But if the line is drawn by a man claiming to be an artist, and if he claims that it is art, who can provide convincing proof that he is wrong? It might be that such work is nonsense, that it represents a sort of panic and that the panic is unnecessary. It may be, however, that in the world as it is, such questions have to be asked, and answers have to be found. Perhaps we have come to the end of a period when art took certain forms, was exhibited in certain ways, and was sold by certain agents to certain purchasers. Perhaps art must now find new forms and be appreciated and enjoyed in new ways. Towards the end of the twentieth century, one can only say that art is treading strange and unfamiliar paths.

But the artist by his nature is someone whose sensitivity (on which we depend for certain kinds of important news about what is happening to us) leads him to follow new trails that often turn out to be reassuringly old ones. Just as to many people, a hundred years ago, Impressionism looked very much like madness, so to many, today, Land Art (to which that trench dug across the desert belongs) seems an absurdity. Yet aerial photography has shown that 2,000 years ago people living at the foot of the Andes, in South America, drew immense geometrical patterns – perhaps using brooms to do so – on the floor of the valley that was their home.

Bruce Lacey: *Oh Boy, Oh Boy, am I living!* Tate Gallery. (*Photo: Tate Gallery*)

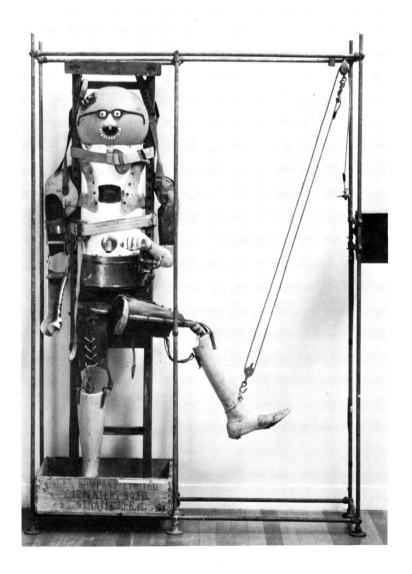

Music

The Romantic Revolution

If we turn now to the story of music in modern times, we shall discover that in certain ways it resembles the story of the visual arts. And again, the roots of it all lie in the Romantic revolution. In the nineteenth century music was created, and enjoyed, for its own sake. Does that seem an obvious remark? But it is obvious because we still think of the arts in Romantic terms. Roughly speaking, pre-Romantic music had been seen as having a social or religious use, as a splendid embellishment of the lives of those people who had the leisure to enjoy it or engage in it. In the nineteenth century music became a means of expressing the creative individuality and ideas of the composer. It was then that the concert became a feature of cultured life, that the modern orchestra came into being, that musical instruments were developed into their powerful modern forms and techniques of performance became immensely more sophisticated.

Already, in that century, there were developments that challenged the traditional ideas on which Western music had been based. Richard Wagner (1813–1883) set out to create, in his massive operas, forms that would embrace music and drama, and in doing so he enlarged the grammar of music. So did Claude Debussy (1862–1918), who can be fairly described as a musical Impressionist. Just as Monet and his followers provided a radically new experience for the eye, so Debussy provided a radically new experience for the ear: his music did not hang together in the way that music had always hung together in the work of his predecessors. Compare any music by Johannes Brahms (1833–97), who was among the last great composers to use the traditional grammar of music, with anything by Debussy. A symphony by Brahms moves forward from idea to idea; it begins with a statement that, as it were, opens the subject, and prepares us for a final statement which will bring the subject to a close. One follows a very clear, forward-moving path of ideas. With Debussy it is different. It has been said that you can best understand what Debussy did if you study one of his great orchestral tone poems (the very idea of a 'tone poem' was new), *La Mer*. This is a description of the sea in its main moods – calm, brisk, stormy – which is very like Monet's paintings of a scene in different lights. The music does not start an idea, develop it and complete it, as in a symphony by Brahms. The sea moves, certainly – the waves roll and advance and retreat – but the sea continues to occupy the same space. In the music there is movement, but at the same time there is no movement. What Debussy's music did – all his music, and not this tone poem only – was to discover new connections between one sound and another. In traditional music, the connections had been of the kind that moved a musical argument from one idea to the next. In Debussy's music, the connections were subtle ones, and we follow them with our senses, rather than with our minds.

What late nineteenth-century composers like Wagner and Debussy (who had very different purposes) were doing was expanding the very language of music.

They gave it greater freedom, and made acceptable new ideas of harmony and melody. They profited from the increased size and power of the nineteenth-century orchestra and the increased range of the nineteenth-century musical instrument. The word 'tone' in that phrase 'tone poem' was important. The sheer tone of music became important in itself, which it previously had not been. And, as in the other arts, new ideas were absorbed that sprang from the discovery of non-Western music; and these were reinforced by a very important nineteenth-century development – a new interest in folk music and in very much earlier Western music. Much of the ancient folk music of Europe follows a grammar different from that of music composed by trained professional musicians. For example, it is full of dissonance – that is, the deliberate use of musical language that, instead of aiming for harmony, aims for discord. Almost all the composers of distinction in the late nineteenth century became interested in the folk music of their own regions, and so introduced into their own work sounds, patterns and types of musical phrase that had for centuries played no part in formal and composed, as distinct from folk, music. This was, by the way, part of a general movement that we have looked at elsewhere in this book – the trend towards nationalism. All sorts of pressures in modern times have driven men, and musicians among them, to set a new value on national identity. Folk music was an ingredient in that identity. Just as painters learned to value the art of distant peoples formerly dismissed as 'primitive', so musicians learned to value the 'primitive' music of their own countries.

What all this added up to was an enormous, quite sharp change in musical ideas that happened around the turn of the century. It strengthened the view of certain composers who began work at that time that the traditional grammar of music was no longer able to express important ideas. It had all become too obvious . It was worn out, they argued. (It is important, however, to remember that even then certain very fine musicians, for instance the Austrian Gustav Mahler, the English Edward Elgar, the German Richard Strauss and the Finn Jean Sibelius, continued with success to use the old language.)

Atonal Music

We can shorten a long and complicated story by looking at the work of a few very influential composers. The first is Arnold Schoenberg (1874–1951). To describe what he did as simply as possible, one could say that he abandoned the old traditional tonality, the grammar on which music had long been based in the West, and replaced it with a grammar in which every sound, every interval between sounds, had the same value. It was as if we were to change the intonations with which we speak. When we talk, part of the meaning of what we say depends on the stresses with which we speak – the rhythms of speech. Schoenberg changed the stresses and the rhythms. He introduced a new sense of order among sounds. It was, in a way, a development of what Debussy had done – the creation of new connections between one sound and another. Anton Webern (1883–1945) went further, reducing sound to its very essentials. Other important names in this revolution are those of Alban Berg (1885–1935), who merged this new language with elements of the older one, and Paul

Hindemith (1895–1963) who invented another new system based, he claimed, 'upon the natural laws of sound'.

It was Hindemith who invented the term *Gebrauchmusik*, which in German means 'practical music', and was based on the idea that it was as important to take part in the making of music as to sit in an audience listening to it. Just as in the visual arts, as we have seen, there has been a strong movement to close the gap between art and its public, so there has been a similar movement in twentieth-century music. Perhaps the greatest name here is that of a very remarkable American, Charles Ives (1874–1954), who said that he was not driven, like the other composers we have looked at, to make a clean break with the musical language of the past. Nevertheless, his is thoroughly revolutionary music, with enormous new ideas behind it. Among those ideas was the notion that one ought to think of music in terms of space. He arranged his groups of instruments in such a way that the space they occupied, in relation to other groups, was itself an important element in the effect of the music. He was strongly opposed to people simply sitting and passively listening to music. He dreamed of, though he never actually composed, an immense symphony to be played and sung by thousands of performers – ideally, he wanted the whole of humanity to join in – not in a concert hall, but in an enormous setting of fields and mountains. He mixed popular music, marches and hymn tunes, with very complex music – so complex that several sections of his orchestra might simultaneously be performing different passages, with subtly interlocking but different rhythms.

Charles Ives stands for much that has been happening in music in our century – that struggle to close the gap between composer, performer and listener; the attempt to bring together the popular and the complex; the exploration of amazing new languages. His experiments with space in the making of music have been taken up by many others. Edgard Varese (1883–1965), for example, has written a work that is designed for a sound-space thought of as a complete circle: that is, the listener would be totally surrounded by the music.

Stravinsky

And just as in the visual arts, as we have seen, there was one dominant figure who reflected in his work all the experiments of his time – Pablo Picasso – so there was such a figure in the story of modern music – Igor Stravinsky (1882–1971), whose outstanding quality may be that, like Picasso, he was a parodist of genius. To parody, of course, is to imitate – and it is perhaps an important thing to say about the arts in modern times that, alongside all the novelty that has marked them, there has been a strong element of really creative and original imitation. That might sound a sort of nonsense – to talk of *original* imitation – but the point is that modern art, to a degree never true of previous periods, has looked back as much as it has looked forward, and has mingled its parodies – its sometimes half-mocking imitations of the past – with its genuinely fresh inventions. There are many reasons for this, but perhaps the chief reason is that an age when men are uncertain about their future, and when they are groping for a new and more universal language, is bound also to be an age when they refer back, with a sort of experimental curiosity, to what has gone before. It can be said that in the musical language of the twentieth century Stravinsky restated some of the musical ideas and structures of the past. He has been called neo-Classical because many of his allusions have been to pre-Romantic music; but, like Picasso, he brought enormous originality and individuality to these, as it were, restorations. We shall see that something like this has been happening, too, in modern literature. It all ties up with what we have observed as the great concern of the artist in modern times – to re-examine the purposes and the material of art. To put it in yet another way, artists are much more self-conscious than they were. If the nineteenth century was a great period when they let themselves go, artistically, the twentieth century is one in which they have been asking questions such as: What is it all about?

Electronic Music

If the first half of our century was musically concerned with creating a new language (which contains twisted echoes of the old one), the second half has been marked by the enormous effects of technology. What the camera was to the visual arts, and the cinema and television to the written arts, the development of magnetic tape, the long-playing record and stereo have been to the most recent music. The invention of tape, which brought with it the possibility of creating sounds electronically – not man-made – and can be almost infinitely manipulated, has transformed the world of music. Again, this development had its roots in the past. Long before the expansion of audio technology, indeed before the First World War, a group of Italian artists who called themselves the Futurists gave concerts that consisted of the production of pure noise (one Futurist actually built a noise machine). The Dadaists, whose work in the visual arts we have already looked at, gave performances in which isolated sounds and pitches, chosen at random, were produced according to a score in which each had a fixed duration. We can take, as our example of a musician who has used audio-technology in an outstanding fashion, the American John Cage (b. 1912). He has used every technological device for creating sound, and has been a pioneer of *musique concrète* – music produced electronically. Today, the live performer has re-entered the scene; when all this began, composers like Cage were fascinated by the possibility of producing music with no intervention at all by a live interpreter. Such sound could be absolutely shaped and controlled: it could (through the use of tape loops) produce infinite repetition of chosen sounds. Cage has also been a pioneer in the use of electronic apparatus to extend and manipulate live sound – a field in which he learned a great deal from pop music, just as pop music has learned much from the experiments of 'serious' musicians. A musical equivalent now exists of the minimalism that we noticed as a feature of modern art – it is music that dwells at length on tiny isolated experiences of sound. There is also musical maximalism, into which everything is thrown – musical drama, voices, instrumental sounds, *musique concrète*, random sound (chosen in some cases by the throwing of dice).... Again we find modern art in an immensely fluid state of experiment, and engaged in the complicated task of mastering all the new techniques and media available to it.

Stockhausen

Randomness, the overthrow of all order, has been a characteristic of much of this late twentieth-century music, but there has been a strong reaction against it of late. It has been noticed, reasonably enough, that it is no more humanly true to let things happen as they will, by chance, or as the dice or a computer suggests, than it is to impose order upon them. But one of the outstanding modern names in music, that of Karl-Heinz Stockhausen (b. 1928), is associated with the term 'indeterminacy', which means that, if the music is not totally random, it has nothing like traditional shape (a beginning, a middle and an end), and varies from performance to performance. As an example, his work called *Stimmung* (*Mood*) is performed by six vocalists who, for precisely an hour and a quarter, utter sounds into microphones – bits of words, vowels, scraps of poetry – and those sounds are manipulated electronically by someone who cannot perhaps be described by the traditional term 'conductor'.

It would be wrong to give the impression that modern music is totally dominated by experiment of this kind. Though the traditional tonality (the key system) that we know in the music of Mozart and Beethoven and Brahms is employed by fewer and fewer composers, it is by no means exhausted – the best of modern British composers, Benjamin Britten (1913–76) worked successfully within it. There are other important strands of development: Bela Bartók (1881–1945), for example, developed in twentieth-century terms the marriage of folk idiom and tonality that was begun in the work of nineteenth-century musicians like Anton Dvorak (1841–1904). But the main movement in modern music, undoubtedly, is towards new languages of sound, new grammars (that is, new ways of using language), and towards the expansion of musical experience, so that it includes the new technological effects, bridges the gap between 'popular' and 'serious' music, and moves towards a new kind of universal music – not Western music, nor African, nor Japanese or Chinese, but a music that embraces them all.

Literature

Realism

To understand what has happened in literature in the last hundred years or so, we might start with a statement like this: that in the middle of the nineteenth century, Realism was well established – especially in the novel. What is meant by Realism? It is the belief that the task of the writer is to provide a picture of the actual world, and of the way people actually behave. Read a novel by, say, George Eliot (1819–80), and you find yourself in a world, created by words, that is plainly real, in the sense that the scenery is solid, and is thoroughly described; the people who move through that scenery – inside their houses, through streets and across the country – are just as firmly based; we are told of their clothes and faces, their mannerisms and the way they walk. The writer is a kind of photographer, and his skill lies partly in his ability to convince the reader that things happened just like that, in just that sort of setting. But the aim of most writers of the middle years of the nineteenth century, and for some time after that, was to create an illusion, and at its best it was a very convincing illusion, of everyday reality. This is true even when the writer, as for instance the great novelist Charles Dickens, is in fact doing other things as well as establishing that illusion of real life.

Dickens was a great fantasist – in many respects his stories display reality as it might appear in a distorting mirror: his characters are larger, more grotesque, more extraordinary than most people actually are. When, for example, Dickens wrote his novel *Dombey and Son* in 1846–7, he certainly drew a very convincing picture of the London of the time, of the operations of a great commercial enterprise, of the manners and dress and speech of mid-nineteenth century Londoners; but he was also writing a marvellous parable, as it were, about money, and the passion for accumulating money, and how that passion may be in conflict with other emotions – of love, for example: love of a father for a child, or of a man for a woman. These other levels at which Dickens' writing can be read have given his novels a new importance to readers in the late twentieth century, which is not essentially an age of Realism at all. But though one could go on pointing to this or that respect in which the great mid-nineteenth-century novelists were more, or less, than Realists, the fact remains that the chief intention in the writing of the time was to create literary works which *mimicked* the real world; the word for it is *mimetic*. The aim was to provide a copy of the real thing – an illusion, because it could not absolutely be done; but the attempt to do it was at the very heart of the writing of the time.

In some senses, the greatest Realist of them all was the Russian novelist Count Leo Tolstoy (1828–1910): perhaps no one has come so close to writing about life in such a way that, as we read, we seem to be involved not so much in a novel as in life itself. He was able most vividly to represent the *feel* of life as we have all experienced it: the everyday weight and texture of it, the way our minds work, the tangle of motives that lie behind our actions. But if you want to measure the extent to which, inside the Realistic novel, other, different elements may be present, read another great Russian, Feodor Dostoyevsky (1821–81). Dostoyevsky is a Realist, in the sense that he too creates the feel of an everyday world in which men and women go about their everyday affairs. But Dostoyevsky's real interest is in the inner life of his characters, what goes on in their heads and their hearts: he was interested in what happens when people follow their ideas and feelings to their limits. So as well as being Realistic, Dostoyevsky's novels are wild, strange, extraordinary, being concerned with the stormy, passionate oddity of human nature.

So, during the great era of nineteenth-century Realism, all sorts of other forces were at work: the seeds of very different attitudes to writing were germinating. We have, in some ways, to be simple in the way we look at these matters: it was *simply* true that Realism was the most important literary outlook of the time. But we have to avoid being too simple: inside Realism there were unrealistic elements that were, as we shall see, later to bear very remarkable and unexpected fruit.

Already, in the second half of the nineteenth century, literature, like the other arts, was under pressure from new ideas and new attitudes. The world of science, for example, was subtly nudging men's minds in new directions. One effect of science was to change Realism into Naturalism. This grew very largely out of the work of Charles Darwin, who in his *The Origin of Species* introduced a very disturbing cat among the placid pigeons of mid-Victorian attitudes. Darwin demonstrated the links between man and other animals: suddenly it was no longer possible to believe that man was a unique creation, put down in the world from the beginning *as man*, with no roots elsewhere in the animal creation. Suddenly room had to be found in man's view of himself for the notion that human beings are simply a specialized branch of animal life, and that they evolved out of other animal forms. We see in the section on Science and Technology that Darwinism, with its notion of the survival of the fittest, had an enormous effect on thinking about science itself, and about the economics and industrial life of human beings. It had a similarly powerful effect on writers: there were Naturalist novelists – the most outstanding was the Frenchman Emile Zola (1840–1902) – who based their pictures of human existence on the perception that man is an animal engaged in a furious struggle to survive ... just as Darwin seemed to have described him.

Just as no one was a perfect Realist, so no one was a perfect Naturalist. In his great novel *Germinal*, which is concerned with the desperate struggle for survival of French miners in the 1880s, their pursuit of better working and living conditions ferociously opposed by the rich men who owned the mines – in this novel Zola was certainly seeing life, as it were, through Darwin's spectacles. It *was* a cruel struggle for survival, but he was unable to prevent certain Romantic feelings about life from shaping his story. The men and women in *Germinal* are not wholly animals, driven by animal passions and hungers; they have ideals and dreams, some feel for others a kind of love or sympathy that is not easily accounted for by the basic idea, taken from Darwin, that behind all the behaviour patterns of men lie simple animal drives and compulsions. Another word for the theory that inspired the Naturalist writers is 'determinism', which means that man's behaviour has no real freedom but is always determined by motives above which, in the end, he cannot rise. The true Naturalist would have to believe that men are never free to break out of this pattern of animal self-seeking; and even the greatest Naturalist in literature, Emile Zola, did not really believe this, totally.

The Neo-Romantics

So we have Realism turning into a narrower form of itself, Naturalism. The next twist of the story is the emergence of attitudes, among writers, that were totally opposed to the whole philosophy of which Realism and Naturalism were products. And here we stand where we did in the story of the modern visual arts, when we saw that things began to dissolve, to break down – all the old, solid attitudes were shattered. It ties in, too, with the similar revolution in music. For what happened now, throughout Western literature, roughly between 1885 and 1905, was that the very ideas on which Realism and Naturalism had been based – including the idea that a writer ought to attempt to create, in his writing, a sense of everyday, common reality – were abruptly rejected.

Among other things, there was a reaction against the idea that art of any kind was photographic. The writers were just as affected as the painters by the spread of photography. A writer – so many novelists and poets felt at the end of the century – ought to be looking for the mysterious pattern under the surface of human behaviour. The truth about the surface was not the only truth – it was not even an important truth. What mattered was the inner life of men – their dreams and emotions. Realism had been based on a belief that the actual world provided the really important setting for the human story; it drew its strength from the enormous confidence that was felt all over Europe in the middle of the nineteenth century – confidence in the forward march of human society, the positive achievements of science. The Realists believed that man was treading a path whose name was progress. Things would get better and better, more and more solid. These successors of theirs, whose writing set the tone of the last years of the century, believed something quite different. They reacted against all that confidence – pointing to the wars that were bedevilling the life of late nineteenth-century Europe (wars in which science, in terms of hideously improved weaponry, was displaying another and darker side of its achievement). The neo-Romantics, as these end-of-the-century writers are sometimes called (they looked back in history, past the Realists with their interest in solid human facts, to the Romantics with their passion for the inner life of the individual) – the neo-Romantics turned the world of the Realists upside down. Where the Realists had cultivated the idea of progress, the neo-Romantics cultivated the idea of standstill; what was important in human life, they held, was simply not capable of getting better and better. In any case, civilization was not growing: it was in decay. The Realist interest in order – in the establishment, for example, of well-organized social systems – was replaced by the neo-Romantics with an interest in disorder and break-down. Many of them led lives of some desperation and of deliberate decadence ('decadence' was another name for this movement) – believing that an individual's existence ought to mirror the process of decay in which they held that civilization was involved. From the rationalism that had been the mark of the middle of the century they turned to religion, especially Catholicism; if they were not positively religious, they were negatively so – cultivating, for example, a topsy-turvy belief known as satanism, which involved the worship of the dark and, in the conventional view, evil forces in life. (The French poet Baudelaire's most famous book was called Les Fleurs du Mal – Flowers of Evil.) They were drawn to the erotic – that is, to the world of the senses at its darkest and most unrestrained. There was a cult of the forbidden, the unrespectable: an example – in the visual arts, but he was closely associated with writers – is the work of the young English draughtsman Aubrey Beardsley (1872–98), many of whose superbly stylish black-and-white drawings are celebrations of the gross and sinister side of human appetites. The neo-Romantics cultivated also the idea of love that is hopeless and doomed. *Fin-de-siècle* – end-of-the-century – was the French term for it all, and it equated the century's end with the end of all positive and forward-looking belief. These writers also gave a twist to the Romantic concern with the individual, transforming it into a cult of the self – a kind of narcissism: that is, one's deepest interest was in one's own existence, not in that of others. (This was obviously another form of the reaction against all those nineteenth-century ideas which saw human society as capable of improvement through human co-operation and altruism – the readiness to subordinate one's interests to those of the mass of men and women.) In a perverse way, again reacting against ideas of improvement, they admired the sheer ugliness of urban life.

It may sound an altogether sick and despairing kind of literature, and in many ways, of course, it was; yet it was also, in many respects, a brilliant and, technically, immensely interesting literature. Much of the poetry written under the inspiration of these ideas was sensitive and memorable: in the movement, for example, known as Symbolism, poetry learned to be fascinatingly allusive, mysterious and musical. The great German poet Goethe once said that all eras in a state of decline and dissolution are subjective – that is, people see the world in terms of their own thoughts and feelings; all progressive eras are objective – that is, people see the world as a reality quite separate from themselves. Whether civilization was actually in a state of decline or not at the end of the nineteenth century, many of the most sensitive human beings alive at the time – including these writers – felt that it was; and, in accordance with Goethe's theory, they turned inwards and became subjective.

When a change came, coinciding more or less with the birth of the twentieth century, it was inspired largely by new discoveries in science.

The Twentieth Century

The first of these discoveries was the quantum theory (see *Science and Technology*), whose foundations were laid in 1900. This is a theory, in physics and chemistry, that assumes (to put it as simply as possible) that the energy possessed by a physical system cannot take on a continuous range of values, as had been allowed in classical physics, but is confined to discrete (that is, disjoined and discontinuous) ones that depend on the dimensions of the system, its masses and charges. To the unscientific reader, the important fact here is that, for the first time, and with strict scientific authority, the world was acknowledged to be, in some of its important operations, discontinuous: that is, one thing does not necessarily follow from another. How should this affect writers and the makers of literature, many of whom have no scientific training? The truth is that great new ideas established by specialists always do find their way into the consciousness of artists – writers among them. We have seen this happening in the worlds of the visual arts and music. New ideas also belong to the general texture of what is happening at any particular time, and the quantum theory chimed in with a feeling that writers had, that the twentieth-century world was so different from the world of the past (even the fairly recent past) that there was scarcely any continuity between old and new.

On top of the first statements of the quantum theory there came, in 1905, Einstein's special theory of relativity, which, as we see in the section on *Science and Technology*, turned the classical world of physics inside out. The point to hang on to, in all this, is that great uncertainties, great novelties in man's view of the workings of the physical world, were being introduced, one after another; and that writers absorbed the general fact that things no longer were as, for so long, they had seemed to be. Alongside these upheavals in science were published Freud's first important works: in 1900, *The Interpretation of Dreams*; in 1901, *The Psychopathology of Everyday Life*. We have seen already what impact Freud's ideas had on painters and musicians: and these ideas, the essence of them being found in these two books (vital reading for anyone who wants to understand the modern world), had a similar effect on poets and novelists. Freud, indeed, always drew very deeply, in his work, on literature; he recognized that the most sensitive writers had always, instinctively, understood the truths about human consciousness that he was discovering, and formulating, in his work as a psychologist and psycho-analyst. He was particularly struck by the human truths that are to be found embodied in the mythological stories invented by primitive people and refined by those who followed. He named the 'Oedipus complex', an important element in his account of the development of the individual, after a character from Greek mythology. Oedipus was the Theban king who was unable to avoid the fate prophesied for him – that he would kill his father and marry his mother; this story seemed to Freud an imaginative account of the truth he had established clinically – that a child is deeply drawn to the parent of the opposite sex and resents the parent of the same sex, whom the child regards as a rival. The new importance attaching to mythology as a result of Freud's work was strengthened by the publication, between 1890 and 1915, of *The Golden Bough*, by a Scottish social anthropologist, Sir James Frazer (1854–1941). What Frazer did was to collate, and to discover the connections and resemblances between, a great mass of mythical material. He showed, for example, that the story at the heart of Christianity, of the god who dies and is resurrected, is to be found in a multitude of other mythological stories from many different sources scattered all over the world. *The Golden Bough* had an enormous effect on the way literature was written. It is not too absurd to say that it reinforced the effect on writers of the revolution in thinking started by the quantum theory. This may seem unlikely, because the quantum theory, as we have seen, suggested that things may be discontinuous: whereas Frazer's work may seem to suggest the opposite – that ancient man and modern man, in their different ways, discover exactly the same human truths, thus establishing a sort of obstinate continuity of human ideas. But in fact *The Golden Bough* reinforced the effect of the quantum theory because it, too, undermined the old idea that one thing not only followed another, but was an improvement on the thing it followed. If, as *The Golden Bough* seemed to suggest, man simply arrived, at all periods of history, at the same ideas and truths, even if he found different ways of expressing them, then man was forever in much the same position; and this again suggested that the old respect for chronology, for time advancing, for today being different from and probably better than yesterday, was unjustified.

These, at any rate, are some of the general ideas that lie behind the literature of the twentieth century: without looking at them, we cannot understand the literature itself.

James Joyce

These ideas lie, for example, behind some of the great novels of the century. They lie behind *Ulysses*, published in 1922 by the Irishman, James Joyce (1882–1941). From the age of twenty-two, Joyce made his home on the continent of Europe – like curiously many literary figures of our time, he was an exile. But his writing drew without exception on his experience of life in Ireland, and especially in Dublin. *Ulysses* treats of happenings on a single day in Dublin in the summer of 1905; the narrative is so organized that it has powerful echoes of Homer's *Odyssey*, the story of Hamlet, the biblical legend of the exodus from Egypt. It has passages that are in the traditional style of the novel – bare, direct narrative; it is full of parodies – of other writers, of popular song; it has long dream sequences that certainly owe their existence to the view of the importance of dreams newly articulated by Freud; it takes the reader deep into the consciousness of the characters; it devotes long passages to interior monologue – that is, to the voice in a character's head in which he engages in talk with himself. It is not possible to imagine *Ulysses* being written in an earlier century. Its attitude to time – though it is pinned to a single day, it is in fact a vast jumble of memories, a series of fascinating journeys through the past lives of its characters – is a twentieth-century attitude, stemming from those doubts about the sequence of things that, as we have seen, were embodied in the new scientific theories of the century. In its obsession with the links between the everyday and the mythical, it obviously draws upon that interpretation of the mythical found in *The Golden Bough*. (Everywhere you look, the same myths, obviously rooted in the sameness of human experience – in ancient Greece or Egypt, Hamlet's Denmark, or Dublin in 1905.) In its use of parody, *Ulysses* is like the painting of Picasso, the music of Stravinsky; as we have seen, both of these artists had the same compulsion to parody the art of the past. And in its attempts to represent the flow of consciousness inside a character's head, Joyce's novel brings together many strands of twentieth-century innovation and experiment.

'Stream of consciousness' is the term for this last device – and though there are anticipations of it in earlier literature, it was not really explored until this century. It had, of course, been the practice of novelists to give an account of the thoughts of their characters, and throughout the nineteenth century the techniques for doing this had grown more and more subtle. They were at their most complex and lifelike, perhaps, in the novels of Henry James (1843–1916) – a very great writer indeed. But the stream of consciousness was another matter altogether. It accepted (what the work of Freud had emphasized) that human consciousness is a very strange affair, and that though we can make sense of the convention, in the novel, that what passes through a man's mind consists largely of thoughts that can be expressed logically in words, what in fact forms our consciousness is a marvellous jumble of images, memories, half-thoughts, sensations, much of it without the benefit of words – or of coherent sentences – and much of it prompted, a great deal of the time, by association rather than by logic: that is, one memory, feeling, thought, sparks off another, rather than following according to logical connections.

Ulysses is, then, one of the key works of twentieth-century literature. The devices used by Joyce have been taken further by others, but the source remains greater than all the streams that have flowed from it. In his novel, Joyce touches on yet another device that he was to explore for the rest of his creative life – a device that rests on the understanding (again, Freudian in origin) that language itself undergoes extraordinary transformations in our dreams and in the depths of our consciousness. When we looked at what had been happening in the visual arts, we saw that a Surrealist painter like Magritte paints a train puffing out of a fireplace – not so much a piece of nonsense as a reference to the fact that our minds (as if they were punning) can put two related images together (in this case, the images of the smoking fire and the smoking steam locomotive) without finding anything really odd in it. (This doesn't cover the whole story, so far as Magritte's picture was concerned; as well as wishing to surprise us, so to speak, by showing us how unsurprising his image was, he also wished to give us a small moment of terror. How horrifying if a train did come steaming out of the fireplace! It is on this combination of simple acceptance and nasty shock that Surrealism depends for its effects.) Magritte also put ideas disconcertingly together: so we have a man standing among rocks – and the man himself *is* a rock. All this belongs to the world of the pun, of one word reminding us of another, of words sliding into one another: or new words getting themselves invented in our imaginations. It goes back to Lewis Carroll and his Jabberwock:

> Twas brillig, and the slithy toves
> Did gyre and gimble in the wabe....

But it was Freud who established that the pun, the play on words, is an important element in the activity of our conscious and subconscious minds. In his last great novel, *Finnegan's Wake*, published in 1939, James Joyce used a language formed in this manner, that is by the pressure of the pun-making aspect of dreams: it is a language forged out of several European and classical tongues. The objection to it, perhaps, is that it takes more reading than most readers can afford to give – but if it is a dead end, it is a glorious one. The first page contains what is perhaps the longest word in all literature; the sentence including it is worth quoting: 'The fall (bababadalgharaghtakamminarron-nkonnbronntonnerronntuonnthunntrovarrhounawnskawntoohoohoordene-nthurnuk!) of a once wallstrait oldparr is retaled early in bed and later on life down through all christian ministrelsy.'

Proust

Another great novelist whose work has been at the same time an end in itself and a source of inspiration to others writing in our time is the Frenchman Marcel Proust (1871–1922). Proust laboured for fourteen years, between 1913 and 1927, on an immensely long novel, published in seven volumes, that is based on his own childhood, spent in the countryside in the north of France and in Paris. *A la Recherche du temps perdu* (literally, *In Search of Lost Time* – though the English translation is called *Remembrance of Things Past*) is a great novel for its style, though this is inimitable: perhaps no one has ever written longer sentences more musically. The style had a purpose: those long sentences enabled Proust to catch up in them many related sensations and memories. In this, too, lies the novel's greatness: for it was another, and supremely successful, device for reflecting that truth about human consciousness to which Freud had drawn attention – that it works largely by association, one thought or sensation recalling another. Though the objective element in the novel is very strong – it gives a perfectly real picture of life in upper-class French society at the turn of the century – the subjective element is even stronger; that is to say, Proust is concerned with the way that reality is filtered through our individual approach to it. Absurd, perhaps, to try to reduce so great a novel to a single idea: but *A la Recherche* is a reminder that every one of us, in the end, fashions his own reality.

The work of these giants, Joyce and Proust, helped to lay the foundations of what has been called Modernism. Like all these terms, it is a difficult one to apply exactly. It included, for example, the work of the Austrian poet Rainer Maria Rilke (1875–1926), who in some ways was a Romantic; he believed, for example, that his pen was directed, when he wrote verse, by some visiting spirit, or by great men of the past – so he subscribed to the Romantic idea of inspiration. But Rilke did new things with language, as all the Modernists did: and indeed one simple way of describing this great movement (at its height in the 1920s) was that it set out to remove from the literary use of language an accumulation of stale phrases and worn-out usages. The English critic and poet T. E. Hulme said that writing must be 'dry, hard, clearly defined' and that it must avoid 'any facile humanity or "life"'. The poet who, in English, most brilliantly carried out this operation of removing sloppiness and staleness from the language of poetry was T. S. Eliot (1888–1965). Eliot's *The Waste Land* drew, like other work we have been looking at, on the new fascination with myth; it is indeed dry, hard and clear in its definition, and when it appeared in 1922 it was felt by many to be almost anti-poetic, as well as perversely difficult to read. It is difficult now to understand how anyone could have felt such things of *The Waste Land* – which is a measure of the success of Modernism. Eliot and other poets such as the American Ezra Pound (1885–1972) and the Irishman W. B. Yeats (1865–1929) hammered out a new language for poetry. 'Hammered' is perhaps the wrong word, since it suggests a noisy workshop. What they really did was to reject a poetic language that had become lazily commonplace and replace it with a language so taut, so refined, so austerely refreshed, that for a long time it was widely regarded as ugly and even shocking. As the novelist and poet D. H. Lawrence said: 'If you cannot read my verse, blame your ear, which has got a habit.'

D. H. Lawrence

Lawrence (1885–1930) is another very great writer of the time. He splendidly summed up much that has been said here about modern writing here when he wrote: 'It suits the modern temper better to have its state of mind made up of apparently irrelevant thoughts that scurry in different directions, yet belong to the same nest; each thought trotting down the page like an independent creature, each with its own small head and tail, trotting its own little way, then curling up to sleep.' Lawrence, beginning in the great tradition of Realism – his autobiographical novel, *Sons and Lovers*, is, among other things, a deeply real account of life in a mining village in the English Midlands at the turn of the century – was drawn, like other writers we have looked at, to the examination of human consciousness below the ordinary surface of things. The novel until then had largely described men and women in terms of their obvious characteristics and their conscious thoughts. This, Lawrence felt, was only the surface, and in many respects it was a partly false surface. Shame, fear and our notions of what is conventional oblige us to present to the world a carefully managed and manipulated surface; to Lawrence, what mattered was the flow of feeling *below* the surface. Opinions differ as to whether he succeeded in the difficult task he set himself, which was to represent the men and women in his novels, not in the old terms of character and personality, but in terms of the warm, dark, uncensored flow of feeling – especially of sympathy and its opposite. But whether, strictly speaking, he *was* successful is probably, given his genius – few writers have been so sensitive to human emotions, or have so marvellously described the life of the senses – an unimportant question. What Lawrence certainly did for his readers was to make them infinitely more aware than they had been of the deep sources of their feelings and their thoughts. In his own way, and though he had reservations about the work of Freud (it was all right as a theory, he said, but when you began to apply the theory you were only doing something as mechanical as the application of older ideas about human consciousness had been), Lawrence helped to fix in people's imaginations the essential drift of Freud's ideas: which was that human truth lies deeper than used to be believed.

So we can say that, in literature, the early decades of the century saw a refreshment of language – especially that of poetry – and an increasing inclination to find the important truths of human existence in the myth and in the deeper layers of consciousness.

Ibsen

There were other trends. In the theatre, Realism had its triumph in the work of the Norwegian Henrik Ibsen (1828–1906), who wrote superb dramas exploring social themes (for example, the rise of a new mood among women in *A Doll's House*) which were also deeply concerned with the way people are moulded by their experiences and their environment. Ibsen was not entirely a Realist; some of his greatest plays (especially *Peer Gynt*) are poetic or semi-poetic, and are profound explorations of the human soul. The Irishman George Bernard Shaw (1856–1950) wrote his plays from a socialist viewpoint, and devoted himself to pressing the claims of rationalism – a view of life in which the intellect and intelligence are regarded as supremely important – and what he called uncommon sense. No one has been more successful in writing plays that contain splendidly lively characters, but are fundamentally plays about ideas.

H. G. Wells

Wells, another socialist, projected much that he had to say in the form of science fiction. A man of impatient temperament and enormous energy, Wells represented – in some ways even more urgently than Shaw – the belief that people had only to resolve to be sensible, to apply their minds to their problems, to educate and inform themselves, and to make rational use of the great powers offered to them by science, to achieve a universal state of peaceful, purposeful happiness. In later life, and as he observed the obstinacy with which men followed their old, foolish courses – the Second World War came as a bitter blow to the ageing writer – Wells lost heart; he once said that his epitaph should be: 'I told you so.' His work plays its part in the curious seesaw of human belief which has been the mark of our century and especially the mark of its literature; in some writing, the seesaw goes up – this is the belief in the improveability of human beings – and in some, it goes down – this being the belief that life, aided by science, gets worse and less manageable, not better and capable of greater control.

The 1930s

In the 1930s – an appalling decade – the seesaw moved, up and down, very sharply. Writers in Europe were divided, then, by the single enormous political issue of the time: the struggle between the complex of ideas that centred on the left, with Communism at its heart, and the other cluster of ideas that was right-wing and had as its core the various forms of Fascism. In a darkening and increasingly frightened world, neutrality was difficult. Anyone who lived through that time feels bound often to say to young people that, bad though the world has been since the Second World War, it has never been quite so bad as it was in the 1930s. Then, it was possible to feel that world affairs had fallen into the hands of positive madmen. Hitler and Mussolini, the main spokesmen of European Fascism, seemed to be, in important respects, insane: that is, they converted their animosities – their hatred of intellectuals, socialists and, in Hitler's case, Jews – into murder. Literature was, like most human activities at the time, polarized by the feeling that total light, or total dark, lay on one side or the other. It is curiously possible to see the division in terms, very much sharpened, of the old conflict between Classical and Romantic. The writers whose main allegiances were Classical ones – that is, they believed that civilized standards rested on a feeling for order, law, respect for religion and an acceptance of inevitable social difference – were inclined away from socialism, and so *towards* Fascism. The great test case in the 1930s was the Civil War in Spain, and writers as fine and civilized as T. S. Eliot were supporters of the Fascist cause in that bitter war. Most writers were on the other side. In Britain, a group of writers – W. H. Auden (1909–73), Cecil Day Lewis (1904–72) and Stephen Spender (b. 1909) among them – wrote what was essentially left-wing literature; with hindsight one can see that much of this was based on an over-simple view of the forces involved. Much of this literature was rooted in a belief that the Soviet Union was, or was on the way to becoming, a Communist utopia (that is, a state in which perfectly happy relations exist between the State and the people).

George Orwell

Out of disillusionment with that view has come a much more complicated and subtle political literature, an important figure being George Orwell (1902–1950), who came to doubt (and rather more than to doubt) the Soviet myth when he himself fought in the Spanish Civil War. Orwell's brilliant fable, *Animal Farm*, suggests that the Russian Revolution, instead of realizing its aim of bringing about equality between people, merely replaced one tyranny with another. Perhaps Orwell's great importance was that he drew attention, more forcefully than any other writer, to the political misuse of language. He was fascinated by the gulf between what politicians say they are doing, and what they actually do: and if people all over the world are now sceptical and watchful when it comes to judging political ideas – often expressed in what Orwell called 'double-think' – then George Orwell is partly to be thanked. His novel *Nineteen Eighty-Four*, published in 1949, is what is called a dystopian novel: that is, it describes the reverse of a utopia. It warns its readers that the dictatorships of the twentieth century have built up an appalling expertise in simply deceiving people, and taking their freedom from them while pretending to do something quite different.

Nineteen Eighty-Four really belongs to an important strand of late-twentieth-century writing which has developed out of the older forms of science fiction. As the world changes faster and faster, and becomes more puzzling and dangerous, more and more writers have tried to look into the future and to offer their warnings of what might happen if current tendencies continue. An example is the young English writer, Michael Moorcock, who has written four novels describing the adventures of Jerry Cornelius. Cornelius is sometimes black, sometimes white; he even changes his sex; he dies, in some episodes, but is restored to life in others; he lives in the past, but also in the future; and he moves through a world that is constantly being destroyed by wars and revolutions, and yet is constantly being re-created. These novels tell us much about the preoccupations of modern writers. In, usually, a less extreme and fantastic fashion than Moorcock, they have begun to doubt the continuity of things – that is, that history is really logical, with one event following another. Like the artists and musicians we have looked at, they find the world today a confused and confusing place, in which the whole history of mankind is in the melting pot.

The Literature of the Absurd

Since the Second World War, literature has tended more and more to have this character: that is, it sees human nature as being out of harmony with what used to be called good sense, or reason, and also with any idea of sensible purpose. Writers tend, in fact, to be fascinated nowadays by what seems to be *absurd* in human conduct; and indeed, one important movement in post-war drama has become known as the Theatre of the Absurd. This is really an offshoot of Surrealism (we have seen already how great an effect the Surrealists have had on all the arts). A leading figure is the dramatist Eugène Ionesco (b. 1912), half French, half Romanian, who has said that modern man 'is lost', and that all his actions have become 'senseless, absurd, useless'. So, for example, Ionesco imagines in one of his plays that men and women, one by one, turn into rhinoceroses, but try to ignore this remarkable change in their condition. Here he is pointing to the way in which, as he sees it, people may be persuaded by dictatorships to become steadily less human, but keep up the pretence that nothing has happened.

Brecht

A great name in the theatre of our century is that of Berthold Brecht (1898-1956), a German who was a Marxist, but always an awkward one, and who made more forceful use than any other writer of an idea he called 'alienation'. This meant that the writer no longer set out to persuade the audience that what was happening on the stage was true. Instead, he wrote his play so that the audience was constantly reminded that it *was* only a play, and so that the spectator should be free to be critical and have second thoughts about what was being represented. It is easy enough to see how this fits in with all the other modern ideas in literature that we have been looking at. Again, there is the reaction against Realism – against the notion that what the writer has to do is to build up, in his plays or novels, a convincing model of the world as it really is, or as it really seems to be. Again, reality is being questioned. Again, we are being asked by a writer to decide for ourselves what is real and what is not – or whether it is possible to make that distinction.

Existentialism

Casting doubt on old assurances and old certainties – that is what most of literature today, like most of the other arts, is engaged in doing. It does it in the drama and novels associated with the idea of 'existentialism'. This idea has a complicated history, but roughly speaking it holds that man inhabits a universe that is quite absurd. For all that, he can become meaningful if he will only choose to exist as himself – as he really and truly finds himself to be. The trouble is that he is always attempting to escape from the freedom that would enable him to make such a choice. He is always choosing, not to be himself, but to be exactly like his neighbours. He is like Ionesco's rhinoceroses who pretend that they are still human beings. Important writers who have built their work around this idea are the Frenchmen Albert Camus (1913–60), who wrote one of the most memorable novels of our time, *The Plague*, and Jean-Paul Sartre (b. 1905). Another playwright who has cast doubt on older ideas about the way we behave is the Englishman, Harold Pinter (b. 1930), whose chief interest is in our failure to communicate with one another. Although there are great exceptions, *on the whole*, in the literature of the past, men and women were shown talking to each other, listening, replying, attentively, to the point. Pinter's plays offer a different picture of the way people relate to one another. In them, as often as not, his characters follow parallel lines of thought; they are shut up in their own private worlds, and only *seem* to be conversing, exchanging thoughts, answering one another. This view of the individual imprisoned in his own private existence, only fitfully aware of other people, is expressed most memorably by the Irish novelist and playwright, Samuel Beckett (b. 1906). Beckett has the bleakest possible view of human life. Man is in the condemned cell, waiting to die, to be extinguished; his memories, worn smooth by being constantly turned over, fill his tormented head. The only weapon he possesses is the language in which he expresses those memories, his regrets, his desperation: but it is a useless weapon. It wins him no battles. It brings him no triumphs.

How appallingly dismal, the reader may think. And it is true that much of the literature of our century is dark and tormented and filled with doubt and despair. Yet it has to be said that the effect on a reader, or a playgoer, may not be in the least depressing. The fact is that art itself, when it is good art, has an enlivening influence on us. In one of Beckett's latest plays, not much more than ten minutes long, the only lighted, visible thing on the stage is an actress's mouth: we watch the mouth repeat, again and again, at the speed of panic, a handful of desperate phrases. In fact, the image is unforgettable. Instead of being cast down by this strange, sad, brief play, the audience is likely to be stimulated by it as by some brilliantly expressed poem.

In literature, as in the other arts, our time has seen the beginnings of universality. That is to say, though we continue to think of American literature, British literature, Russian literature and so on, these literatures are far less separate than they used to be. Ideas and influences pass rapidly from one to another. And some of the most remarkable modern writing comes from corners of the world that not long ago were hardly regarded as being sources of literature of any kind. As a rough proposition it is true that until the second half of the twentieth century, the great names in literature tended to come from Europe or America. To take three names almost at random in the novel: the supremely creative Thomas Mann (1875–1955) was German; Franz Kafka (1883–1924), who gave his name to that nightmare feeling we have all experienced that we are being hunted down for some unspecified crime, was Czech; and Ernest Hemingway (1898–1961), who changed the whole style of story-telling, was American. But now, in the novel, the great names include Jorge Luis Borges (born 1899) from the Argentine; Yasunari Kawabata (1899–1972) from Japan: and Patrick White (b. 1912) from Australia.

The Future

The literary map is changing, fast. And indeed, one of the most exciting developments in literature in the twentieth century has followed from the ending, nearly everywhere, of the colonial era. Virtually new literatures have sprung up: in the Caribbean, for example, and especially in Africa. Until the African countries won their independence, much of the writing about Africa was the work of Europeans. What is more, in the African schools it was European literatures that were taught: in the French-controlled territories, for example, the literature of metropolitan France; in the British colonies and dependencies, English literature. This meant that African writers in, say, Nigeria or Kenya tended to write poetry in the manner of Wordsworth or Shelley (modern English poets were rarely taught), and prose modelled on the style of the Victorians. Africa was thought to have no literary traditions of its own. The truth is that though large areas of the continent had no tradition of written literature, they had a long and marvellous tradition of oral, or spoken, literature. Two things happened at independence. The first was that young writers turned to their own, purely African tradition, recognizing that it must be made the basis of a genuinely African literature; they began to build on the rich deposit of folklore and oral poetry, and to reflect in their use of English the rhythms and other characteristics of their vernaculars (that is, the African languages they spoke among their own people – the continent has over 300 such languages). They also set out to write the story of the African past, including the colonial story, as seen from the inside, through African and not European eyes. Within the past twenty years Africa has produced a handful of fine novelists (including Chinua Achebe from Nigeria and Ngugi Wa Thiongo from Kenya), poets and playwrights (especially Wole Soyinka and Christopher Okigbo, both Nigerians – Okigbo was killed, tragically young, in the Biafran War). And there are new French-African and Portuguese -African literatures.

It is quite certain that during the next century not only will the world's older literatures be deeply influenced by the newer ones, but the whole tone of the world's poetry, its novels and its drama, will undergo strange and wonderful changes: simply because the world has become a smaller place, and because, as with the other arts, very little now happens in literature out of sight, tucked away or isolated.

Prominent People

Abercrombie, Sir Patrick (1879–1957), British architect and town-planner. He was consulted on the re-planning of Plymouth, Hull, Bath and other cities, and produced a plan for Greater London in 1943.

Achebe, Chinua (b. 1930), b. in eastern Nigeria; Achebe is the foremost Nigerian writer, and probably the best known writer of black Africa. His books so far are: *Things Fall Apart, No Longer at Ease, Arrow of God, A Man of the People, Girls at War* (stories), *Beware Soul Brother* (poems) and *Morning Yet on Creation Day* (essays).

Albee, Edward (b. 1928), American dramatist who touched on the Theatre of the Absurd with *The Zoo Story* (1958) and *The American Dream* (1961), and social criticism in *The Death of Bessie Smith* (1959), and scored a major commercial success with *Who's Afraid of Virginia Wolf?* (1962). Later plays include *Tiny Alice* (1964) and *A Delicate Balance* (1966).

Andersen, Hans Christian (1805–75), Danish writer, best known for fairy tales such as *The Tin Soldier, The Emperor's New Clothes, The Ugly Duckling* and *The Tinder Box*, although he wrote many other books in his lifetime, including a genially egotistical autobiography.

Anouilh, Jean (b. 1910), French playwright of deeply pessimistic outlook, who divides his plays into two categories – the fatalistic *pièces noires* and the romantic fantasies, *pièces roses*. He has frequently reworked classical themes, as in *Eurydice* (1942), *Antigone* (1944) and *Romeo et Jeannette* (1946). Other well-known plays include *L'Invitation au château* (1947), *Pauvre Bitos* (1956), *Becket* (1959), and *L'Hurluberlu* (1959).

Apollinaire, Guillaume (Wilhelm Apollinaris Kostrowitzki) (1880–1918), b. in Rome of Polish extraction, he won French nationality after serving in the First World War. Hit in the head by a shell splinter, he was trepanned, but died in the Paris influenza at the end of the war. A restless and experimental poet, described by his friend André Billy as 'Baroque', he was a great friend and champion of the cubists, and of Picasso, and he invented the term 'Surrealism'.

Arnold, Matthew (1822–88), English poet, critic, and educational reformer; Professor of poetry at Oxford 1857–67. Among his poems is *The Scholar Gypsy*; of his forty works, *Culture and Anarchy* (1869) is best known.

Auden, Wystan Hugh (1907–73), English-born American poet and essayist. In the 1930s he was one of a group of poets, such as Spender and MacNeice, who were drawn to, and then repelled by, Communism; his first book of poems appeared in 1930 and was well received. He then wrote a group of verse plays with the novelist Christopher Isherwood: *The Dog Beneath the Skin* (1935), *The Ascent of F6* (1936 and *On the Frontier* (1938), attempting modern social and political themes. With political disillusion came a tendency to irony and anti-climax. He succeeded C. Day Lewis as Professor of poetry at Oxford 1956–61.

Austen, Jane (1775–1817), one of the major English novelists; she spent the first twenty-five years of her life at her father's Hampshire vicarage. After her father's death she moved to Chawton, near Alton, and it was here that she wrote her great works. Four stories were published anonymously during her lifetime: *Sense and Sensibility* (1811), *Pride and Prejudice* (1813), *Mansfield Park* (1814) and *Emma* (1816). *Northanger Abbey* and *Persuasion* were published in 1818, when the authorship of the whole six was first acknowledged. She wrote of her work: 'The little bit (two inches wide) of ivory on which I work with so fine a brush, as produces little effect after much labour.'

Balzac, Honoré de (1799–1850), French novelist of vast energy and influence, and author of eighty-five novels in twenty years. He gave his novels the overall title of *La Comédie humaine*; they depict the appetites and passions of the new social class born of the revolution and of Napoleon's regime. Among his masterpieces are *La Recherche de l'absolu*, *Le Père Goriot*, *Les Illusions perdues*, *Les Paysans* and *Eugénie Grandet*.

Barbusse, Henri (1874–1935), French novelist and Communist journalist; born at Asnières of an English mother, he fought in the First World War and exposed its horrors in *Le Feu* (1916), translated as *Under Fire*. He also wrote *L'Enfer*.

Barrie, Sir James Matthew (1860–1937), Scottish author and dramatist. He first made a name as a novelist and essayist, drawing his material from the working-class life and backgrounds of his childhood. The most famous of his plays, though not the most characteristic, *Peter Pan*, appeared in 1904 and has become an institution. Less cloying are his social comedies, *The Admirable Crichton* (1902) and *What Every Woman Knows* (1908).

Bartok, Bela (1881–1945), Hungarian composer, b. Transylvania. Deeply interested in folk-song, he made important collections of Magyar, Slovak and Romanian folksongs. With his strong personal style and powerful intellect, he transformed traditional influences into highly original music. Most important in his output are undoubtedly his string quartets, which cover most of his creative life.

Baudelaire, Charles Pierre (1821–67), French poet of sombre imagination, analytic power and haunting rhythm, best known for his *Les Fleurs du mal* (1857); *Les Paradis artificiels, opium et haschisch* (1860), with translations from Poe and De Quincey; *L'Art Romantique*, essays; and *Petits pöemes en prose*, fine prose poems. He died in poverty and ill health.

Beardsley, Aubrey Vincent (1872–98), British artist who became famous for his posters and illustrations in *The Yellow Book* (1894), and for illustrations to Wilde's *Salome* and Pope's *The Rape of the Lock*. His works are a perfect expression of the Art Nouveau of the period.

Beckett, Samuel (b. 1906), Anglo-Irish dramatist and novelist, most distinguished of the English dramatists of the Absurd. His world is drastically limited, peopled chiefly by old men awaiting their death, and conceived with the intensity and haunting power and suggestiveness of the true poet. He lives in Paris and writes mostly in French, saying that an acquired language makes it easier to write without style. His plays are *Waiting for Godot*, his masterpiece; *Endgame* (1957), *Krapp's Last Tape* (1958), *All That Fall* and *Embers* (for radio); *Happy Days* (1962), *Play* (1963); his latest play is *That Time* (1975). His novels, establishing him as one of the great novelists of the century, include *Murphy* (1938), *Watt* (1953), *Molloy* (1955), *Malone Dies* (1956) and

The Unnameable (1958). In 1969 he won the Nobel Prize for literature.

Beerbohm, Sir Max (1872–1956), critic and caricaturist, master of irony and satire. His works include *Zuleika Dobson* and *A Christmas Garland*, and he contributed to the *Saturday Review*.

Beethoven, Ludwig van (1770–1827), among the very greatest of composers, b. of Flemish ancestry at Bonn, where his father was a tenor singer at the Elector's court; at seventeen he went to Vienna to study under Haydn, was recognized by Mozart, and settled there, without any official appointment, for the rest of his life. From 1798 he became increasingly deaf as a result of congenital syphilis, and he died of dropsy at the age of fifty-six. Between 1805 and 1808 he composed some of his greatest works: the oratorio *Mount of Olives*, his opera *Fidelio*, and the *Pastoral* and *Eroica* symphonies, besides a number of concertos, sonatas and songs. The nine symphonies rank as the greatest ever written, and the pianoforte sonatas and string quartets are unequalled in beauty and creative power.

Bellini, Vincenzo (1801–35), Italian operatic composer, b. Sicily. His melodies were admired by Chopin. His best-known operas are *I Capuleti ed i Montecchi* (1830), *La Somnambula* (1831), *Norma* (1832) and *I Puritani* (1834).

Belloc, Hilaire (1870–1953); a French barrister's son, he became a British subject in 1902 and was Liberal MP for Salford 1906–10. A versatile writer whose works include *The Bad Child's Book of Beasts*, *The Path to Rome*, *Hills and the Sea*, *Cautionary Tales*, and historical studies of Danton, Robespierre and Richelieu. Like many writers who use a language not their first, he achieved memorable and witty rhymes, and once wrote: 'When I am dead, I hope it may be said: "His sins were scarlet, but his books were read." '

Bennett, Enoch Arnold (1867–1931), English author who wrote of the pottery towns in north Staffordshire where he was brought up. His novels include *The Old Wives' Tale* (1908), *Riceyman Steps* (1923), and the trilogy *Clayhanger*, *Hilda Lessways* and *These Twain* (1910–16). Successful plays were *Milestones* (1912) and *The Great Adventure* (1913).

Berg, Alban (1885–1935), Austrian composer whose best-known work is the three-act opera *Wozzeck* (1925), based upon a drama by Bücher, which has become a modern classic. He studied with Schoenberg 1904–10.

Bergson, Henri Louis (1859–1941), French philosopher, who exercised a huge influence on literature. His principal works are: *Essai sur les données immédiates de la conscience* (1888), translated as *Time and Free Will*; *Matière et mémoire* (1896); *Le Rire, essai sur la signification du comique* (1900); *L'Evolution créatrice* (1907); and *Les Deux sources de la morale et de la religion* (1932). He expounded the theory of creative evolution and the life force. Nobel Prize winner 1927.

Berlin, Irving (b. 1888), American composer of popular songs, b. Russia; pioneer of both ragtime and jazz music. His songs include *Alexander's Ragtime Band*, *Always*, *What'll I Do?*; his musicals include *Annie Get Your Gun* and *Call Me Madam*.

Berlioz, Hector (1803–69), French composer. He was a prime figure in the French Romantic movement. In Italy he became acquainted with Liszt and Mendelssohn, and it was abroad that he was first acknowledged. Described as 'the perfect painter in music', Berlioz's works extend to twenty-six opus numbers. The dramatic cantata *The Damnation of Faust* is his most popular work; he also wrote the symphony *Romeo and Juliet* and the operas *Benvenuto Cellini, Beatrice and Benedict* and *The Trojans*; *The Requiem (Grand Messe des Morts)* and *Te Deum*.

Bernhardt, Sarah (1844–1923), French tragedienne. She became a member of the Comédie Française in Paris in 1870. After 1876 she made frequent appearances in London, America, Europe etc., earning vast sums of money. Established as the leading actress of the day with her performances as Cordelia in *King Lear* and the Queen in *Ruy Blas*, her other successes included *Phèdre, La Dame aux camélias, Fédora, Theodora* and *La Tosca*. She founded the Théâtre Sarah Bernhardt in 1899.

Bizet, Georges (1838–75), properly Alexandre César Léopold, French composer, chiefly remembered for his opera *Carmen* (1875), from the story by Merimée.

Björnson, Björnstjerne (1832–1910), Norwegian poet, dramatist and novelist. His work provides an image of Norwegian life from the period of the sagas (*Kong Sverre*) to contemporary problems (*Over Aevne*), and he wrote the national anthem. Nobel Prize for literature, 1903.

Blake, William (1757–1827), English poet, mystic, and artist, son of a hosier. His first book of poems, *The Poetical Sketches by W.B.* (1783) is full of exquisitely spontaneous lyrical power. This, the *Songs of Innocence* (1789), and the *Songs of Experience* (1794) include the finest examples of his poetry; but those who admire him as 'the greatest mystic poet of the western world' set great store by the 'Prophetical Books', which include *The Marriage of Heaven and Hell* and *The French Revolution* (1791). A solitary and deeply religious man, he hated materialism and the hypocrisy of the church. He produced his own books, engraving on copper plates both the text of his poems and the illustrations. His finest artistic work is to be found in the twenty-one *Illustrations to the Book of Job*, published in 1826, when he was nearly seventy; they are unequalled in modern religious art for imaginative force and visionary power.

Bloch, Ernest (1880–1959), composer, whose music is characterized by Jewish and oriental themes. Born in Geneva, he became a naturalized American.

Boito, Arrigo (1842–1918), Italian poet and composer. He wrote his own and other libretti including Verdi's *Otello* and *Falstaff*; published songs, lyrical dramas, and novels; and was a senator.

Bond, Edward (b. 1935), English playwright, son of a labourer. His plays are full of strange and powerful images and obsessive violence. His first play, *Saved* (1965), won notoriety because of the depiction on stage of a baby murdered in its pram by a gang. His other plays include *Early Morning* (1968), *Narrow Road to the Deep North* (1968), *Black Mass* (1970) and *Lear* (1971).

Bonnard, Pierre (1867–1947), French painter of landscapes, still life, and nudes, a colourist and skilled draughtsman. A member of the so-called Nabi group of painters.

Borges, Jorge Luis (b. 1899), Argentine poet, critic, and short story writer. His works include *A Personal Anthology* and *Labyrinths*.

Borodin, Alexander Porfyrievich (1833–87), Russian composer who taught chemistry and founded a school of medicine for women. In a busy professional life he wrote two symphonies, two string quartets, the symphonic sketch *In the Steppes of Central Asia* and the opera *Prince Igor*.

Brahms, Johannes (1833–97), German composer, son of a double-bass player. His works (about 120 in all) are marked by ascetic earnestness and regard for pure musical form. As a song-writer he had no living equal, and as a pianist was unrivalled in the performance of his own works and those of Bach. He has been described as 'a romantic spirit controlled by a classical intellect'.

Brecht, Bertold (1898–1956), German dramatist and poet, perhaps the most original and vigorous dramatist and producer of the century. After early experimental plays, such as *Baal* (1918) and *Jungle of the Cities* (1921), his Marxist preoccupations came to the fore with *The Threepenny Opera* in 1928, a 'musical' with a score by Kurt Weill. Brecht left Germany in 1933, went to America in 1941, and returned to East Germany after the war. Between 1937 and 1945 he wrote some of his greatest plays: *Galileo* (1937), *Mother Courage* (1939), *The Good Woman of Setzuan* (1938–40), *Puntila* (1940), *The Resistible Rise of Arturo Ui* (1941) and *The Caucasian Chalk Circle* (1943–5). After 1949 Brecht consolidated the famous Berliner Ensemble in East Berlin, where he developed his influential techniques of production.

Brieux, Eugène (1858–1932), French dramatist whose realistic plays deal with social evils, such as venereal disease in *Les Avariés* (*Damaged Goods*).

Britten, Edward Benjamin (1913–1976), English composer who did more than anyone to establish English music on the international scene. *Peter Grimes* (1945), *Billy Budd* (1951), *Gloriana* (1953) and *A Midsummer Night's Dream* (1960) all showed his mastery of stage technique, as did his chamber operas, *The Rape of Lucretia* (1946), *Albert Herring* (1947) and *The Turn of the Screw* (1954). He was closely associated with the Aldeburgh festival and his work is still the core of festival programmes.

Bronte, Charlotte (1816–55), forceful English novelist, daughter of an Anglican clergyman of Irish descent, incumbent of Haworth, Yorkshire. She published under a pseudonym *Jane Eyre* (1847), which was at once successful, and was followed by *Shirley* (1849) and *Villette* (1852), her own favourite. Her sister Emily (1818–48) wrote poetry and also the novel *Wuthering Heights*; and Anne (1820–49) wrote *Agnes Grey*.

Brooke, Rupert (1887–1915), English poet who died on active service during the First World War; his *Poems* appeared in 1911; *1914 and Other Poems* in 1915; his dissertation on *John Webster* in 1916. Though few, his works showed promise and included the poems *Grantchester* and *The Soldier*.

Browning, Elizabeth Barrett (1806–61), English poet. In her youth she seriously injured her spine, and the shock of losing her brother and friends, drowned in a boating accident, increased her confinement. Her marriage to Robert Browning led to some recovery; in her lifetime her works were more read than those of her husband. They include *Cry of the Children* (1844), *Aurora Leigh* (1856) and the beautiful love poems, *Sonnets from the Portuguese*.

Browning, Robert (1812–89), English poet. Because of his involved and difficult style his reputation grew slowly. In *Strafford* and *The Blot on the 'Scutcheon* he attempted drama also. In 1846 he married Elizabeth Barrett and they settled in Florence. His words include *Dramatis Personae* (1864) and his masterpiece *The Ring and The Book* (1869).

Bruch, Max (1838–1920), German composer and conductor, best known for his G minor violin concerto.

Burns, Robert (1759–96), Scottish poet. The son of a small farmer, his first poems published in 1786 were at once successful, and he bought a farm. These poems, including *The Address to a Mouse*, would alone place Burns as the greatest of popular poets. He wrote simply, with tenderness and humour; among his best known poems are *The Jolly Beggars, Auld Lang Syne, Scots Wha Hae, Comin' Through the Rye* and *The Banks of Doon*.

Busoni, Ferruccio Benvenuto (1866–1920), Italian pianist and composer of three operas – *Die Brautwahl* (1908–10), *Turandot* (1917) and *Doktor Faust*, which was unfinished at his death. He lived in Germany, and wrote much orchestral and chamber music, and works for the piano.

Butler, Samuel (1835–1902), English novelist and satirist, author of *Erewhon* and *Erewhon Revisited*. Other works include *The Fair Haven, Life and Habit* and *Evolution Old and New*, in which he attacked Darwinism. His autobiographical novel, *The Way of all Flesh*, was published after his death.

Byron, 6th Baron (**George Gordon Byron**) (1788–1824), English Romantic poet who deeply influenced European literature and thought. His first work, *Hours of Idleness* (1807), is probably the worst first book ever written by a considerable poet, and was violently attacked by the *Edinburgh Review*. He retaliated with *English Bards and Scotch Reviewers* a year later, and caused a sensation. His *Childe Harold's Pilgrimage* appeared in 1812. After much travelling, unhappy love affairs, and frequent scandal, he went to help the Greeks in their struggle for independence and died of rheumatic fever at Missolonghi.

Camus, Albert (1913–60), French writer, native of Algiers. He was active in the Resistance movement in France during the Second World War; later he became associated with the existentialist school of philosophy, and it was Camus who first enunciated the concept of the Absurd. His best known novels are *L'Etranger, La Peste* and *La Chute*, along with his philosophical essays *L'Homme revolté* and *Le Mythe de Sisyphe*. His plays include *Le Malentendu* (1944), *Caligula* (1945), *L'Etat de siège* (1948), based on *La Peste*, and *Les Justes* (1949). In 1957 he received the Nobel Prize for his 'penetrating seriousness' which has 'thrown light on the problems of human conscience'. He was killed in a car crash.

Carlyle, Thomas (1795–1881), Scottish author. Of peasant stock, he went to Edinburgh University, but later lived mainly in England where he lectured. Influenced by Goethe and German literature he wrote a book on *Schiller* (1825). His *The French Revolution*, which established his reputation as a literary genius, appeared in 1837. Other well known works include *Sartor Resartus, Heroes and Hero worship, Cromwell's Letters and Speeches* and *The History of Friedrich II*.

Cézanne, Paul (1839–1906), French Post-Impressionist painter, the son of a wealthy banker and tradesman. He developed a highly original style, using colour and tone in such a way as to increase the impression of depth. This was in direct contrast to the work of the Impressionists. He said that he wanted 'to make of Impressionism something solid and durable like the art of the Museums'. He was perhaps the greatest painter of the last hundred years.

Chagall, Marc (b. 1887), Russian (Jewish) painter, a forerunner of Surrealism. Using unusual juxtapositions and very rich colour, most of his subjects were poetic evocations of Russian village life, but he came increasingly to paint religious pictures. His later work includes stained glass windows for a synagogue near Jerusalem, and mosaics and tapestry for the Knesset (the Israeli parliament) in 1966. He has lived in Paris for most of his life.

Chaplin, Charles Spencer (1889–1977), first international screen star, with more than forty years' achievement. He was born in London, his mother being a music-hall singer; he made his début at five. In 1910 he went to America; and with the Keystone Company in Los Angeles (1914–15) he made films in which his early hardships are reflected with humour and pathos. He is known the world over for his characterizations of the little man: bowler hat, moustache, walking stick, baggy trousers and funny, waddling walk. His films included *Shoulder Arms, The Kid, The Gold Rush, City Lights, The Great Dictator, Modern Times* and *Limelight*. In 1953 he went to live in Switzerland. His *Autobiography* appeared in 1964.

Chekov, Anton (1860–1904), Russian dramatist and supreme short story writer. His plays include *The Cherry Orchard, Uncle Vanya, The Seagull* and *The Three Sisters*. His stories include *The Steppe, The Sleepyhead, The Post, The Student* and *The Bishop*.

Chirico, Giorgio de (1888–1978), Italian painter. Founded the quasi-Surrealist *pittura metafisica* movement at Ferrara in 1917. In the 1930s he abandoned his 'modern' ideals and returned to a form of imitation of the Old Masters.

Chopin, Frédéric François (1810–49), Polish pianist and composer, son of a French father and Polish mother. He has been called 'the poet of the piano' because of the originality and delicacy of his playing. Mendelssohn called him 'a truly perfect virtuoso'. His relationship with George Sand, the writer, lasted for seven years; he died of consumption at Paris. On a groundwork of Slavonic airs and rhythms, notably that of the mazurka, Chopin raised superstructures of the most fantastic and original beauty; his compositions comprise fifty mazurkas, twenty-seven etudes, twenty-five preludes, nineteen nocturnes, thirteen waltzes, twelve polonaises, four ballades, four impromptus, three sonatas, two piano concertos and a funeral march.

Clair, René (b. 1898), French film producer whose early films, full of wit and satire, include *Sous les toits de Paris* (1929) and *A Nous la liberté* (1931).

Clare, John (1793–1864), English labourer who became a poet. Starting outdoor work at the age of seven, he enlisted in the militia (1812), associated with gypsies, in 1817 worked at a lime-kiln, but was discharged for 'wasting his time in scribbling'. *Poems Descriptive of Rural Life and Scenery* and *The Village Minstrel* were among his publications. He died a poor man in the county lunatic asylum.

Cocteau, Jean (1891–1963), French dramatist, poet, novelist, film-maker and designer. He first made a name for himself as a poet but in 1912 made friends with Diaghilev, in Paris with his Russian ballet, and produced a group of ballets and mimes (*Parade*, 1916; *Le Bœuf sur le toit*, 1920), followed by a wide variety of plays. He made films, some adapted from his own plays; others, like the haunting *Orphée* (1950), original. He was the supreme showman among French dramatists. His books include *Opium* and *Les Enfants Terribles*.

Coleridge, Samuel Taylor (1772–1834), English poet, critic, and friend of Wordsworth; he was the son of a vicar and grammar school master. He and Wordsworth planned and published the influential *Lyrical Ballads* (1798), in which they set out a poetic philosophy; Coleridge's contribution was *The Ancient Mariner*. His other works included *Christabel, Kubla Khan* (1816), *Sibylline Leaves* (1817).

Colette (Sidonie Gabrielle Claudine Colette) (1873–1954), French novelist, author of the 'Claudine' stories, *Chéri* (1920), *La Fin de Chéri* (1926), *Mitsou* (1919) and *Gigi* (1945).

Collins, William (1788–1847), English landscape and figure painter.

Collins, William Wilkie (1824–89), elder son of the above; originally called to the bar, he made the acquaintance of Dickens (his brother Charles married Dickens' younger daughter) and contributed to *Household Words* from 1855. It was in this periodical that he published in 1860 *The Woman in White*, making him practically the first English novelist to deal with the detection of crime. He also wrote *The Moonstone* (1868).

Compton-Burnett, Ivy (1892–1969), English novelist whose eighteen novels deal, largely in dialogue, with family relationships and include *Pastors and Masters, Men and Wives, A House and its Head, Manservant and Maidservant*.

Conrad, Joseph (1857–1924), Polish-born English novelist. He did not learn English until he was an adult. He became a master mariner in the British merchant service, and began to write novels after he left the sea in 1884. His chief works are *Lord Jim* (1900), *Typhoon* (1902), *Heart of Darkness* (1902), *Nostromo* (1904), *The Secret Agent* (1907), *Under Western Eyes* (1911).

Constable, John (1776–1837), English landscape painter. A master of landscapes, he found his scenes within a few miles of his home in Suffolk, and spent long periods alone in the fields, sketching and painting. His work was more popular in France than in England at the time and affected the Barbizon school and Delacroix. Among his most famous paintings are *The Hay Wain, Flatford Mill, The Cornfield* and *View on the Stour*.

Corot, Jean Baptiste Camille (1796–1875), French landscape painter whose main sketching-ground was at Barbizon, in the Forest of Fontainebleau. Around 1840 he asserted his full individuality and developed his style, characterized by great breadth and delicacy. Among his masterpieces are *Dance of the Nymphs, Homer and the Shepherds*, and *Orpheus*.

Coward, Noel (1899–1973), English dramatist, actor and composer, the most polished author of high comedy since the death of Wilde. His plays include *Hay Fever* (1925), *Private Lives* (1930), *Blithe Spirit* (1941) and *Present Laughter* (1942).

Cowper, William (1731–1800), English religious poet, whose work is characterized by simplicity and tenderness, in contrast to his own life which was full of melancholy and attempted suicides. His best known poems are *John Gilpin* and *The Task*.

Cox, David (1783–1859), English landscape painter, son of a blacksmith. Best known for his watercolours; his works can be seen in the Birmingham Art Gallery and the Tate Gallery.

Crabbe, George (1754–1832), English narrative poet of grim humour; saved from debt by Burke, a generous patron, he entered the Church. His works include *The Village* (1783), *The Parish Register* (1807), *The Borough* (1810) and *Tales of the Hall* (1819). Byron said of him: 'Though nature's sternest painter yet the best.'

David, Jacques Louis (1748–1825), French painter of classical subjects, such as the *Oath of the Horatii* (1784), *Death of Socrates* (1788) and *Brutus Condemning his Son* (1789). An ardent republican, he voted for the death of Louis XVI and was artistic director of the great national fêtes founded on classical customs. His masterpiece, *The Rape of the Sabines*, appeared in 1799; in 1804 he was appointed court painter by Napoleon, but after the Bourbon restoration he was banished as a regicide in 1816 and died in Brussels.

Davies, William Henry (1871–1940), Welsh poet, autobiographer and novelist. He spent some years tramping, both in England and America, lost a leg, and took to selling his pamphlets of verses on the streets. Shaw discovered him, wrote a preface to *The Autobiography of a Super-Tramp* (1907) – the best of his prose books – and established him.

Day Lewis, Cecil (1904–72), Irish poet, novelist, critic, and detective-story writer as 'Nicholas Blake'. Professor of poetry at Oxford 1951–6, he succeeded Masefield as Poet Laureate in 1958.

Debussy, Claude Achille (1862–1918), composer and leader of the French Impressionist school in music. Among his works are *Suite bergamasque*, containing the popular *Clair de lune; L'Après-midi d'un faune*, inspired by a poem of Mallarmé, and *La Mer*. His one opera, *Pelléas et Mélisande*, was based on Maeterlinck's drama.

Degas, Edgar (1834–1917), one of the greatest French Impressionist painters, also a sculptor; the son of a banker. He painted subjects from everyday life – ballet girls, working girls, models dressing and bathing, café life, the racecourse. Technically, he was one of the greatest experimenters and innovators in nineteenth-century art.

Delacroix, Ferdinand Victor Eugène (1798–1863), the major painter of the Romantic movement in France. He broke with traditional French Classicism, being an admirer of Constable, and painted animal subjects, battles, hunts and portraits of intimate friends such as Chopin.

De la Mare, Walter John (1873–1956), English poet, novelist and essayist. His work has great charm and he was an outstanding children's writer. His novels, especially *Memoirs of a Midget*, have been compared by Graham Greene to those of R. L. Stevenson.

Delibes, Clément Philibert Léo (1836–91), French composer of much graceful music, including operas, of which *Lakmé* is the best known, and ballets, among them *Coppélia*.

Delius, Frederick (1862–1934), English composer of German parentage, the only important English disciple of the French Impressionist school. His music, highly idiosyncratic in idiom, was more readily received in Germany than in

England until promoted by Sir Thomas Beecham. After growing oranges in Florida and studying music in Leipzig, Delius settled in France. He composed several operas, concertos and symphonic poems.

De Quincey, Thomas (1785–1859), English essayist and critic, friend of Wordsworth and Southey. In 1821 his *Confessions of an English Opium-eater* appeared in the *London Magazine*, and at once made him famous.

Dickens, Charles (1812–70), the most popular English novelist of the nineteenth century – perhaps of any period. When his father was imprisoned for debt in London, Dickens worked in a blacking factory at the age of ten. At twenty-two he became a journalist and in 1836 the first number of the *Pickwick Papers* appeared in serial form (as most of his novels were first to appear). From then onwards his enormous energy and output continued: *Oliver Twist* (1837–9, in *Bentley's Miscellany*), *Nicholas Nickleby* (1838–9), *The Old Curiosity Shop* (1840–1) and *Barnaby Rudge* (1841). He lectured in America, concerned himself with many public issues, gave public readings – and continued to produce a stream of novels and other works: *American Notes* (1842), *Martin Chuzzlewit* (1843), *Christmas Tales* (1843–8), *Dombey and Son* (1846–1848), *David Copperfield* (1849–50), *Bleak House* (1852–3), *Hard Times* (1854), *Little Dorrit* (1855–7), *A Tale of Two Cities* (1859), *The Uncommercial Traveller* (1861), the Christmas numbers in *Household Words* and *All the Year Round*, *Great Expectations* (1860–1), *Our Mutual Friend* (1864–5) and *The Mystery of Edwin Drood* (1870, unfinished). Lord David Cecil has said: 'It does not matter that Dickens' world is not life-like; it is alive.'

Dickinson, Emily (1830–86), American poet whose writing has a mystic quality. She lived a quiet and secluded life, and her poems were published posthumously. They are: *Poems*, 1890; *Poems*, 1891; *Poems*, 1896; *The Single Hound* (1914), and *Further Poems* (1929).

Dodgson, Charles Lutwidge (1832–98), English writer and mathematician. Under the pseudonym Lewis Carroll, he wrote poems and books for children, including *Alice's Adventures in Wonderland* (1865) and *Through the Looking-glass* (1872). These books, which were illustrated by Tenniel, among many others, rapidly became a nursery classic, and have been widely translated and exhaustively interpreted. He also published *The Hunting of the Snark* (1876) as well as books on mathematics. Dodgson was also a pioneer photographer.

Donizetti, Gaetano (1797–1848), Italian composer. The best-known of his sixty operas are *Lucia di Lammermoor*, *La Fille du régiment*, *La Favorita*, *Lucrezia Borgia* and *Don Pasquale*.

Doré, Gustave (1833–83), artist and (notably) book illustrator. He painted scriptural subjects and illustrated Dante, Rabelais, Balzac, Milton, Tennyson and La Fontaine. Between 1850 and 1870 Doré earned £280,000 by his pencil. His *London: A Pilgrimage* is a memorable collection of teeming London scenes, a pictorial representation of the world of Dickens, whom Doré greatly admired.

Dostoyevsky, Feodor Mikhailovich (1821–81), Russian novelist, the son of a surgeon. Having graduated from the military engineering school of Leningrad, he resigned his commission to devote himself to literature, he published *Poor Folk* in 1846. Joining revolutionary circles in St Petersburg, he was condemned to death in 1849, was reprieved at the last moment from the firing squad, and spent years of hard labour in Siberia. His experiences are recorded in *Letters from a Dead House* (1861–2), which was followed by his masterpiece, *Crime and Punishment* (1866), *The Idiot* (1866), *The Possessed* (1871) and *The Brothers Karamazov* (1880). He explored the dark places of the human spirit to a degree not previously attempted.

Dumas, Alexandre (Dumas *père*) (1802–70), French Romantic novelist, among whose many works are *The Three Musketeers*, *The Count of Monte Cristo* and *The Black Tulip*.

Dumas, Alexandre (Dumas *fils*) (1824–95), French dramatist, son of the above; author of some highly successful social dramas, of which the best known is *La Dame aux camélias* (1848).

Dvořák, Antonin (1844–1904), Czech composer, son of a butcher. His music is rich in folk-song melodies of his native land; his first work to attract attention was *Stabat Mater* which he conducted in London in 1884. His cello concerto of 1895 is perhaps his crowning achievement, and he wrote nine symphonies. His New World symphony was composed in New York, where he was head of the National Conservatoire 1892–5. He died in Prague.

Eisenstein, Sergei Mikhailovich (1898–1948), Russian film director, one of the giants of cinema. His films include *The Battleship Potemkin*, *Alexander Nevsky* and *Ivan the Terrible*.

Elgar, Sir Edward (1857–1934), English composer, especially of choral-orchestral works for festivals. His oratorios include *The Kingdom*, *The Apostles*, and *The Dream of Gerontius*; over the score of the latter the composer wrote, 'This is the best of me.' He also wrote *The Enigma Variations*, *Pomp and Circumstance* marches, and the symphonic poem *Falstaff*.

Eliot, George (1819–80), the pen-name of Mary Ann (later Marion) Evans. The daughter of a land agent, she was born near Nuneaton. After the death of her parents she began to write for the *Westminster Review*, and in 1851 she became its assistant editor. Her first successful novel, *Adam Bede*, appeared in 1859. It was followed by *The Mill on the Floss* (1860), *Silas Marner* (1861), *Romola* (1863), and *Felix Holt* (1866). In 1871–2 appeared *Middlemarch*, considered by many the greatest English novel ever written. She also wrote *Daniel Deronda* (1876). She lived with the writer George Lewes from 1854 until his death twenty-five years later. (Although Lewes had been deserted by his wife it was not then possible to obtain a divorce.) She married after Lewes' death, but herself died a few months later in Chelsea.

Eliot, Thomas Stearns (1888–1965), poet and critic; American-born, he became a British subject in 1927. *Prufrock and Other Observations*, his first book of poems, appeared in 1917; *The Waste Land*, published in 1922, established Eliot as a major poet; *The Hollow Men*, *Ash Wednesday*, and *Four Quartets* appeared after his conversion in 1927 to a mystical Anglicanism. He wrote two verse dramas, *Murder in the Cathedral* and *The Family Reunion*. He described himself as 'classicist in literature, royalist in politics, and Anglo-Catholic in religion'. Nobel Prize winner 1948.

Falla, Manuel de (1876–1946), Spanish composer whose music is highly individual with a strong folk-song element. Perhaps his most typical works are the two ballets *Love the Magician* (1915) and *Three-Cornered Hat* (1919).

Faulkner, William (1897–1962), American novelist. His novels *The Sound and the Fury, As I Lay Dying, Light in August, Absalom, Absalom!* and *Intruder in the Dust*, depict the American South. Nobel Prize winner 1949.

Fauré, Gabriel Urbain (1845–1924), French composer and teacher. His works include chamber music, nocturnes and barcarolles for piano, an opera *Pénélope*, some exquisite songs, and a famous *Requiem*.

Field, John (1782–1837), Irish composer of nocturnes, who settled in Russia in 1804 as a music teacher, returned to London in 1832, but died in Moscow. A pupil of Clementi and teacher of Glinka, his work served as a model for Chopin.

Fitzgerald, Edward (1809–83), English poet who translated the *Rubaiyát* of Omar Khayyam in 1859.

Fitzgerald, F. Scott (1896–1940), American novelist and short-story writer. He came from a rich, aristocratic Catholic family and achieved success with his first (autobiographical) novel, *This Side of Paradise* (1920). He wrote of his generation in the 1920s, which he defined as the 'jazz age', in books such as *The Stories* (collected in 1951). *The Great Gatsby* (1925), *Tender is the Night* (1934), *The Crack-Up* (1936) and the unfinished *The Last Tycoon* (1941).

Flaubert, Gustave (1821–80), French novelist, creator of *Madame Bovary* (1857). Other works were *Salammbô* (1862), *L'Education sentimentale* (1869) and *Bouvard et Pécuchet*, which appeared after his death.

Fonteyn, Dame Margot (Mme Roberto Arias) (b. 1919), prima ballerina of the Royal Ballet and foremost English dancer. Her appearances with the Russian dancer Rudolf Nureyev have thrilled audiences all over the world.

Forster, Edward Morgan (1879–1970), English novelist, author of *Where Angels Fear to Tread, The Longest Journey, A Room with a View, Howard's End, A Passage to India*. OM, 1969.

Frost, Robert (1874–1963), American poet; his best-known poems include *Stopping by Woods on a Snowy Evening, Birches, The Death of the Hired Man*, and *After Apple-Picking*.

Fry, Christopher (b. 1907), English poet and dramatist of Quaker family; author of *The Lady's Not for Burning, Venus Observed* and *The Dark is Light Enough*.

Fugard, Athol (b. 1933), South African playwright, actor and director (he is half-Afrikaans). Among his works are *The Blood Knot, Boesman and Lena, Sizwe Bansi is Dead* and *The Island*.

Galsworthy, John (1867–1933), English novelist and playwright, author of *The Forsyte Saga* (1906–22). Nobel Prize winner 1932.

Gaskell, Mrs Elizabeth Cleghorn (1810–65), English novelist, who published anonymously ten novels including *Mary Barton* and *Cranford*. She also wrote *The Life of Charlotte Brontë*, a masterpiece of English biography.

Gauguin, Paul (1848–1903), French painter of enormous influence, being one of the main sources from which non-Naturalistic twentieth-century art has emanated. He travelled a great deal, and died at Atuana in the Marquesas. His rejection of Western life had led to his departure for Tahiti, and to his efforts to express through an art free from the conventions of the Naturalistic tradition the simplicity of life among 'primitive and unspoiled' people.

Gautier, Théophile (1811–72), French poet and novelist, an extreme Romanticist. He wrote a celebrated novel, *Mademoiselle de Maupin*, with a defiant preface.

Gide, André (1869–1951), French writer of many short novels – he called them *récits* – in which he gave expression to his struggle to escape from his Protestant upbringing: *The Vatican Cellars* (1914), *The Immoralist* (1902), *Strait is the Gate* (1909), *La Symphonie pastorale* (1919), and his great *Les Faux-Monnayeurs* (*The Counterfeiters*), written in 1926. In his memoir *Si le grain ne meurt* he tells the story of his life up to his marriage. The narratives of his travels in Africa led to a reform in French colonial policy. Nobel Prize winner 1947.

Gielgud, Sir John (b. 1904), English actor and producer, member of the Terry family, to whom the present popularity of Shakespeare is largely due. A fine actor, his Hamlet was the performance of his generation and as early as 1934 his production and performance at the New Theatre had broken all records since Irving. Still a masterly performer.

Gilbert, Sir William Schwenck (1836–1911), English humourist and librettist of the Gilbert and Sullivan light operas. First known as the author of the *Bab Ballads*, which appeared in the magazine *Fun*, from 1871 he collaborated with Sir Arthur Sullivan and together they wrote thirteen operas, including *HMS Pinafore*, *The Mikado*, *The Gondoliers* and *The Yeomen of the Guard*.

Gillray, James (1757–1815), English caricaturist who produced upwards of 1,500 political cartoons between 1779 and 1811. They are full of broad humour and keen satire aimed against the French, Napoleon, George III, the leading politicians and the social follies of his day.

Gissing, George Robert (1857–1903), English novelist whose sombre novels deal with the degrading effect of poverty. The best known is *New Grub Street*.

Glazunov, Alexander Constantinovich (1865–1936), Russian composer, a pupil of Rimsky-Korsakov. The first of his eight symphonies was composed when he was sixteen.

Glinka, Mikhail Ivanovich (1804–57), Russian composer, a founder of the Russian national school of composition, best known for his operas; also wrote orchestral, church and chamber music.

Goethe, Johann Wolfgang von (1749–1832), German poet, dramatist, thinker. Considered by many a 'great European' in the tradition of Shakespeare and Dante. A man of immense energy, vision and curiosity, his interests included anatomy and botany and the study of optics. He wrote many beautiful lyrics in widely varied styles, and novels, plays and ballads; his best-known work however is *Faust*, which was composed over many years, its theme being man's search for happiness. Goethe was happy in marriage, and found in Schiller a dear and close friend.

Gogol, Nikolai Vasilievich (1809–52), Russian novelist and dramatist. One of the best of Russian comedies is his *The Government Inspector* (1836), exposing the corruption, ignorance and vanity of the provincial officials. His masterpiece, *Dead Souls* (1837), is a tremendously comic novel which deals with the absurdities of provincial life.

Gorky, Maxim (Alexei Maximovich Peshkov) (1868–1936), Russian writer. From the age of ten he worked at many trades, being a pedlar, scullery boy, gardener, dock hand, tramp and railway guard – experiences described in *My Childhood*. Involved in strike troubles and imprisoned in 1905, he lived abroad till 1914. Never wholly at ease during the Revolution, he was highly critical of Lenin. His death may have been ordered by Stalin. The second part of his autobiography, *In The World*, appeared in 1918, and the third, *Reminiscences of my Youth*, in 1924.

Gounod, Charles François (1818–93), French composer, known for his operas *Faust* (1859), and *Roméo et Juliette* (1867), and his comic opera *Le Médecin malgré lui* (1858).

Goya y Lucientes, Francisco José (1746–1828), Spanish painter and etcher. He became court painter to Charles III in 1786. His portraits are painted with ruthless realism; his series of etchings *Los Caprichos* are savagely satirical attacks on manners and customs and abuses in the church, while *The Disasters of War* express his hatred of the cruelty and reaction of his day.

Grass, Günter (b. 1927), German (born Polish, in Danzig) novelist, poet, dramatist. His novels include *The Tin Drum, Dog Years, Cat and Mouse, Local Anaesthetic, The Diary of a Snail, The Flounder*; his play is *The Plebians Rehearse the Uprising*.

Graves, Robert Ranke (b. 1895), English poet, novelist, critic, and autobiographer, of Irish–Danish–German ancestry. Author of *Goodbye to All That*, written after the First World War, and of distinguished historical and mythological novels including *I, Claudius* and *Claudius, the God*. He was also possibly the best love poet of his generation.

Greene, Graham (b. 1904), English novelist and journalist, whose many novels – *Brighton Rock, The Power and the Glory, The Heart of the Matter, The Quiet American, A Burnt Out Case, The Comedians* – and films: *Fallen Idol, The Third Man* – deal with moral problems in a modern setting from a Catholic standpoint. It has been said of him that although he is a converted (1927) Catholic, he is at heart a 'romantic anarchist'.

Grieg, Edvard Hagerup (1843–1907), Norwegian composer. His works are mainly for the pianoforte, and in small forms, but include a sonata and a concerto for pianoforte, three violin sonatas, numerous songs, and some orchestral suites, such as *Peer Gynt*.

Grimm, the brothers Jakob Ludwig Karl (1785–1863) **and Wilhelm Karl** (1786–1859), German philologists and folklorists, best known for their *Fairy Tales*. Jakob published a notable philological dictionary, *Deutsche Grammatik* (1819). The brothers also projected the vast *Deutsches Wörterbuch* (a dictionary) which was completed by German scholars in 1961.

Hamsun, Knut (Knut Pedersen) (1859–1952), Norwegian author who was a shopkeeper, teacher, tram conductor and farmer in America and Norway before he gained fame as a novelist. His *Growth of the Soil* gained him the Nobel Prize in 1920, although his masterpiece is *Mysteries*, written twenty-five years earlier. During the war he welcomed the Nazis and visited Hitler, which gives an unpleasant angle to the 'Nietzschean' quality in his work.

Hardy, Thomas (1840–1928), English novelist and poet; first practised as an architect and in 1863 gained the prize and medal of the Institute of British Architects. *Desperate Remedies* (1871) was his first novel, and his first great work was *Far from the Madding Crowd* (1874). A series of novels followed, including *The Trumpet Major*, *The Mayor of Casterbridge*, *Tess of the D'Urbervilles* and *Jude the Obscure*. In 1809 he completed a dramatic poem, *The Dynasts*, whose central figure is Napoleon. His poetry, although belonging to the nineteenth century, has persisted as a powerful influence into the twentieth century.

Hauptmann, Gerhart (1862–1946), German dramatist and novelist. His play *The Weavers* (1892) deals with a revolt of 1844 and has a collective hero. He won the Nobel Prize in 1921.

Hawthorne, Nathaniel (1804–64), American author. His works include *The Marble Faun*, *The Scarlet Letter* and *The House of the Seven Gables*. He was a friend of Herman Melville.

Haydn, Franz Josef (1732–1809), Austrian composer, son of a poor Croat wheelwright, he belongs to the Classical period of Bach, Handel and Mozart. The 'father of the symphony', he did more than any other composer to separate instrumental music from vocal music, as an independent art. Much of his life was spent as musical director to the princely Hungarian house of Esterhazy, and many of his most beautiful symphonies and quartets were written in this family's service. His two great oratorios, *The Creation* and *The Seasons*, were written in old age.

Hazlitt, William (1778–1830), English essayist and critic. A great controversialist, a master of epigram and burning invective and withering irony. His writings include *The Characters of Shakespeare's Plays* (1817), *Table Talk* (1821), *Plain Speaker* (1862) and *The Spirit of the Age* (1825).

Hegel, Georg Wilhelm Friedrich (1770–1831), German idealist philosopher, whose name is associated with the dialectic method of reasoning with its sequence of thesis–antithesis–synthesis. He studied theology at Tübingen with his friend Schelling. He taught philosophy at Jena, Nuremberg, Heidelberg and Berlin. His first important work was the *Phenomenology of the Spirit* (1807), followed by his *Logic* (1812–16), and later by the *Philosophy of Right*, embodying his political views. He died of cholera.

Heine, Heinrich (1797–1856), German (Jewish) lyric poet. In 1826–7 the first and second volumes of the *Reisebilder* were published, with two further volumes in 1830–1. *Das Buch der Lieder* created excitement throughout Germany and these two works are considered his masterpieces. He lived mostly in Paris, drawn by the Revolution; he married a Parisienne and died there of a lingering spinal paralysis.

Hemingway, Ernest (1898–1961), American novelist of varying calibre, but of much originality and great achievement. His best work was written in the 1920s, and includes his short stories, his first novel *The Sun Also Rises* (1926) and *A Farewell to Arms* (1929). Awarded the Nobel Prize in 1954, he committed suicide in 1961.

Hesse, Hermann (1877–1962), German (later – 1923 – Swiss) writer of fiction, poet and essayist. Perhaps best known for his novels, which are currently enjoying a revival, his poems, short stories and essays are also very fine. Among his novels are *Peter Camenzind* (1904), *Rosshalde* (1914), *Demian* (1911), *Siddartha* (1922), *Steppenwolf* (1927), and *The Glass Bead Game* (1943). He won the Nobel Prize in 1946.

Hindemith, Paul (1895–1963), German composer and viola player. He is associated with the movement for *Gebrauchsmusik*, which regarded music as a social expression. His numerous works include chamber and ballet music, songs and symphonies, the oratorio *Das Unaufhörliche* and the operas *Die Harmonie der Welt*, *Cardillac* and *Mathis der Maler*.

Hokusai, Katsushika (1760–1849), Japanese artist of the Ukiyo-e (popular school). He excelled in landscapes.

Hölderlin, Johann Christian Friedrich (1770–1843), German poet whose works include the novel *Hyperion* and the elegy *Menon's Laments for Diotima*. Described as a 'somewhat pathological genius', in his middle years he became insane.

Holst, Gustav Theodor (1874–1934), British composer of Swedish descent. His works include the suite, *The Planets*, *The Hymn of Jesus*, an opera, *The Perfect Fool* and a choral symphony.

Hopkins, Gerard Manley (1844–89), English poet who became a Jesuit in 1868. His poems, none of them published in his lifetime, were concerned with religious experience and written with originality and skilful innovations in rhythm.

Hughes, Richard (1900–76), Welsh novelist, playwright and poet. His first success was the novel *A High Wind in Jamaica* (1929), followed at long intervals by *In Hazard* (1938), and *The Fox in the Attic* (1961). This last was the first of a trilogy to be entitled *The Human Predicament*: the second volume, *The Wooden Shepherdess*, appeared in 1973, but Hughes died before the work was completed. He also wrote some excellent children's stories.

Hughes, Ted (b. 1930), English poet. His works include *The Hawk in the Rain* (1957), *Lupercal* (1960), *Wodwo* (1967) and *Crow* (1970); he has also written prose and verse for children.

Hugo, Victor Marie (1802–85), French poet, dramatist and novelist, who headed the Romantic movement in France in the early nineteenth century. His dramas include *Hernani*, *Lucèce Borgia*, *Ruy Blas* and *Le Roi s'amuse*, His novels, *Les Misérables*, *Les Travailleurs de la mer* and *L'Homme qui rit* were written while he was living in exile in Guernsey.

Hunt, William Holman (1827–1910), English artist, one of the founders of the Pre-Raphaelite movement, which aimed at detailed and uncompromising truth to nature. His best-known picture is *The Light of the World* (1854).

Huxley, Aldous (1894–1963), English novelist, writer of twenty novels of which *Point Counter Point* (1928) is perhaps the best and *Brave New World* (1932), a brilliant dystopia, the best known.

Ibsen, Henrik Johan (1828–1906), Norwegian playwright and poet, who dealt with social and psychological problems and revolutionized the European theatre. His chief works are *A Doll's House*, *Ghosts*, *The Wild Duck*, *Hedda Gabler*, *The Master Builder*, *John Gabriel Borkman*, and the poetic drama, *Peer Gynt*.

James, Henry (1843–1916), American novelist whose work is noted for intellectual subtlety and characterization, and includes *The American, Daisy Miller, The Portrait of a Lady, The Spoils of Poynton, The Wings of the Dove, The Ambassadors* and *The Golden Bowl*. Living mainly in England, he became a naturalized British subject in 1915.

Janáček, Leoš (1854–1928), Czech composer and conductor, and student of folk music, the son of a village schoolmaster and creator of a national style. His fine operas are the fullest expression of his original genius, the best known being *Jenufa*.

Jefferies, Richard (1848–87), English naturalist of poetic perception, author of ten books including *The Gamekeeper at Home* and *The Life of the Fields*.

John, Augustus Edwin (1878–1961), British (Welsh) painter and etcher. He travelled much in England and France, often gypsy-fashion, and was always a passionate opponent of academicism in art and life. His brilliant portraits include those of Lloyd George, Bernard Shaw and T. E. Lawrence.

Joyce, James (1882–1941), Irish author, educated by Jesuits. His book of stories, *Dubliners*, appeared in 1914 and he spent ten years writing the novel *A Portrait of the Artist as a Young Man*, which finally appeared in New York in book form in 1916. His masterpiece, *Ulysses*, is a tragi-comic, passionate affirmation of life, and is one of the richest books of the century. *Finnegan's Wake* is a difficult but heroic failure. He also wrote a play, *Exiles*.

Kafka, Franz (1883–1924), German-speaking Jewish writer, b. Prague, who introspective work, the bulk of which was not published till after his early death from tuberculosis, has had a notable influence. His life can be glimpsed from his *Diaries*, published by his friend and biographer Max Brod; some of his best work is contained in the short stories, such as *Metamorphosis, Investigations of Dog* and *A Hunter Artist*; his novels are *The Trial, America* and the unfinished *The Castle*.

Keats, John (1795–1821), English poet who in his short life (he died of tuberculosis) produced poems notable for richness of imagination and beauty of thought. They include his lovely odes – *On a Grecian Urn, To a Nightingale*, and *To Autumn, On Melancholy, On Indolence*, and *To Psyche*; and the narrative poems *Isabella*, and *The Eve of St Agnes*. A friend of Shelley, he died in Rome, requesting the epitaph: 'Here lies one whose name is writ in water.'

Kierkegaard, Sören Aaby (1813–55), Danish philosopher and religious thinker, whose views have influenced contemporary existentialism. His most famous books are *Either-Or* (1843) and *Stadia on Life's Way* (1845).

Kipling, Rudyard (1865–1936), English writer, b. India. Much of his vivid work, popular in his day, portrays English rule in India, and at the time of his death he was detested by many critics (though not readers) as an arch-imperialist. He won the Nobel Prize in 1907. His books include *Kim* (1901) and *Stalky and Co.* (1899). Among his books for children are *Just So Stories* (1902), and *The Jungle Book* (1894). Some of his finest work can be found in his short stories.

Klee, Paul (1879–1940), Swiss artist whose art of free fantasy, perhaps the most poetic of modern times, is best defined in his own words 'taking a line for a walk'.

Kodály, Zoltán (1882–1967), Hungarian composer and teacher. He worked closely with Bartók in the collection of Hungarian folk tunes, many of which he used in his own music. His works include the *Peacock Variations* for orchestra, the choral *Psalmus Hungaricus* and *Te Deum*, and the opera *Háry János*.

Kokoschka, Oscar (b. 1886), Austrian portrait and landscape painter. Between 1908 and 1914 he developed a highly imaginative Expressionist style and, after teaching in Dresden, he travelled widely before settling in England. His paintings, particularly town views, are vivid in colour and of a restless energy of drawing.

Lamb, Charles (1775–1834), English essayist. A clerk in the East India Office, he devoted his life to his sister Mary, who was of unstable mind; nevertheless, in 1807 they wrote together their *Tales from Shakespeare* for children – Mary taking the comedies and Charles the tragedies. He is chiefly known for his *Essays of Elia*, and for his letters, which are full of humour and tenderness. His criticism is subtle and original, and he was largely responsible for the revival of Elizabethan poetry and drama.

Landor, Walter Savage (1775–1864), English writer. A great friend of Southey, he is chiefly remembered for his *Imaginary Conservations* (1824–9), and for his poems. A man of fierce temper, he was expelled from Rugby school and from Oxford; had an unhappy married life, and lived for many years in Italy, dying in Florence.

Larkin, Philip (b. 1922), English poet and novelist, whose works include *The Less Deceived* (1955), *The Whitsun Weddings* (1964) and *High Windows* (1974). It has been said of him: 'He has the distinction of being the last Englishman to write a viable non-Expressionist body of poetry.'

Lawrence, David Herbert (1885–1930), English novelist, poet, playwright and critic, born a miner's son. One of the most influential figures in European literature and life of this century, he remains controversial. His interpretations of emotion on a deeper level of consciousness have led to accusations of Fascism, but also to praise for honesty; he had been seen as sexually liberating, and also as puritanical. His novels include *The White Peacock, Sons and Lovers, The Rainbow, Women in Love* and *Lady Chatterley's Lover*; he is perhaps at his best in his poems and short stories. His plays have recently come into their own on the stage.

Leacock, Stephen Butler (1869–1944), Canadian humourist, formerly head of the political economy department of McGill University. Among his stories are *Nonsense Novels* (1911) and *Sunshine Sketches of a Little Town* (1912).

Le Corbusier (1887–1965), pseudonym of Charles Edouard Jeanneret, Swiss architect, whose books and work (especially his Unité d'Habitation at Marseilles and the new Punjab capital at Chandigarh) have widely influenced town planning.

Leigh-Hunt, James Henry (1784–1859), English poet and essayist. His writings are probably less memorable than his friendships – with Keats and Shelley, Lamb, Byron, Moore, Coleridge, Dickens and Carlyle.

Leoncavallo, Ruggiero (1858–1919), Italian composer, famous for his opera *I Pagliacci* (1892).

Lermontov, Mikhail Yurevich (1814–41), Russian poet and novelist of Scottish extraction, who was exiled to the Caucasus for a revolutionary poem addressed to Tsar Nicholas I on the death of Pushkin. He has been called the poet of the Caucasus. His novel, *A Hero of our Time* (1839) is said to have occasioned the duel in which he lost his life.

Lewis, Sinclair (1885–1951), American writer of novels satirizing small-town life and philistinism. His works include *Main Street* (1920), *Babbitt* (1922) and *Elmer Gantry* (1927). He was the first American to win the Nobel Prize, in 1930.

London, Jack (1876–1916), American novelist, was successively sailor, tramp and gold miner before he took to writing. Remembered for his adventure stories, *Call of the Wild* and *White Fang*, he also wrote an interesting and prophetic novel of totalitarianism, *The Iron Heel*, and a study of London's East End called *The People of the Abyss*. His philosophy of 'tooth and claw' and the survival of the fittest was too close to Fascism for some people, but he struggled to reconcile it with a kind of socialism. He committed suicide.

Lorca, Federico García (1899–1936), Spanish poet and dramatist of Andalusia. Among his works are *Llanto por Ignacio Sánchez Mejías* (1935), an unforgettable lament on the death of a bull-fighter, and *Canción de Jinete*. He was brutally murdered by Franco sympathizers at the outbreak of Civil War.

Lowell, Robert (1917–77), American poet, author of the verse play *The Old Glory*, and *Life Studies*, an autobiographical volume in verse and prose.

MacDiarmid, Hugh (1892–1978), pseudonym of Christopher M. Grieve, Scottish poet, leader of the Scottish literary revival. His finest poem, written in Scottish dialect, is *A Drunk Man Looks at the Thistle* (1926). In 1928, he helped found the Scottish Nationalist Party.

Mackenzie, Sir Compton (1883–1972), British comic writer whose works include *Carnival* (1914), *Sinister Street* (1913–14), and *Guy and Pauline* (1915), as well as a monumental autobiography *My Life and Times* (ten volumes) (1963–71). His novel *Whisky Galore* (1947) was made into a famous film. Like MacDiarmid, he was a founder-member of the Scottish Nationalist Party.

MacNeice, Louis (1907–63), Irish poet, playwright and translator who was educated and lived in England. He was friendly with Auden and Spender, and his translations of *Agamemnon* (1936) and Goethe's *Faust*, Parts 1 and 2 (1951) are outstanding. He worked with the BBC and wrote several allegories for radio, such as *The Dark Tower* (1947).

Maeterlinck, Maurice (1862–1949), Belgian poet, dramatist and prose writer. Among his plays is *Pelleas et Mélisande* (1892), which Debussy made into an opera, and *L'Oiseau bleu* (1908), which won him the Nobel Prize in 1911.

Magritte, René (1898–1967), Belgian Surrealist painter whose pale and drily painted works have a dream-like clarity.

Mahler, Gustav (1860–1911), Austrian composer and conducter of Jewish parentage, and one of the most important figures in twentieth-century music. He wrote beautiful songs, and his ten symphonies are vast in length and variety.

Mallarmé, Stéphane (1842–98), French poet who became well known through his translation of Poe's *Raven* (1875). In prose and verse he was a leader of the Symbolist school; his best-known poem is *L'Apres-midi d'un faune*.

Malraux, André (b. 1901), French novelist whose works include *La Condition humaine* (1933), about the 1927 Shanghai revolution in which he was involved;

Le Temps du mépris (1935) and *L'Espoir* (1937). Later he became de Gaulle's Minister of Culture and produced *Antimémoires* (1967).

Manet, Edouard (1832–83), French painter, friend of Zola, whose Impressionist pictures include *Olympia, Le Déjeuner sur l'herbe* and *Un bar aux Folies-Bergère.*

Mann, Thomas (1875–1955), German writer who won world recognition with his first novel, *Buddenbrooks*, at the age of twenty-five. Opposed to the Nazis, he left Germany in 1933 to live in Switzerland, and then settled in America, becoming a US citizen in 1944. Other works are *The Magic Mountaan* (1924), the *Joseph* tetralogy and the unfinished *Felix Krull*. His short stories include *Tonio Kröger* and *Death in Venice*. He won the Nobel Prize in 1929.

Mansfield, Katherine (1890–1923), short story writer, b. New Zealand, whose work was influenced by Chekhov's short stories. Her husband, J. M. Murray, edited her *Journal* (1927) and her *Letters* (1928), which contain some of her finest writing. She died of tuberculosis.

Manzoni, Allessandro (1785–1873), Italian novelist and poet, whose historical novel *I Promessi Sposi* (*The Betrothed*) won his European fame, and has been described as the most notable novel in Italian literature.

Mascagni, Pietro (1863–1945), Italian composer, son of a baker, whose brilliantly successful one-act opera, *Cavalleria Rusticana*, was produced in 1890.

Masefield, John (1878–1967), English poet, novelist and critic. His best-known works are *Salt-Water Ballads* (1902) and *Reynard the Fox* (1919); he also wrote some fine children's books. He became Poet Laureate in 1930.

Massenet, Jules Emile Fréderic (1842–1912), French composer who made his fame with the comic opera *Don César de Bazan* in 1872. He also wrote songs, orchestral suites, oratorios and operas.

Matisse, Henri (1869–1954), French painter, member of a group known as Les Fauves (the wild beasts) because of their use of violent colour and colour variation to express form and relief. His main work, painted on the Riviera, consists of a long series of odalisque and still-life subjects.

Maugham, William Somerset (1874–1965), British writer, b. Paris. His first novel, *Liza of Lambeth* (1897) is about the London slums, and was followed by *Of Human Bondage* (1915), *The Moon and Sixpence* (1919), and *Cakes and Ale* (1930). He was a master of the short story and his work reflects his travels in the East. In both World Wars he served as a British agent.

Maupassant, Guy de (1850–93), French writer whose novels and short stories include *Boule de Suif, La Maison Tellier* and *La Parme*. A leader of the Naturalist school, he excelled in short stories and wielded a considerable influence on later writers.

Mauriac, François (1885–1970), French novelist, playwright and poet, most of whose work is set in or around his native Bordeaux. His novels include *Le Baiser au lépreux* and *Le Noeud de vipères*. Nobel Prize winner 1952.

Melville, Herman (1819–91), American novelist who became a sailor, but in 1842 deserted from a whaling ship at the Marquesas Islands, where for four months (he claimed) he was the prisoner of a savage tribe in the Typee valley. His *Typee* (1846) and *Omoo* (1847) record his adventures. Most celebrated for his novel *Moby Dick* (1852), Melville also wrote *Mardi, Pierre, or the Ambi-*

guities, *The Confidence Man*, *Redburn*, *White Jacket*; and some superb short stories, notably *Billy Budd* and *Bartleby the Scrivener*.

Mendelssohn-Bartholdy, Felix (1809–47), German composer, grandson of the philosopher Moses Mendelssohn. He belongs with Chopin and Schumann to the early nineteenth-century Classical–Romantic school. A boy genius – many of his finest works were written before he was twenty – he knew Goethe, Weber and Moscheles. At sixteen he wrote the opera *Comacho's Wedding*, and a year later his *A Midsummer Night's Dream* overture appeared. An eminent pianist and organist.

Meredith, George (1828–1909), English writer. His novels include *The Ordeal of Richard Feverel*, *The Egoist*, *Evan Harrington*, *Diana of the Crossways* and *The Amazing Marriage*. His poetry has received renewed attention; the main works are *Modern Love* and *Poems and Lyrics of the Joy of Earth*.

Mickiewicz, Adam (1798–1855), Polish revolutionary poet, whose masterpiece is the epic *Pan Tadeusz* (1834), a brilliant delineation of Lithuanian scenery, manners and beliefs. He died in Constantinople.

Mill, John Stuart (1806–73), English philosopher. A member of Bentham's utilitarian school, his main work is *On Liberty* (1859), which advocates a kind of social and political freedom, while warning against the tyranny of the majority. *The Subjection of Women* (1896) advocates women's suffrage. He was godfather to Bertrand Russell.

Millet, Jean François (1814–75), French painter of rural life, son of a peasant; his works include the famous *Sower* (1850) and *The Angelus* (1859). He also produced many charcoal drawings of high quality.

Modigliani, Amedeo (1884–1920), Italian painter and sculptor, who lived mainly in Paris. His *Cellist* of 1910 won him recognition; his portraits and figure studies tend to elongation and simplification, and reveal a style based on African sculpture as well as on his Italian heritage. Possibly the greatest Italian artist of the twentieth century, he was handsome, amorous, and addicted to drink and drugs. He said, 'I am going to drink myself dead,' and he did.

Monet, Claude (1840–1926), French painter and a leading Impressionist, the term being derived in 1874 from his landscape *Impression: Sunrise*, and used at first derisively. Monet was the member of the group who practised for the longest time the principles of absolute fidelity to the visual sensation – the truth of retinal sensation – and painting directly from the object, if necessary out of doors. From 1890 he painted series of pictures of one subject, under various conditions and at different times of day – the *Poplars*, the *Haystacks*, and the *Water Lilies* among them.

Moore, George (1852–1933), Irish novelist, son of an MP, whose works include *Confessions of a Young Man* (1888), an account of his years in Paris and a masterpiece of ironic self-criticism; *Esther Waters* (1894), a realistic and moving story which made him famous; *Evelyn Innes* (1898) and *Sister Teresa* (1901), as well as a number of superb short stories and plays.

Moore, Henry (b. 1898), English sculptor and draughtsman who uses a semi-abstract style. From 1940 he made many drawings of underground air-raid shelters and of coal miners; his sculptures, which place him as the most eminent living sculptor, are to be seen in many cities of the world. His earliest major work was the *North Wind* (1928) for the London Transport Board head-quarters.

Mussorgsky, Modest Petrovich (1839–81), Russian composer whose great opera *Boris Godunov* (1874), based on Pushkin's drama, placed him among Russian masters. His piano suite *Pictures at an Exhibition* was orchestrated by Ravel. He lived in poverty and died a prey to drugs.

Nabokov, Vladimir (1899–1977), Russian émigré novelist who wrote in Russian until 1937; he became an American citizen in 1945, and later lived in Switzerland. He achieved international fame with *Lolita* (1955), and his other novels include *Laughter in the Dark*, *The Gift* and *Pnin*; he also wrote short stories.

Naipaul, V. S. (b. 1932), West Indian (of Indian parentage) novelist who lives in England. His early novels and stories about Trinidad were outstanding: they include *The Mystic Masseur* (1957) and *A House for Mr Biswas* (1961). *An Area of Darkness* (1964), about his visit to India, shows him to be an excellent journalist.

Nielsen, Carl (1865–1931), Danish composer who wrote six symphonies, highly individual concertos for the flute and clarinet, four string quartets and two operas – the dramatic *Saul and David* (1902) and a delightful comedy, *Maskarade* (1906), full of lyrical music.

Nietzsche, Friedrich Wilhelm (1844–1900), German philosopher, a pastor's son, in his younger years influenced by Wagner and Schopenhauer. From 1878 he began in a long series of works to expound a revolutionary philosophy denouncing all religion and treating all moral laws as a remnant of Christian superstition, cherishing the 'virtues of the weak'. His ideal, the 'superman', is to be developed by giving unbridled freedom to the struggle for existence, knowing no pity. His doctrines are expounded in *Thus Spake Zarathustra*, *Beyond Good and Evil* and *The Will to Power*. He became insane in 1889, and lived out the last of his life in great pain and courage. The Nazis perverted his philosophy to justify their Fascist excesses.

Nijinsky, Vaslav (1892–1950), Russian dancer, one of the Ballets Russes company which included Pavolva, Karsavina and Fokine, brought by Diaghilev to Paris and London before the First World War. In *Les Sylphides*, *Le Spectre de la rose* and *L'Après-midi d'un faune* he won a supreme place among male dancers.

Nureyev, Rudolf (b. 1939), Russian dancer, defector from the Soviet Union, famous for his performances with Dame Margot Fonteyn and for his athletic and brilliant interpretations of great ballet parts.

O'Casey, Sean (1884–1964), Irish dramatist who, before turning to literature, had been an extreme left-wing activist and took part in the Easter 1916 uprising. The Abbey Theatre took him up in 1919 and staged his three masterpieces, the realistic and lyrical *Shadow of a Gunman* (1923), *Juno and the Paycock* (1924) and *The Plough and the Stars* (1926). His later plays include *The Silver Tassie* and *Red Roses for Me*.

Offenbach, Jacques (1819–80), German (Jewish) composer who settled at Paris, and is mainly known for his light operas, especially *The Tales of Hoffman*.

Olivier, Baron (Laurence Kerr Olivier) (b. 1907), British actor and director, especially famous for Shakespearian roles. He has also produced, directed and played in films, including *Henry V, Hamlet* and *Richard III*. In 1962 he was appointed director of the National Theatre in London, and in 1970 received a life peerage. One of the theatres in the new National Theatre building on the Thames is named after him.

O'Neill, Eugene Gladstone (1888–1953), American playwright who, after spending his adventurous youth in sailing, gold-prospecting and journalism, first won success in 1914 with the one-act play *Thirst*. In 1920 and 1921 he won the Pulitzer Prize for *Beyond the Horizon* and *Anna Christie;* he also wrote *Strange Interlude, Mourning Becomes Electra, The Iceman Cometh* and *Long Day's Journey into Night*. Nobel Prize winner 1936.

Orwell, George (real name **Eric Arthur Blair**) (1903–50), English novelist, critic and journalist, b. India, who was educated at Eton and joined the Burma Police (1922–7) instead of going to university. His first book was *Down and Out in Paris and London* (1933), followed by *Burmese Days* (1934), in which he settled his account with imperialism; *A Clergyman's Daughter* (1935) and *Keep the Aspidistra Flying* (1936). *The Road to Wigan Pier* (1937) was followed by his involvement in the Spanish Civil War, where he was seriously wounded. On his return he wrote the fine *Homage to Catalonia* (1938), followed by the nostalgic *Coming Up for Air* (1939). His allegory of Stalinism, *Animal Farm* (1945) made him famous and was followed by his final dystopian masterpiece, *Nineteen Eighty-Four* (1949). A man of great intellectual courage, who refused easy answers, he died of tuberculosis when only forty-seven.

Paganini, Niccolò (1782–1840), Italian violinist, son of a porter. He gave his first concert in 1793, began his professional tours in Italy in 1805, and in 1828–31 caused a great sensation in Austria and Germany, Paris and London. A virtuoso, he revolutionized violin technique.

Palmer, Samuel (1805–81), English landscape painter and etcher, a follower of Blake whom he met in 1824. His 'Shoreham Period' (1826–35) was the moment of perfect balance between inner and outer vision; after it, his life became one 'of dreadful tragedy', according to his son.

Pasternak, Boris Leonidovich (1890–1960), Russian poet and writer who published his first poems in 1931. Although the novel *Dr Zhivago* is his most famous – it was banned in Russia – his prose masterpiece is the earlier *Detstvo Luvers* (trans. as *Childhood*). He was awarded the Nobel Prize in 1958, but was not allowed to receive it by the Soviet authorities.

Peacock, Thomas Love (1785–1866), English novelist. His work, which is mainly satirical, includes *Headlong Hall* (1816) and *Nightmare Abbey* (1818).

Pérez Galdós, Benito (1843–1920), Spanish novelist and dramatist, born in the Canary Islands and brought up in Madrid. He has been compared to Balzac for his close study and portrayal of all social classes, especially in the series of forty-six short historical novels, *Episodios nacionales*.

Picasso, Pablo Ruiz (1881–1973), Spanish painter, son of an art teacher. He received his early training in Catalonia and settled in Paris in 1903. He and Braque were the originators of analytical Cubism (*c.* 1909), but Picasso's restless genius would never allow him to be trapped by any one style. Perhaps his best-known single work is *Guernica*, painted at the time of the Spanish Civil War, expressing the artist's loathing of Fascism and the horrors of war. He was never allowed to return to Spain, and his last years were spent mainly in the south of France. His genius extended to sculpture, ceramics and the graphic arts, and he designed decor and costumes for the ballet, notably the Diaghilev Russian Ballet in Rome in 1917. No painter has more radically changed the nature of modern art.

Pinter, Harold (b. 1930), leading English playwright, of Cockney Jewish background, who made his name with *The Caretaker* (1959), followed by *The Birthday Party* (1960), *The Homecoming* (1965), *Landscape* and *Silence* (1969), *Old Times* (1971) etc. His film scripts include *The Servant*, *The Pumpkin Eater*, *Accident* and *The Go-Between*.

Pirandello, Luigi (1867–1936), Italian dramatist and novelist, b. Sicily. He was a prolific writer: besides his novels he wrote nearly fifty plays, nearly 250 short stories, and two critical works. His play *Six Characters in Search of an Author* (1921) brought him international fame and he won the Nobel Prize in 1934.

Pisarro, Camille (1830–1903), French Impressionist painter (of Spanish–Jewish descent), b. in St. Thomas, Virgin Islands. In 1874 he took part in the first Impressionist exhibition in Paris, and was the only one to exhibit in all eight. His output was enormous and covered all the techniques of the time; of all the Impressionists he was the most consistent.

Poe, Edgar Allan (1809–49), American poet and story writer. His poems include *The Raven*, *To Helen* and *Annabel Lee*, and his stories, often weird, wild and fantastic, include the collection called *Tales of the Grotesque and Arabesque* (1839), *The Murders in the Rue Morgue* (1841), *The Gold Bug* (1843) and *The Masque of the Red Death* (1842). He deeply impressed Baudelaire and the 'Decadents'.

Pound, Ezra Loomis (1885–1972), American poet and critic, best known for his *Cantos*, and his translations of Provençal, Latin, Chinese, French and Italian poets. Still a controversial figure, his intermittent bursts of insanity led him to embrace Italian Fascism and to see Mussolini as a figure of hope in a decaying world.

Priestley, John Boynton (b. 1894), English novelist, critic and playwright. His works include the novels *The Good Companions*, *Angels Pavement* and the plays *Dangerous Corners*, *Time and the Conways*, *I Have Been Here Before* and *The Linden Tree*.

Prokofiev, Serge Sergeievich (1891–1953), Russian composer whose music has a strong folk-song element, rich in melody and invention. He has written operas: *The Love of Three Oranges*, *The Betrothal in a Nunnery* and *War and Peace* – the last written in the face of strong pressure from the Soviet authorities; ballets: *Romeo and Juliet* and *Cinderella*; symphonies, chamber music, and the music for Eisenstein's films *Alexander Nevsky* and *Ivan the Terrible*.

Proust, Marcel (1871–1922), French novelist and critic, whose most famous novel is *A la Recherche du temps perdu*, a work of great psychological depth which deals with the nature of memory better than any other novel of the twentieth century. He was a friend of Bergson, whose ideas assisted him.

Puccini, Giacomo (1858–1924), Italian composer whose operas include *Manon*

Lescaut, La Boheme, Tosca, Madame Butterfly, The Girl of the Golden West, and *Turandot* (completed by a friend).

Pushkin, Alexander Sergeievich (1799–1837), Russian writer whose place in Russian literature ranks with Shakespeare's in English. He wrote in many forms – lyric poetry and narrative verse, drama, folk tales and short stories. Musicians have used his works as plots for operas – the fairy romance *Ruslan and Ludmilla* (1820) was dramatized by Glinka; the verse novel *Eugene Onegin* (1828) and the short story *The Queen of Spades* were adapted by Tchaikovsky, and the tragic drama *Boris Godunov* formed the subject of Mussorgsky's opera. Like Lermontov, who was also exiled, he was inspired by the wild beauty of the Caucasus. He was killed in a duel defending his wife's honour.

Quasimodo, Salvatore (1901–68), Italian poet, b. Sicily, son of a railway worker. His works include *La Vita Non è Sogno.* Nobel Prize winner 1959.

Rachmaninov, Sergei Vasilievich (1837–1943), Russian composer and pianist. Best known for his piano music, especially his *Prelude.* He wrote many beautiful songs, and three operas. He left Russia after the Revolution, living mostly in Switzerland and America.

Ravel, Maurice (1875–1937), French composer, pupil of Fauré, one of the leaders of the Impressionist movement. His work, full of colour and ironic humour, gave him the first place among French composers after Debussy's death. He wrote chamber music, piano pieces, songs, operas and ballet music, including *Daphnis et Chloé* (1912), specially commissioned by Diaghilev.

Renoir, Pierre Auguste (1841–1919), French Impressionist painter. He exhibited in the first three Impressionist exhibitions and his works include portraits, still lifes, landscapes and groups, including *La Loge, Les Parapluies, La première sortie* and *La Place Pigalle.* His late works are mostly nudes, or near nudes. He had to stop painting near the end of his life because of crippling arthritis.

Richardson, Sir Ralph David (b. 1902), English actor who has worked at the Old Vic, on the West End stage, and at Stratford-on-Avon, and appeared in many films, including *South Riding, Anna Karenina* and *The Fallen Idol.* He has often played with great success opposite his friend John Gielgud.

Rilke, Rainer Maria (1872–1926), Austrian lyric poet, b. Prague, and one of the greatest poets of the century. His work culminated in the *Duino Elegies* (1912–22) and *Sonnets to Orpheus* (1923), which both gave a new musicality to German verse. He also wrote the terrifying 'city' novel, *The Notebook of Malte Laurids Brigge* (1910).

Rimbaud, Jean Nicholas Arthur (1854–91), French poet. In his brief poetic career (four years from about the age of sixteen) he prepared the way for Symbolism (*Bateau Ivre, Les Illuminations*) and anticipated Freud (*Les Déserts de l'armour*). He became intimate with Verlaine and at eighteen had completed his memoirs, *Une Saison en enfer.* He then renounced literature and travelled – in Abyssinia he dealt in arms and ivory, had a leg amputated after a bad wound, and died at Marseilles on his return.

Rimsky-Korsakov, Nikolai Andreievich (1844–1908), Russian composer whose works include the operas *The Maid of Pskov, The Snow Maiden, Le*

Coq d'or, and the the symbolic suite *Schéhérézade*. He was a brilliant orchestrator and recorded many works, including Borodin's *Prince Igor*.

Rodin, Auguste (1841–1917), French sculptor. He produced great biblical and symbolical groups – *Eve*, *The Burghers of Calais*, *La Guerre*, and *La Porte d'enfer*, a huge bronze door for the Musée des Arts Décoratifs, unfinished at his death – but is best known by *The Thinker* and his statues of Balzac and Victor Hugo.

Rossetti, Dante Gabriel (1828–82), English poet and painter, son of Gabriele (1783–1854), an exiled Italian author who settled in London in 1824. Dante formed the Pre-Raphaelite brotherhood with Millais, Holman Hunt and others; their aim was a return to pre-Renaissance art forms. His first major work was the *Girlhood of Mary Virgin*; his adherence to the tenets of the brotherhood was, however, very short-lived. His subjects were drawn mostly from Dante and from a medieval dream world also reflected in his verse, of which *The Portrait* and *The Blessed Damozel* were written in his nineteenth year. He married Elizabeth Siddal in 1860; in 1862 she died of drugs and he became a recluse and drug addict. His sister, Christina Georgina (1830–94) wrote poetry, including *Goblin Market*.

Rossini, Gioacchino Antonio (1792–1868), Italian operatic composer, the son of a strolling horn-player. His operas include *The Barber of Seville* (1816), *Otello* (1816), *La Cenerentola* (1817), *The Thieving Magpie* (1817), *Semiramide* (1823) and his greatest work, *William Tell* (1829). He had great success in Paris and London and in 1836 he retired to Bologna, where he raised Bologna's Liceo Filarmonico (now the Conservatorio Statale di Musica G. B. Martini) to a high position. His last years were spent in Paris.

Rousseau, Henri (1844–1910), influential French painter, called 'Le Douanier' because he had been for some years a customs official. He had a direct, simple and hauntingly naive vision and painted large and complicated pictures; he used the Paris botanical gardens as inspiration for his jungle scenes.

Ruskin, John (1819–1900), English author and art critic. His *Modern Painters*, in five volumes, was issued over a period of years, the first volume containing a strong defence of Turner; he also helped to establish the Pre-Raphaelites. Other notable works include *The Seven Lamps of Architecture* and *The Stones of Venice*, both attempting to introduce a new concept of domestic architecture. Ruskin College at Oxford, the first residential college for working people, is named after him.

Russell, 3rd Earl (Bertrand Arthur William Russell) (1872–1970), English philosopher, mathematician and essayist, celebrated for his work in the field of logic and the theory of knowledge, and remembered for his moral courage, belief in human reason and his championship of liberal ideas. He published more than sixty books, including *The Principles of Mathematics* (1903), *Principia Mathematica*, in collaboration with A. N. Whitehead, three volumes (1910–13), *The Problem of Philosophy* (1912), *The Analysis of Mind* (1921), *An Inquiry into Meaning and Truth* (1940), *History of Western Philosophy* (1945), and a number on ethics and social problems. His *Autobiography* (three volumes) appeared 1967–9. Nobel Prize winner 1950.

Saint-Saëns, Charles Camille (1835–1921), French composer, for twenty years organist at the Madeleine in Paris. His compositions include symphonic and chamber music and the opera *Samson and Delilah*, which was produced by Liszt at Weimar in 1877.

Sand, George (1804–76), pseudonym of the French writer Armandine Lucil Dupin. After nine years of married life she left her husband and went to Paris to devote herself to literature. Her publications are extensive and varied, and include the fine novel *Mauprat*, *Consuelo*, rural studies, and an autobiography, *Histoire de ma vie*. Her complete works run to over 100 volumes. She was the mistress of Alfred de Musset and Chopin.

Santayana, George (1863–1952), American philosopher and poet, b. Madrid of Spanish parentage. His excellent novel *The Last Puritan* (1935) became a bestseller; the essential philosophical works are *The Life of Reason* (1905–6), *Scepticism and Animal Faith* (1923), and *The Realm of Being* (1927–40).

Sartre, Jean-Paul (b. 1905), French existentialist philosopher, left-wing intellectual, dramatist, essayist and novelist. His major philosophical work is *L'Être et le néant* (1943, trans. *Being and Nothingness*); his novels, illustrating and confronting the problems of his philosophy, include *L'Age de raison* (1945), *Le Sursis* (1947), and *La Mort dans l'âme* (1949), which make up the unfinished trilogy *Les Chemins de la Liberté*; and *La Nausée* (1938). His plays include *Les Mouches*, *Huis Clos*, *Les Mains Sales*, and *Les Séquestrés d'Altona*. He was awarded, and refused, the 1964 Nobel Prize for literature.

Schiller, Johann Christoph Friedrich von (1759–1805), German dramatist and poet who began his career as a military surgeon. His play *The Robbers*, with a revolutionary theme, was successfully staged in Mannheim in 1782. After a period at Dresden, where he wrote *Don Carlos*, and at Jena, where he wrote a history of the Thirty Years' War, he became the close friend of Goethe and moved to Weimar, where he wrote the *Wallenstein* trilogy, which ranks among the greatest of German plays; *Mary Stuart* (1800), *The Maid of Orleans* (1801) and *William Tell* (1804). Shattered by hard work, poor health and financial problems, he died at the early age of forty-six. As a lyric poet he is not outstanding, but his plays make him a leading figure in the European Romantic movement.

Schlegel, Friedrich von (1772–1829), German critic, prominent among the founders of German Romanticism, whose revolutionary ideas influenced nineteenth-century thought. His brother, August Wilhelm (1767–1845) made remarkable translations of Shakespeare (which established Shakespeare in German), Dante, Calderon, Cervantes and Camoens.

Schoenberg, Arnold (1874–1951), Austrian composer of Jewish parentage, who in 1933 was exiled by the Nazis and settled in America, teaching at Boston and Los Angeles. Among his works are the choral orchestral *Gurrelieder* and *Pierrot Lunaire*, a cycle of twenty-one poems for voice and chamber music. He revolutionized Western music by his twelve-note theory – a system which uses all the notes of the chromatic scale 'and denies the supremacy of a tonal centre', as Schoenberg himself put it. The unfinished *Moses and Aaron* (1932) is perhaps his masterpiece.

Schopenhauer, Arthur (1788–1860), German philosopher important historically for his pessimism, and his doctrine that Will is the creative, the primary, while Idea is the secondary, the receptive factor in things. His chief work is *The World as Will and Idea* (1819). Believing himself the successor of Socrates, he regarded his contemporaries, such as Hegel and Fichte, as charlatans.

Schubert, Franz Peter (1797–1828), Austrian composer, the son of a school-master, and a contemporary of Beethoven. He wrote not only symphonies, operas, sonatas, string quartets, choral music and masses, but also over 600 songs of unsurpassed lyrical beauty. He might almost be called the creator of the German *Lied* as known today. He gave his first and only concert eight months before his death in Vienna at the age of thirty-two.

Schumann, Robert Alexander (1810-56), composer of the early nineteenth-century German Romantic school. He wrote much chamber music, four symphonies, a piano concerto and choral music, but it is his early piano pieces and songs that give constant pleasure. He died in an asylum near Bonn. His wife Clara (1819–96), was one of the outstanding pianists of her time, and she worked incessantly to obtain a hearing for her husband's piano compositions. She was a fine interpreter of Chopin, and played in the major European cities.

Scott, Sir George Gilbert (1811–78), English architect of the Gothic revival style. He restored many churches and cathedrals and designed the Albert Memorial, the Martyrs' Memorial in Oxford, and St Pancras Station and Hotel in London.

Scott, Sir Giles Gilbert (1880–1960), English architect, grandson of the above, designed the Anglican Cathedral in Liverpool and planned the new Waterloo Bridge.

Scott, Sir Walter (1771–1832), Scottish novelist and poet. He was educated for the law, but came to know and love the Border country and people: in 1802–3 he issued a collection of ballads, *Border Minstrelsy. The Lay of the Last Minstrel* (1805) made him the most popular author of the day, and poems such as *Marmion* (1808) and *The Lady of the Lake* (1810) followed. His novels appeared anonymously, beginning with *Waverley* in 1814, and continuing with *Guy Mannering, The Antiquary, Old Mortality, Rob Roy* and *The Heart of Midlothian*. From 1819 he turned also to English history with *Ivanhoe* and *Kenilworth*. In 1826 he became bankrupt but worked heroically to clear his debts.

Scriabin, Alexander (1872–1915), Russian composer and pianist, he relied to some extent on extra-musical factors, such as religion, and in *Prometheus* applied a new and revolutionary theory to music, attempting to unite music and philosophy.

Shaw, George Bernard (1856–1950), Irish dramatist who conquered England by his wit and exposure of hypocrisy, cant and national weaknesses. His first success was *Arms and the Man* (1894), followed by *Mrs Warren's Profession*, written in 1893 but not staged until 1902, and not seen publicly in London until the Lord Chamberlain's ban was lifted in 1925 (it was banned because it concerned prostitution). His other plays include *Man and Superman, Pygmalion, Heartbreak House, Back to Methuselah, Saint Joan, The Apple Cart*, and *Too True to be Good*, and most have important prefaces. He was a superb critic and journalist, and in 1884 he joined the new socialist Fabian Society

(Lenin said of him: 'He is a good man, fallen among Fabians.') Nobel Prize winner 1925.

Shelley, Percy Bysshe (1792–1822), English poet and dramatist. He was a master of language and of literary form, and a passionate advocate of freedom and new thought. Sent down from Oxford for his pamphlet *The Necessity of Atheism* (1811), he came under the influence of William Godwin; and, after his first marriage ended unhappily, married Godwin's daughter Mary Wollstonecraft (1797–1851), herself a writer and author of *Frankenstein* (1818). In the same year began his friendship with Byron. His works include *The Revolt of Islam*, *The Masque of Anarchy* (an indictment of Castlereagh over the Peterloo massacre), and *Prometheus Unbound*, besides lyrics such as *To a Skylark*, *Ode to the West Wind*, and the elegy *Adonais*, suggested by the death of Keats. He lived for some years in Italy and was accidentally drowned while sailing near Spezzia.

Sheridan, Richard Brinsley (1751–1816), Irish dramatist. He was a brilliant writer of comedies, especially *The Rivals*, *The Duenna*, *The School for Scandal* and *The Critic*. He was also an MP, and took part in the impeachment of Warren Hastings; he also made a magnificent defence of the French Revolution in 1794.

Sholokhov, Mikhail Aleksandrovich (b. 1905), Russian novelist, author of *And Quiet Flow the Don*. Nobel Prize winner 1965.

Shostakovich, Dmitri (1906–75), Russian composer whose music is complex and profound, and reflects the struggles of the age in which he lived. His works include operas, ballets, symphonies, chamber music and music for films.

Sibelius, Jean Julius Christian (1865–1957), Finnish composer whose works include seven symphonies, a violin concerto, and several tone poems, notably *Finlandia*, and some based on the Finnish epic poem *Kalevala*.

Sickert, Walter Richard (1860–1942), British artist, b. Munich. He was influenced by Degas and studied under Whistler, and himself influenced later painters. He painted landscape, portraits and genre pictures with equal success.

Sienkiewicz, Henryk (1846–1916), Polish novelist and short story writer; the best known of his novels are *The Deluge*, *With Fire and Sword*, and *Quo Vadis?* Nobel Prize winner 1905.

Sillitoe, Alan (b. 1928), English novelist and short story writer. His short stories contain his best work: among them are *The Loneliness of the Long Distance Runner*, *The Ragman's Daughter*, *Guzman Go Home*, and the recent collection, *Men, Women and Children*. He achieved fame with his first novel, *Saturday Night and Sunday Morning* (1958), which drew on his experiences of his Nottingham working-class background, and was subsequently filmed.

Sinclair, Upton (1878–1968), American novelist whose documentary novel *The Jungle*, based on life in the Chicago slaughteryards, caused a sensation in 1906 and led to reform.

Sisley, Alfred (1839–99), French Impressionist painter of English origin, he painted some enchanting landscapes, such as *Meadows in Spring*. He exhibited at the first Impressionist exhibition in 1874.

Smetana, Bedřich (1824–84), Czech composer and pianist. He was principal conductor of the Prague National Theatre, for which he wrote most of his operas, including *The Bartered Bride* and *The Kiss*. The best known of his other compositions are the cycle of symphonic poems *My Country* and the string quartet *From My Life*. He became totally deaf in 1874, suffered a mental breakdown, and died in an asylum. He was the father of his country's music.

Snow, Baron (Charles Percy Snow) (b. 1905), English physicist and novelist, author of the essay *The Two Cultures of the Scientific Revolution*, and a sequence of novels, *Strangers and Brothers*.

Solzhenitsyn Alexander Isaievich (b. 1918), Russian fiction writer, historian and dramatist. Nobel Prize 1970. He was imprisoned in 1945 and spent the rest of Stalin's lifetime in camps. His first novel, *One Day in the Life of Ivan Denisovich* (1962), telling of his experiences, was published in Russia but no other book by him has appeared there. He was expelled from the Soviet Writers' Union in 1969 and from Russia in 1974; for the time being he has settled in Switzerland. His others works are *The First Circle* (1967), *Cancer Ward* (1969), *August 1974* (1971), *The Gulag Archipelago* (1974), and *Lenin in Zurich* (1975). He has also written short stories and plays.

Southey, Robert (1774–1843), English poet and historian, son of a linen-draper. A friend of Coleridge, he became Poet Laureate in 1813, though his best work is in prose. He wrote histories of Brazil and of the Peninsular War and lives of Nelson, Wesley and others.

Soyinka, Wole (b. 1935), Nigerian (Yoruba) playwright, poet and novelist. With his plays *The Lion and the Jewel* (1963), *Madmen and Specialists* (1971) and others he has established an authentic Nigerian theatre in English – some of his plays were performed at the Royal Court Theatre where he used to work. His controversial prose works *The Interpreters* (1965) and *The Man Died* (1973) are harder to penetrate but, as Achebe has pointed out, Soyinka is always a celebrant of life, even at his most pessimistic.

Spencer, Sir Stanley (1891–1959), English artist of visionary power. His two pictures of the *Resurrection* are in the Tate Gallery. He also painted many times Cookham regatta, Cookham in Berkshire being his native village where he spent most of his life.

Spender, Stephen (b. 1909), English poet who was closely associated with Auden and MacNeice in the thirties. His early poems, full of romantic yearning, are *Nine Experiments* (1928), *20 Poems* (1930) and *Poems* (1933); more recently *The Generous Days* (1971). He has also written fiction, criticism, autobiography, and translated poets such as Rilke and Lorca.

Stendhal, pseudonym of Marie Henri Beyle (1783–1842), French novelist. He was painter, government clerk, soldier and merchant by turns, and accompanied the fatal Russian campaign of 1812. After the revolution of 1830 he was appointed consul at Trieste and Civita Vecchia until 1841, and died in Paris. He had a high reputation as a writer of novels, art and literary criticism, and notes of travel: his main works are *Le Rouge et le Noir* and *La Chartreuse de Parme*.

Stevenson, Robert Louis Balfour (1850–94), Scottish author. He suffered from ill-health and the last five years of his life were spent in Samoa, where he was buried. His main works are: *Travels with a Donkey* (1879), *Treasure Island* (1883), *Kidnapped* (1886), *Dr Jekyll and Mr Hyde* (1886), *The Master of*

Ballantrae (1889), and *The Weir of Hermiston*, unfinished at his death.

Strauss, family of Viennese musicians. Johann Strauss the elder (1804–49), was a composer of dance music, who with Josef Lanner established the Viennese waltz tradition. His son, Johann Strauss the younger (1825–99), although not so good a violinist or conductor as his father, was called 'the waltz king' and composed over 400 waltzes, which include *The Blue Danube* and *Tales from the Vienna Woods*. Two of his brothers, Josef Strauss (1827–70) and Eduard Strauss (1835–1916), were also composers and conductors.

Strauss, Richard (1864–1949), German composer and conductor, the son of a horn-player in the opera orchestra at Munich. He succeeded von Bülow as court musical director at Meiningen, and was director of the State Opera, Vienna. His works include the operas *Salome, Elektra* and *Der Rosenkavalier*, the symphonic poems *Don Juan, Till Eulenspiegel, Don Quixote* and *Also Sprach Zarathustra*, and many songs of lyrical beauty.

Stravinsky, Igor (1882–1971), Russian composer and conductor, pupil of Rimsky-Korsakov. His ballets, *The Fire Bird* (1910), *Petrushka* (1911) and the revolutionary *The Rite of Spring*, which caused a furore in 1913, were written for the impresario Diaghilev. *Oedipus Rex* (1927) is a dignified version of the Sophocles play; in 1951 he wrote *The Rake's Progress*, with a libretto by W. H. Auden and Chester Kallman. A vital figure in twentieth-century music, he said of his work: 'My music is best understood by children and animals.'

Strindberg, Johan August (1849–1912), Swedish writer of intense creative energy. He studied medicine and philosophy, married three times but never happily, was teacher, actor, librarian and journalist, but after 1882 lived solely for literature, mainly abroad. He produced some fifty-five plays, as well as novels, stories, poems and critical essays. His plays include *Lucky Peter, Gustav Adolf, Till Damascus, The Father, Miss Julie* and *The Dance of Death*.

Sudermann, Hermann (1857–1928), German novelist, dramatist, poet and journalist. His works include the realistic drama *Die Ehre* (1888) which made him famous, and *Frau Sorge*, a novel translated as *Dame Care*.

Sullivan, Sir Arthur Seymour (1842–1900), Irish composer, mainly known for the music he wrote for light operas with W. S. Gilbert as librettist; he also wrote sacred music which was popular at the time.

Sutherland, Graham Vivian (b. 1903) British artist, one of the best known of living British painters. An official war artist in 1941, he is primarily a painter of the mood of landscape, but he has also produced important religious works such as the huge tapestry in Coventry Cathedral.

Swinburne, Algernon Charles (1837–1909), English poet and critic. He first won attention with a play, *Atalanta in Calydon*, in 1865, followed by *Poems and Ballads* (1866). *Songs Before Sunrise* (1871), *Bothwell* (1874) and *Mary Stuart* (1881) are among his later works. He was, at the time, the greatest metrical inventor in English literature.

Synge, John Millington ((1871–1909), Irish poet and playwright, a master of poetic language and of idiom. *Riders to the Sea* (1905) and *The Playboy of the Western World* (1907), are his two finest plays. He was a director of the Abbey Theatre, and died tragically young of cancer.

Tagore, Sir Rabindranath (1861–1941), Indian (Bengali) poet, novelist, playwright, son of the religious reformer Devendranath Tagore (1812–1905). His poems, *Gitanjali* (1909) (*Handful of Songs*), introduced by Yeats, gained him the Nobel Prize in 1913, and were followed by *Balaka* (1914) (*A Flight of Wild Cranes*).

Tchaikovsky, Peter Ilyich (1840–93), Russian composer. Among his works are the operas *Eugene Onegin* and *The Queen of Spades* (both from stories by Pushkin); symphonies, including the Little Russian and the Pathétique; ballets, including *Swan Lake*, *The Sleeping Beauty* and *The Nutcracker*, the fantasies *Romeo and Juliet* and *Francesca da Rimini*, the 1812 overture, the piano concerto in B flat minor, the violin concerto in D, and numerous songs. He died of cholera.

Tennyson, 1st Baron (Alfred Tennyson) (1809–92), English poet. He succeeded Wordsworth as Poet Laureate in 1850, his lyrics having brought him fame. *In Memoriam* (1850) reflects his grief for his friend Arthur Hallam. Apart from his lyrics, his longer works include *The Princess* (1847), *Maud* (1855), *Idylls of the King*, and *Enoch Arden* (1864). His publications extended over sixty years, mirroring much of the age in which he lived.

Thackeray, William Makepeace (1811–63), English novelist, b. Calcutta, author of *Vanity Fair*, *Pendennis*, *Esmond*, *The Newcomers*, *The Virginians*, *Philip* and *Lovel the Widower*. He edited the *Cornhill Magazine* from the first number in 1860, his most notable contributions being *Roudabout Papers*. He also wrote *Yellowplush Papers*, *The Book of Snobs* and *The Four Georges* (based on lectures given in the United States).

Thomas, Dylan (1914–53), Welsh poet whose early poetry – *Eighteen Poems* (1934), *Twenty-Five Poems* (1936) and *The Map of Love* (1939) – showed great promise, followed by *Deaths and Entrances* (1946). His radio play *Under Milk Wood* (1954) reached a wide audience. He died in America while on tour, as a result of excessive drinking.

Tippett, Sir Michael Kemp (b. 1905), English composer whose works include the operas *The Midsummer Marriage*, *King Priam* and *Knot Garden*, and the song cycles *Boyhood's End* and *The Heart's Assurance*.

Tolstoy, Leo Nikolaievich, Count (1828–1910), Russian writer and philosopher; born of noble family, he entered the army and fought in the Crimean War. During his time in the Caucasus he wrote *Childhood, Boyhood, and Youth*; *Memoirs of Prince Nekludoff*; and *The Cossacks*. The first of his two great works, *War and Peace* (1865–8), gives a vivid picture of the Napoleonic campaign against Russia. The other monumental novel is *Anna Karenina* (1875–8). Increasingly preoccupied with social problems, he freed his serfs before this was made a legal requirement, lived as poorly as a peasant in his wife's house, and was excommunicated by the Holy Synod for his departure from orthodoxy. His later works include *The Kreutzer Sonata, Resurrection* and *What is Art?*; in the last of these he argued that only that art is good which moves the masses, and to good ends; what is written for the select can only be bad art. In 1910 he suddenly left home, intending to end his days in ascetic seclusion; he fell ill, and died shortly afterwards.

Toscanini, Arturo (1867–1957), Italian conductor. He had a remarkable musical memory, and was long associated with the Metropolitan Opera House,

New York, and La Scala, Milan. He spent the Second World War in exile.

Toulouse-Lautrec, Henri de (1864–1901), French painter whose subject-matter was centred narrowly round the life he led; scenes from dance-halls and cafés in Montmartre, especially the Moulin Rouge series, figures of actresses, prostitutes, female clowns, circus artists, and a great number of nudes, unposed. He was a superb draughtsman and executed a large number of posters which were reproduced by lithography; he subscribed to no theories, and was a member of no artistic or aesthetic movement. His individuality was intensified by the stunted growth that resulted from two broken legs in childhood.

Trollope, Anthony (1815–82), English novelist. His early life was a struggle, the family being supported by his mother's writing. He worked for the Post Office, but managed to produce many novels, portraying in particular clerical life (the Barchester series, including *The Warden* (1855) and *Barchester Towers* (1857)) and political life (the Phineas Finn series). Some of his works first appeared in Thackeray's *Cornhill Magazine*, with illustrations by Millais.

Turgenev, Ivan Sergeievich (1818–83), Russian novelist, friend of Gogol and Tolstoy, whose *Letter on Gogol* (1852) led to imprisonment and seclusion on his own estate till 1855. He published poems in 1843, but it was *A Sportsman's Sketches* (1846) that made him famous, especially for their vivid pictures of serfdom. In *Fathers and Sons* (1861), *Smoke* (1867) and *Virgin Soil* (1876), he dealt with the triumph of Slavophile ideas. He died in exile in Paris.

Turner, Joseph Mallord William (1775–1851), English landscape painter, a barber's son. He entered the Royal Academy and was at first a topographical watercolourist. Later he turned to oils and became a master of light and colour, achieving magical effects, especially in depicting the reflection of light in water. His works include *Crossing the Brook* (1815), *Dido Building Carthage* (1815), *Ulysses Deriding Polyphemus* (1829), *The Fighting Téméraire* (1839), and *Rain, Steam and Speed* (1844). He was violently criticized as his style became more abstract – 'pictures are nothing, and very like', said one critic – which led to Ruskin's passionate defence of him in *Modern Painters*. He left nearly 300 paintings and nearly 20,000 watercolours and drawing to the nation, and bequeathed his savings (£140,000) to found an asylum for distressed artists.

Twain, Mark (real name **Samuel Langhorne Clemens**) (1835–1910), American humourist. First a printer, then a Mississippi pilot, he adopted his pseudonym from the call of the man sounding the river in shallow places ('Mark twain' meaning 'by the mark two fathoms'). His *Innocents Abroad* (1869) was the result of a trip to Europe and established his reputation as a humourist. Among his books are *Tom Sawyer*, *A Tramp Abroad*, *Huckleberry Finn* and *Pudd'n-head Wilson*.

Undset, Sigrid (1882–1949), Norwegian novelist, daughter of an antiquary, author of *Jenny*, the trilogy *Kristin Lavransdatter*, set in the fourteenth century, and *Olav Audunsson*. Nobel Prize winner 1928.

Valéry, Paul (1871–1945), French poet and essayist, strongly influenced by the Symbolist leader, Mallarmé. His poems include *La Jeune Parque* (*The Young Fate*), *Le Cimetière marin* (*The Cemetery by the Sea*), *La Pythie* (*The Pythoness*), and *Charmes*.

Van Gogh, Vincent (1853–90), Dutch painter, son of a pastor, who created some of the most colourful pictures ever painted. With passionate intensity of feeling he painted without pause – starting only in 1880 – whatever he found around him – landscapes, still lifes, portraits. The vivid colours and writhing, flame-like forms are completely expressive of his tormented sensibility. A life of pain, sorrow, poverty and, often, despair led to insanity and, at the age of thirty-seven, he shot himself.

Vaughan Williams, Ralph (1872–1958), English composer. He studied under Max Bruch in Berlin and under Ravel in Paris; he wrote nine symphonies besides a number of choral and orchestral works, operas (including *Hugh the Drover* and *Riders to the Sea*), ballets, chamber music and songs. He also published many English folk songs.

Verdi, Giuseppe (1813–1901), Italian composer. His early works include *Nabucco, Ernani, I Due Foscari* and *Macbeth*, popular because of their patriotic and revolutionary themes, reflecting Verdi's peasant background; a middle period represented by *Rigoletto, Il Trovatore, La Traviata, Un Ballo in Maschera* and *Don Carlos*; to the last period of his life belong *Aïda* (1871), *Otello* (1887), and the brilliant comic opera *Falstaff* (1893).

Verlaine, Paul (1844–96), French poet, one of the first of the Symbolists, also known for his memoirs and confessions. His works include *Poèmes saturniennes* (1865), *Les Fêtes galantes* (1869), *Sagesse* (1881), and *Romances sans paroles* (1887). He was imprisoned for two years in Belgium for shooting and wounding his friend Rimbaud. He died in poverty in Paris.

Verne, Jules (1828–1905), French pioneer of science fiction whose works include *Five Weeks in a Balloon, Twenty Thousand Leagues under the Sea, A Journey to the Centre of the Earth* and *Around the World in Eighty Days*.

Wagner, Richard (1813–83), German composer, one of the most controversial composers in musical history. He achieved a new type of musical expression in his operas, believing 'music-drama' to be a fusion of all the arts – music, literature, painting – in one entity. He made use of a device known as the *leitmotiv* and was his own librettist. His originality and modernism and his sympathy with the revolutionary party led to twelve years' exile, but he was supported by Liszt, young King Ludwig of Bavaria, and Nietzsche. He began writing the operatic cycle *Der Ring des Nibelungen* in 1853 but it was not until 1876 that the whole of the drama was performed at Bayreuth under the conductor Hans Richter. His operas include *The Flying Dutchman, Rienzi, Tannhäuser, Lohengrin, Tristan und Isolde, Die Meistersinger* and *Parsifal*, a religious drama. He married Liszt's daughter Cosima, formerly the wife of his friend Hans von Bülow. He died at Venice.

Walton, Sir William Turner (b. 1902), English composer whose works include concertos for string instruments, two symphonies, two coronation marches, *Façade* (set to Edith Sitwell's poem), and an oratorio, *Belshazzar's Feast*.

Waugh, Evelyn (1902–66), English satirical writer, author of *Decline and Fall, Vile Bodies, The Loved One, Scoop, Brideshead Revisited* and the trilogy *Sword of Honour*.

Weber, Carl Maria Friedrich Ernst von (1786–1826), German composer who laid the foundation of German Romantic opera. His reputation rests principally on his three operas, *Der Freischütz* (1820), *Euryanthe* (1823), and *Oberon*

(1826). He was also an able pianist, conductor and musical director.

Weill, Kurt (1900–50), German composer of satirical, Surrealist operas, including *The Threepenny Opera* (whose librettist was Brecht, with whom he regularly worked), and musical comedies such as *Lady in the Dark* (1941) and *One Touch of Venus* (1943). In 1936 he settled in America; he was married to the singer-actress Lotte Lenya.

Wells, Herbert George (1866–1946), English author, son of a cricket professional. He believed in progress through science and his long series of books includes romances of the Jules Verne variety (*The Time Machine, The Island of Dr Moreau, The Invisible Man, The War of the Worlds*), sociological autobiography (*Love and Mr Lewisham, Kipps, Tono-Bungay, The History of Mr Polly*), and popular education (*Outline of History, The Shape of Things to Come*). He was an early and successful educator of 'the common man'. He was also a founder member of the Fabian Society. *Experiment in Autobiography* was published in 1934.

Whistler, James Abbott McNeill (1834–1903), American artist who studied in Paris and settled in England. His eminence as an etcher and dry-pointer is even more widely recognized than his reputation as a worker in colour. Among his main works are studies of the Thames and a portrait of his mother.

White, Patrick (b. 1912), Australian novelist and playwright, Nobel Prize winner 1973. His novels include *The Aunt's Story* (1948), *The Tree of Life* (1955), *Voss* (1957), *Riders in the Chariot* (1961), *The Solid Mandala* (1966), *The Vivisector* (1970) and *The Eye of the Storm* (1973).

Whitman, Walt (1819–92), American poet. He led a compulsively wandering life and did hospital work in the Civil War. He seemed unable to find free expression for his emotions until he hit upon the curious, irregular, incantatory measures of *Leaves of Grass* (1855), originally a small quarto of ninety-four pages, which grew to nearly 400 pages. Other works are *Drum Taps*, and *Democratic Visas*.

Wilde, Oscar Fingall O'Flaherty Wills (1854–1900), Irish author, dramatist and wit; son of a Dublin surgeon and leader of the cult of art for art's sake. His works include poems, fairy tales, short stories and witty comedies – *Lady Windermere's Fan, A Woman of No Importance, The Ideal Husband* and *The Importance of Being Earnest*. In a libel action he was convicted of homosexual practices and imprisoned for two years, during which he wrote the poem *The Ballad of Reading Gaol*. He also wrote a novel, *The Picture of Dorian Gray*.

Wilson, Edmund (1895–1972), American critic, author of *Axel's Castle* (1931), *The Triple Thinkers* (1938), *To the Finland Station* (1940), *The Wound and the Bow* (1941), *The Shores of Light* (1952) and *The Dead Sea Scrolls* (1955).

Wodehouse, Pelham Grenville (1881–1975), English humourist, creator of Jeeves in the Bertie Wooster stories (eg *My Man Jeeves* (1919), *The Code of the Woosters* (1938)). He wrote over 100 books.

Wolf, Hugo (1860–1903), Austrian song-writer. In his settings of over 300 German lyric poems, including many by Mörike and Goethe, he achieved complete union of poetry and music. He lived much of his life in poverty and eventually lost his reason and died of an incurable disease.

Woolf, Virginia (1882–1941), English writer, daughter of Sir Leslie Stephen and wife of Leonard Woolf with whom she founded the Hogarth Press which published, among others, Eliot, Freud, and Virginia's own novels. Her works include *To the Lighthouse*, *Mrs Dalloway*, *The Waves* and *A Room of One's Own*.

Wordsworth, William (1770–1850), English poet. He was educated at Cambridge, and in 1798 issued, with Coleridge, *Lyrical Ballads*; he settled at Grasmere with his sister Dorothy (1771–1855), to whose insights his poems owe much. In 1843, after Southey's death, he became Poet Laureate. He wrote an enormous body of work, some of it very poor and often cruelly parodied, but his best poems are outstanding, including his sonnets, the *Ode on the Intimations of Immortality* and *The Prelude*.

Wright, Frank Lloyd (1869–1959), American architect, initiator of horizontal strip and all-glass design. His buildings include the Imperial Hotel, Tokyo and the Guggenheim Museum, New York.

Yeats, William Butler (1865–1939), Irish lyric poet and playwright, a leader of the Irish literary revival. His plays were performed in the Abbey Theatre which he helped to found, and include *Cathleen Ni Houlihan*, *The Hour Glass* and *Deidre*. His poetry, influenced variously by Blake, French Symbolism and Eastern mysticism, includes *The Second Coming*, the *Byzantium* poems, *Easter 1916*, *The Tower*, *The Two Trees* and *Dialogue of Self and Soul*. Nobel Prize 1923.

Zadkine, Ossip (b. 1890), Russian sculptor working in France, who makes play with light on concave surfaces. His works include *Orpheus* and the public monument *The Destruction of Rotterdam*.

Zola, Emile Edouard (1840–1902), French novelist, b. Paris of Italian descent. In the later years of the Empire he formed with Flaubert, Daudet, the Goncourts and Turgenev a sort of informal society, out of which grew the Naturalist school. His series *Les Rougon-Macquart* portrays in a score of volumes the fortunes of one family, and includes the novels *L'Assommoir*, *Nana*, *Germinal* and *La Bête humaine*. He was a champion of Dreyfus, writing the famous letter starting, 'J'accuse'; he was accidentally suffocated by charcoal fumes in 1902.

8

The World since 1945

Summary of Chapter

Since 1945, when the Allied powers achieved final victory over Hitler's Germany and Japan, great political and economic changes have occurred. Old empires have fallen. New forces of nationalism have swept the world. Our world has been dominated by two 'superpowers', America and Russia. This chapter looks at some of these great movements – movements whose course is still at work in the world today.

The Legacy of the Second World War

The Second World War made a tremendous impact on world politics. By 1945, the armies of the victorious Allies occupied most of the territories over which war had been waged. Western Europe was largely under the control of Anglo-American forces, with the French back in control of their own country and sharing responsibility for the administration of Germany with the 'Big Three' – Britain, the USA and the Soviet Union. Eastern Europe came under Russian influence as the Red Army advanced across Europe towards Germany throughout 1944 and early 1945. Southern Europe was controlled by the Big Three. Britain predominated in Greece and Turkey (until 1947 when her responsibilities were transferred to the US), Italy was under joint Anglo-American administration, and some countries like Yugoslavia and Bulgaria were under the control of regimes friendly to the USSR. Elsewhere in the world the European pattern was repeated. All three of the major Allies had armies of occupation in the Far East and the Middle East, though not in equal proportions. Only areas like Africa south of the Sahara, and Latin America, were relatively unaffected by the war, and as we shall see, this was to change within fifteen years. Of the three major powers, only the USSR was to emerge from the war with territories greatly in excess of those it possessed at the beginning of 1939. It was able to keep those which it had gained in the Nazi–Soviet agreement of August 1939, thus recovering the bulk of the territories taken from the Tsarist Russian Empire at the end of the First World War. Britain and America were later to withdraw from the territories they occupied, in some cases altogether, in others leaving military installations behind. They did not, however, annex any of the territories they had conquered in the war.

Economic Changes

Wars, and modern wars especially, involve the expenditure of great effort and tremendous resources on destruction rather than creation. The state of the belligerent nations' economies at the war's end reflected this sad and simple fact. The economic development of all the major participants was restrained or retarded, and their relative economic strength underwent a substantial alteration.

Of the four great European nations – Britain, France, Italy and Germany – all except Britain were at some time occupied and compelled to use productive capacity for the benefit of the occupying power's war effort. All but France used large amounts of manpower in the armed services, with consequent loss of life and production. All four nations saw fighting over their respective territories – Britain by air, the others by both air and land. Consequently, and unlike the First World War, civilian casualties occurred in substantial numbers in Britain and Germany, and in all four countries direct and often substantial damage to industry retarded output during and for many years after the war.

In absolute terms there can be no doubt that it was the USSR who suffered most as a result of attacks by land and air. The conflict had destroyed 1,700 towns and 70,000 villages, and left 25 million homeless; 20 million died – 60,000 starved to death at the siege of Leningrad alone. Recognizing this, the Allies agreed at the end of the war that Russia should receive relatively much higher compensation than the others from the industries of defeated Germany. The Allies could not agree on the exact amounts and this was to become one of the reasons why the war-time co-operation between the Allies was to lead after the war to mistrust and nearly to armed conflict.

Even wealthy America, whose territory was virtually untouched by hostilities, paid a heavy price for her participation in the war. As well as fighting with American troops and equipment against the Japanese in the Pacific and the Germans and Italians in Europe, she provided much of the equipment for front-line Allied forces and food for hungry Allied civilians. For several years after the war, acute shortages of foodstuffs and other goods, such as cars, washing machines and furniture, reminded Americans of the cost of involvement in foreign conflicts. Nevertheless, of all the victorious nations, America's relative economic position was the most significantly improved. The USA was the only power with sufficient wealth to assist the recovery of the devastated nations of Europe and the Far East. Its success in doing so is witnessed by the rapid post-war growth of Japan and Western Europe, especially when compared with the development of other regions which failed to receive such assistance.

New Political Institutions

Almost as soon as the war ended, plans for restructuring international relations were developed and discussed by the Allied powers. Their first and most important aim was to ensure that such a conflict would not occur again. The principles upon which the British and the Americans wished to base the post-war settlements were set out in the United Nations Declaration of July 1941. These principles were rather vague and subject to different interpretations at the hands of skilful negotiators. Those which referred to the conditions governing transfers of territory were to cause particular trouble between the Soviet Union on the one side, and Britain and America on the other. But this declaration envisaged the future United Nations Organization. This organization, which

The Birth of the United Nations. President Truman of the United States addresses the 16th Plenary Session of the San Francisco Conference – which led to the formation of the United Nations – on 25 June 1945. (*Photo: Camera Press, London*)

today has well over 150 members, with its headquarters in New York City, was created as a result of two conferences in August, September and October of 1944 in Dumbarton Oaks near Washington DC.

The San Francisco Conference of June 1945 was held to establish the structure and procedure of the new United Nations. The members of the organization would comprise the General Assembly, while the five major Allied powers were given permanent places on the Security Council, the remaining places being allocated on a rotating basis to the ordinary members. The conference was the scene of discord between the major powers over the participation of certain states, as well as bitter argument over the voting procedures to be used by the Security Council.

The purpose of the United Nations Organization was to provide a meeting-place for the nations of the world in which rapid and peaceful solutions to international crises could emerge from debate and enjoy the guarantee of the member states. Like its predecessor, the League of Nations, the United Nations inspired much hope as an alternative to the competitive power politics that were felt to have caused the two World Wars. The controversy that arose at the San Francisco Conference was an early indication of the difficulties that the organization would face in discharging these responsibilities, and like many plans conceived in the comradeship of war, the colder atmosphere of the peace thwarted their full implementation. Our later discussion of the United Nations will show that it was not as ineffective as the League, but not as successful as its most ardent advocates hoped it would be.

An international conference at Bretton Woods, New Hampshire in July 1944 recommended the creation of two new institutions concerned with world trade and finance. Their aims have been much more modest than those of the UN and their record correspondingly more successful. They are the International Bank of Reconstruction and Development (often referred to as the World Bank), and the International Monetary Fund (the IMF). The former was set up in December 1945 to promote the economic development of the member states by encouraging and making investments. The latter exists to promote international co-operation in trade and finance and to help preserve stability in currency exchanges, which was regarded as an essential precondition of steadily expanding trade. The Bretton Woods Conference considered the lack of such organizations before the war to have contributed to the lack of international economic co-operation that had bedevilled relations between otherwise friendly states such as Britain and America, and that had prevented wealthy nations from intervening in the economies of states such as Germany, where economic depression had done much to pave the way for militarist and aggressive governments.

The aftermath of war produced political circumstances that in turn gave rise to other international organizations, military and economic, which will be described later. First let us examine the nature of those political circumstances.

Political Alignments

If anything should surprise us about the relations between the Western powers (Britain and the USA) and the USSR, it must be the degree of co-operation they sustained during the war rather than the conflict between them that followed it. Britain had actively sought to crush the Russian Revolution by sending British troops to fight in the ensuing Civil War. The character of the Communist regime that emerged from that war was very different from the regimes of both Britain and America. Certain of its features, for example its opposition to religion and its refusal to tolerate private property, seemed to threaten two of the most fundamental characteristics of Western society. Founded in war, the new regime acquired a well-deserved reputation for ruthlessness amounting to brutality, and its intolerance of dissenting political and philosophical views seemed the very antithesis of the free and democratic state it claimed to be. Before the war influential people in both Britain and America saw little important difference between Nazi Germany and Soviet Russia, a view which the Nazi-Soviet agreement of August 1939 tended to reinforce. An eloquent expression of this attitude was given by Harry S. Truman only five years before he met Stalin as an ally at the Potsdam Conference; 'If we see that Germany is winning,' he said, 'we should help Russia, and if Russia is winning we ought to help Germany, and that way let them kill as many as possible, although I don't want to see Hitler victorious under any circumstances.' It was not the best spirit with which to start a new partnership. The

Russians interpreted these and other indications of Anglo-American distaste as a positive threat to their safety. This, added to their ideological contempt for and hostility towards such bastions of capitalism and imperialism, made them view their war-time partners as inevitable enemies, the struggle with whom might be postponed, but not in the long run avoided.

The first sign of trouble during the war concerned the future western boundary of the USSR. In the summer of 1942, during negotiations for a treaty of alliance with Great Britain, the Soviets requested assurances regarding their boundary with Poland. Britain was prepared to make these assurances, but the Americans were adamantly opposed to any agreements before the official peace conferences. The Russians gave way because the British indicated their unwillingness then, or at any other time, to side against the Americans on a major issue. Another issue which historians consider to have significantly influenced inter-Allied relations was the constant postponement of the second front campaign which Britain and America had pledged themselves to open. For a long time the Allies in the West did not consider themselves able to make successful landings on the coast of France, and were not prepared to suffer heavy casualties simply to reassure their Eastern ally. The Russians, bearing the brunt of the land war in Europe, could not help feeling bitter at the postponement of much-needed assistance; but they also must have realized that the Anglo-American postponement would be a useful lever in future bargaining over other issues.

Because of the American refusal to consider extensive inter-allied agreements before the war had been won, the major issues were left to be dealt with by the leaders of the Big Three at three conferences – the Teheran Conference of November–December 1943, the Yalta Conference of February 1945, and the Potsdam Conference of July–August 1945. If these conferences had succeeded in producing agreement on the range of issues discussed, it is likely that much of the subsequent hostility could have been avoided. At each of the three meetings the troublesome questions of the frontiers of Poland and Germany were tackled without any substantial agreement being reached. Though Russia was to have its way in Poland, it was mainly because the other two powers were unwilling to use force to hinder it – not because they agreed. In the case of Germany, only temporary arrangements for occupation were made. Germany's eventual partition into two separate states, later to be ranged against one another in hostile alliances, is proof of the Allies' failure to come to terms with one another's interests.

The basis of disagreement between Britain and America on one side, and Russia on the other, lay in their different views of what would produce maximum security in the post-war years. Russia, feeling that it had been the victim of an international conspiracy before the war, was determined to control the areas through which it had been twice invaded during the twentieth century. This meant ensuring friendly governments in Eastern Europe and a weak and, if necessary, divided Germany. America and Britain opposed the creation of spheres of influence in Europe, believing these to have been partly responsible for the failures of the inter-war period. They wanted a more orderly system for the resolution of international disputes such as would be provided by an effective United Nations Organization. They opposed any attempt by the Russians to control the internal affairs of the states on her western and later on her Chinese border, but could not provide her with effective and convincing alternative guarantees. The Western powers interpreted the unilateral measures taken by Russia first in Europe, then in Iran in the Middle East, and by 1949 in China, as merely the first steps in a campaign to spread Communism throughout the world. All the old pre-war hostility was resumed and added to it was what statesmen called the lesson of 'appeasement' (the policy of making concessions to Nazi Germany followed by Britain and France before the war) – namely that the more an aggressor's claims were conceded the more numerous those claims would become. America resolved to help the Western European states recover from the war by economic assistance through the Marshall Plan of 1947, and through participation in the military co-operation that became the North Atlantic Treaty Organization in 1949. They also decided to support Chiang Kai Shek against the Communist Chinese led by Mao Tse Tung after the failure of American attempts (1947–8) to arrange a compromise between them. In 1947 Churchill spoke of an 'Iron Curtain' dividing Europe. By 1950 and the Korean War, divisions of interest between the Western and Eastern sections of the war-time alliance existed throughout the world, with profound effects on the developments of international relations for the next quarter of a century.

The Rise of the Superpowers

Before the Second World War, the name 'great power' was accorded to the largest and most influential of the world's nations. Before the First World War these nations were all European; after that war America joined the group. By 1945 however, with the severe weakening of the European states, the term 'superpower' came into use. Initially it was a phrase coined by an American journalist to describe the Big Three – the USA, Great Britain and the USSR. But as the full extent of Britain's dependence on the USA for economic and military assistance became clear, the term became confined to America and Russia. By 1947, and the onset of the 'Cold War', these two nations were distinguished from all others in three main respects. Firstly, they were militarily stronger by a large margin than the third most powerful nation in the world, Britain. Secondly, both countries were leading members of identifiable and mutually exclusive groupings of states, soon to become formal military alliances and economic associations. Thirdly, they were by 1947 the only two major states that were not economically dependent upon other governments. Russia was receiving payment in the form of reparations from Germany and had been receiving substantial economic assistance from the USA, but with the termination of that assistance and the refusal of the Russians to participate in the 'European Recovery Programme' or Marshall Plan of 1947, the USSR was left with influence over the economies of its Eastern European satellites, but without economic dependence on the USA. Before discussing the course of relations between the superpowers let us first examine these three distinguishing features separately and in more detail.

USA Military Strength

The United States reduced the size of its armies very rapidly after the surrender of Japan. But the war had hastened the development of nuclear weaponry, whose destructive force became very clear after their use against the Japanese cities of Hiroshima and Nagasaki. The development of nuclear weapons was an Anglo-American project, and soon after the full implications of the extraordinary power of nuclear bombs became known, President Truman decided against sharing with the Soviet Union the secrets of their manufacture. So until the early 1950s America and Britain were the only two nuclear powers in the world. The advantages and drawbacks of nuclear weapons became clearer to American strategists during the Korean War. In the summer of 1950 fighting broke out between the northern (pro-Communist) and southern (pro-American) sections of that partitioned country. The United States contributed the bulk of a United Nations force to defend the south against the north. The fighting raged for three years with the American forces invading the north but being repelled by Chinese troops, eventually settling for a return to the boundaries that prevailed before fighting broke out. Despite strong pressure from some military advisers the President declined to use nuclear weapons.

The reason for this was that the great destructive power of nuclear bombs restrained Presidents from using them unless the circumstances were so serious that they could be sure of public support for the immense loss of life that would follow. This was a weakness in that it showed nuclear weapons to be unusable in circumstances where, on narrow military grounds, they would assure advantage if not victory over the enemy. When the use of nuclear weapons was thus prevented America lost much of her theoretical military superiority, and had to fulfil her obligations at great cost in American lives. It was also a weakness in that it seemed to have encouraged the USSR to confront the United States, not directly, for that would risk direct retaliation against the USSR, but indirectly through smaller, or weaker friendly states. But the Korean War also showed the great advantage of having nuclear weapons. It is likely that the Chinese and North Koreans agreed to a ceasefire only because President Eisenhower threatened to use nuclear weapons if they did not. This was an example of the value of nuclear weapons as a deterrent. They might not be usable in all circumstances, but the possibility of their being used was enough to persuade adversaries to back down. From this time onwards America has developed both nuclear weapons and more conventional types of armaments, using the former only as a threat and the latter in actual armed conflicts.

Map 8. The Korean War, 1950, confirmed the division of Korea along the 38th Parallel into the pro-Communist north and the pro-Western south.

The Political Position of the USA

As the deterioration in relations between the USA and the Soviet Union grew more pronounced in the years after the war, America adopted the role of the principal member of a group of states determined to prevent or even reverse the expansion of Communist government. It was felt that Russia was the leader of a world communist movement whose eventual aim was the domination of the world. By 1947 the USA had adopted the doctrine of 'Containment' – meaning the prevention of Communist expansion at any point in the world. This signified the acceptance of responsibility for the security of governments under attack by Communist movements anywhere in the world and led directly to America's involvement in the Korean and Vietnam wars. This policy was most explicitly formulated in a speech by President Truman on 12 March 1947, that later came to be called the 'Truman Doctrine'. He urged Americans to commit themselves to defending 'free peoples' against 'totalitarian regimes'. That this marked the beginning of a long-sustained policy is demonstrated by its similarity to a speech made over thirteen years later by President Kennedy, in which he pledged himself to 'Let every nation know ... that we shall pay any price, bear any burden, meet any hardship, support any friend, oppose any foe to assure the survival and success of liberty.' This type of global commitment has been formalized by America's participation in several alliances. In 1949 America signed the North Atlantic Treaty which created NATO, a military alliance between the USA, Canada, Denmark, France, Iceland, Italy, Luxembourg, the Netherlands, Norway, Portugal, Great Britain, and later the Federal Republic of Germany. In 1951 it signed a similar one with Australia and New Zealand known as the ANZUS pact, and in 1954 the South East Asia Treaty Organisation (SEATO). In addition to these treaty organizations America has treaties with several individual countries, notably Japan.

Economic Relations of the USA

As a result of its influence in the World Bank and the International Monetary Fund (IMF), the USA lies at the centre of the network of economic relations between the participating states. In addition to these formal responsibilities, the stability of the US dollar made it the most important form of payment in international trade, replacing for practical purposes gold, which was used before the Second World War. This made America responsible in an equally important but less clear way for the health of the world economy. Since the stability of its currency was important to other nations' trade, America's domestic economic policy had to take careful account of other countries' problems. This consideration prevented successive American Presidents from acting as decisively as they might have liked, until President Nixon devalued the dollar in 1971. So not only was America the only country that could provide the funds necessary to promote economic recovery after the war; it is still the single most important economic unit in the world despite the recent fall in the value of the dollar and the wealth of the oil-rich Middle East.

USSR Military Strength

Though the Soviet Union did not demobilize its armies with the same rapidity as the United States following the defeat of Germany and Japan, it did decrease its forces from approximately $11\frac{1}{2}$ million men in 1945 to 3 million men in 1948. With much of the USSR's industrial capacity destroyed in the war, and in view of the technological backwardness of the Soviet arms industry, America's military superiority over the Soviet Union was not seriously questioned until the presidential election campaign of 1959–60. Even then many of the fears expressed about a 'missile gap' between the USA and the

USSR turned out to be unfounded. Russia did acquire nuclear weapons in spite of America's decision not to supply information. Most of the secrets were passed on to the USSR by scientists disillusioned with American foreign policy or simply in need of money; thus by 1949 the Soviet Union had managed to explode a nuclear device. It was not until several years had passed that a weapons system capable of use against the USA was developed. The USSR is a much larger country than the USA in terms of space, and, as it has land borders with many different nations it is not surprising that it has developed a much larger 'conventional' army than that of the USA. But it has also achieved virtual equality in nuclear strength, and the Soviet navy, now the most extensive in the world, is almost entirely a post-war creation.

Political Position of the USSR

One of the major disputes between the USA and the Soviet Union focused on the latter country's demand for 'friendly governments' in the Eastern European states on its western borders. Russia required such governments, it was argued, because it had been invaded through those areas on two occasions in the twentieth century and would never feel secure until assured of some influence over the foreign policies of its neighbouring states. But such an arrangement could not be made if countries were to have truly free elections. Many people in those countries not only disliked Communism – they were also traditionally hostile to Russia, whoever ruled her. Thus in Poland, Romania, Bulgaria, Hungary, Yugoslavia, the Eastern part of Germany, and, after 1947, Czechoslovakia, governments either overtly Communist or pro-Communist were installed with some measure of Russian assistance. To consolidate its influence in these countries Russia signed agreements of 'Friendship and Mutual Assistance' with Poland, Yugoslavia, Romania, Finland and China; it also signed a much more important 'Treaty of Friendship, Co-operation and Mutual Assistance' with Albania, Bulgaria, Hungary, the German Democratic Republic (East Germany), Poland, Romania and Czechoslovakia, in Warsaw during May 1955. This Treaty became known as the Warsaw Pact and is a military alliance between the Communist-governed states of Eastern Europe equivalent and opposed to the North Atlantic Treaty Organization. Russian alliances and alignments came under much stress during the 1950s and 1960s. In 1953 rioting broke out in East Germany. The most serious trouble came in 1956 when a rebellion against Soviet influence in Hungary had to be crushed by the Russian Red Army. In the same year violence between Russia and Poland was only narrowly averted. By 1963 Russia's relations with the People's Republic of China had deteriorated badly. The two countries ceased to co-operate economically, diplomatically and militarily, while China's best friend in Europe, Albania, left the Warsaw Pact. In 1968 the regime of Alexander Dubček in Czechoslovakia was toppled on Soviet orders because it had shown an unacceptable degree of political independence. Russia also sought to associate itself with the so-called Third World of poor, and in some cases, newly independent nations in Asia, Africa and the Far East through giving economic assistance, supplying arms and offering diplomatic support.

The Hungarian revolution. Budapest 1956: burning the red flag in Petofi Square. (*Photo: Camera Press, London*)

Economic Position of the USSR

The USSR declined to participate in the World Bank or the International Monetary Fund; neither would it accept assistance from the Marshall Plan which did so much to restore the health of the West European economies after the war. Until the late 1960s the USSR's economic relations concentrated on the states in the Communist bloc and those in the Third World with whom it was on good terms. A trading organization similar to the European Economic Community or Common Market was established in 1949. It was called the Council of Mutual Economic Assistance or Comecon, but was, until 1953, little more than a paper organization designed to compensate its members for the Marshall Plan assistance that Stalin forbade them to accept. After the inauguration by President Nixon of the policy of détente a process of gradually increasing economic contact with the West was hastened. Agreements concerning trade between the USSR and the USA have been accompanied by the opening of Eastern European markets to Western commerce, a process we may expect to continue as long as political relations continue to improve, and as long as the relative backwardness of Soviet and East European technology stimulates demand for western knowhow and products.

Conclusion: Relations between the Superpowers 1945–79

There seem to have been four distinct phases in Soviet–American relations since the Second World War. From 1945 until late 1947 there was a possibility that issues arising out of the war might be amicably or at least acceptably settled. With the formulation of the Truman Doctrine and the Soviet Union's refusal of economic assistance, a period of acute political hostility began which was not mitigated by any common economic interest and lasted until Stalin's death in 1953. During those years American society exhibited the most profound revulsion for and suspicion of Communism. They had seen their troops fighting the Chinese in Korea, and regarded that hostility as merely a part of a global bid for supremacy that could surface anywhere at any time. After Stalin's death the Soviet government underwent a period of introspection as rivals struggled for the leadership. When Khruschev emerged victorious in 1956 he denounced many of the aspects of Stalin's leadership and appeared willing to make a break with the past. Though he seemed also to be willing on occasions, such as the Cuban missile crisis of October 1962, to go to the brink of war, it was he who derided the view that war with the West was inevitable and desirable, and often argued that Russia could benefit from co-operation with the West in economic and technical matters. The fourth period began with the Nixon policy of détente.

The co-operation begun by Khruschev has developed into one that is more extensive in scope, and institutionalized by agreements on trade, and on consultation in situations of political interest to both states. Their relationship has come to resemble what one commentator has called an 'adversary partnership', in which the tremendous military and political power of the states has given them a common outlook on certain political questions that makes co-operation rather than conflict the most prudent policy from their respective points of view, if not from that of their allies.

The March of World Communism

Introduction

Before the Second World War, there existed only one state governed by an explicitly Communist administration, the Union of Soviet Socialist Republics (USSR). There had been attempts elsewhere in Europe to impose Communist rule by force. In Hungary, a Communist regime under the leadership of Bela Kun survived for almost a year before being crushed in 1919. In Germany at about the same time, the Spartacists attempted to overthrow the infant Weimar Republic, but without success. Lenin and the Bolshevik revolutionaries had expected the rapid collapse of established governments all over Europe. But other countries, though weakened by the war, had not suffered the privations that had made Russia so fertile for revolution. In addition to this consideration, the political leadership of the larger European nations was more responsive to popular feeling than were the Russian royal family. Consequently these nations were better equipped to anticipate and tackle matters causing popular unrest. Thus, in the absence of the use of force, and effective propaganda, the Russian Revolution was destined to be the exception in post-First World War politics, rather than the first act in a general European rebellion against the old pre-war order. Recognizing this, after Lenin's death in 1924 the Soviet Union concentrated on building 'socialism in one country'. Though Russia exerted influence abroad, and particularly in China through the Communist International or Comintern, its energies were primarily devoted to imposing the rule of the Communist party in Russia, and building up the Soviet economy at a ruthless pace. After the Second World War, the situation was vastly changed. Victorious Soviet armies controlled European territories as far west as East Germany and Austria and as far south as Albania. Between 1945 and 1948 East Germany, Poland, Czechoslovakia, Hungary, Yugoslavia, Romania, Bulgaria and Albania became Communist. In 1945 the Baltic states of Estonia, Latvia and Lithuania were annexed by the USSR. In the Far East, the cessation of hostilities between Chinese and Japanese forces was the signal for a resumption of fighting between the pro-Communist forces of Mao Tse Tung and the Nationalist forces led by Chiang Kai Shek. In other parts of the world small colonial territories were the scene of preparations for struggles against the rule of colonial powers that would produce a form of alliance against Western Europe and North American influence between the Communist bloc and the nationalist movements in the newly independent states.

Eastern Europe

'This war is not as in the past. Whoever occupies a territory also imposes on it his own social system as far as his army can reach.' With these words to a Yugoslav Communist in 1944, Stalin summarized the policy that was to guide Soviet actions in the territory occupied by his armies in Europe in the years since the Second World War. With the single exception of Austria whose fate was settled by the Austrian State Treaty of 1955, all the countries under Russian control in 1945 are still controlled today by governments based on the Soviet model and subservient to the Soviet Union. The technique employed by the Soviet Union was the creation of 'Popular Front' regimes, comprising the pro-Soviet representatives of various political organizations within the countries concerned. It is noticeable that in the two countries where the Communist governments were founded by national leaders who rose to prominence during the war – ie Albania and Yugoslavia – the Soviet Union failed to establish the absolute political control that was to characterize its relations with other East European states. The technique of using 'Popular Front' regimes was applied in Poland, East Germany, in 1947 in Czechoslovakia, in Romania and in Bulgaria. Perhaps even more indicative of Stalin's determination to secure control of the region was the process of political consolidation that occurred during the early 1950s, with a general purge of pre-war political figures, as well as of the leaders of the Church. Not satisfied with this, Stalin then turned his attention to those communists who had risen to prominence independently of Soviet assistance. Laszlo Rajk in Hungary, Traicho Kostov in Bulgaria, and Vladimir Clementis in Czechoslovakia are but three examples. In addition to these Communists, others were attacked in the course of an anti-Zionist anti-Israeli campaign which was unleashed in the Soviet Union in 1951–2. Economic consolidation was secured by compelling the export of produce from the Eastern European satellites at prices much lower than those offered on the international market. Soviet 'advisers' were installed in some ministries, especially those concerned with internal security and finance.

After Stalin's death in 1953, these countries enjoyed a respite from the terror that arrest and imprisonment had created, but they saw no softening of the basic control exerted by the Soviet leadership. When Khruschev emerged in 1956 as the most powerful of the new Soviet hierarchy, he instigated a period of criticism of Stalin's methods of government. In a secret speech to the Soviet Party Congress in 1956, which quickly became known to the public, he denounced the methods of terror that had been employed to secure the co-operation of people within the Soviet Union and Eastern Europe. The impact of these revelations on the Eastern European states was immediate, and far from passive. In both Poland and Hungary, the notion of 'separate roads to socialism' led to open protests against the Soviet Union's influence. In Poland there were riots in which over fifty people were killed. In Hungary such demonstrations were actually *supported* by the police and army. A new government led by Imre Nagy left the Warsaw Pact, and established a multi-party system. All this ended early in November when the Soviet Red Army entered Hungary, crushing the government and executing many of its members. The developments of 1956 were important for the future in two respects. Firstly it was clear that any attempt to dismantle the apparatus of Communist rule, or to leave the Communist bloc, would be thwarted by force, and would produce no more than verbal support from the West. Secondly, reforms which did not threaten the 'leading role' of the Communist party, and which indicated a willingness to remain within the Warsaw Pact, would apparently be tolerated. After 1956 most of the changes that took place in Eastern Europe followed this pattern. There were however, some exceptions. In Romania the leaders of the Communist Party were able to use the conflict between China and the Soviet Union to increase their country's economic and political independence from the USSR. They have been notably successful in doing so, but mainly because they did not attempt to accompany the change in their international position with a change in their policy on political liberties within Romania. This was not so in Czechoslovakia. There, pressure for internal reform grew steadily from 1961 onwards. When, in January 1968, Alexander Dubček became First Secretary of the Czechoslovak Communist Party (the most important political position in the country) the pace of reform increased rapidly. There was immediate acceptance of the desirability of allowing factions to form within the party, censorship was abolished, and non-party political organizations were allowed to function. The powers of the secret police were curbed and the role of the national assembly or parliament was greatly increased. But this form of responsiveness to the wishes of the people was a threat, not only to the Soviet leadership, but to the hierarchies that dominated other Eastern European nations, notably East Germany. The forces of the Warsaw Pact mounted an invasion of the country in August 1968, which resulted in the purge of all the reformist elements and the imposition of a government more favourable to the interests of their fellow Communist party bureaucracies.

The Russians in Prague. In proud defiance Czechs walk past Soviet tanks, their heads averted. (*Photo: Stefan Tyszko/Queen, Camera Press, London*)

Today, as in 1945, Eastern Europe is effectively under the control of the Soviet Union. Future developments in the Eastern European nations must, it seems, take place with the consent of the Soviet Union if they are to have any chance of success. In the absence of assistance from the Western powers the people of Eastern Europe do not have the strength to oppose so determined an adversary as the leadership of the Soviet Communist Party. In Eastern Europe the pace of political change will be determined by that prevailing in the USSR, unless something happens greatly to weaken its power to control the destiny of its 'satellites'.

China

Communists had been in control of areas of China since 1927. From that time until 1949, the Chinese Communists waged an almost constant struggle for survival against either Chinese Nationalists led by Chiang Kai Shek, or Japanese invaders, and sometimes both. The Communist movement originated in the reforming Nationalist Party created after the First World War by Sun Yat Sen. Associated with this movement were such young radicals as Mao Tse Tung, Chou En Lai and Lin Piao, later to become the leaders of Communist China. When their conflict with the forces led by Chiang Kai Shek erupted in Shanghai in 1927, the Communists moved away from the cities into remote provinces where Chiang's forces would have difficulty following them. There, conflict with Chiang abated during the years of their joint campaign against

Chinese adulation of their Communist leaders; here pictures of Hua and the dead Mao Tse Tung are brandished at a mass rally held to confirm and applaud Hua's position as leader. (*Photo: Camera Press, London*)

the Japanese (1936–1945), but was quickly resumed after the defeat of Japan. Despite American efforts to reach a compromise between the groups, fighting continued until the Communists seized full control of the Chinese mainland, forcing Chiang Kai Shek to retreat to the island of Formosa, which remains independent of Communist China to this day.

The victory of the Chinese Communists was seen in the West, and particularly in the United States, as a victory for Soviet-led world Communism. This view was reinforced when the Chinese government signed a 'Treaty of Friendship, Alliance, and Mutual Assistance' with the USSR in February 1950. They seemed to be as firmly under the control of the Russians as were the Communist states of Eastern Europe. During the following decade, relations between the Chinese and Soviet Communist leadership appeared to be as close as ever. It has subsequently become known that relations between the two countries were under considerable strain throughout the period; and by 1960, signs of political tensions that continue to divide the two largest communist states became visible. The reasons for the so-called 'Sino-Soviet split' are manifold and complex, but we may summarize them by using two categories – ideological and diplomatic divisions.

The ideological disagreement between the two countries centred on attitudes towards the world's largest non-Communist powers. Before 1956 it was central to the ideology of the Communist bloc that non-communist states were hostile, and that a war between East and West was both inevitable and desirable. With

America's acquisition of nuclear weapons, this view became more and more difficult to hold as the likely consequences of nuclear war became apparent. As Khruschev came to display the changing attitude towards the West by, for example, his visit to the USA in 1959, so Chinese suspicions of the Soviet Union's willingness to stand by it in an international conflict became stronger. These suspicions were shown to be justified during the two Sino-Indian wars (1959 and 1962), when the Soviet Union stayed neutral or actually supported China's opponent. Another ideological disagreement concerned their respective 'paths to socialism'. Through campaigns such as the Great Leap Forward, the Chinese indicated that they had developed an independent conception of how best to construct socialist society, a conception that threatened to undermine the Soviet Communist party's dominance of the international Communist

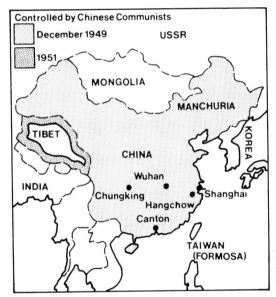

Map 9. China under Communism.
Map 10. China and her neighbours, 1951–79.

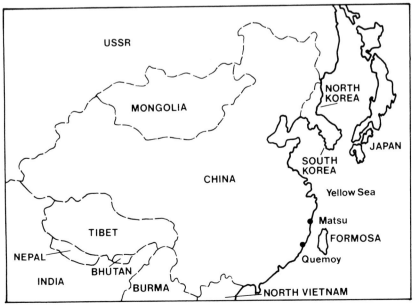

movement. Diplomatic friction between Russia and China was much older than the Communist movements in either of those countries. In the course of several armed conflicts during the nineteenth century, Russia had acquired territories which the Chinese Communists said, and still say, rightfully belong to China. Disputes over these territories reached a climax when fighting broke out between Soviet and Chinese troops on the Sino-Soviet border in 1967. There can be no doubt that this issue was one of the reasons why relations between the two countries deteriorated throughout the years preceding the armed clashes. This issue, like many of the ideological ones, remains unresolved and thus a continuing source of hostility between the two most powerful and populous states governed by Communist parties. Other issues will remain to make any Sino-Soviet détente hard to construct – the apparent racial prejudice felt by many Russians for Chinese people; the heavy concentration of Soviet forces along the Sino-Soviet border, over forty divisions in 1975; and perhaps most important of all, the attitudes of mutual hostility generated by years of sustained propaganda, difficult to reverse even in the most totalitarian of countries. The effect of the Sino-Soviet dispute on the development of Communist government has been to diminish the authority of the leadership offered by the Soviet Union in Eastern Europe, namely Albania and Romania; to provide an alternative focus for pro-Communist sympathizers in the West; and of course to split the solidarity of Communist countries in the face of capitalist nations.

The Non-Ruling Parties

A brief mention of the Communist parties that have sought but failed to gain power is necessary to complete a survey of post-war Communism. Communist parties exist in almost all democratic societies. In Western Europe the Communist Party in France and in Italy has consistently secured substantial electoral support. In France Communists have in the past held ministerial office, while in Italy substantial areas are run by local governments dominated by freely elected Communist officials. It is not inconceivable that both countries will, at some time in the future, be administered by national governments in which the Communists play a significant role. Indeed, both the Italian and the French Communist parties have made considerable efforts to dissociate themselves from some aspects of Communist government in Eastern Europe in order to allay fears that a vote for the Communist Party might be a vote against freedom. In countries like Britain and West Germany, which have a strong national tradition of social democracy, the Communist Party has been almost pathetically unsuccessful in gaining electoral support. In Britain this has led the Communist Party to develop the policy of working for 'a Labour government committed to socialist policies' and to activity within the country's trade union movement. Elsewhere in the world actual Communist parties, or parties committed to Communist programmes of extensive nationalization and single-party government, are strong but not yet in power. A good example is the Indonesian Communist Party which is reputed to enjoy the support of some 35 per cent of voters.

Conclusion

Apart from the developments described above, Communist government has influenced the political development of states that could not accurately be described as Communist. One-party rule is a concept central to the management of politics in Communist states, and is a feature of the government of many of the new, post-colonial states, especially of those which have developed the strongest links with the USSR, such as Algeria, Iraq and Angola. Secondly, the central control of economic development, first fully exerted in Stalin's Russia, has become an accepted path to economic development. While this is not entirely attributable to the Communist example, the success with which both Russia and China have accomplished rapid economic growth has clearly influenced developing countries' style of economic management in a way that Japan's, for example, has not. Lastly, it should be noted that whereas before the start of the Second World War Communism was a little-understood political theory in the West, the post-war period has seen a massive increase in the amount of literature available at all levels about the history of Communism and its contemporary practice.

The End of Empire: Decolonization since 1945

Introduction

The dissolution of the colonial empires is one of the most distinctive features of international politics since the Second World War. Not only did it lead within a short space of time to the creation of many new states, but it also transformed the international role of the older ones, such as Britain, France and Belgium, and influenced the nature of relations between the world's major powers. It was the empires of four nations that provided the substance of decolonization – Britain, France, Belgium and Portugal. Though the individual circumstances vary in which these colonial empires disappeared, certain general causes of the process were common to them all.

Internal Pressure for Independence

The existence of pressure from within colonies had been in evidence since the 1920s. Almost all colonies experienced some economic growth, bringing with it the development of urban societies, and expanding responsibilities for the indigenous peoples. There was also a general increase in the number of people receiving education, though this was more a feature of the British and French Empires than of the Belgian and the Portuguese. The Second World War created its own form of encouragement for independence movements. Many of the colonial powers were cut off from certain of their dependencies, in others they had to share facilities with other nations, which gave the local inhabitants a deeper acquaintance with the outside world. The contribution to the war effort by some of the dependencies was given in exchange for assurances regarding future political reforms or independence. This was so with the British in India, and with the French in West Africa. At the same time the war itself tended to weaken the authority of the colonial powers. Their system of relations seemed to have failed completely, and the feeling of superior ability that coined such phrases as the 'White Man's Burden' or the 'Civilizing Mission' was shared less and less by the young and educated future leaders of the colonial peoples.

External Pressures

All the colonial powers except Portugal had been participants in the Second World War, and the costs of that struggle expressed themselves through weakened economies and loosened control over most colonial possesions. At the same time, the priorities imposed by the need to recover from the war accorded the colonies less and less importance. There had been a reorientation of international power towards the USSR and the USA. Both these powers were anti-colonial as a matter of principle or ideology, and agreements between the Big Three during the war, such as the Atlantic Charter (1942) had referred to a new world order that did not include the old-style colonial relationships. As the Cold War began, the Western European states became more and more preoccupied with European and, later, North African defence. Finally, the moral climate that prevailed after the Second World War was very different from that which preceded it. Notions of the equality of all nations, which were enshrined in the Charter of the United Nations, provided the legitimization of opposition to continued colonial rule, and served to weaken the will to resist among those who wanted to retain colonies but who became aware of the increasing difficulty of doing so.

The Different Empires

Responses to these developments varied between the imperial nations.

Britain opted almost immediately after the war for a policy of gradual but eventually total transfer of power. The question was not whether, but when and in what manner, independence should take place. Considerable momentum was given to the pace of British decolonization by two events – the independence of India in 1947, and the Anglo-French invasion of the Suez Canal zone in Egypt in 1956. India's success demonstrated to many for whom independence was a dream that it could become a reality. An independent India was not just a source of inspiration to others, it also provided diplomatic support, and with its policy of non-alignment with any of the major powers, an alternative friend for the new states that were to follow it. The Suez invasion was important because it revealed a deep insensitivity on the part of the

Egypt, November 1956. The world continued to condemn or support the British and French action in the Canal zone, but these are the facts – what bombardment and air attack have meant to the inhabitants of Port Said and the surrounding area. Here a British soldier helps Egyptians with the rubble in a Port Said street. (*Photo: Radio Times Hulton Library*)

British political leadership towards the nature and hopes of the new national governments in control of the Third World. Though there were to be other sources of friction in other parts of the world, the Suez affair created suspicions and hostility that tended both to poison relations between Britain and its possessions and to bind those countries more closely together against the metropolitan powers. Events such as these disrupted the planned timetable for withdrawal. It had been hoped that independence would follow a considerable increase in education, the transfer of more responsibility in the government and commerce of the territories, and the development of stable political parties which, together, would be able to manage a parliamentary system similar to Britain's. It was expected that this would take considerable time, yet in the years between 1957 and 1964 the colonies now known as Ghana, Nigeria, Tanzania, Uganda, Kenya and Zambia gained their independence from the British Empire, while Rhodesia declared her independence illegally rather than accept independence based upon the same principles as were applied in these other countries. In the same period two important non-African dependencies also gained their independence – Cyprus and Malaysia. In both areas Britain's departure was an unhappy one, with violence characterizing the changing political order.

The aims of British decolonization were threefold and it is against them that its success must be assessed. The new nations were to be friendly, stable and

Independence Celebrations: Dr Nkrumah dances with the Duchess of Kent at a state ball. (*Photo: Information section, the High Commissioner for Ghana*)

democratic in that order of importance. Their friendliness was to be secured by their participation in the British Commonwealth, their stability was to be facilitated by the proper education of the new leaders in politics and government, and their democratic character was to flow from the constitutional arrangements with which the countries began their political life. On the first count, friendliness, decolonization has been moderately successful. Though Britain has often stood on the opposite side to many of her ex-dependencies at the United Nations, and though the issue of British policy in southern Africa has not been as hostile to the governments of South Africa and Rhodesia as many of the Commonwealth African states would like, relations have rarely been severed altogether – disagreements have been accepted as part of the consequences of the unusual 'special relationship' between Britain and her ex-possessions, and not a reason for ending it. The aim of stability has not been so satisfactorily achieved. In most of the countries formerly under colonial control, violence has characterized political conflict at some time during their brief history as independent states. In Nigeria and Pakistan civil war has killed many, in several African republics the government has changed hands as a result of military intervention, and in Cyprus the conflict between Greek and Turkish communities that raged during the struggle for independence still prevents life on that troubled island from enjoying the promise of long-term stability. It follows from what has been said about the stability of ex-colonies that the hopes held out for the spread of democracy have not been justified by events. In many of the countries political immaturity allied to unusually deep divisions within the nations produced tensions that economic deprivation has emphasized, making the political climate uncongenial for the forms of government that has evolved slowly over the centuries in Britain.

France's defeat at the hands of the Germans in 1940 constituted an enormous blow to her prestige in her colonial possessions from which she never fully recovered. Her attempts to do so can be associated with major political disasters – the collapse of the fourth Republic, and the beginning of American involvement in Vietnam, formerly French Indo-China. These attempts began in 1944 with the Brazzaville Declaration concerning future relations between France and her African dependencies. This created a French Union in which France was to have overall responsibility for the territories, but in which certain administrative tasks and minor policy decisions would be devolved to local officials. In 1958 these responsibilities were more clearly defined in the new constitution of that year. A 'French Community' was created in which the overseas territories were granted full internal self-government while France retained responsibility for defence, foreign policy and general economic planning. Only one country, Guinea, voted against this constitution and opted for independence, probably encouraged by the nearby example of Ghana. But this one dissenting voice was enough to make the other African dependencies think again. Despite the fact that Guinea was penalized by the withdrawal of French technical and economic aid, twelve new African states emerged out of the French African empire. In the Middle East, France retreated gracefully in some cases and under extreme duress in others. It granted independence to the Lebanon in 1946 without more than persuasion from the British. But independence for Morocco (March 1956) and Tunisia (also March 1956) followed intense and sometimes violent resistance to French rule from the nationalist opposition within both countries. But it was in Algeria that French decolonization experienced its most painful phase. Algeria was actually a part of metropolitan France, not a colony, and was regarded by many as a part of France like any area of the mainland. But the Algerian National Liberation Front, supported with finance and weapons by the USSR and China, waged a long guerrilla struggle. Independence came on 3 July 1962, but only after the fiercest opposition of the French inhabitants of the region and their supporters at home. Almost as disruptive for French colonial policy was the struggle waged to regain control of her Indo-Chinese possessions. Despite the fact that France had lost control of the region to the Japanese during the Second World War, the French were determined to reassert themselves. In doing so they faced the opposition of organized political groups in Vietnam, Laos and Cambodia, all of which had declared their independence with the encouragement of the Japanese in 1945. In 1946, the revolutionary leader Ho Chi Minh broke off negotiations with the French and began the guerrilla war that was to continue unabated for almost thirty years. The French received co-operation from a regime led by Emperor Bao Dai, who signed an agreement which granted Vietnam partial independence within the French Union, a measure that was also accepted by governments in Cambodia and Laos. But by that time the indigenous leaders of the three countries were irreconcilably split, and no agreement on anything less than absolute independence would be acceptable to all political groups. In 1950 President Truman announced that the USA was send-

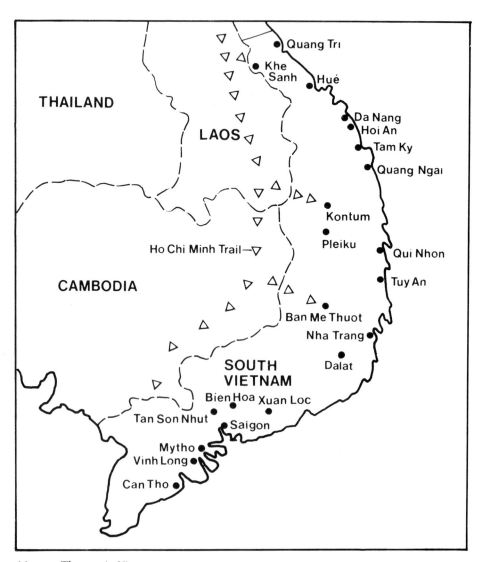

Map 11. The war in Vietnam.

ing economic and military aid to the French; though this increased in volume it failed to secure the defeat of the guerrilla forces, and thus began the long and eventually disastrous American involvement in the political struggle. At the Geneva Conferences of 1954, after the disastrous blow suffered by France at the battle of Dien Bien Phu, the French accepted the independence of the region; henceforth it was the USA that was to be the principal external power engaged in Indo-China.

Belgium and Portugal were even less prepared to decolonize than either Britain or France. Their departure from Africa (which is where most of their possessions were) was correspondingly even more tumultuous. Belgium's most significant possession was the Belgian Congo, now renamed Zaire; and its departure led directly to the first of the two major civil wars in a large African country. When the inevitability of decolonization became apparent with the independence of French and British African possessions, the Belgian government decided to grant independence to the Congo without further delay. But since they had excluded native Congolese from participation in the country and done little to prepare them for the task of governing a large, complex society it was not surprising that, within a month of independence being granted, law and order in the various regions broke down completely. In July the district of Katanga seceded from the country taking with it a third of the country's population and most of its wealth. Fighting continued between Katangan and Congolese forces for two years, until December 1962 when Katanga was reunified with the Congo.

The independence of Portuguese African territories did not come to pass until 1975. The cost in terms of men, money and international isolation led to a military coup d'état in Portugal itself in April 1974. The aim of those who effected the coup was the rapid withdrawal of Portuguese forces from Angola and Mozambique, and the transfer of power from the Portuguese authorities to local administration. The long years of opposition to Portugal had given rise to organizations such as Frelimo in Mozambique, which provided a nucleus for the new government. In Angola three factions, UNITA, the MPLA and the FNLA fought to control the country. With the assistance of 13,000 Cuban troops it was the MPLA which took over full control of the country in early 1976.

Conflict in the Middle East

Since 1945, the Middle East has been the scene of perhaps the most dramatic military and political upheavals that have taken place anywhere in the world. To understand these complex conflicts, it is necessary to look backwards in time to the 1914–18 war. Prior to 1914, the countries of the Middle East formed part of the ailing Ottoman Empire. During the First World War, and with the encouragement of the British army officer, T. E. Lawrence or 'Lawrence of Arabia', who was an architect of the Arab rebellion, the Arabs were helped to throw off the Turkish yoke. The result was the Arab rebellion and the collapse of the Ottoman Empire. After 1918 much of the Middle East came under British or French influence: the British were given mandates under the League of Nations over Palestine, Jordan and Iraq and the French were given Syria. To these basic facts of history have been added two major new dimensions – the rise of Arab nationalism and the creation of the independent state of Israel.

The single most important event in the history of Zionist aspirations to create an independent homeland in Palestine is the Balfour Declaration, the promise given in 1917 by the British Prime Minister to the Zionist leader, Chaim Weizmann, of a home for Jews in Palestine. There had been pogroms in central Europe before the outbreak of the First World War, and throughout its course the position of Jews on the Continent had certainly not improved. Most lived poverty-stricken lives in ghettos. Zionists faced with increasing anti-semitism began lobbying for the creation of a single Jewish homeland at the end of the nineteenth century. Although they had considered Uganda, the focus soon moved to Palestine. Theodore Herzl, founder of the World Zionist Organization, negotiated, although unsuccessfully, with the Ottoman Government to obtain a charter for the region before the First World War.

The Balfour Declaration of 1917 slightly conflicted with the British mandate over Palestine which had also of course to be concerned with Arab interests, but the British did their best to try to resolve both Jewish and Arab wishes. Jews were admitted into Palestine. In 1919 the country had been populated almost entirely by Arabs; now Jews were allowed to settle in limited annual quotas. Arab revolts in 1921 and 1929 were put down by British troops stationed in Palestine to keep order. In the former, anti-Jewish violence on a significant scale was first manifested in Arab rioting which produced sporadic bloodshed. In the latter things became more serious – 250 Jews and Arabs were killed and over 500 wounded. Clearly as the number of Jews in Palestine increased annually, so the tension was rising between the two groups. The Hope-Simpson and the Passfield Reports of 1930 both recommended the suspension of Jewish immigration, but neither were implemented in the face of Zionist opposition. With the rise of Nazism in Germany and its spread throughout Europe as Hitler's powers grew, there was clearly a case for allowing Jews to escape from the persecution prevalent on the Continent. Illegal immigration now increased and the flow of Jews into Palestine in the 1930s grew and grew. The worst outbreak of trouble occurred in 1936. The Arabs still had not secured national independence and had been further angered by the increased numbers of Jews arriving in what they considered to be their homeland. A rebellion broke out which took British armed forces three years to quell. The Peel Commission was set up to study the situation. It suggested in its report of 1937 that partition was the only answer. However, nothing was done, except the introduction of restrictions on immigration in 1939.

The failure of the Arab revolt over these three years created the conditions for the ultimate success of the Jewish cause. When war broke out in September

1939, the British were clearly at pains to settle the issue at least temporarily so that they could concentrate their efforts on defeating Germany. The Jews took advantage of Britain's pre-occupation to mobilize a force of 20,000 men (known as the Haganah) and to press for the setting up of an independent Jewish state. From 1939 onwards this official Jewish military organization struck at the British with acts of sabotage and terrorism. During the war more Jews arrived in Palestine, at a time when the Arab leaders of a vast anti-British conspiracy being plotted in Iraq, under one of their chief religious leaders the Grand Mufti of Jerusalem, were informing the Germans of their desire to settle the Jewish question in Palestine in accordance with the Arabs' national and racial interests. Britain tended to ally itself with the Arabs, while the United States (with its huge Jewish population, especially in New York) was increasingly pro-Zionist.

The end of the war in 1945 meant that the major powers were now free to turn their attention more fully to Middle East questions. In a sense the Arab countries there have never allowed them to turn away since. It was now clear to the Western Powers that the Jews had suffered terribly at the hands of the Germans during the war and that they needed a new homeland. Palestine was really the only candidate. Britain considered that the solution was to partition the country. The riots of the interwar years had shown that a bi-national state was impracticable. The Jews were vastly outnumbered in 1946. The Haganah consisted of only 20,000 men and 4 tanks, while the Arabs had 90,000 infantry and 200 tanks.

Britain decided it could not solve the question alone and in 1947 turned the matter over to the United Nations, which came up with a plan for partition and an international force based at Jerusalem. This proved unacceptable to the Palestine Arabs and neighbouring Arab states and war broke out between them and the Jews in 1948.

By this time, of course, many Arab states had achieved either complete or partial independence. Jordan had become free from British control in 1946. The Amir Abdullah now ruled the country, though with British and later American support. Iraq had been fully independent for some years, though the British also maintained some of their old influence. Egypt had been granted formal independence at the end of the Second World War, but was not autonomous in practice. Again Britain retained considerable influence and stationed several thousand troops there. The system of government was that of a constitutional monarchy, but the exercise of power was the product of a three-sided tug of war in which the King, the Wafd (the leading political party) and the British were the major contenders. The underlying conflicts of Egyptian society began to erupt into violence with increasing frequency, while a growing inflation rate caused additional insecurity and hardship for the poor. The Moslem Brethren, the Islamic revival movement with political and nationalist ambitions, had made inroads into the Wafd's support and was then at the height of its powers. Clashes between the Brethren and the Government grew more frequent and violent, until 1948 when the government was forced to outlaw and dissolve the organization.

In Saudi Arabia independence had been secured by 1945 and the country was ruled by King Abd al-Aziz Ibn Saud. He had formed close ties with the United States through the war. Libya had been an Italian colony, but in 1942 had been liberated by the British and French who now occupied the country. Morocco, Tunisia and Algeria were all French colonies and continued to be administered as such, though they all had growing nationalist movements. In 1947 Algerian nationalists formed an underground terrorist group later to become the National Liberation Front (FNL).

Meanwhile the fighting between the Arabs and the Jews had intensified. Egypt was involved as was Jordan. But the characteristic disunity amongst the Arabs that was to recur in later wars against the Israelis was already in evidence. Arab armies were relatively successful in the first period of the fighting, but their lack of co-ordination enabled the Jews to hold out. A short cease-fire was imposed by the United Nations. Then the Israelis attacked and took parts of Jordan. Egypt was then attacked and beaten, an armistice being arranged in January 1949. The borders were then established where the fighting had stopped. Israel had been created and was an independent state.

Israel was now far bigger than any UN plan had allowed for and there was no homeland for the Palestinian Arabs. The remaining lands were divided between Egypt and Jordan. Jordan acquired a large Palestinian population, including refugees which it proved difficult to integrate. Egypt which had taken the Gaza strip, established there a Palestinian government, laying claim to the whole of Palestine. Egypt then imposed a blockade on Israeli shipping in the Gulf of Aqaba and closed the Suez Canal, thereby denying the Israelis access to many markets. Israel ignored the UN's order that Palestinian Arabs should be allowed to return peacefully to their homelands.

The Arab refusal to accept Israel's existence as a Jewish state was heightened by the arrival of General Abdel Nasser as ruler of Egypt in July 1952, as the result of a military coup. He became a catalyst for pan-Arabism (the term used to signify greater political union between Arab States). Egypt turned more and more towards the Eastern block. Until July 1955 Egypt's armed forces were equipped with British armaments, but now Nasser ordered Stalin tanks, MIG fighters, and Czech rifles. Sums of over £12 million and perhaps as much as £30 million were involved in the procuring of new equipment. In October 1955 a joint Syrian–Egyptian military command was established and five months later King Hussein dismissed General John Glubb (Glubb Pasha, as he was known) as commander-in-chief of Jordan's armies.

Supplies of arms to the two sides continued apace, with Israel receiving extensive supplies from France, among others. On 26 July 1956 Nasser nationalized the Suez Canal Company. Britain stopped all sales of armaments to the Egyptians and Eden as Prime Minister called up 20,000 army reservists. Reinforcements were sent to the Mediterranean ready to mount an attack on the Canal Zone. Though the Egyptians were clearly in the majority and possessed quite a lot of modern hardware, her troops were not as well trained as the British. Joining forces with the French, assisted by an Israeli paratroop drop in Sinai, an attack was mounted on 29 October 1956. However, as a result of pressure from the United Nations and world opinion, Britain and France were forced to withdraw their forces and in their place a UN Emergency

Force under General Burns was built up. The Israelis withdraw from their positions captured in Sinai. British and French citizens were also obliged to leave the area, though of course the Suez Canal remained closed.

From 1956 to 1966 there was an uneasy peace in the Middle East. On 14 July 1958 a Russian-backed revolution occurred in Iraq and the King and his Prime Minister were murdered. On the following day US Marines were air lifted to Lebanon, and shortly after this British paratroopers were landed in Jordan. Egypt, though continuing to criticize Israel vehemently, actually adopted a passive policy in order to be able to slowly build up her military strength. The main conflicts during this decade were in the Yemen and then in Aden. A civil war broke out in the latter between various nationalist groups while Britain acted as a peace-keeping body. Eventually independence was granted to Aden in November 1967 and British forces withdrew. While this was going on there had been a gradual escalation in the main conflict between the Arabs and the Jews. National service in Israel had been increased from twenty-six to thirty months. Egypt intensified its terrorist activities against Israel and concluded a defence agreement with Syria. Israel took punitive action and on 13 November 1967 a large force with tanks and armoured cars rolled over the Jordan border and attacked Samu, a large village. An air battle followed against the Syrians who had been bombarding Israeli farm-workers in the de-militarized zone near Galilee. Still raids continued by Syrians and the El Fatah organization. Nasser was drawn into the conflict as the Syrians appealed to him for assistance. He ordered the UN peace-keeping force to withdraw, which they did without complaint. A defence pact was signed with Jordan and the stage was set for the Six Day War.

Israel decided on a pre-emptive strike. An air attack was launched on 5 June at 7.45 a.m., thereby beating the Egyptians' starting time. Israeli tanks and motorized infantry were also on the move to engage the enemy. The Israelis were vastly outnumbered by the Arab forces facing them – the Egyptian forces alone were larger. It proved to be a lightning mechanized war. In four days the Israelis had broken Egypt's Sinai Army of 100,000 men, thousands of vehicles were taken and several hundred Russian tanks destroyed. In the battle for the Golan Heights, against the Syrians, 1,000 attackers were killed and a further 5,000 were taken prisoner by Israeli forces. In total 390,000 regular Arab troops had been engaged against Israel together with 1,800 tanks, while there had been a mere 264,000 in Israel's army (mostly reservists) and only 800 tanks. Israel had confirmed her independence and indeed had now succeeded in extending her borders.

The period from 1967 till the Yom Kippur War of 1973 was another time of uneasy peace, with the United States and Russia continuing to back their respective sides. Terrorism continued and even spread to European countries themselves. Hijackings, bombings and random attacks became increasingly common. By 1973 Nasser had died and Anwar Sadat had taken over as Egypt's leader. Public opinion was mounting in the Arab states, revenge and the re-capture of territory was demanded and so Sadat agreed to another offensive. Again the Arabs had the larger forces and this time the advantage of surprise. On 6 October 1973 specially trained Egyptian forces crossed the Suez

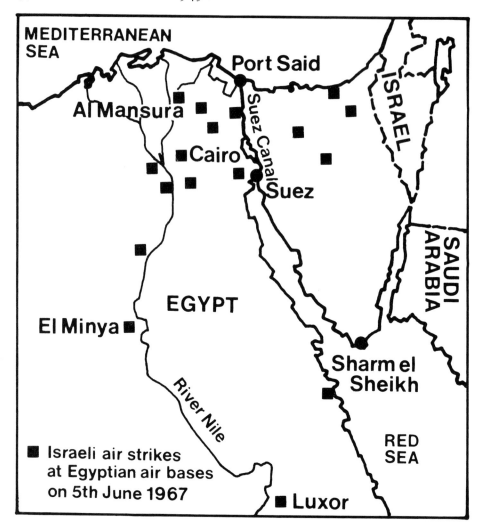

Map 12. The Arab–Israeli War, 1967.

Canal and attacked the Bar Lev defensive line. Air and missile strikes followed and the Egyptians penetrated Sinai. However, the Egyptians were slow in seizing the vital passes into central Sinai and allowed the Israelis time to regroup and prepare a counter-attack. On the northern front the Syrians had again attacked in Golan. Since their forces were weakest here, the Israelis decided to fight the Syrians first. They yielded ground slowly and then halted their forces, driving the enemy back with the aid of reinforcements and air power. This time the Syrians held on and the front stabilized. Then the Israelis counter-attacked in the south and proceeded to inflict a massive defeat on Egyptian tanks. Paratroops landed on the other side of the Canal and divided the Egyptian Second and Third Armies. A cease-fire was rapidly negotiated by the Egyptians just as the Israelis were on the brink of another military victory. There had been the threat of actual involvement of Russian troops in the area, countered by an American nuclear alert. Though Israel had clearly won this war, she had lost a large number of trained pilots and some tank commanders as a result of the extensive Egyptian use of ground-to-air missiles. Air supremacy was now shown to be vulnerable to surface air missiles.

Terrorism really had its origins in the Middle East crisis. It was used by the Popular Front Palestinian movement to try to secure parts of Palestine now occupied by Israel for the large number of former Arab inhabitants settled throughout the Middle East. In July 1968 this group made its first attack on an El Al aeroplane and forced it to fly to Algiers rather than its destination of Rome. There the hijackers demanded the release of the 1,200 Palestinian guerillas held in Israel. Other PFLP attacks on El Al aircraft took place in 1968 and 1969 and were then extended to the airlines of other countries. The security forces, however, had some success and by 1970 several Palestinian guerillas had been captured. In September as many as five airliners were attacked by PFLP groups and although one failed and Leila Kaled was taken prisoner, a second hijacking secured her release. One aircraft was blown up in Cairo; others, one carrying 500 hostages were flown to Dawson's Field in Jordan. Seven terrorists were released in exchange for the passengers and the planes were blown up.

Following King Hussein's attack on the Palestinian movement in Jordan in September 1970, even more extreme groups were formed, including the Black September Organization. They carried out hijackings at Aden and Tel Aviv. A climax to this violence occurred in September 1972 when members of this group massacred eleven Israeli athletes at the Munich Olympic village.

While Israel remains a possible protagonist in a further Middle East war, the Lebanon has been the scene of a prolonged civil war. The fighting has essentially been between left-wing Moslem groups and right-wing Christians who were trying to maintain their economic and political ascendancy; the war has been concentrated in the capital Beirut. It began in September 1975 and has continued in a desultory fashion ever since. Israel warned that she would not tolerate the invasion of Syrian troops at the invitation of the Moslems, and a cease-fire was arranged temporarily in 1976, with Syrian troops occupying limited areas along the Lebanese border. Despite a series of truces the fighting has gone on and in one year as many as 15,000 were killed. As yet there seems no solution to this problem.

The whole future course of the Middle East will largely depend on the peace initiative launched by Egypt's President Sadat in November 1977 and taken up by Israel's Premier, Menachem Begin. At the historic Camp David Summit Meeting in America in 1978, the main elements of a peace treaty between Egypt and Israel were assembled. But whether a wider peace between all the Arab states and Israel can be worked out remains an unanswered question.

The Arms Race

The post-war period has witnessed the renewal of two developments that have characterized Great Power relations since before the First World War – an arms-building race between the major hostile alliances and nations, and renewed attempts to construct international agreements to limit the number and type of new weapons. Some of these agreements have concerned the testing and development of new weapons, others have prohibited altogether certain types of weapons, and still others have concerned the imposition of final limits to the volume of weapons of almost all types. Agreements have also been signed which are designed to prevent the spread of the arms race to new areas of the world – so-called non-proliferation treaties. All of these agreements will be examined in some detail below. Before doing so, let us examine some general aspects of military development since the Second World War.

Firstly, the volume of armaments in existence has increased dramatically. Not only have the superpowers and their allies engaged in a process of arms-hoarding unparalleled in history; the states that have come into existence have all acquired some form of military establishment. In certain areas of persistent conflict, for example the Middle East, the Indian subcontinent and Indo-China, the volume of armaments has increased drastically. The reasons for militarization vary. In some cases prestige has been associated with armaments which have not been justified by political conflict. In others, the expansion of the armed forces has occurred because of the political importance of the military. In others the dominant cause has been the existence of local and international conflict over territory or ideology. It is hardly surprising therefore that the military have come to play an increasingly prominent role in the politics of developing countries. The expansion of armaments in these areas has been facilitated by the willingness with which the arms-manufacturing countries such as the USA, France and Britain have exported weapons. They do so for the economic benefit of expanded trade, and for the increased political influence that the supply of arms is thought to confer. Only nuclear weapons have not been available for purchase, and even these have been developed by some smaller powers such as India as a result of the export of nuclear reactors designed for peaceful purposes. It is difficult not to conclude that the increase in armaments in these countries has of itself increased tensions and therefore the likelihood of war amongst developing nations. This contrasts with the overall effect of the massive rearmament of the superpowers which has been designed primarily to deter war by making its consequences so severe that no limited policy goals such as the acquisition of new territory, or the change of a government allied to one or other of the powers, could justify them. The power of the nuclear deterrent has been illustrated on several separate occasions during the past twenty-five years. In Korea, it was probably the threatened use of nuclear weapons (by the USA) that brought the war to a halt. During the Suez crisis of 1956, the apparent preparedness of the USSR to support Egypt with nuclear power had a strong influence on the Anglo-French decision to withdraw.

The 1962 Cuban missile crisis was probably the closest that the superpowers have come to a nuclear war – once again the threatened use of nuclear retaliation was responsible for forcing the Soviet Union to withdraw her nuclear missiles from Cuba. But though nuclear weapons have never been used except against Japan at the end of the Second World War, and have in practice been a stabilizing influence in certain crises, the possibility that they might one day be used through misunderstanding, and the probability that the existence of nuclear weapons has caused rivalries and mistrust that create tensions of their own, provides strong incentives for those who possess nuclear weapons in large quantities to come to agreements limiting their numbers, and increasing consultation in crisis situations that might lead to their use.

There are further factors that create a common interest in the otherwise hostile superpower relations. The proliferation of nuclear weapons threatens them both. In other words, it is in their interest to preserve their joint monopoly of nuclear weapons. In addition to their military security, the spread of nuclear weapons within their own arsenals has been undertaken at immense economic cost. This consideration is compelling for both the USSR and the USA. The former has a 'controlled' economy which lessens the importance of public opinion and its attitude towards massive defence expenditure. But the continual postponement of improvements in the ordinary Russian's standard of living is closely related to the size of the Soviet defence budget, and even in Russia, continued stagnation in living standards could have serious political repercussions. In the USA, a much richer country than the USSR, the political sensitivity of economic policy is much more influential than in the USSR. Therefore, though there are big differences in their economic ability to finance a continued arms race, the difference in their political systems narrows the economic advantage enjoyed by the USA.

Progress on the control of nuclear weapons did not really begin until after the Cuban missile crisis of 1962. Though this is partly coincidence it seems likely that the closeness with which the world approached nuclear war during the fortnight of crisis persuaded both of the superpowers to confer on the question of increasing communication between them and controlling the growth of weapons. An agreement was reached on the establishment of a direct communication link – the so-called 'hot line' between the Soviet leaders and the American President. This has enabled the two leaders to communicate directly in urgent situations; the mechanism has frequently been put to use and in September 1971 an agreement improving the hot line was signed in Moscow.

The story of the attempt to reach agreements on the control of arms between the superpowers is a continuing one, and one whose relative lack of success is closely related to the political differences between them and to the history of the discovery and development of nuclear weapons. From 1943 until 1946 America and Britain shared information on the secret development of nuclear weapons. The collaboration was ended by the United States Atomic Energy Act of 1946. This legislation was designed to prevent the spread of atomic weaponry, and efforts were also made in the United Nations to secure international control and inspection over the manufacture of atomic energy. These efforts were undermined by the Soviet Union which was determined to develop her own nuclear capacity. To her leaders, America's desire to possess weapons but deny them to others must have seemed an attitude of barely concealed hostility. In 1949 the USSR exploded its first nuclear device and at some time during the early 1950s – exactly when is not clear – it made a usable nuclear bomb. Others followed suit. In 1957 Anglo-American collaboration over nuclear matters was resumed with President Eisenhower agreeing in principle to provide Britain with missiles for its nuclear warheads. In 1960, France, which was excluded by Britain and the USA from a share in nuclear weapon techno-logy, succeeded in manufacturing a bomb of her own. In 1962, America and Britain concluded the Nassau Agreement, by which American Polaris missiles would be placed in British-built submarines. This agreement enabled Britain to participate in the first superpower agreement on nuclear weapons, even though Britain was not strictly speaking a superpower.

The Limited Nuclear Test Ban Treaty of August 1963 banned all nuclear testing in the atmosphere and elsewhere except underground. It is doubtful, however, whether this treaty did anything to hinder the continued development of nuclear weapons. It did succeed in alienating the smaller nuclear powers who were not invited to participate in the agreement – France, and China who exploded her first nuclear device in October 1964 – and who persist in atmo-spheric testing to this day. The next superpower agreement concerned a treaty on principles governing the activities 'of States' in the exploration and use of 'outer space including the moon and other celestial bodies'. Once again this agreement was confined to the superpowers and Britain, and once again the arms control value of the agreement has been strictly limited. A similar treaty concerning the positioning of nuclear weapons on the ocean bed was signed between the USA and the USSR in 1970, as was another prohibiting nuclear explosions in Antarctica in 1959. The treaty which best demonstrates the limited common interests of the superpowers in nuclear matters was signed by them both in 1968. The 'Treaty on the non-proliferation of nuclear weapons' took several years to negotiate. It was designed to prevent the spread of nuclear weapons to other states. But France and China have refused to sign it, and by 1972 only seventy-one nations had ratified it; once again it cannot be regarded as a success. Perhaps the most comprehensive and ambitious attempt to control nuclear weapons is the series of Strategic Arms Limitation Talks, which began in 1969 and are still being held. These talks led directly to the major achievement of arms control discussions since the war – that both sides accepted the principle of having their nuclear installations inspected by satellite reconnaissance. In addition to this form of inspection, an agreement allowing specialists to examine the site of the other side's nuclear tests was signed in April 1976. Other agreements such as the Treaty on the Limitation of Anti ball-istic-Missile Systems of May 1972 established future ceilings for the number of defensive nuclear missiles permitted to each power. Since the talks continue, the agreements so far achieved cannot be properly judged. At present the treaties can best be seen as limited declarations of faith in the outcome of the new round of negotiations, often refered to as 'SALT 2', which may lead to a comprehensive treaty covering all aspects of nuclear armaments.

The Nation State since 1945

Many of the changes that have occurred since the war have affected not only the character of relations between certain states, their friendliness towards one another, their relative strengths, the nature of their disagreements and so forth, but also the very status of the nation state as an agent of international politics. Though the world is still best divisible into nations or states, several developments have reduced the power of individual states and increased the authority of supranational or non-state organizations.

Federalism

Federation of states is not a new concept. It was a recognized form of political organization at the time of the creation of the United States of America 200 years ago. But before the Second World War federation had been one of many internal systems adopted by what we loosely call nation states. This often entailed the reorganization of a country's political structure, but it seldom meant what it has come to mean since 1945 – the amalgamation of separate states into larger political groupings. The three areas in which such federations or amalgamations have been or are being attempted are Africa, Western Europe and the Arab Middle East.

Africa

The decolonization of Africa was in a way the triumph of old-style nationalism. From a group of colonial empires founded and developed mostly during the nineteenth century emerged a large group of modern states with defined boundaries, and central governments for the most part in full control of the states' recognized territory. But the boundaries were based on the rather arbitrary division of territory into effective administrative units during the colonial era, which often produced tribal or ethnic clashes, and did not ensure the economic unity of the new countries. These considerations, and the feeling that separate African states would always be too weak to acquire a strong voice in international affairs led Kwame Nkrumah, first President of Ghana, to propose pan-Africanism – the federation of as many as possible of the African states. These proposals were debated in the early 1960s with interest but no great conviction. Too many local obstacles stood between a general acceptance of the principle and its practical application. In place of pan-African federation, co-operation and co-ordination of policy in Africa has been fostered by a regional organization established in May 1963, called the Organization of African Unity. All the African states excepting South Africa and Rhodesia belong to the organization, which has become the effective voice of Africa in world affairs. The organization demonstrates the need amongst smaller states for collective policy-making in order to express opinions with sufficient weight to make them generally heard. In these matters, traditional diplomacy between individual countries has been replaced by collective, regional negotiation.

Europe

For somewhat different reasons this development is also visible in Western Europe. The development of Western Europe institutions was closely concerned with the past history of the continent. The pilot institution of the Common Market, or European Economic Community, was established not only to secure more efficiency in the production of steel and coal, but according to the then French Foreign Minister, Robert Schumann, to 'change the destiny of regions that have long been devoted to the production of war armaments of which they have themselves been the constant victims'. The Treaty of Rome, signed by France, West Germany, Italy, the Netherlands, Belgium and Luxembourg on 25 March 1957, established the Common Market and envisaged the creation of a common European parliament, and full co-operation between the member nations on a range of issues including agriculture, economics, finance and foreign policy. In January 1972 Britain, Denmark and Ireland signed a treaty of accession to the Common Market that made those countries full members, increasing the total number to nine. Over the two decades since it came into existence, the EEC has seen a trend towards the harmonization of its members' policies on foreign affairs, economics and trade. It has also been responsible for the creation and strengthening of institutions such as the European parliament, which might one day perform several of the functions now the responsibility of national parliaments. Exactly how far and how fast these developments continue will depend on factors too unstable to predict. One can at this stage note that the continuation of European integration is proceeding at a cautious rate, but at the same time those who most strongly oppose European federation are becoming less influential.

The Middle East

The third major post-war experiment in international federation took place in the Middle East and was the least successful of them all. In 1958 a merger was arranged between the states of Egypt and Syria, to form the United Arab Republic. This experiment was designed to create the nucleus of an Arab nation that would eventually comprise all the Arab territories in the area. Its failure was caused by local rivalries about religion and ideology, and strong disagreements as to the proper distribution of power within any such federation. Subsequent attempts to revive the spirit of pan-Arabism have been equally unsuccessful, but this does not mean that interest in such a political realignment will not continue.

All these experiments with their differing causes and degrees of success have in common the recognition that a far higher degree of international co-operation is necessary for the successful execution of ever more complex and interrelated policies. This level of interdependence is continuing to rise, and with it the need for international co-ordination which will inevitably sustain interest in the merger of separate states.

Though regional federation or transnationalism has been a significant factor in the transformation of the role of the state in international politics, it has not been the only one. The United Nations, though by no means an attempt to diminish the importance of the state, has served as an occasion for the construction of interstate political alignment, not as in the past on very specific matters, but on general issues. The term the 'Third World' came into use at a conference of non-aligned nations in 1955, but it has been reinforced by the persistent alignment of new and poor nations in the debates of the General Assembly of the UN.

A more specific but no less interesting form of international co-operation has been seen in the growth of organizations of states with common economic interests. In Europe the EEC, the European Free Trade Association (EFTA) and the North Atlantic countries that participate in the General Agreement on Tariffs and Trade (GATT) set the pattern for other groups. Among these, the Organization of Petroleum Exporting Countries (OPEC) has had a dramatic effect on the international standing of its members, particularly after they forced oil-consuming nations to accept a fivefold increase in the price of their most important source of energy, following the war between Israel and the Arab states of Egypt, Syria, Iraq and Jordan of October–November 1973. Other groupings such as the Andean Pact of western South American states have come into existence to promote economic co-operation between their members, and to enhance their collective strength in relation to the outside world. One may safely predict that the number and influence of such organizations will increase in the future, and that as a result of doing so diplomacy will gradually change from being a dialogue between individual states into a dialogue between types of states at many different levels of activity.

Since 1945 the term 'devolution' has become important in the vocabulary of contemporary politics. It means the distribution of power away from the centre of a political unit to its regions. This phenomenon is, in some ways, similar to the demands for independence in the European empires made by nationalists in the nineteenth and early twentieth centuries, since both are largely a product of dissatisfaction with remote and insensitive central governments. The difference is that these earlier demands were for total independence, but devolutionists want to transform the internal political structure of the state by redistributing power within it. In Britain the discussion of devolution has centred upon the government of Wales, Scotland and Northern Ireland. Those who want devolution demand that certain local areas be given responsibility over certain matters presently under the control of central government. In France, Belgium, Spain and Italy similar debates based on similar arguments are taking place. It is clear that in all of these countries in varying degrees the central governments will soon relinquish to local bodies certain of their responsibilities. Thus as well as being changed by external co-operation between governments, the state is being changed in some areas by internal pressure for internal change. It seems likely that central governments will be less able than in the past to act on behalf of their nations without more extensive consultation between more numerous representative bodies. This in turn will make the process of constructing foreign policy even more sensitive to domestic politics than has been the case in the past, and is yet another factor contributing to the increasing complexity of the modern international system.

Perhaps the most direct and dramatic challenge with which the modern state has been confronted has come from terrorism. Though by no means a new activity, the use of violence for political ends has become wider in scope and tactically more effective since the war than at any time before. There are two reasons for this. Firstly, the nature of modern life has been more conducive to terrorists than to those opposing them. The vast amount of information now reaching ordinary people through the press, radio and television has provided terrorists in 'open' societies – ie those which do not practice censorship – with an easy method of publicizing their cause, and communicating with people with whom they need to negotiate. Secondly, the availability of modern weapons and the vulnerability of ordinary people to them has provided terrorists with a much larger number of useful and accessible victims than have been available in the past. One terrorist with one hand grenade can do millions of pounds' worth of damage, and kill hundreds of people in front of an audience of tens of millions. In itself this change in the strategic ability of the individual terrorist does not threaten the power of states. But when that strategic power translates into political power, when the use of untraditional terrorist power is effective in securing traditional political goals, then a new factor enters the traditional relationships between states. Examples of this are abundant. In 1975, for the first time, the leader of the Palestinian Liberation Organization was invited to address the United Nations on the Middle Eastern question. The PLO does not control a recognized territory, nor therefore does it represent

The child soldiers of the Palestinian refugee camps; trained from the age of seven on, boys and girls will be trained front-line soldiers when they reach fifteen. (*Photo: Ron McKay, Camera Press, London*)

in the traditional sense a recognizable population. Its influence, and therefore its presence at the United Nations, derived from its ability to wield force, which it had done through hijacking, attacks on villages, and engagement with the Israeli and Jordanian armies. It was speaking as a state, *to* states, but without the characteristics of a state. It has diplomatic representatives with many governments and organizations, and its leaders are regarded by many governments as diplomatically immune from prosecution, as are the recognized diplomats of conventional states. Other terrorist organizations, such as the Irish Republican Army, have been able to exact either recognition from official governments who negotiate with them directly, or political influence through political figures who advocate their cause in national parliaments or international organizations.

Developments such as these are of great importance for the future. Yet the nature of international politics, being increasingly complex, becomes increasingly difficult to anticipate. So far as one can see, terrorism will continue while the existing international system fails to provide either the flexibility in which the conflicting and often extreme political views of terrorist groups can be accommodated, or effective combined action against those who usurp the role of representation, traditionally the province of the territorial or national state. All the signs are that anti-terrorist co-operation is diminishing rather than increasing. It is probable therefore that the future of terrorism as a political phenomenon will be determined by the development of new institutions in the international arena, and the sorts of policies that they produce.

The Principles of Economics

These political trends in post-war politics which we have been examining must also be seen in the context of the world economic system in which we work. Economics is a subject many people find difficult to comprehend – partly, no doubt, because of not being certain what 'economics' is defined as.

Defining Economics

Most famous economists, like Adam Smith, Karl Marx, Alfred Marshall and John Maynard Keynes have offered definitions of what economics studies and why it is important to us. The kind of definition that these economists, and most others, offer is fairly clear. Economics examines how man attempts to satisfy his material needs by putting to use the limited supply of natural resources in the world.

Economics, therefore, covers many different activities – the operations of production, distribution and consumption of goods and services, and the institutions (like the government) whose objective it is to see through these operations. Now, because of the limit nature imposes on the resources available to man, economics is constantly concerned with the problem of choice. In short, we see how the individual may get as much satisfaction as possible when he is forced to choose between, say, going to the pub, and spending his limited income at the cinema. But not only does the economist analyse man's behaviour when subject to the constraints of nature and institutional intervention (eg the government's taxes), he also examines the consequences for society as a whole of such behaviour at the individual level.

In discussing the world of economics, several terms and concepts occur. Such terms as capitalism, Communism and inflation are discussed below. The section concludes with a short explanation of key economic theories. Economics is, then, both a 'positive' and 'normative' science; and there is a further important distinction which we must make. Studying the interaction of individual agents and producers, and seeing how this leads to a supply of, and demand for, each good and service in the economy, is called microeconomics. When, by contrast, we 'aggregate' (or add together) many agents and goods and examine what happens to them as a group, we are studying macroeconomics. The rate of inflation, level of employment and a country's balance of payments are all macroeconomic variables. Let us return to microeconomics, and the crucial problem of choice.

How the consumer deals with the problem of choice

Each consumer in the economy assigns 'degrees of usefulness' or *utility* to the goods and services available for his consumption (how these goods and services become available we shall see later). This scale of preferences, or preference ordering, helps him, or her, choose which goods to buy. Although the utility of a good seems similar to its usefulness, we should remember that utility does not imply that a good will benefit its consumer. All it says is that a consumer requires the good for some purpose or other; a hallucinatory drug will have utility for the addict, but it may well harm him.

Can we measure utility? Some economists, early this century, thought that we could, but it was soon discovered that to measure utility was not necessary. The consumer needs only to be able to rank goods and services in their order of preference. Utility of a good, to the consumer, does not remain constant as his stock of that good increases. Rather, the utility falls. A simple example is the consumption of a meal; further food will have little utility if the consumer has already eaten a hearty meal. There is, for each good and individual, a point beyond which the money representing the price of another unit of that good could be more beneficially spent on something else.

Now, the last unit that we buy of any good is the marginal unit and possesses marginal utility. As this marginal utility falls with greater consumption (the example in the last paragraph) of a good, there is said to be diminishing marginal utility. How does this affect the amount of a good the consumer is willing to buy? First, the consumer will compare the utilities of goods. But more important will be their marginal utilities when he considers *how much* to buy of each good. So the second stage of making the choice will involve the consumer in ensuring that the marginal utility of his expenditure on each of his purchases is the same. If this condition holds, the consumer will have no preference for any of the various ways of spending his money; he cannot gain more satisfaction by spending in a different way. To see how plausible is this 'rule' for maximizing satisfaction, or, as the economist calls it, utility, let us take a case where marginal utilities are not equal. If the consumer would benefit more from spending 50p on cigarettes than on beer (remember this is his assessment of utility), he will not be happy unless he buys the cigarettes – their marginal utility is greater. Yet where marginal utilities are equalized, such a gain cannot be made.

All we have said above is that the economist uses a rule to describe how man maximizes the satisfaction obtainable from his limited income; there has been no mention of prices and how they are determined. But it is not difficult to see how the marginal utility and the price of a good are related.

The theory of demand

Intuitively, it seems that the consumer will buy a good, taking its price as something he cannot influence, as long as its utility to him exceeds what he must sacrifice (ie some of his income) to make the purchase. Now, if the utility of a good falls as the consumer's stock of the good increases, it might be thought that he would prefer to pay less for each additional unit. Yet he simply cannot do this, both because the marginal pound of potatoes is precisely the same as all other pounds of potatoes, and because one individual consumer, we are assuming, is not able to influence prices – he or she must take them as given. What the consumer pays is a price low enough to induce him to purchase the marginal unit of that good. In short, where the consumer has no influence on prices, he will pay a price equal to the marginal utility of that good to him.

Now, the economist is unable to assess a want that is not backed by the ability to pay, and his concern is with *effective demand*. We may define this demand as a want combined with the capacity to pay for what the consumer wants. The relation between the price of a good and the demand for it is not difficult to see, remembering our rule about marginal utilities being equal. If the price of potatoes falls, the marginal expenditure on potatoes will now buy more potatoes than before, and the consumer can increase his utility by spending more on potatoes and less on some other good. Exactly the reverse is the case if the price of potatoes increases; the consumer will 'substitute', for potatoes, something cheaper.

With some goods, however, because they are *necessities* (rather than luxuries which we are able to do without, such as cars and televisions), this *law of demand* does not operate in the same way. Bread and potatoes are examples where, despite a substantial change in price, the consumer's demand changes little, if at all. There is said to be *inelastic* demand for these necessities. Conversely, where demand changes appreciably in response to a price change we say that it is *elastic*. Whether there are substitutes for the good whose price has changed will also influence the elasticity of demand. Thus, if butter increases in price, demand may increase for margarine because it is a close substitute. Economists also talk of 'normal' goods and 'Giffen' goods. The former are goods for which demand increases as the consumer's income rises, while the latter describes goods where the reverse occurs. Potatoes sometimes are an example of a Giffen good (named after the economist who first spotted the phenomenon) – when consumers can afford nothing more exciting, they must serve as a staple diet. But as income rises, fewer potatoes are purchased.

A short summary of how the consumer maximizes satisfaction from his spending

We have seen, then, that the consumer purchases a good until the point at which the cost, in terms of the amount of his income he has used up in making his payment, just balances the satisfaction he obtains from the good. He follows this rule for every good, so that there is no better position he could achieve by switching his spending from one good to another, when he sets prices equal to marginal utilities.

What we have said describes how man goes about satisfying his wants, and gaining as much pleasure as he can from his limited income. But we have said nothing about how these goods and services that man needs come into being. To find out, we must look at *the theory of production*.

The theory of production

In the theory of production, the economist examines the supply side of the economy to see precisely how firms combine the natural resources at their disposal to produce the goods and services people need. Traditionally, production has been thought of as existing purely for the purpose of satisfying a human want. Thus first there must be a want, and then production is set in motion to satisfy this want. But with the growth of advertising and the 'conditioning' of the consumer to induce in him a want for a good he had not before thought of, the traditional account may not be as accurate as it once was.

Nonetheless, production of goods and services is undertaken, in either case. Sometimes, production is a very simple process, involving just one man, say, picking fruit and satisfying his want in that way. But all production involves the factors of production. These factors are land, labour, capital and enterprise.

The first two factors are, perhaps, the easiest to understand in operation. For example, a man working a plot of land involves land and labour being used to produce a good. In fact, the economist normally takes the factor of land to mean all natural resources and not just the area on which the production takes place, ie mineral deposits, vegetation, water and wind. Capital is one of the most difficult concepts to define in economics.

We might define capital as any material resource used in production, which is not land or labour. That should suggest that to constitute capital, some natural resource has to be 'worked into' a different form for the purpose of aiding further production. A tractor is capital, because it has been produced to help produce other things. Combining land, labour and capital makes possible extremely sophisticated forms of production, eg a car assembly line, but these three factors would not be capable of such production without the addition of the fourth factor we mentioned: that is, enterprise.

Enterprise is required to bring together land, labour and capital in the right quantities, to decide what to produce, originally, and to supply the good to the market in the right quantity and at the right time. For this task of acting as the link between the consumer and the unco-ordinated factors of production – land, labour and capital – the entrepreneur (that is, whoever provides the enterprise) takes profit as his reward. He, or she, must also face the risk of failure if his plans backfire. We can see why advertising is important to the entrepreneur; for, having decided what to produce, he is primarily concerned with pointing out the exact nature and advantages of his product. This will enable him to sell his good at a price sufficient both to cover his costs incurred in production, and to provide a profit.

There is a law regarding the returns to factors of production, which is broadly equivalent to the law of diminishing marginal utility we met earlier. If we consider the factor of land, there will come a point in its cultivation (we are thinking simply in terms of a plot of land) beyond which the return to every application of labour and capital is lower than the return to previous applications. This seems quite plausible, if we think of the land becoming 'exhausted' by the repeated applications. Such less-than-proportionate returns are called *diminishing returns*, and their existence is guaranteed by the *law of diminishing returns*.

At what point should the entrepreneur stop hiring other factors of production to enable him to supply his good to the market? The answer is: at all the points where the cost of using an 'input', such as land, labour or capital, is just equal to the return that input realizes. Labour is, therefore, hired by the entrepreneur until the point at which the wage paid to the last employee equals his marginal contribution to output, or marginal product. Labour is often referred to as a variable factor of production, and land a fixed factor, for the entrepreneur can vary the quantity of labour he uses, whereas although the quantity of land can be changed, once production is started on a piece of land, it is fixed.

When these factors of production are set to use, they provide both consumer goods such as bread, potatoes and cars, various forms of personal service (eg medical and dental services), producers' goods (eg machinery and tools), and commercial services such as shipping and insurance. Some of these activities satisfy wants directly, while others, like producer goods, satisfy them indirectly through what they, in turn, produce.

In deciding precisely how much of a good or service to supply to the market, the costs of production are crucial. It is to them that we must now turn.

The costs of production

There are costs in every type of business – agricultural, extractive or manufacturing, and in those professions which supply services to the market. We can divide costs into two main sections – fixed costs and variable costs. The idea behind this division is simple. Fixed costs are those costs that remain, in total, the same as output changes. Thus, if a businessman works in a factory with a fixed rent, this rent will not vary with output – whether he produces a small output or a large one, he must pay the same rent. Insurance premiums and rates are precisely the same, and their overhead charges will still have to be met, if the factory is producing nothing.

Conversely, variable costs change as output varies. Doubling output will leave fixed costs unchanged, but more materials will be required to enable this increase in output to take place. Such expenses constitute the entrepreneur's prime costs. But these two types of costs do not exhaust the total costs of production. Allowances must also be made for a so-called 'normal' profit, which, as we saw earlier, is the very special reward for risk-taking. This profit may be regarded as a 'supplementary' cost.

It seems clear that an entrepreneur will stay in business only if he covers both his fixed and variable costs, including a normal profit. One of his problems is that if, for a short time, he is producing very little, he must still meet his fixed costs. And if it is found that covering these fixed costs is consistently beyond the business, then the entrepreneur would lose less by closing down altogether. Yet it is a difficult decision for him to make, since he may well expect an upturn in the near future when the business will more than recover the losses it is making during the 'bad' period. To assist him in deciding how much to produce and whether to keep his business running, the economist uses a rule analogous to the 'price equals marginal utility' rule for the consumer. This rule, for the producer, is that his price must cover his marginal costs. The marginal cost of supply is the cost of adding another unit to the supply of that good.

Now the efficiency of firms in supplying goods differs – some have better equipment than others, more experienced management and so on; less competent firms will only just be able to match marginal costs at the prevailing price, while others will make larger profits. However, all firms will follow the 'price = marginal cost' rule. If a firm does not, and is producing output at a point where price is greater than marginal cost, then, by expanding output further, the producer can increase his profits. Conversely where marginal cost exceeds price, by reducing output the entrepreneur will no longer lose on those units – provided he stops contracting at the level of output where price equals marginal cost.

How can some firms earn a profit, and others not, we may ask, if all firms set price equal to marginal cost? The difference between the firms is that the more efficient will be producing at a lower *average* cost, which, if it is well below price, will enable them to earn a larger profit. We must remember that average cost is equal to total cost to the firm (both fixed and variable) divided by the level of output, so even though the cost of producing the marginal unit equals price, the gains being made on all other units will permit a profit to be made.

Price, we saw above, affected the demand for a good or service in a certain way. Is there a similar rule in the case of supply? Let us consider the supply of goods and services.

The supply of the goods and services that we, as consumers, buy

The supply of a good or service is what producers actually offer for sale, at any time. What is supplied, and the total stock of a commodity, may well differ, if the good is one that does not perish. But in the case of perishable stocks, the entrepreneur will try to ensure that as much of his stock as possible comes on to the market. Changes in prices will affect the quantity of what is supplied, though there will be a delay between the change in price and change in supply. Agriculture is a good example of this phenomenon.

An increase in the price of any crop will induce an increase in its supply (that is, broadly, the 'law' of supply, and a fall in price will tend to reduce supply), but not immediately. For to realize this increase in supply, more of the crop must be planted in order that next year's crop will be greater. Therefore, the higher price today may not induce a higher supply next season; which may mean next year.

The ease with which supply can be changed in the face of price changes depends upon the *elasticity* of supply. For those goods in elastic supply, a fall in price will quickly lead to a reduction in supply, and vice versa. But for agricultural produce, as we saw earlier, and also manufactured goods that take a long time to plan and produce, such as ships and large machinery, a rapid adjustment in supply is not possible – supply is inelastic to price changes.

As we might expect, however, even for those goods whose supply is elastic, it is likely that demand will respond faster to a change in price, and therefore that the relation between demand and price will, in the short run, be the dominant influence in the market for a good. In the longer run (we will discuss these concepts in more detail later) influences from the supply side, due to changes in the cost of production, may well be more important and outweigh changes in demand.

Before looking at the concept of a market in more detail we must briefly mention what the economist refers to as 'opportunity cost'. That is, the costs of production have been described above in terms of measurement by money – for the use of capital, the entrepreneur must pay a money rent, for labour, a money wage and so on. Yet we must not over-estimate money's importance in the economic system – many simple communities have functioned without money and used barter instead. In these communities production still involves cost. So how can we measure cost without referring to money?

The economist's answer is to say that the true, or 'opportunity', cost of producing a good or service is the alternative goods that could have been produced with the resources used in the production of that good. It is the production you 'forgo' (by using the resources necessary for the production that is actually undertaken) that accurately reflects the true cost of supplying the output.

Equilibrium in the market

People often think of a market as simply a place where goods are bought and sold at a set of prices. But in economics we do not mean by the term market a place where such transactions are conducted. A market, to the economist, is a set of concepts which describes how buyers and sellers contact each other, how rival sellers compete, how rival buyers compete and how prices are established. Perhaps the simplest explanation of what constitutes a market is to say that there is a market for a good or service, if that good or service can be bought and sold, and there are some buyers and some sellers of that good or service.

How good the flow of information between buyers and sellers is, will determine how competitive the market is – in a perfect market, competition is entirely free, everyone knows what quantities are available at what prices, and no one buyer or seller is large enough to exert any influence on the market price. No market in the real world is perfect, but certain markets come quite close to the definition; those where goods are in almost universal demand, transportable and easily graded. Commodity markets in cotton, wool and rubber provide examples of such markets. We have described what a 'market' means in economics, but what determines (a) the value of a good traded in a market, and (b) its price?

The 'value' of a good is a tricky concept, although it seems quite simple. Some economists have distinguished between the value in use of a good, and its value in exchange for other goods and services. Thus air is extremely useful to all of us, and without it we would die, yet because its 'price' is zero (eg it is a free good), its value in exchange is negligible. We will confine our attention to a good's value in exchange for other commodities. This is quite straightforward, for if 2 lb of potatoes can be exchanged for 4 lb of turnips, the value of one lb of potatoes in terms of turnips is two. Such an example suggests that the value of a good or service denotes a relationship between one good and another. Further, if one good is in plentiful supply, and another relatively scarce, we might expect the latter to be worth many units of the former. In fact we can generalize to say that where demand far exceeds supply for a good or service, this good or service will have a high value, but conversely, a plentiful supply with little demand means the value of the good will be low.

The connection between the value we talked of in the last paragraph, and price should be readily apparent. For all market prices do is express this value in money terms. A high price means a high value; many units of a cheaper good must be foregone to purchase an expensive food. As yet we have not answered our question about the determination an equilibrium price in the market. To do so, all we need to remember is that an equilibrium price is one that balances supply and demand in the market for the good, or service, in question.

Consider the example of potatoes again. Each seller will be able to supply a certain quantity of potatoes at different prices, one such schedule might be:

    100 lb supplied at 12p/lb
     80 lb supplied at 10p/lb
     60 lb supplied at 8p/lb

Adding together all such schedules, we will derive a total supply of potatoes in this market, at various prices. Naturally enough, producers are able to supply a greater quantity when the price is higher and they have more 'in revenue' to cover their costs. Similarly buyers will have a schedule of prospective purchases, only this will reflect the law of diminishing marginal utility so that demand falls as the price increases. The two aggregate schedules might have the following price/quantity combination in common:

600 lb will be supplied at 10p/lb
600 lb will be demanded at 10p/lb

At this combination, with demand and supply balancing, 600 lb will be sold and 600 lb bought. In short, there is an 'equilibrium' price in the market for potatoes; can there be more than one price for potatoes in our market? The answer is no, for if there were, then adjustment to a common price would immediately take place. In our free market, where there is perfect information, a price higher than the equilibrium price would become obvious to buyers (because of the flow of information) who would buy nothing at this more expensive level. This would induce the producer to lower his price to the equilibrium level.

Although, at the 'market-clearing' price for potatoes, all potatoes supplied are purchased, this does not mean that all demand for, and supply of, potatoes is exhausted. Some producers will have stocks left over, which they were prepared to sell only at higher price, and these will be retained for another day, while the buyers who were prepared to purchase more potatoes, but only at a lower price, will postpone satisfaction of their wants in the hope of a future fall in price.

Market price may vary from one week to another, day to day, or even hour to hour (as in the stock market), so it would be wrong to think of the equilibrium price as one that is fixed and unchanging. Instead, we should think of it as varying according to the conditions prevailing at any particular time. Fluctuations in the prices of perishable goods are particularly common (eg fruit and vegetables); if trade is bad on a particular day, producers may be inclined to sell at very low prices to stave off the danger of the goods deteriorating, and also to save carting the produce home again. There is likely to be more stability in the prices of durable goods. What role do these prices, determined by demand and supply, play in economic activity?

The importance of prices

Prices tell entrepreneurs who are considering what to produce in the future (eg whether to produce a different good) what goods or services it may be profitable to supply. That is, because prices reflect relative scarcities they act as a signalling device to entrepreneurs in a free market. But, we may ask, if prices, in some market, fluctuate considerably, how can an entrepreneur have any idea about what price will be ruling in the market, when his production is available? Fortunately, for the producer considering at what costs his production needs to be supplied, there is, in most markets, a kind of 'normal' price around which day-to-day fluctuations occur.

So in the type of market we have been examining, with many sellers and buyers, and perfect information, the producer will have an indication of the price his supply is likely to realize.

Production takes time, as we have seen already, so this 'normal' price is one producers expect to see established over a period of time, and to remain in force. As one might expect, normal price tends towards the costs of production. Why? The answer is that in the longer run, when producers are able to vary the inputs they use (eg the size of factory and number of labourers), they will supply a certain output at minimum costs of production, given the technology available.

But if, say, because of an increased demand, market price exceeds this normal price, in the short run, so that increased profits can be made in the industry, what will happen? Competitors will be attracted into the industry, because they can supply the good at a price below its present level. Thus supply will increase, and price will fall. If price falls, temporarily, below the 'marginal costs of production level', because of this increased output, some producers will leave the industry (they cannot afford to stay in it) and move towards more profitable industries. In this case, supply will contract and price move back up towards the 'normal' level. As the preceding analysis suggests, the greater the elasticity of supply in a market, the less divergence is there likely to be from the 'normal' price level, or the 'marginal cost level'. Alternatively, in the antiques market, supply, and therefore price, is not related to cost. The price for which an antique is sold depends entirely upon what collectors are willing to pay.

Underlying what we have said about demand and supply in the perfectly competitive market is that supply exerts a stronger influence in the long run (when we allow producers to vary the capital inputs they use), though changes in demand do so when the entrepreneurs cannot vary their fixed costs.

Degrees of competition in the market for goods and services

Our discussion in the preceding section concentrated upon a free and perfectly competitive market where no one firm or buyer was able to influence prices *on his own*. Instead each producer and consumer, because of his 'atom-like' size and contribution to total activity, was forced to 'take' price as given, something beyond his control. The individual consumer, then, must decide what he is willing to buy as the market-determined price changes, and the producer must calculate, given his costs, what he can afford to supply at the various prices. Crucial to the working of this market in the way described is the competition among buyers and sellers, and the freedom to compete.

Perfect competition is only one type of competition, and really a limiting case, since the assumptions we must make to facilitate its operation are very strong. A perfect market of this category cannot exist in the real world, and agriculture is perhaps, the nearest approximation to it. Most common in the real world in many industries nowadays are large firms who, acting together, can exert some influence on price and what is supplied to the market. They compete with one another in a limited way, but have the power to protect their control of the industry by preventing other firms from entering it. The danger to them of more firms entering is that this will 'compete away' the profits which previously they controlled. In the car, detergent and washing machine industries there are only a few suppliers, who control what cars are produced, in what quantities they are supplied and at what price to sell them. Economists call this type of market, where a few suppliers exercise control over prices, and construct barriers to entry into their industry, an *oligopoly*. Such a market is a good example of one that is imperfectly competitive. But there is *some* competition amongst producers.

If a firm has complete control over what is supplied to the market in a particular good, it is said to be a monopolist. British monopolists like the National Coal Board, the Central Electricity Generating Board and British Rail have, in some respects, more power than oligopolists. A consumer cannot purchase coal, electricity or a rail ticket from one of several suppliers and choose to deal with the firm which charges the lowest price. This element of choice which a competitive market preserves is lost in a monopolized market, where the monopolist has the sole right to deal in that particular good or service. Prices are established in a completely different way in a monopoly; indeed, prices are *fixed* by the monopolist and not subject to the conditions of free competition.

State-owned or nationalized industries such as the NCB, CEGB and BR mentioned above have an *absolute* monopoly in the provision of their respective goods and services, but this is very unusual in private industry. Even very large private firms such as ICI, although able to control the price of some chemicals because their proportion of total supply is so high, do not have the same absolute control. Despite his supply control the monopolist cannot control demand – he must concentrate on either supply or price. The elasticity of demand for his product, and the conditions of production of his product, will determine whether he charges a high price or not. When we talk of the conditions of production we are referring to whether the industry is subject to increasing or decreasing returns. Monopoly price will probably be low if there are increasing returns operating in the industry and demand is elastic. For, with increasing returns, costs per unit of output will fall as output increases. Therefore, a large demand at a low price will produce the greatest net revenue.

The mistake is sometimes made of assuming that monopoly price must be high, but, as in the previous example, the monopolist can sometimes gain more by holding his price down and inducing a large demand, so as to spread his fixed costs over many units of output. We mentioned increasing returns earlier, and the law of diminishing returns. Are the two laws compatible? They are, because increasing returns, due to economies of scale (the greater efficiency of large-scale production) can only enable falling average costs up to a certain level, beyond which diminishing returns will set in. There are only a certain number of large-scale economies available at any given time, and eventually, if the firm produces on a very large scale, these will be exhausted. Nonetheless, there is no reason why the monopolist should choose to operate his plant at a level of output where diminishing returns have started – rather he will, as we have seen, seek to exploit the benefits of large-scale production by producing at a point of increasing returns.

One further aspect of the monopolist's market power we should mention is that of price discrimination. The monopolist may charge his customers different prices, in the pursuit of increasing profits. British Rail, for example, operates cheaper fares for pensioners and students, in the hope of attracting more custom. Such price discrimination will not be possible however in those markets where the good sold in the 'cheaper' market can be resold (at a higher price, clearly) in the 'dearer' market. The price discrimination operated in the National Health Service is safe from this danger, since a patient cannot resell a doctor's services at a higher price.

An important example of monopoly worth mentioning, because of its consequences, is that of trade unions in the labour market. The trade unions are capable of operating an effective monopoly of the supply of labour, in some modern economies. But such a monopoly is not secure from pressure on its policies, which may come even from members. For example, a trade union in a certain industry may attempt to establish a minimum wage – a wage below which no labour will be supplied. So if the trade union can ensure that its members do not damage the policy by offering their labour at a wage below the minimum, employers will be in the position of having to pay at least this minimum wage to hire workers. Yet if employers are simply unable to employ all workers at this wage, there will be excess supply in the labour market and consequent downward pressure on the minimum wage. We will discuss the possible consequences of this position later.

But before we move on to macroeconomics questions about inflation, unemployment and the balance of payments, we will discuss briefly the role that money has played in our analysis of the economic system.

Money's role in the modern economy

Most people's idea of money is connected with the monetary unit the society in which they live happens to use. British people in 1979 think of money as 5p and 10p pieces, or £1 notes etc, and French people think of money as francs. But there is no reason why money should consist of a particular currency; anything that serves as a 'medium of exchange' and is widely accepted and used in this role will suffice. Serving as a means of exchange, ie so that we can give money in exchange for some article or service that we require, is one of money's roles in a modern economy, but there are others. Because we are often uncertain about what we would like to buy and because people who sell things for money are not always in immediate need of the things they could get in exchange, money serves as a store of value. Actually, the presence of uncertainty immediately means that we need money. Why is this?

If people were certain about what prices goods would be sold at tomorrow and further into the future, and were willing to barter with one another, there would be no need either for money as a store of value or to facilitate the exchange of goods and services. Introducing uncertainty about the future course of prices, however, and thus a lack of information about the future, suggests the need for something that can be put on one side for use at a later date without loss of value. Money also serves a third vital role, as a unit of account – a unit by means of which we can measure and record the value of things exchanged.

Now there is no particular justification for using paper notes and metal coins as money. In the past, gold was a satisfactory form of money both because everyone accepted it in exchange for goods and services, and because, over long periods, its value was pretty steady. But the supply of gold was found to be unstable (depending on the success or failure of mining concerns) and its use as a 'money' expensive. Therefore paper money began to replace gold early in the twentieth century, though for many years the paper notes used by the Bank of England were fully convertible into gold coin or bullion. This right to convert a Bank of England note into gold has long since gone, as it has in all modern economies except insofar as most countries back their currencies with reserves of other currencies and gold held by the government or central bank.

Bank of England notes and coins in Britain are legal tender and thus legally valid in the settlement of a debt. Yet they form only a small fraction of the total money supply; the bulk is composed of bank deposits subject to cheque. A cheque enables a bank to transfer a stated amount of money from the account of one person to another, and although a cheque is not legal tender, it is often acceptable in the payment of debts. Just as demand and supply determine the value of other goods, so they do in the case of money, but we will postpone discussion of the demand for money until we look at inflation later. Although it has been suggested that we could do without money in our economy and rely upon barter instead, our lives are made much easier by money. In a barter economy, a 'double coincidence of wants' is required before any exchange of goods can take place, so that if a dentist wants to buy a car, he must find a car-dealer with toothache – not an impossible task, but a very difficult one, and one that money makes unnecessary.

The economy as a whole

In the previous discussion we have studied the economic actions of individuals as consumers and producers, and how their interaction determines market prices for goods and services. This study of microeconomics is to be compared with macroeconomics, and it is to the most important aspects of macroeconomics that we now turn.

Inflation

When we talked of money's role in the modern economy we suggested that there was a certain money supply comprising bank notes, coins and bank deposits, being used at any particular time to effect transactions. Now there is a relation between the demand for, and supply of, money that determines its value (or its purchasing power over commodities) in exchange. The demand for money is based on the needs of individuals in the economy to carry out transactions – the housewife requires money to buy the shopping, businessmen must carry some stock to enable them to purchase investment goods, and the student needs money to buy books or a pint of beer! In fact, not only the level of economic activity or 'trade' may effect the demand for money. More sophisticated theories, such as the American economist Milton Friedman's, suggest that the amount of money desired by individuals is also related to the rates of return on goods like stock market shares, government securities and bank deposits (deposit accounts and not current accounts).

Thus if people can earn a high rate of return by investing in the stock market, they will be less inclined to hold their resources in money. But we will simply think of the level of income determining the individual's demand for money. One unit of money is used in more than one transaction; a 5p piece goes from the shopper's purse into the shopkeeper's till, from there into another shop till and so on. The number of times this happens is referred to, by the economist, as the velocity of circulation of money. We can say that one 5p piece involved in twenty transactions is doing the equivalent work of twenty 5p pieces involved in one transaction each. It is, broadly, the relations between the total supplies of goods and services and money that tell us what the value of money will be, provided that the velocity of circulation is constant. So if the quantity of goods increases while the money supply (notes, coins and current accounts) remains unchanged, in order that these goods can be sold, their price in terms of money must fall, and the value of money will increase. Every unit of money will buy more goods than it did before; a pound of potatoes which did cost 10p may now cost only 8p.

In the opposite situation, where the money supply is increased but the quantity of goods stays the same, prices will tend to increase. But we cannot say that this observation has the status of an economic law, in the way that returns diminished with an increased application of factors of production. This is only one explanation of 'inflation' which describes the phenomenon of rising prices. The value of money falls during an inflation but a moderate rise in prices may not be harmful. Rising prices often encourage producers to employ more workers and machines for the purpose of expanding output, since profit margins are widening; fixed costs do not rise at all, or at least less than the prices of the goods the producer sells. But *rapidly* rising prices are less welcome to everyone. Those people whose income is fixed (like old age pensioners) find they can buy fewer goods, trade unions are likely to become aggressive about demanding higher wages to 'keep pace' and the economy will be unable to sell as many goods abroad as it could previously. This last problem will lead to balance of payments difficulties as we shall see below.

Although some economists blame the money supply for causing inflation, others hold trade unions responsible. The suggestion of these economists is that trade unions force up wages which employers must pay, employers 'pass on' these higher costs in higher prices, which in turn induces further wage demands. And so the wage-price spiral develops. We shall not enter into the question of which argument is the most powerful, except to say that elements of both theories are present in most modern economies.

Despite the danger of inflation, money is still a great help to us, with our transactions, and given the complexity of many of these transactions, a banking system is a necessary part of a modern economy.

The banks

In Britain, the so-called Big Four clearing banks – Barclay's, Lloyd's, National Westminster and the Midland – fulfil a number of highly specialized functions. Not only do they act as 'vaults' (which was the only function of the earliest banks) where money can be deposited, but also they lend to, and borrow from, both the public and government. 'Discounting' bills of exchange and accepting bills on behalf of customers is another function of a modern bank of deposit. Such banks of deposit do not issue notes – in Britain this note issue is controlled by the Bank of England. A clearing bank (called such because it 'clears' cheques drawn on its customers' accounts) also acts for its customers in undertaking stock and share transactions and in discharging the duties of executor of wills, trustee or referee on a customer's character.

Perhaps the most important role that the clearing banks play is as a link between those individuals who want to save and those who want to borrow; the banks mobilize funds for the use of industry. Without such an institution this co-ordination of the decisions made by small lenders and borrowers would be impossible.

The government's, or state's, role in modern economies

When we talked of inflation, we hinted at one of the reasons for the intervention of the government or state in modern economies. Briefly, we may say that the government's role is twofold – firstly, to provide those goods and services that private enterprise finds unprofitable and therefore does not provide, and secondly, to regulate the economy with the aim of safeguarding the jobs of the population. Under the first heading comes the provision of such services as the army, navy, police force, civil service, education, public health services, public parks and recreation facilities. These are mostly services for which private production is unsuited – eg the police force is a service which, society considers, should be available to all, but this might not be the case if this protection had to be purchased from a private producer.

The government's second role is a more exacting task for it must so gauge its intervention that the economy remains in a position of near full employment, without inflation and, as we shall see below, balance of payments problems.

When we consider together the actions of all producers and consumers in the economy, there will be both an aggregate demand and aggregate supply schedule for the output our economy produces. Just as these schedules intersect at some 'equilibrium' price and quantity combination in one small market, so they do when we consider all sectors together as one vast market. Now a certain 'quantity' of labourers, managers, car-workers, directors and executives will be required to produce this output. But this number may not be equal to the number who would like to, and are able to, work at this level of wages – in short there may not be, indeed there is not likely to be, full employment.

The government's ability to achieve full employment will depend upon how predictably businessmen respond to the changes in taxes it imposes. For the two main 'methods of regulation', for the government, are changing its own spending and changing the taxes it charges to finance this spending. Increasing its spending will help increase employment, for it will boost total demand in the economy for private producers' output, and the government may even directly increase employment by building more hospitals, roads and swimming pools. When the government spends more than it receives in taxes, the difference is called 'the government (or sometimes public sector) borrowing requirement'. It can borrow from the public by issuing government securities at a certain rate of interest, which are 'redeemed' – at some future date the government pays back the sum it borrowed. Some stocks are 'undated', which means that the holder will never be paid back by the government, but he can sell his stock in the gilt-edged market; War Loan is one of the most famous British undated stocks.

Modern economies do not exist independently of each other – Britain, for instance, trades goods and services with France, Germany, Japan and most countries in the world. International trade is a vital part of economic activity and we must examine its importance.

Why countries trade with each other; is it of benefit?

All trade, whether within the same country or between countries, arises from the same cause – the fact that specialization enables greater production of goods, and that trading amongst specialized areas benefits all. From South America we import bananas and other tropical products because we cannot produce them as efficiently. Similarly, Britain exports machinery to countries unable to supply machinery at a comparable cost. The economist describes the advantages obtainable from trade in the 'law of comparative costs'. Thus a country exports those goods in which it has a greater relative advantage. So even though Britain could produce some of the products it imports, because it is more beneficial to concentrate production in those industries of lowest comparative cost, we do so. Such a principle of specialization operates in all forms of production and explains the localization of industries in districts of a country.

It is by competing with one another that countries discover whether or not they have a comparative advantage – the production of a particular good or service. Competition amongst countries in the production of goods and services also reflects whether comparative positions have changed – the invention of a new technique in one country may mean that it can now supply a good at a cost below that of rivals, when before it could not. Given the prices of imports and exports there is a certain relationship between the volume of exports (goods and services sold to foreign countries) that are required to pay for a certain volume of imports. This relationship the economist calls the terms of trade. If exports from Britain are being purchased at quite a high price relative to imports, only a low volume of exports need be sold to 'finance' the importing of goods and services. Then the terms of trade are said to be favourable, and vice versa.

When a country consistently buys more goods and services from abroad than it exports in return, it will be running a deficit on international account, or an adverse balance of trade. Thus, a country importing more goods and services than it is exporting, must pay for this trade deficit either by losing gold and currencies from the reserves or borrowing the balance from creditor countries. The International Monetary Fund will also tide a country over a bad period, when it is struggling to maintain its international competitiveness (because of high prices, say) by making a loan, usually subject to certain conditions being fulfilled.

Fluctuations in countries' exchange rates will help iron out differences in the costs at which they can supply various goods. Thus Britain's £ sterling has declined slowly but consistently against other currencies since the Second World War, which has tempered the rise in relative costs of production in Britain. A devaluation, in effect, automatically cuts the prices of a country's exports since it reduces the value of the currency in which these prices are expressed, vis-à-vis other currencies.

Prominent People

Adenauer, Konrad (1876–1967), Chancellor of the West German Federal Republic 1949–63; founder and chairman of the Christian Democratic Party 1945–66.

Allende, Salvador (1908–73), a Marxist socialist, elected President of Chile in 1970. Taking over a country whose industries were largely controlled by America, Allende set about nationalizing industrial concerns, including the mines. In 1973 a right-wing military junta, with American backing, overthrew Allende's government and Allende was killed.

Attlee, Clement Richard (1883–1967), Labour Prime Minister of Britain 1945–51; he was MP for Limehouse from 1922, having lectured at the London School of Economics and served as a mayor of Stepney. His government helped to create the welfare state and granted independence to India.

Auriol, Vincent (1884–1966), French politician, President of the Fourth Republic 1947–54.

Ayub Khan, Mohammed (1907–74), Pakistani military leader, President of Pakistan 1958–69.

Azikiwe, Nnamdi (b. 1904), Nigerian statesman; President of Nigeria 1963–6.

Bevan, Aneurin (1897–1960), British (Welsh) socialist politician, architect of the National Health Service which came into operation in 1948. A powerful and passionate orator, he expressed his detestation of 'the vermin in ermine' (a reference to the House of Lords).

Beveridge, Lord (William Henry) (1879–1963), British economist. Drew up the Beveridge Plan, published in 1942, which formed the basis of the present social security services.

Bevin, Ernest (1881–1951), British trade union leader, who later became Foreign Secretary under Clement Attlee. He was assistant general secretary of the Dockers Union, later general secretary of the Transport and General Worker's Union; Minister of Labour 1940–5, and Foreign Secretary 1945–51.

Bhave, Vinova (b. 1895), Indian reformer, leader of the Sarvodaya movement. A follower of Gandhi, in 1951 he began a walking mission to persuade landlords to help landless peasants. In four years, 4 million acres of land were redistributed.

Brandt, Willy (b. 1913), first Social Democratic Chancellor of the Federal Republic of Germany, 1969–74, who resigned after a close aide was exposed as an East German spy. He won the Nobel Peace prize in 1971.

Brezhnev, Leonid Ilyich (b. 1906), succeeded Khruschev as first secretary of the Soviet Communist Party in 1964; formerly President of the Supreme Soviet of the USSR.

Bulganin, Nikolai Alexandrovich (b. 1895), Soviet Prime Minister 1955–8; Defence Minister 1947–9, 1953–5. Retired 1960.

Butler, Baron (Richard Austen Butler) (b. 1902), British Conservative politician who brought in the Education Act of 1944 and helped secure Conservative acceptance of the welfare state. An unsuccessful candidate for the Premiership.

Carter, James Earl (b. 1924), President of the United States since 1977.

Castro, Fidel (b. 1927), Cuban revolutionary and premier since 1959. After two unsuccessful attempts, he succeeded in 1959 in overthrowing the police state of the corrupt president dictator Fulgencio Batista. A former lawyer, Castro's experiences as a guerrilla fighter turned him into a Marxist and he has initiated reforms in agriculture, industry and education, and repulsed American economic dominance. His acceptance of Russian support led to the 'missiles crisis' of 1962.

Chiang Kai Shek (1887–1975), Chinese general and statesman; with the fall of the Manchu dynasty in 1911 he became military adviser to president Sun Yat Sen and, after the latter's death (1925), he became commander of the Kuomintang army and President, 1928–31. Torn between fighting the Japanese invaders and the Chinese Communists, but intent above all on holding on to power and wealth, he was defeated by the Communists and retired to Formosa in 1949.

Chou En Lai (1898–1976), Chinese revolutionary statesman, administrator and diplomat. He organized revolt in Shanghai in 1927, formed a close partnership with Mao Tse Tung, took part in the long march of 1934–5, and became Prime Minister of the new China in 1949.

Couve de Murville, Maurice (b. 1900), French diplomat; General de Gaulle's Foreign Minister 1958–68.

Cripps, Sir Stafford (1889–1952), British Labour statesman. As Chancellor of the Exchequer in post-war Britain his programme was one of austerity.

De Gasperi, Alcide (1881–1954), Italian politician who founded the Christian Democrat Party; Prime Minister 1945–53.

Douglas-Home, Alexander Frederick (Lord Home of the Hirsel) (b. 1903), Conservative Prime Minister, 1963–4; Foreign and Commonwealth Secretary 1970–4.

Dulles, John Foster (1888–1959), US Secretary of State in the Republican administration 1953–9. His foreign policy was inflexibly opposed to negotiation with Russia and to American recognition of China.

Eden, Robert Anthony (1st Earl of Avon) (1897–1976), British statesman. He entered Parliament in 1923; became Foreign Secretary in 1935; deputy Prime Minister in 1951; and succeeded Sir Winston Churchill in 1955. His Suez policy divided the country and he resigned in 1957.

Eisenhower, Dwight David (1890–1969), American general and statesman. He was C-in-C Allied Forces North Africa 1942–3; and in Europe 1943-5; and was Republican President of the USA 1953–61.

Elizabeth II (b. 1926), Queen of England, ascended the throne in 1952 on the death of her father George VI.

Gaitskell, Hugh Todd Naylor (1906–63), Labour politician and economist. He represented Leeds South from 1945; was Chancellor of the Exchequer 1950–1; and leader of the Labour opposition from 1955 until his untimely death in 1963.

Gandhi, Indira (b. 1917), daughter of Nehru, succeeded Shastri in 1966 to become India's first woman Prime Minister. From 1975, when investigations into corruption in her government looked certain to unseat her, she was virtual dictator of India, until her election defeat in 1977. She has since attempted a political comeback.

Gaulle, Charles de (1890–1970), French general and statesman, first president of the Fifth Republic 1959–69. In the Second World War he refused to surrender (1940), and raised and led the Free French forces. Coming to political power in 1958 he based his government on personal prestige and use of the referendum in place of parliamentary approval. Taken by surprise by the uprising of students and workers in 1968, he resigned after losing the referendum in 1969. He survived a number of assassination attempts, and his influence still motivates a large section of older French people.

Giap, Vo Nguyen (b. 1912), Vietnamese general who defeated the French at Dien Bien Phu (1954) and withstood American intervention in the Vietnam War which followed; deputy Prime Minister and commander-in-chief North Vietnam.

Gromyko, Andrei Andreevich (b. 1908), Russian diplomat who has served as Foreign Minister since 1957. He was ambassador to Britain 1952–3.

Guevara, Ernesto 'Che' (1928–67), revolutionary leader, b. Argentina. A former doctor, he took part in the Cuban guerrilla war and became a minister in the Cuban government 1959–65. He believed it vital to initiate the liberation of all southern America and led a band of guerrillas against American-trained Bolivian troops. Disagreements with Bolivian revolutionaries increased the problems, and he was captured and executed by Bolivian soldiers.

Hammarskjöld, Dag (1905–61), Swedish statesman who became secretary-general of the United Nations in 1953. He was killed in an air crash while attempting to mediate in a dispute between the Congo and the secessionist province of Katanga. The possibility of sabotage has never been completely ruled out. Posthumous Nobel peace prize.

Heath, Edward Richard George (b. 1916), leader of the British Conservative party from 1965–75, and Prime Minister 1970–74. His government negotiated the terms of Britain's entry into the EEC and in 1971 passed the controversial Industrial Relations Act. In 1972 his government took over direct rule of Northern Ireland and in 1974 cut the working week in most industries to three days. Deciding to confront the miners, who were planning a national strike, Heath called an election on the issue 'Who governs Britain?' The Labour Party won the election and in 1975 he was replaced by Margaret Thatcher as leader of the Conservatives.

Ho Chi Minh (1892–1969), leader of the Vietnam revolutionary nationalist party of Indo-China, which struggled for independence from France during and after the Second World War. In 1945 the independent republic of Vietnam was formed with Ho Chi Minh as President. In 1954 the decisive victory over the French at Dien Bien Phu led to the Indo-China armistice, signed in Geneva, and the Communists occupied Hanoi. Intent on uniting all Vietnam, Ho sent troops against the south and the war with America escalated. With victory in 1975, the southern capital of Saigon was renamed Ho Chi Minh City in honour of the late President.

Jinnah, Mohammed Ali (1876–1948), Pakistani statesman. Born in Karachi, he became president of the Moslem League, and in 1947 established the Dominion of Pakistan, becoming its first governor-general.

Johnson, Lyndon Baines (1908–73), President of the United States 1963–9. He became President on Kennedy's assassination and, after the 1964 elections, was inaugurated as the 36th President. A Texan, he followed a progressive policy at home, but his achievements were clouded by the escalated war in Vietnam.

Kaunda, Kenneth (b. 1924), African leader of international standing, son of Christian missionaries. He has been President of Zambia since independence in 1964.

Kennedy, John Fitzgerald (1917–63), President of the United States, 1961–3; the youngest holder of the office and the first Roman Catholic to be elected. Popular because of his youth, good looks, energy and heroic war record he gave the American people a sense of purpose and hope. He opposed racial discrimination and initiated a new era in East-West relations, but his foreign policy sowed the seeds of the Vietnam War and his record over Cuba was clouded. He was assassinated in Dallas in November 1963, and his death is still surrounded by controversy and doubt. His younger brother Robert was also assassinated while campaigning for the presidency in 1968.

Kenyatta, Jomo (1893–1978), African leader who in 1953 was convicted with five other Kikuyu of organizing the Mau Mau in the fight for independence, and was imprisoned. In 1964 Kenya became an independent republic with Kenyatta as President.

Khruschev, Nikita Sergeyevich (1894–1971), Russian statesman who became leader of the Soviet Union after Stalin's death; first secretary of the Soviet Communist Party, 1953–64; Prime Minister 1958–64. At the 20th Soviet Communist Party conference he denounced Stalin's policy and pursued a policy of relaxation both in home and foreign affairs. Relations with America improved but those with China became strained. The confrontation over the Cuban missile bases in 1962 put Khruschev to the severest test, and in 1964 his posts were taken over by Brezhnev (first secretary) and Kosygin (Prime Minister). Khruschev said of the Cuban crisis: 'They talk about who won and who lost. Human reason won. Mankind won.'

King, Martin Luther (1929–68), American clergyman and black integration leader; awarded the 1964 Nobel peace prize for his consistent support of the principle of non-violence in the struggle of blacks for civil rights; he also supported campaigns against the war in Vietnam. Assassinated in a motel in Memphis, Tennessee by James Earl Ray, who was given a ninety-nine-year prison sentence.

Kissinger, Henry (b. 1923), American statesman of German Jewish parentage. In 1973 he became the first non-US-born citizen to be appointed US Secretary of State. In 1971 he secretly arranged President Nixon's trip to China; after the Vietnam War, and the Paris peace talks, the Nobel peace prize was awarded to Kissinger and the North Vietnamese Le Duc Tho, who refused the award. Kissinger has arbitrated frequently between the Arabs and Israel in the Middle East, in Cyprus, and, towards the end of his career, in Africa; he was also implicated in the CIA involvement in Chile, which led to the overthrow of the democratically elected president Allende by the military junta.

Kosygin, Alexei Nikolayevich (b. 1904), succeeded Khruschev as chairman of the council of ministers of the USSR (Prime Minister) in 1964.

Liaquat Ali Khan (1895–1951), leader of the Moslem League (1946) and first premier of Pakistan in 1947. He was assassinated.

Lie, Trygve (1896–1968), Norwegian politician who became first secretary-general of the United Nations, 1946–52.

Luthuli, Albert (1899–1967), African non-violent resistance leader, ex-Zulu chief. Nobel Peace Prize 1960. Killed in train accident.

Macmillan, Harold (b. 1894), British Conservative politician, Prime Minister 1957–63. His speech on the financial situation in 1959 contained the famous phrase, 'You've never had it so good,' and his 'wind of change' speech in 1960 hailed African independence.

Makarios III (1913–77), Greek Orthodox archbishop and Cypriot national leader. Deported by the British to the Seychelles in 1956, he returned in 1957 to become President of the newly independent republic in 1960. In 1974 Greek-led Cypriot rebels overthrew the government and Makarios fled. The rebels' demands for union with Greece were thwarted by the invasion of Turkish forces, and Makarios returned to resume as President of the Greek section in the divided island.

Mao Tse Tung (1893–1976), Chinese national and Communist leader. Born in Hunan, of rural origin but with university training, he understood how to win peasant support for a national and progressive movement. Attacked by Chiang Kai Shek, he led his followers on the 'long march' to north-west China, where they defeated both Japan and the Kuomintang forces and proclaimed a People's Republic in 1949. Mao resigned the chairmanship in 1959, but came to the fore again in 1966–8, leading the cultural revolution. A man of great intelligence, strength and subtlety, Mao's reputation was based upon his ability first as a military theorist (of guerrilla warfare): second as a political philosopher (adapting Marxism to Chinese needs): and, third, as a more ardent champion of world revolution than Russia.

Marshall, George Catlett (1880–1959), American general. He was US chief of staff 1939–45, and originated the Marshall Aid plan for European reconstruction in 1947. Nobel prize for peace 1953.

Mendes-France, Pierre (b. 1907), French politician, premier 1954–5, but defeated on his North African policy. He was a critic of de Gaulle.

Menzies, Sir Robert Gordon (1894–1978), Australian Liberal statesman, premier 1939–41, 1949–66.

Montgomery of Alamein, 1st Viscount (Bernard Law Montgomery) (1887–1976), British field-marshal; commanded 8th Army in North Africa, Sicily and Italy 1942–4; C-in-C, British Group of Armies and Allied Armies in Northern France, 1944. He served as Deputy Supreme Allied Commander Europe (NATO) 1951–8.

Nasser, Gamal Abdel (1918–70), leader of modern Egypt and of the Arab world. A colonel, he led the 1952 military coup that deposed King Farouk, becoming President of the new Egyptian Republic in 1956 and of the United Arab Republic in 1958. His nationalization of the Suez Canal in 1956 led to the short-lived attack by Britain and France. Israeli–Arab hostility culminated in the 'six day' June war of 1967, after which Nasser named himself Prime Minister of the UAR. He carried out reforms to bring his people out of feudal backwardness, and with Russian help and finance carried out the building of the Aswan High Dam.

Nehru, Pandit Jawaharlal (1889–1964), Indian national leader and statesman, first Prime Minister and Minister of Foreign Affairs when India became independent in 1947. A leading member of the Congress Party, he had been frequently imprisoned for political activity. Under his leadership India made advances, and in world affairs his influence was for peace and non-alignment. He once said: 'The only alternative to co-existence is co-destruction.'

Nixon, Richard Milhous (b. 1913), Republican President of America 1969–72, winning in 1969 by the narrowest margin since 1912, and being re-elected in 1972 by a near-record landslide. He was elected to Congress 1946; to the Senate 1951; Vice-President 1952; re-elected 1956. The Vietnam War was escalated under Nixon, and he ordered the dropping of more bombs than any other man in the world's history. Of the first moon landing in 1969 he said: 'This is the greatest week in the history of the world since the creation.' He visited Russia and China, but in 1972 the Watergate scandal became uncontrollable, Nixon could not cover up his involvement, and on 9 August he became the first President to resign from office in mid-term.

Nkrumah, Kwame (1909–72), Ghanaian leader, first premier of Ghana when his country achieved independence in 1957, and President in 1960. His government was personalized and he promoted the pan-African movement. Aware of the dangers of neo-colonialism, he sought solutions applicable to Ghana's problems, but unsound finance and dictatorial methods led to a military coup, and Nkrumah died in exile.

Nyerere, Julius (b. 1922), Tanzanian leader. He became first premier of Tanganyika on independence in 1961, and President in 1962. In 1964 he negotiated its union with Zanzibar, forming the United Republic of Tanzania. As Tanzania is a poor, largely agricultural country, he organized the 'ujumaa', or collective farm system, looked to Communist China for help in building roads and railways and, with the Arusha Declaration, ensured that government ministers did not own companies or lose contact with the life and work of the people. Following this declaration banks, insurance, and some food and import/export businesses were nationalized. A strong advocate of African unity, Nyerere was one of the founder members of the Organization of African Unity.

Pompidou, Georges Jean Raymond (1911–75), French administrator and politician who succeeded de Gaulle as President of France in 1969.

Sadat, Anwar (b. 1918), President of Egypt who initiated peace moves in the conflict with Israel in December, 1977.

Salazar, Antonio d'Oliveira (1889–1970), Portuguese dictator who became premier in 1932. He kept the Portuguese people in a state of atrophied feudalism, and continued the costly imperialist wars in Portuguese Africa.

Shastri, Shri Lal Bahadur (1904–66), Indian politician who became Prime Minister of India after the death of Nehru in 1964. He died of a heart attack at the end of the Soviet-sponsored Tashkent talks.

Spaak, Paul Henri (1899–1972), Belgian statesman and a founder of the Common Market. First president of the UN General Assembly in 1946, and of the Assembly of the Council of Europe 1949–51; secretary-general of NATO 1957–61.

Thant, Sithu U (1909–74), Burmese diplomat; secretary-general of the United Nations 1962–72.

Thorez, Maurice (1900–64), French Communist leader from 1930 and especially after the Second World War.

Tito (Josip Broz) (b. 1892), Yugoslav leader. In 1941 he organized partisan forces against the Axis invaders, liberated his country, and carried through a Communist revolution. In 1945 the Federal People's Republic of Yugoslavia was proclaimed, with Tito as Prime Minister, and in 1953 he became President. He has successfully pursued an independent line for his country, on the right of the Eastern bloc, and he supported the Czech liberation drive in 1968 before the Russian invasion. In 1970 he announced that he would be succeeded by a collective leadership.

Truman, Harry S. (1884–1972), 33rd American President 1945–53. He inherited the presidency on the death of Roosevelt in 1945 when he took the decision to drop the first atom bomb; he won the election in 1948. He intervened in Korea, dismissed General MacArthur, and created the Atomic Energy Commission.

Weizmann, Chaim (1874–1952), Israeli leader, b. Poland. He came to England in 1903 and taught chemistry at Manchester. He helped to secure the Balfour Declaration (1917), promising a Jewish national home, and was president of the Zionist Organisation and the Jewish agency 1920–30. In 1948 he became first President of Israel.

Wilson, Sir James Harold (b. 1916), British Labour statesman. He entered Parliament in 1945 as member for Ormskirk and was elected for Huyton in 1950. He became leader of the Labour Party in 1963 after Gaitskell's death, and was Prime Minister 1964–70, won the early 1974 election with a minority government, and in the second election in the autumn won a narrow majority over all other parties. He resigned early in 1976, and accepted a knighthood and the Order of the Garter.

Index